Environmental Safety and Health Regulations

Joel M. Haight, Editor

American Society of Safety Engineers
Des Plaines, Illinois, USA

Copyright © 2012 by the American Society of Safety Engineers
All rights reserved.

Copyright, Waiver of First Sale Doctrine
All rights reserved. No part of this work may be reproduced or transmitted in any form or by any means, electronic or mechanical for commercial purposes, without the permission in writing from the Publisher. All requests for permission to reproduce material from this work should be directed to: The American Society of Safety Engineers, ATTN: Manager of Technical Publications, 1800 E. Oakton Street, Des Plaines, IL 60018.

Disclaimer
While the publisher and authors have used their best efforts in preparing this book, they make no representations or warranties with respect to the accuracy or completeness of the contents, and specifically disclaim any implied warranties of fitness for a particular purpose. The information herein is provided with the understanding that the authors are not hereby engaged in rendering professional or legal services. The mention of any specific products herein does not constitute an endorsement or recommendation by the American Society of Safety Engineers, and was done solely at the discretion of the author. Note that any excerpt from a National Fire Protection Association Standard reprinted herein is not the complete and official position of the NFPA on the referenced subject(s), which is represented only by the cited Standard in its entirety.

We encourage comments and suggestions for improving this text. Please email to Manager, Technical Publications at: techpubs@asse.org

Library of Congress Cataloging-in-Publication Data

Environmental safety and health regulations / Joel M. Haight, Editor.
    p. cm.
  ISBN 978-1-885581-69-3 (alk. paper)
  1. Environmental law--United States. 2. Public health laws--United States. 3. Safety regulations--United States. I. Haight, Joel M., editor of compilation.
  KF3775.E76 2013
  344.7304'6--dc23
                    2012043226

Managing Editor: Michael F. Burditt, ASSE
Editor: Jeri Stucka, ASSE
Text design and composition: Cathy Lombardi
Cover Design: Image Graphics

Printed in the United States of America

18 17 16 15 14 13   6 5 4 3 2 1

ENVIRONMENTAL SAFETY AND HEALTH REGULATIONS

Contents

Foreword	iv
About the Editor and Authors	vii
Chapter 1: Air Pollution Control and Mitigation Anthony J. Joseph and Tyler Nguyen	1
Chapter 2: Water and Wastewater Judy Freeman	35
Chapter 3: Solid Waste William S. Fink	61
Chapter 4: Hazardous Waste Salvatore Caccavale, Barry R. Weissman, Thomas S. Butler, Jr., and Judy Freeman	89
Chapter 5: Hazardous Material Spills and Response George and Cherie Walton	125
Chapter 6: Hazard Communication and Right-to-Know Regulations James M. Miller	169
Chapter 7: Management Systems Robert R. Stewart	225
Index	251

Foreword

THE CHAPTERS IN THIS BOOK discuss the major areas of U.S. environmental regulations. Each chapter also presents management practices and principles in: applied sciences and engineering controls, cost analysis and budgeting, performance measurement, and benchmarking criteria and best practices.

Federal air quality legislation dates to the enactment of the Air Pollution Control Act of 1955, but it was not until over a decade later, with the Congressional passage of the Air Quality Act in 1967, that the federal government actually gained enforcement power against air polluters. Amendments to what was later termed the Clean Air Act authorized federal departments to set standards for auto emissions, establish air-quality control regions, set compliance deadlines for stationary source emissions, and authorize research on low-emission fuels and automobiles. The 1967 law also gave the states a role in identifying regional sources of air pollution. A major change in addressing air pollution control was ensured with the passage of the Clean Air Act of 1990. Congress directed the EPA to improve the reduction of air toxics by utilizing a technology- and performance-based approach to major sources of air pollution followed by a risk-based approach to address residual risks. This approach provides a level economic playing field by ensuring that those companies employing cleaner processes and good emissions controls are not placed at an economic disadvantage. While the 1990 Clean Air Act Amendments failed to address two increasingly prominent global air pollution problems: greenhouse gas emissions, and mercury pollution from coal-fired power plants, it did have far-reaching impacts, a number of which are discussed.

Two landmark pieces of legislation, the Clean Water Act (CWA) and the Safe Drinking Water Act (SDWA), have had profound impact on what can be discharged into America's waterways and the quality of water in the public water supply. The 1987 CWA limits discharges into the nation's waterways through a permit program (National Pollutant Discharge Elimination System or NPDES). How this system works, specifically with regard to discharges to public sewer systems and publicly owned treatment works, is discussed. The EPA regulates both direct and indirect discharges based on the best available technology. EH&S managers must know and understand the permitting systems in force in their states.

The collection, management and treatment of solid waste are essential activities that are necessary for a safe, healthy and vibrant society. However, the tasks associated with solid waste management are inherently dangerous. The category of "Refuse and Recyclable Material Workers" ranks as the 6th most dangerous occupation by the U.S. Dept. of Labor. As a safety professional you need to understand the tasks and the associated regulatory environment surrounding solid waste management. In addition, as safety professionals actively managing safety programs for personnel involved in solid waste activities and assisting to protect our natural resources, we are faced with a great social responsibility.

Solid waste is not a glamorous topic, but it is one each of us contributes to each day. Have you ever thought about what happens after you are asked to take out the garbage? Your job may end after placing the trash bag in the garbage can in the alley or the end of the driveway, but someone else's job is just beginning. The list of workers includes, but is not limited to: garbage collector; garbage truck driver; transfer station workers; landfill operators; landfill heavy equipment operators; civil engineers; landfill constructors; etc. There is an entire profession that keeps our society free from piling up with garbage. How important is this profession? A mayor of a major metropolitan city once said that if the garbage is picked up, the streets are plowed of snow, the potholes are filled and the water is running, he is doing his job. Everything else is secondary. Maintaining public health and safety by keeping the garbage picked up and hauled away is one of the primary functions of a city public works department.

Managing our environment doesn't only mean being good stewards of the air and water, but also of the land. A large majority of the solid waste that is generated goes into landfills. A much smaller amount of the solid waste stream is recycled for beneficial re-use. The goal of this chapter is to provide you with an introduction to the Bureau of Labor Statistics (BLS) on the solid waste industry; an introduction to the U.S. EPA solid waste regulations; historic waste handling procedures and definitions; items necessary for developing a landfill safety plan; and issues to be considered at waste management and recycling facilities. This chapter on solid waste management safety has been designed to provide you with a better understanding and appreciation for this oftentimes under-appreciated line of work.

It was not until the passage of the Resource Conservation and Recovery Act in 1976, followed by the Hazardous and Solid Waste Amendments (collectively known as "RCRA"), that the United States for the first time codified and regulated the disposal of materials that were determined to be a danger to human health and the environment. Any business that generates, transfers, or disposal of regulated hazardous waste must comply with the RCRA regulations. In addition, facilities required to maintain Material Safety Data Sheets per OSHA's Hazard Communication Standard must file with their state emergency response commission, their local fire department and their local emergency planning commission. Information is presented on the four series of hazardous waste codes and classifications of their characteristics based on ignitability, corrosivity, reactivity and toxicity. The information presented on generator categories, selection of shipping and disposal facilities. labeling, recordkeeping, and training provides an introduction to the regulations and management practices.

Regulation of spills and releases of hazardous chemicals is not limited to the EPA; both the U.S. Department of Transportation and OSHA are frequently involved as well. OSHA regulations apply to the safety and health of workers involved in the cleaning up of spills, including treatment and disposal of waste products and residues, and DOT regulations apply to the transportation of the hazardous materials resulting from the spill. Depending upon the location, chemical involved and whether the incident involved a pipeline or in certain transportation accidents, the incident must be reported to the National Response Center. In addition to the toxicity and quantity of the chemical involved, factors affecting the severity of spill also include the nature of the affected area or environment, including the hydrology and geology as discussed. The authors of the chapter on spills and response list a number of excellent sources for training and for benchmarking a response plan. They also discuss measures of response readiness and performance appraisal criteria. The authors also discuss risk assessment and how answers to the assessment can be used to help plan the best response to chemical spills and releases. Best practices in spill prevention and response must begin with assessing a spill prevention and response plan based on federal standards, including EPA regulations, HAZWOPER requirements, and OSHA regulations, which are all discussed. Hazard assessments, followed by determination of the best hazard reduction approach, must be integrated into the planning process for the plan to be most effective. The authors do an excellent job of providing an overview of key elements to developing a written spill response plan. They also discuss decontamination of the personal protective equipment (PPE) and other equipment which should be part of a decontamination plan. The chapter concludes with an introduction to DOT requirements for drivers and equipment operators involved with the transportation and/or handling of hazardous materials.

The Hazard Communication Standard discussed in Chapter 6 was enacted by OSHA in order that employees know the identities of the chemicals and the associated hazards of those chemicals to which they are exposed in the workplace. Furthermore, under the law they have a right to know what protective measures are available to prevent adverse effects from occurring. The rules specifically address the evaluation and communication of chemical hazard information to workers. One of the key documents required by the HazCom standard, the Material Safety Data Sheet (MSDS), will give way to a more organized and comprehensive Safety Data Sheet (SDS) under the revised HazCom Standard, which meets the requirements of the Global Harmonization System (GHS). Author Dr. James Miller discusses five tasks that embody the essence of how to comply with the HazCom Standard as required by OSHA. The author points out at the beginning of the chapter that besides the OSHA requirements, there are a number of other standards and practices in place that address hazard communication in the workplace. These he discusses in some detail toward the end of the chapter.

In the last chapter, "Management Systems," author Robert Stewart examines the business case for environmental compliance. He points out that the first environmental management systems (EMS) were derived from popular management concepts linked to quality control, such as ISO 14001. He also notes the long-standing support of the U.S. EPA as a form of injunctive relief to facilitate remedial actions and ensure ongoing compliance. To qualify for injunctive relief (i.e., to assure ongoing compliance), a company's EMS must follow the guidelines listed in the U.S. EPA's "Enforcement Agreement Guidance." The Guidance details 12 necessary components referred to by the EPA as a model for developing and improving an EMS. The federal government is actively involved in developing EMSs as federal facilities, and organizations that self-audit are shielded from excessive financial and legal liability. An EMS is most often based on the Plan-Do-Check-Act principle, which the author discusses in terms of specific EPA directives.

ISO 14001 "Environmental Management System" certification sets a framework for a company to develop and implement an environmental management system recognized internationally. Automakers such as Ford require its preferred production suppliers' manufacturing facilities to be ISO certified. Although specific reductions in pollution emissions are not mandated under ISO 14001, companies are required to set pollution reduction objectives.

Since an ISO EMS registration is reviewed annually, the process provides benchmarks for sustainability measures such as tons of scrap recycled, and energy use reduction targets. As the author points out, companies that pursue a strategic environmental management initiative to minimize emissions and environmental impact often do so in pursuit of competitive business advantages.

ABOUT THE EDITOR

In 2009, Joel M. Haight, Ph.D., P.E., was named Branch Chief of the Human Factors Branch at the Centers for Disease Control and Prevention (CDC)—National Institute of Occupational Safety and Health (NIOSH) at their Pittsburgh Office of Mine Safety and Health Research. He continues in this role. In 2000, Dr. Haight received a faculty appointment and served as Associate Professor of Energy and Mineral Engineering at the Pennsylvania State University. He also worked as a manager and engineer for the Chevron Corporation domestically and internationally for eighteen years prior to joining the faculty at Penn State. Hehasa Ph.D. (1999) and Master's degree (1994) in Industrial and System Engineering, both from Auburn University. Dr. Haight does human error, process optimization, and intervention effectiveness research. He is a professional member of the American Society of Safety Engineers (where he serves as Federal Liaison to the Board of Trustees and the ASSE Foundation Research Committee Chair), the American Industrial Hygiene Association (AIHA), and the Human Factors and Ergonomics Society (HFES). He has published more than 30 peer-reviewed scientific journal articles and book chapters and is a co-author and the editor-in-chief of ASSE's *The Safety Professionals Handbook* and the John Wiley and Sons, *Handbook of Loss Prevention Engineering*.

ABOUT THE AUTHORS

Thomas S. Butler, Ph.D., CSP, CHMM, is a principal of Butler Health and Safety Inc., San Pedro, CA.

Salvatore Caccavale, B.S., CPE, CHMM, serves as the Vice President of Safety and Health for First Group America (passenger transportation) based in Cincinnati, OH.

William S. Fink, CIH, CSP, CHMM, is the Corporate EHS Manager for Oneida Total Integrated Enterprises (OTIE).

Judy Freeman is President, of Green SEED Energy, a company that develops and markets integrated solutions for bio-energy production. She is also Special Projects Manager with Gabriel Environmental Services, Inc., of Chicago, IL. She has been involved in the environmental and waste industries for over 26 years. She is past administrator of ASSE's Environmental Practice Specialty.

Anthony J. Joseph, Ph.D., was Professor and Director of Environmental, Health and Safety programs at the University of Connecticut.

James M. Miller, P.E., Ph.D., is President of Miller Engineering Associates of Ann Arbor Michigan and an Emeritus Professor of Industrial and Operations Engineering at the University of Michigan.

Tyler Nguyen, CSP, REP, is the Principal Safety and Environmental Compliance Specialist for Santa Clara County, California. He is also Past President of the American Society of Safety Engineers, Greater San Jose chapter.

Robert Stewart, M.S., CIH, CSP, is EHS Director for Oldcastle Building Products, Atlanta, GA.

Cherie C. Walton, CSP, is co-owner and Vice President of Reactives Management Corporation.

George C. Walton, M.S., CHMM, is founder and co-owner of Reactives Management Corporation.

Barry R. Weissman, REM, CHMM, CHS-IV, CIPS, CSP, is Corporate Manager—Health & Safety with Benjam in Moore and Company in Flanders, NJ.

Air Pollution Control and Mitigation

1

Anthony J. Joseph and Tyler Nguyen

LEARNING OBJECTIVES

- Develop a better awareness of the air pollution problem and the need for prevention and control.

- Be able to identify regulatory and compliance issues related to controlling and preventing air pollution associated with industrial operations.

- Internalize basic information for assisting, evaluating, and selecting air pollution control equipment and systems.

- Become familiar with guidelines for evaluating air pollution control systems and programs.

REVIEWING THE DEVELOPMENT of environmental issues over the past century, it can be said that the first period was characterized by the growth of a conservation movement that focused mainly on protection of wild and scenic areas and a general appreciation of nature in a rapidly urbanizing world. This began in the 1890s and lasted until the early 1960s. The second development, which lasted from roughly 1964 until the early 1990s, focused primarily on pollution control and remediation—reducing *point source* emissions into air, land, and water. Today, recognizing that air pollution is not simply industrial emissions, but a by-product of the social demands of living, pollution prevention is the method of dealing with environmental degradation.

The information presented in this chapter was extracted primarily from published works, such as the *Handbook of Environmental Health and Safety* (Koren and Bisesi 1995) and *Air Pollution Control* (Cooper and Alley 2002), as well as those found on the Environmental Protection Agency (EPA) Web site (www.epa.gov). Additional information was extracted from the chapters on air pollution and air pollution control in the *Encyclopaedia of Occupational Health and Safety* (ILO 1993) and from the *Handbook of Environmental Health and Safety Principles and Practices* (Koren 2003).

AIR POLLUTION CONTROL APPROACHES AND MEASURES

Two approaches are used for control and prevention of harmful effects from poor air quality:

1. air quality management
2. best practicable means

Air quality management aims at the preservation of environmental quality by prescribing the tolerated degree of pollution, leaving it to the public and local communities to devise and implement programs and actions that will ensure that the maximum accepted degree or level of pollutants in the air is not exceeded.

The best practicable means approach stresses that the air pollutant emissions should be kept to a minimum. This is defined through emission standards for single sources of air pollution. An emission standard is a limit on the amount or concentration of a pollutant emitted from a source.

In the author's opinion, among the many factors that must be considered in order to select the most adequate air pollution control strategy are:

- geographical situation and meteorology
- number of sources and their relative location to each other and to the surrounding communities
- type of sources and effluents
- characteristics of the pollutants involved
- degree of control required
- socioeconomic aspects and priorities

HISTORY OF AIR POLLUTION

The following is a historical review of air pollution and a statement of the importance of controlling air pollutants.

Notable Incidents

Air quality issues prior to and including industrial contributions were primarily concerned with *air abatement* issues. These included residential fuels, burning of coal, peat, and wood in urban areas, with contributions from trade industries such as metallurgy, ceramics, tanning, smelting, and woodworking. Kanarek (2004) noted that, between the 1880s and the 1940s, the United States saw no penalties for violation of early laws prohibiting the burning of peat and coal during designated times, for ore smelting in 1900–1930s that created pollutants such as sulfates, lead, zinc, and nickel, or for increased smog from electrical power plants and motor vehicles.

In the 1930s, Meuse Valley, Belgium, experienced a disastrous air pollution event caused by a combination of industry, dense population, and climatic conditions. Considered one of the first modern air pollution events, Meuse Valley, a densely populated and highly industrialized area, experienced a climatic event during the winter—high barometric pressure that created a thermal inversion. This temperature inversion restricted stack emissions from an industrial plant from dissipating into the atmosphere. The result was an inversion layer within the valley, consisting of smog comprised of sulfur dioxide and sulfuric acid mist; the evaporation of water from the nearby river also contributed to this development. Sixty-three people died, along with cattle, rats, and birds. Others experienced sore throat, shortness of breath, cough, phlegm, nausea, and vomiting.

In 1952, the Great London Smog occurred as a result of (among other factors) Londoners burning bituminous (soft, high-sulfur) coal. This led to:

- a temperature inversion, creating five days of the worst smog ever seen (smog = smoke + fog)
- a halt in public transportation
- a spike in the death rate and increased instances of bronchitis, coronary disease, myocardial degeneration, and pneumonia

Another historic air pollution incident occurred in 1948 in Donora, Pennsylvania. Located in the Monongahela River Valley, Donora was an industrialized city of approximately 14,000 people that had a steel mill industry, which smelted ore and burned coal within blast furnaces. On October 26, a stable temperature inversion, lasting nearly six days, trapped sulfur dioxide and zinc emissions within the valley, resulting in twenty deaths and hundreds of illnesses, with over 1500 requiring medical assistance. The U.S. Public Health Service became involved in what was recognized as air-pollution-caused incidents. There is some controversy as to the cause of the deaths—either fluorides or sulfur mists—and it is a question that is still unresolved today. Other notable air pollution incidents include the 1976 Seveso, Italy, dioxin release that exposed tens of thousands of humans and farm animals; the 1984 methyl isocyanate release in Bhopal, India, which was reported to have killed over two thousand people; the Chernobyl radioactive release in Russia in 1985; and the most recent World Trade Center disaster on September 11, 2001, which released asbestos and particulate matter, contributing to what is referred to today as the "World Trade Center Cough."

History of Pollution-Related Regulations

The Air Pollution Control Act of 1955

Enacted on July 14, 1955, the Air Pollution Control Act (P.L. 81-159) was the first federal legislation to address the national environmental problem of air pollution. It was "to provide research and technical assistance relating to air pollution control" (AMS 2002), providing funds for research in air pollution. The act "left states principally in charge of prevention and control of air pollution at the source" (Schnelle and Brown 2002). It declared that air pollution was a danger to public health and welfare, but preserved the "primary responsibilities and rights of the States and local government in controlling air pollution" (EPA 1955). The act set the federal government in a purely informational role, authorizing the U.S. Surgeon General to conduct research, investigate, and pass out information "relating to air pollution and the prevention and abatement thereof" (EPA 1955). However, the Air Pollution Control Act of 1955 contained no provisions for the federal government to actively combat air pollution by punishing polluters (Schnelle and Brown 2002).

California was the first state to act against air pollution. The metropolis of Los Angeles had begun to notice deteriorating air quality. Several geographical and meteorological problems unique to the Los Angeles area exacerbated the air pollution problem. Under the Air Pollution Control Act of 1955, research was federally funded to assist states in assessing air pollution sources and identifying the range of general health effects on urban populations.

Clean Air Act of 1963 and Amendments (1965–1969)

Eight years later, Congress passed the Clean Air Act of 1963 (CAA 1963). This act dealt with reducing air pollution by setting emissions standards for stationary sources such as steel mills and power plants. The CAA 1963 was the first federal legislation to address air pollution control. It established a federal program within the U.S. Public Health Service and authorized research into techniques for monitoring and controlling air pollution. In 1967, the Air Quality Act was passed in order to expand federal government activities. In accordance with this law, enforcement proceedings were initiated in areas subject to interstate air pollution transport. As part of these proceedings, for the first time the federal government conducted extensive ambient monitoring studies and stationary source inspections. Mobile sources of air pollution were not covered, although they are the largest source of many dangerous pollutants. Amendments to the Clean Air Act were passed in 1965, 1966, 1967, and 1969 (EPA 1971; Kanarek 2004).

These amendments authorized the Secretary of the Health, Education, and Welfare (HEW) Department to set standards for auto emissions, expanded local air pollution control programs, established air-quality control regions (AQCR), set air-quality standards and compliance deadlines for stationary source emissions, and authorized research on low-emission fuels and automobiles. Again, funding was made available to states and local authorities to assist in implementing programs, enforcing regulations, and supporting research programs into pollution control technologies.

The 1965 amendment created the President's Science Advisory Committee, which published a report entitled "Restoring the Quality of our Environment" (EPA 1971). The report identified numerous major sources of environmental contamination: municipal and industrial sewage, animal wastes, municipal solid wastes, mining wastes, and unintentional releases, which included automobile exhaust, smokestack emissions, pesticide mists, and agricultural chemicals that drained into waterways, among other things. The main report contained subpanel reports on soil contamination, the potential for global warming by carbon dioxide, the effects of chlorinating wastes, the health effects of environmental pollution, and the effects of pollutants on organisms other than man. Also in 1965, automobile emissions were added under the Motor Vehicles Air Pollution Control Act (EPA 1971; Kanarek 2004). Standards mirroring the California auto emissions requirements, which included emission control devices such as catalytic converters, were set as guidelines for other states to follow.

One of the first attempts toward identifying regional contributions of air pollution was made through the Air Quality Act of 1967. States were given regional designations by the Secretary of Health, Education, and Welfare and were tasked with identifying regional contributions affecting air quality. Regional boundaries were set, which created published criteria for sulfur oxide (SO_x) emissions and particulate matter. Also coming into play was the inclusion of climatic influence on the interboundary transport of air pollutants, including to and from Mexico and Canada.

Clean Air Act of 1970 (CAA 1970)

The year 1970 brought about the most radical environmental steps to date. The National Environmental Policy Act (NEPA) was formulated to emphasize a need for active participation of the national government in the protection of natural resources (EPA 1970). NEPA served as the conduit for the formation of two historic governmental agencies, the Council on Environmental Quality (CEQ) and the EPA, resulting in the passage of the CAA 1970. The enforcement of the CAA 1970 was the responsibility of the EPA.

The provisions within the CAA 1970 created:

- *The National Ambient Air Quality Standards* (NAAQS), establishing the six criteria pollutants: SO_x, nitrogen oxide (NO_x), particulate matter (PM10), lead, volatile organic compounds (VOCs), and carbon monoxide (CO)
- state implementation plans (SIPs) for the identification and regulation of stationary and mobile sources of pollution
- new source performance standards (NSPS) for all major stationary sources of air pollution
- requirements for best available control technology (BACT), including engineering technology to reduce pollutants, as well as requirements for administrative compliance through alternative fuels
- regulation of eight *National Emission Standards for Hazardous Air Pollutants* (NESHAPs): asbestos, vinyl chloride, radio nuclides, arsenic, mercury, beryllium, radon, and benzene
- increased enforcement authority of the EPA
- control technology guidelines (CTGs) for specific-source industrial categories

The CAA 1970 sought to tighten standards for air pollutants and enforcement that had failed under the 1967 Air Quality Act. By 1970, fewer than three dozen air quality regions had been designated, as compared to the anticipated 100. Not a single state had developed a full pollution control program. The CAA 1970 went from regional to national air quality standards, with Congress imposing statutory deadlines for compliance with emission standards.

1977 Amendments to the 1970 Clean Air Act

The amendments of the 1970 CAA, written in 1977, added provisions that utilized monitoring data to categorize air quality within regional boundaries. Areas were designated as attainment, nonattainment, or unclassified (EPA 1970; Kanarek 2004). The prevention of significant deterioration (PSD), an amendment to maintain regions that currently met or exceeded the NAAQS, was also established. The amendments required construction permits for new or modified stationary sources categorized as *major*, to include the installation of BACT for large industries and power plants. The 1977 CAA amendments, while tightening some standards under the PSD, also relaxed the enforcement authority of the EPA at the state level, allowing individual SIPs to set extended timeframes for implementing air quality emission standards for vehicles and industry.

Clean Air Act of 1990 (CAA 1990) and Amendments

Since 1970, the CAA has provided the primary framework for protecting the environment and people from the effects of air pollution. The CAA requires the EPA to significantly reduce daily, "routine" emissions of the most potent air pollutants. These routine emissions are defined as substances that are known or suspected to cause serious health problems such as cancer or birth defects. The CAA 1990 refers to these substances as "hazardous air pollutants," commonly referred to as toxic air pollutants or, simply, air toxics. Prior to 1990 the EPA set standards for each toxic air pollutant, based on its particular health risks. This approach proved difficult and minimally effective at reducing emissions. As a result, when amending the CAA in 1990, Congress directed the EPA to use a technology- and performance-based approach to significantly reduce emissions of air toxics from major sources of air pollution, followed by a risk-based approach to address any remaining, or residual, risks (EPA 1990; Kanarek 2004).

Standards are developed under the technology-based approach for controlling the routine emissions of air toxics from each major type of facility within an industry group (or source category). These standards are known as maximum achievable control technology (MACT) standards. They are based on emission levels already achieved by the better-controlled and lower-emitting sources in an industry. This approach provides a level economic playing field by ensuring that facilities employing cleaner processes and good emission controls are not disadvantaged by competitors with poorer controls.

In setting MACT standards, the EPA does not generally prescribe a specific control technology. Instead, whenever feasible, the agency sets a performance level based on technology or other practices already used by the industry. Facilities are free to achieve these performance levels in whatever way is most cost-effective for them. The deadline for companies to submit detailed applications for permits, under which state air agencies would determine their hazardous air pollutant (HAP) emission limits on a case-by-case basis, was scheduled for May 15, 2002; on April 5, 2002 it was extended to May 15, 2004. The promulgation delay by the EPA forced industry and the state air agencies to make MACT determinations in the absence of a specific rule, or based on proposed rules, rather than a final rule. Due to the dynamic nature of this standard, it was advisable to evaluate its applicability on a case-by-case basis as it applies to a facility. The EPA projected that, once fully implemented, these standards would cut emissions of toxic air pollutants by nearly 1.5 million tons yearly.

The CAA 1990 and its amendments introduced some major changes, holding states responsible for implementing and enforcing the act; conducting hearings for permits to build power or chemical plants, and setting fines for violating air pollution limits. However, the ultimate responsibility for enforcing the CAA remains with the EPA. States were allowed to establish standards more stringent than federal standards and were also required to develop SIPs. These plans provide information on how the state will comply with the requirements of the CAA. States are required to involve the public through hearings and commenting opportunities in the development of their SIP. The EPA must approve all SIPs. In states with no approved SIP, and the federal CAA is enforced.

In 1990, provisions written in the previous titles of CAA 1970 were enhanced to include nine more titles (EPA 1990):

1. Attainment of the 1970 *National Ambient Air Quality Standards* (NAAQS), and timeframes for compliance
2. New emission reductions from mobile sources of air pollution
3. Emission control standards for the 189 identified toxics under the *National Emission Standards for Hazardous Air Pollutants* (NESHAP)
4. Acid rain deposition and transport from sources of SO_x and NO_x
5. Permit requirements for stationary sources
6. Identification and reduction of stratospheric ozone-depleting chlorofluorocarbons (CFCs)
7. EPA enforcement rights
8. Miscellaneous issues
9. Research programs aimed at the reduction of air pollution

The 1990 Clean Air Act Amendments (CAAA) introduced the "Haze and Visibility Rule," later adopted in 1999, which seeks to reduce smog and soot problems by emphasizing PM10 and ozone. Congress also introduced another version of control technology for both stationary and mobile sources called "best available retrofit technology" (BART), which was applied to 26 source categories and was finalized in April 2005 (EPA 2005a).

A somewhat controversial emissions trading initiative was introduced in 2003 by the Bush administration as an alternative to provisions in the CAA of 1990. The Clear Skies Act (CSA) was introduced in Congress in 2005, though never passed as law; it was supposed to dramatically and steadily cut power-plant emissions of three of the worst air pollutants (EPA 2005c). President Bush indicated that the CSA would do the following:

- Cut sulfur dioxide (SO_2) emissions by 73 percent from current emissions of 11 million tons to a cap of 4.5 million tons in 2010 and 3 million tons in 2018.
- Cut emissions of nitrogen oxides (NO_x) by 67 percent, from current emissions of 5 million tons to a cap of 2.1 million tons in 2008 and 1.7 million tons in 2018.
- Cut mercury emissions by 69 percent—the first-ever national cap on mercury emissions. Emissions would be cut from current emissions of 48 tons to a cap of 26 tons.

Opponents contended that the emissions trading under the CSA would change the CAA limits. CSA would loosen the cap on NO_x to 2.1 by 2008; and on SO_x (acid rain) emissions to 4.5 million tons by 2010. There is no limit set on CO emissions because it is a voluntary program. By the fifteenth year of the Bush plan, there would be an estimated 450,000 more tons of NO_x, one million more tons of SO_x, and 9.5 more tons of mercury in the environment (Sierra Club 2004). The Bush administration has declined signing the Kyoto Protocol, a global warming reduction document entered into by other countries (West 2005). The CSA is a separate U.S. plan allowing the President to manage ozone and NO_x emissions independently of international scrutiny (Kanarek 2004; EPA 2005c; Montague 1999).

FEATURES OF THE CLEAN AIR ACT AMENDMENTS OF 1990 (CAAA 1990)

The federal CAAA 1990 was expanded from six titles to nine. The intent of CAA 1970 was to enhance air quality management with the introduction of specific pollutant criteria, state monitoring programs, stationary permitting, and federal enforcement rights. It failed to address improvements to human health and the environment from acid rain, regional smog, and air toxics, resulting in the amendments. Unfortunately, the 1990 amendments failed to address two increasingly prominent global air pollution problems: greenhouse gas emissions and mercury pollution. Carbon dioxide (CO_2) is the most important of these emissions, and, as noted earlier, electric power plants emit one-third of the total carbon dioxide emissions in the United States. Mercury pollution from coal combustion is becoming a crucial regional and global issue because of contamination of essential food supplies (Wooley 2000).

Major features of the CAAA 1990 are discussed under the following headings:

- *National Ambient Air Quality Standards* (NAAQS)
- Mobile Sources: Vehicle Emissions
- Hazardous Air Pollutants (HAPs)
- Acid Deposition
- Stratospheric Ozone and Global Climate
- Air Pollution Control Research

National Ambient Air Quality Standards (NAAQS)

In 1971, then-EPA-administrator William Ruckelshaus announced that NAAQS had been established. The standards applied to six criteria pollutants:

- sulfur oxides (SO_x)
- particulate matter (PM10, particulate matter 10 microns or less in diameter)
- carbon monoxide
- photochemical oxidants (ozone)
- nitrogen oxides (NO_x)
- hydrocarbons (ozone precursor)

This occurred in response to the requirement that the administrator publish, within thirty days of December 31, 1970, air quality standards for mobile and stationary sources that contribute to air pollution. By 1978, the EPA had revised the NAAQS to include lead as a recognized health hazard, particularly for children.

In 1978, the EPA published a list of nonattainment areas within the country, regions that had not met the NAAQS for the six specified criteria. Many reports across the country indicated that the targeted deadlines were unattainable as originally envisioned. In addition, it appeared that the Clean Air Act Amendments of 1977 (CAAA 1977) did not provide the most

TABLE 1

Six Criteria Pollutants, Major Emission Sources, Chemical Interactions, and Potential Control Technologies

Criteria Pollutant	Source(s) & 1997 Emission Estimates (short tons per year)	Basic Chemical Reactions	Control Technology/ Main Options
Sulfur dioxide (SO_2) Corrosive gas	Transportation: 1.4 Fuel Combustion: 17.3 Industrial Processes: 1.7 Miscellaneous: 0.0 Total: 20.4 % of 1970 Total: 65%	Reacts in the atmosphere to form acid rain $S + O_2 \rightarrow SO_2$ $SO_2 + H_2O \rightarrow H_2SO_4$	Scrubbing
PM10 Particulate matter, as a solid or vapor between 0.1–0.00005 mm	Transportation: 0.7 Fuel Combustion: 1.1 Industrial Processes: 1.3 Miscellaneous: 0.0 Total: 3.1 % of 1970 Total: —	Coarse: road dust, sea spray, construction Fine: fossil fuel combustion from autos and industry	Mechanical separators, fabric filters, electrostatic precipitators, and wet scrubbers.
Carbon monoxide (CO) Odorless gas emitted from fossil fuel combustion, primarily autos	Transportation: 67.0 Fuel Combustion: 4.8 Industrial Processes: 6.1 Miscellaneous: 9.6 Total: 87.5 % of 1970 Total: 78%	CO does not react readily in the atmosphere $CO + O_2 \rightarrow CO_2$	Promote complete combustion or oxidation.
Ozone (O_3) Troposphere ozone gas is a contributor to smog	Transportation: 7.7 Fuel Combustion: 0.9 Industrial Processes: 9.8 Miscellaneous: 0.8 Total: 19.2 % of 1970 Total: 70%	$NO + HC + Sunlight \rightarrow NO_2 + O_3$	Reduce emissions of its precursors
Nitrogen dioxide (NO_2) Reddish-brown gas generated from fossil fuel combustion	Transportation: 11.6 Fuel Combustion: 10.7 Industrial Processes: 0.9 Miscellaneous: 0.3 Total: 23.5 % of 1970 Total: 116%	$NO + HC + O_2 + Sunlight \rightarrow NO_2 + O_3$ (ozone) $NO_2 + H_2O \rightarrow$ nitric acid (acid rain) $NO_2 +$ cation $\rightarrow$ particulate matter	Combustion modifications and flue gas treatment.
Lead (Pb) Toxic blue-gray metal	Transportation: 0.00052 Fuel Combustion: 0.00050 Industrial Processes: 0.0029 Miscellaneous: 0.0 Total: 0.0039 % of 1970 Total: 1.7%	Tetraethyl-lead in gasoline $Pb(C_2H_5)_4$	Substitution

(Adapted from Fleagle and Businger 1980)

effective means to handle the problems associated with ozone nonattainment areas. Under CAAA 1990, designated nonattainment areas were given clarification that revised the mechanism used to meet attainment deadlines. The previously defined nonattainment areas were further subcategorized based upon severity of pollution, deadlines were revised, and sanctions, originally reserved for nonattainment, were used to ensure compliance with the CAA 1990.

Criteria Pollutants

Table 1 presents the six criteria pollutants, major emission sources, chemical interactions, and some potential control technologies.

NAAQS Nonattainment Areas

The CAAA 1990 required states to revise their SIPs to meet the national primary and secondary ambient air quality standards. Title 42, Section 7410, states that "Each State shall . . . submit to the Administrator . . . after the promulgation of a national primary ambient air quality standard . . . a plan which provides for implementation, maintenance and enforcement of such primary standard in each air quality control region within such State." Additionally, under the prevention of significant deterioration (PSD) requirements within the act, states must prohibit any source which contributes significantly to nonattainment in, or interfere with the maintenance by, any state with respect to any such national primary or secondary ambient air quality standard. Classifications within regions where the six criteria pollutants of the NAAQS apply were identified as nonattainment, attainment, and reclassified. Within the nonattainment classification were further area classes identified as marginal, moderate, serious, severe, or extreme for the particular criteria pollutants for ozone. The designated areas within regions were also required to address cross-jurisdictional air pollution. "The boundaries of serious, severe, or extreme nonattainment areas located within metropolitan statistical areas (MSAs) or consolidated metropolitan statistical areas (CMSAs) are to be expanded to include the entire MSAs or CMSAs." This led to an expansion of geographic areas classified as "nonattainment" (DOE OHSS 1996).

The EPA maintains a Web site providing yearly data from different geographic areas within the United States. Air quality data can be retrieved for the entire country by EPA region, state, and county. The data includes emission and monitoring information on pollution sources and concentrations. Emissions data are estimates provided by the computing of annual data from individual sources, such as power plants, industry, and vehicles. Monitoring data is compiled from designated outdoor monitoring stations situated in 4000 strategic areas throughout the country. Ambient air quality information is supplied to the EPA by the states, and a yearly summary for individual stations is generated.

Monitoring sites report data to the EPA for six air pollutants termed *criteria pollutants* because of the requirement that the EPA describe the characteristics and potential health and welfare effects of these pollutants. It is on the basis of the criteria that standards are set or revised. These are:

- carbon monoxide (CO)
- nitrogen dioxide (NO_2)
- ozone (O_3)
- sulfur dioxide (SO_2)
- particulate matter—PM10 and PM2.5, which are acronyms for particulate matter consisting of particles smaller than 10 and 2.5 micrometers, respectively.
- lead (Pb)

One might expect that the EPA would track emissions of the same six criteria air pollutants. However, ozone is not emitted directly but forms through chemical reactions of organic compounds with nitrogen oxides in the air, mediated by sunlight. The EPA tracks emissions of lead only as a hazardous air pollutant, defined as a pollutant to which no ambient air quality standard is applicable and that may cause or contribute to an increase in mortality or in serious illness. Ammonia reacts with nitric and sulfuric acids in the atmosphere to form fine particulate matter, so the EPA tracks ammonia emissions. Thus, the EPA tracks emissions data of the following air pollutants (EPA 2004b):

- carbon monoxide (CO)
- sulfur dioxide (SO_2)
- particulate matter (PM10 and PM2.5) and three precursors/promoters of criteria air pollutants:
- volatile organic compounds (VOC)
- nitrogen oxides (NO_x)
- ammonia (NH_3)

Mobile Sources: Vehicle Emissions

The CAA 1970 required emission reductions from automobile exhaust—considered a major contributor to nitrogen oxides (NO_x), hydrocarbons (HCs), and carbon monoxide (CO).

The act directs the EPA to prescribe the following (EPA 1971):

- standards to reduce emissions of CO and HC by 90% from 1970 model levels in the 1975 model autos
- NO_x standards, reduced by 90% from 1971 model levels, to take effect in 1976 model year
- a description by companies of the basic techniques being explored to meet emission standards

EPA sent this requirement to 28 automobile manufacturers; however, delays in meeting the CAA 1970 requirements occurred in part because of the failure of the automobile industry to meet emission-reduction standards and in part because of the energy crisis of the 1970s. By 1975, the oxidation catalytic converter was introduced on newer vehicles. Additionally, gasoline suppliers were to reformulate leaded gas (introduced in 1923); the purpose was to eliminate lead by the introduction of alternative fuels. Even with the phase-out of leaded gasoline in the United States by 1986, it was estimated that the use of lead had deposited seven million tons of nondegradable lead throughout soils, water, and indoor soot (Western Houston Association Issues 2003). Note that between 1975 and 1988 there was a 99 percent reduction in leaded gas.

The CAAA 1990 set more stringent emission standards for automobiles and some categories of light trucks for further reduction in pollutants from mobile sources. CAAA 1990 also required:

- stricter emission standards
- stricter standards for gasoline and diesel fuel
- programs for enforcement of the development of vehicles designed to operate on "clean" fuels (methanol, ethanol, propane, natural gas, and electricity)

The CAAA 1990 also used emission standards compliance in the levying of major highway funding to the states under Transportation Conformity (Section 176(c)). This encourages states to continue to reduce emissions of the six criteria pollutants (NAAQS), in keeping with the maintenance of attainment areas, primarily by encouraging programs within their SIPs that promote car-pooling, gas conservation, and mass transit.

Hazardous Air Pollutants (HAPs)

Hazardous air pollutants, or air toxics, are known or suspected to cause cancer or other serious health problems related to (for example) reproduction and birth and also to affect the environment adversely. The presence of HAPs in the air is more localized than are the criteria pollutants, and HAPs are usually found at highest levels close to their sources. Examples of air toxic pollutants include benzene (found in gasoline), mercury (from coal combustion), perchloroethylene (emitted from some dry-cleaning facilities), and methylene chloride (used as a solvent by a number of industries). Most air toxics originate from manmade sources, including mobile sources such as cars, trucks, and construction equipment; stationary sources such as factories, refineries, and power plants; and indoor sources such as some building materials and cleaning solvents (EPA 2005b).

In 1985, the EPA set forth a strategy for the identification and reduction of HAPs, or air toxics, from specific major and minor stationary source categories. This applied to operational emissions and accidental releases. The strategy went from focusing on categories of chemicals to focusing on specific pollutants emitted by industry, power plants, and waste combustors. Included in the strategy were mobile sources and fuel refineries. The 1985 strategy outlined the following efforts (EPA 1997):

- expanding the focus of the national air toxics control program from solely regulating individual pollutants to also regulating multiple pollutants from different source categories
- expanding the program to reduce risk in specific communities having air toxic problems
- increasing federal support of state air toxic programs, allowing states to improve their capabilities to deal with air toxics within their borders

- improving emergency preparedness and response at all levels of government for sudden, accidental releases of HAPs
- beginning new efforts to give the public the information needed to prevent, prepare for, and respond to toxic accidents

The CAA 1990 began focusing on HAPs emitted by specific major and area source categories, based upon the size of the industry and its potential to emit toxic air pollutants. The following is a summary of the requirements of Title 42, Section 7412, of the CAA:

- Require emission controls for major sources, defined as stationary sources with the potential to emit 10 tons per year or more of any hazardous air pollutant or 25 tons per year or more of any combination of hazardous air pollutants.
- Regulate 189 (now 188) listed hazardous air pollutants under Title 42, Section 7412.
- Revise the list to include pollutants found through scientific study to adversely affect human health and the environment.
- Identify major or area (nonmajor) categories of emissions in accordance with established emission standards.

Along with the identification of source categories, MACT for the reduction and control of emissions included, but was not limited to, end-of-the stack controls, material substitution, recovery/recycling, and chemical use reductions within processes. Emission standards for source categories that emit HAPs must, within reasonable cost constraints, include provisions to reduce pollutants in accordance with established pollutant limits. Hence, control technology should:

- reduce the volume of, or eliminate emissions of, such pollutants through process changes, substitution of materials, or other modifications
- enclose systems or processes to eliminate emissions
- collect, capture, or treat such pollutants when released from a process, stack, storage, or fugitive emission point
- reduce pollutants through design, equipment, work practice, or operational standards (including operator training or certification)
- employ a combination of the above

When developing a MACT standard for a particular source category, the EPA looks at the level of emissions currently being achieved by the best-performing similar sources through clean processes, control devices, work practices, or other methods. These emission levels set a baseline (often referred to as the MACT floor) for the new standard. At a minimum, a MACT standard must achieve, throughout the industry, a level of emissions control at least equivalent to the MACT floor. The EPA can establish a more stringent standard when it makes economic, environmental, and public-health "sense."

The MACT floor is established differently for existing sources and for new sources.

- For existing sources, the MACT floor must equal the average emission limitations currently achieved by the best-performing 12 percent of sources in that source category, if there are 30 or more existing sources. If there are fewer than 30 existing sources, then the MACT floor must equal the average emission limitation achieved by the best-performing five sources in the category.
- For new sources, the MACT floor must equal the level of emissions control currently achieved by the best-controlled similar source.

Wherever feasible, the EPA writes the final MACT standard as an emissions limit (i.e., as a percent reduction in emissions or a concentration limit that regulated sources must achieve). Emission limits provide flexibility for industry to determine the most effective way to comply with the standard.

Acid Deposition

Acid deposition, or acid rain, is addressed under Title IV of CAAA 1990, which calls for regulatory programs to control emissions of sulfur dioxide (SO_2) and nitrogen dioxide (NO_2). Sulfur dioxide reacts in the atmosphere in the presence of water to form sulfuric acid, and nitrogen dioxide reacts with sunlight to form tropospheric ozone, with atmospheric moisture to form nitric acid, and with cations in the atmosphere to form particulate matter in the form of gases of sulfates and nitrates (PM10 and PM2.5). The primary sources of SO_2 and NO_2 come from the combustion of fossil fuels such as coal and oil used to generate electricity at power plants. EPA regulations require that major sources, such as power plants, install continuous monitoring devices to measure the quantities of emissions. The goal of emission standards was to reduce NO_2 emissions by 10 million tons in 2000 and SO_2 emissions by 10 million tons below the 1980 standards (EPA 2005a).

Emissions trading was established as a form of reduction strategy whereby plants that reduce emissions below their allotted standards could sell their excess to other power plants and industries unable to meet source category emission standards. Under the Acid Rain Program of the Clean Air Markets Division, major reductions of sulfur dioxide and nitrogen dioxide from electric utilities were achieved through a new approach to environmental protection that featured market incentives. This nationwide cap-and-trade method of regulation has resulted in significant environmental progress and cost savings. Under the emissions-trading program, each allowance permits a unit to emit one ton of SO_2 during or after a specified year. For each ton of SO_2 emitted in a given year, one allowance is retired, that is, it can no longer be used. The program acts almost like a stock, where companies and the public may purchase units, resell them, create accounts, or, in some instances, retire the units. Utilities are limited to 8.95 million allowances per year (EPA 2005).

Acid-Rain Deposition Mapping

The U.S. Geological Survey (USGS) provides tracking data and other information on precipitation deposition of rain, sleet, and snow by monitoring location and identifies areas impacted by sulfur and nitrogen deposition. The USGS also includes recent reports and presentations on the effects of pollutant deposition.

Atmospheric Deposition of Air Toxics to the Great Lakes and Coastal Waters

Under the CAAA 1990, the EPA and the Under Secretary of Commerce of Oceans and Atmosphere must create a report that identifies the effects of air toxics on the Great Lakes as well as the Chesapeake Bay, Lake Champlain, and coastal waters. The study must use the existing national monitoring stations for the Great Lakes region and deploy an atmospheric monitoring network for coastal waters. By 1993, and on a biennial basis thereafter, pursuant to Section 7412 (6)(m), the Under Secretary of Commerce for Oceans and Atmosphere must use monitoring data to create a report to be submitted to Congress that identifies atmospheric impacts to the Great Lakes, Chesapeake Bay, Lake Champlain, and coastal waters. The report must:

- assess the contribution of atmospheric deposition to pollution loadings
- identify impacts to the environment and public health of any pollutant that is attributable to atmospheric deposition
- describe the sources of any pollution
- assess whether pollutant loadings cause or contribute to overshooting of drinking water standards or water quality standards
- indicate whether any federal law revisions are required to ensure protection of human health and the environment

Since 1990, the EPA has issued three reports to Congress on the deposition of air toxics and their detrimental effects on the Great Waters (i.e., the Great Lakes, the Chesapeake Bay, Lake Champlain, and coastal waters). In these reports, the EPA lists fifteen pollutants of greatest concern, most of which have a tendency to persist in the environment and accumulate in organisms such as fish. The pollutants of concern are metals (mercury, cadmium, lead), dioxins, furans, polycyclic organic matter, polychlorinated biphenyls (PCBs), pesticides (such as chlordane and DDT/DDE), and nitrogen compounds. Nitrogen compounds from the deposition of air toxics can intensify nutrient enrichment (or eutrophication) of coastal water bodies.

EPA's most recent report, issued in 2000, provides an update on atmospheric deposition of pollutants to the Great Waters and identifies activities that will reduce these pollutants (EPA 2000; Kanarek 2004).

Several of the MACT standards are expected to substantially cut emissions of mercury, dioxins, and other pollutants of concern to the Great Waters from sources such as municipal waste combustors and medical waste incinerators. Compared to the 1990 baseline, these alone account for almost 30 percent of mercury emissions and over 70 percent of dioxin emissions nationwide (EPA 2005a).

Mercury Emissions from Coal-Fired Electric Utilities

Mercury is one of the 188 listed toxic air pollutants. It is of concern because it does not degrade in the environment but persists. The largest emitters of mercury are electric utility plants (primarily coal-fired plants), which are estimated to emit approximately one-third of all manmade mercury in the United States. The EPA reported in 2004 that reduction achievements exceeded expectations. The Institute of Clean Air Companies (ICAC) reported that the air pollution control industry had already achieved commercial readiness of mercury control and measurement technologies and could surpass the level of reductions proposed by the EPA in the December 2003 Utility Mercury Reduction Rule. Multiple mercury control technologies are available at a reasonable cost for a range of coals and equipment. Mercury reductions of 50 percent (24 tons of emissions) are achievable by 2008 to 2010, and with flexibility in the rule, a 70 percent reduction (14 tons of emissions) is achievable. Continuous emission measurement systems (CEMS) for mercury are available and provide the technology needed to document compliance, improve process controls, and support the emissions certainty needed for regulatory flexibility such as trading programs (ICAC 2004).

Integrated Urban Air Toxics Strategy

A key component of future efforts to reduce air toxics is the integrated urban air toxics strategy, released by the EPA in July 1999. The strategy presents a framework to address air toxics in urban areas and builds on the substantial emission reductions already achieved in cars, trucks, fuels, and industries such as chemical plants and oil refineries. The strategy outlines actions to further reduce emissions of air toxics and to improve the EPA's understanding of the health risks posed by air toxics in urban areas. The goals of the strategy are to reduce the risk of cancer by 75 percent and to substantially reduce noncancer risks associated with air toxics from commercial and industrial sources. The strategy also reflects the need to address any disproportionate impacts on sensitive populations, including children, the elderly, minorities, and low-income communities (EPA 1999).

The reduction of SO_2 and NO_2 emissions, both of which had specific timeframes for emissions reduction, is set on a phase-in schedule (Wikipedia 2005b):

- Phase I began in 1995 and affected 263 units at 110 (mostly coal-burning) electric utility plants located in 21 eastern and midwestern states.
- An additional 182 units joined phase I of the program as substitution or compensating units, bringing the total of phase I–affected units to 445. Emissions data indicate that the 1995 SO_2 emissions at these units nationwide were reduced by almost 40% below their required level.
- Phase II, which began in 2000, tightened the annual emission limits imposed on these large, higher-emitting plants and also set restrictions on smaller, cleaner plants fired by coal, oil, and gas, encompassing over 2000 units. The program affects existing utility units serving generators having an output capacity of greater than 25 megawatts, as well as all new utility units.
- The act also called for a 2-million-ton reduction in NO_x emissions by the year 2000. A significant portion of this reduction has been achieved in coal-fired utility boilers that were required to install low NO_x burner technologies and to meet new emission standards.

Stratospheric Ozone and Global Climate

Title VI of CAA 1990 describes the requirements for identifying stratospheric ozone-depleting substances, the monitoring of class I and class II chemicals, and phase-out schedules for these substances. Class I substances include CFCs, or chlorinated compounds, that have mostly been phased out from production, with some exceptions. Class II substances include HCFCs, which are slated for phase-out by 2030. Ozone-depleting potential factors were established by the EPA in determining the effects of the most harmful substances. Federal measures to control emissions that impact stratospheric ozone depletion take the initiative to

- create area classifications of nonattainment for ozone within state and interstate boundaries
- establish control technology guidelines (CTGs) for the reduction or elimination of ozone-depleting gases
- identify the sources of ozone depletion—i.e., volatile organic compounds (VOCs), nitrogen dioxides (NO_2), carbon dioxide (CO_2), and their precursors

Ozone Classifications for Boundary/Interboundary Attainment

Ozone (O_3) is a primary component of smog. Ozone is described in its naturally occurring state and as a toxic chemical pollutant. In the naturally occurring state, ozone exists as a thin layer between the troposphere and the stratosphere, acting as a filter for harmful ultraviolet (UV) radiation. As a toxic chemical, O_3 is created when organic compounds—such as hydrocarbons emitted from the combustion of gasoline and solvents and nitrogen dioxides from fuels combustion—combine with UV rays to form the unstable gas O_3. This can be written chemically as

$$NO_2 + \text{sunlight} \rightarrow NO + O \quad (1)$$
$$O + O_2 \rightarrow O_3$$

In 1989, the CAA prescribed classifications of areas for attainment of design values of ozone concentrations, set in parts per million (ppm). Under Title 42 (Section 7511) of the 1990 CAA, attainment dates for each classification were established for state compliance as presented in Table 2. Anticipating the challenge to achieve these targeted dates, provisions were set for extended dates of attainment and for subsequent reclassifications of nonattainment areas.

Control Technology Guidelines (CTGs)

Sources of volatile organic compounds (VOCs), which include manmade organic compounds such as gasoline, solvents, and other hydrocarbons, received CTGs to begin implementation within three years of the November 1990 CAAA. The amendments brought into regulation an additional eleven source categories for which VOC emissions had not been previously set.

Under the CTGs, the EPA is required to periodically review sources and modify the listing according to the determination of VOC contribution toward ozone attainment. Those source categories that are priority contributors in ozone nonattainment areas include power plants, hazardous waste incinerators, and industries considered major sources (depending upon tons/emissions of VOCs), such as aerospace, shipbuilding, and chemical manufacturing facilities. These major source categories emit VOCs from such operations as degreasing, paint-spraying, and coating operations, with aggregate contributions of 25 tons of VOCs or more yearly. Such facilities are required to implement a progression of control technologies based upon available technology, from RACT to the more aggressive BACT and MACT, as prescribed by CTGs (EPA 1997).

Key Sources of Ozone Depletion

Title 42, Section 7511, of the CAA 1990 further defines the potential of consumer or commercial products to release VOCs. This applies to "any substance, product

TABLE 2

Attainment Dates for State Compliance with Ozone Values

Area Class	Design Value (ppm)	Primary Standard Attainment Date
Marginal	0.121–0.138	3 years after November 15, 1990
Moderate	0.138–0.160	6 years after November 15, 1990
Serious	0.160–0.180	9 years after November 15, 1990
Severe	0.180–0.280	15 years after November 15, 1990
Extreme	0.280 and above	20 years after November 15, 1990

(Adapted from *Federal Register* 2001)

(including paints, coatings and solvents) or article (including any container or packaging) held by any person, the use, consumption, storage, disposal, destruction, or decomposition of which may result in the release of VOCs." This has been of particular importance within industries such as the aerospace industry that ship degreed components that frequently undergo scrutiny for VOC because of the use of chlorinated solvents.

As required under the CAAA, by 1993, the EPA had to generate a report detailing the contribution of various sources under the categories of consumer and commercial products and identify sources with the potential for exceeding ozone levels in noncompliance with NAAQs. These reports divide the source categories into groups with emissions comprising 80 percent VOCs and assign a priority and incremental timeline for VOC reduction.

Although CFCs and HCFCs have received the most international attention, the increasing use of fossil fuels in the United States and, particularly, in developing countries has also been recognized as a major contributor to global warming. The burning of fossil fuels, which include oils, coal, and natural gas, contributes much carbon dioxide to the atmosphere. The estimated CO_2 in the atmosphere has increased since industrialization in the 1860s. Many environmental groups and organizations, such as the Sierra Club, identified the United States as a major contributor to CO_2, stating that "[t]he US has four percent of the world's population yet emits 25% of the global warming pollution. Power plants emit 40% of US carbon dioxide pollution, the primary global warming pollutant. In 1999, coal-fired power plants alone released 490.5 million metric tons of CO_2 into the atmosphere (32% of the total CO_2 emissions for 1999)" (Sierra Club 2004).

There have been a number of new requirements proposed or already implemented regarding greenhouse gas (GHG) emissions. In the United States, on November 8, 2010, the EPA finalized a rule regarding reporting requirements for the petroleum and natural gas industry under 40 CFR Part 98, the regulatory framework for the Greenhouse Gas (GHG) Reporting Program.

This final rule requires petroleum and natural gas facilities that emit 25,000 metric tons or more of carbon dioxide (CO_2) equivalent per year to report annual methane (CH_4) and CO_2 emissions from equipment leaks and venting, and emissions of CO_2, CH_4, and nitrous oxide (N_2O) from gas flaring and from onshore petroleum and natural gas production stationary and portable combustion emissions and combustion emissions from stationary equipment involved in natural gas distribution.

Emerging industries (such as solar panel and semiconductor) and traditional ones (such as aluminum) use perfluorocarbons (PFCs) in their manufacturing processes. PFCs are fluorocarbons, compounds derived from hydrocarbons by replacement of hydrogen atoms by fluorine atoms. PFCs are made up of carbon and fluorine atoms only, such as octafluoropropane, perfluorohexane, and perfluorodecalin. Aluminum and semiconductor industries are greatly affected by controlling PFC emissions (EPA 2011).

Air Pollution Control Research

CAA 1990 provisions included the use of public and private funds for air pollution prevention, especially for

- research
- investigations
- training
- advisory committees for technical issues
- alternate fuels research
- alternative vehicles research

To achieve these provisions, the EPA was required to establish a program that supports the research and transfer of air pollution prevention and control technologies and systems. Specifically, the EPA was required to:

- promote facilities research and monitoring, as well as scientific studies and public surveys into the effects of air pollution on human health
- provide federal technical and financial assistance to the states' environmental protection agencies or other "public or private agencies, institutions and organizations and individuals" (EPA 1990a)

- work collaboratively with the states to identify specific air pollution contributions and sources; identify solutions for preventing air pollution from affecting communities
- create diverse panels of experts (Department of Defense, Department of Energy, the National Aeronautics and Space Administration, and the National Oceanic and Atmospheric Administration) to conduct research analysis
- provide means for training individuals in air pollution recognition and prevention

In addition, the agency was required to collect and distribute results of investigative air pollution studies and reports and to make them available to the public.

Throughout the CAA of 1990, several requirements are given for the generation of reports periodically updated over a series of years. These include:

- air modeling and data management
- atmospheric effects of pollutants
- trend analysis for ozone, VOCs and reactivity, nitrogen dioxides, sulfur dioxides, carbon dioxide, and particulate emissions
- national/international networks dealing with the effects of pollutants on human health and on ecosystems

A large portion of funding has been allocated to to foster a better understanding of the properties of ozone-depleting chemicals for analysis of inventory and chemical reactivity. Every five years the EPA must submit a report to Congress on the progress and effectiveness of monitoring programs, research committees, data generation, and overall regulatory control of air pollution programs.

Clean Air Act Achievements

Total emissions of the six criteria air pollutants identified in the Clean Air Act dropped again in 2003; air in the United States was the cleanest it had been in three decades. Annual emission statistics for these six pollutants are considered major indicators of the quality of the nation's air because of their importance for human health and the existence of their long-standing national standards.

Emissions have continued to decrease even as the U.S. economy has increased by more than 150 percent. Since 1970 (changing numbers to reflect the 1970 baseline), the aggregate total emissions for the six pollutants (carbon monoxide, nitrogen oxides, sulfur dioxide, particulate matter, volatile organic compounds, and lead) have been cut from 301.5 million tons per year to 147.8 million tons per year, a decrease of 51 percent. Total 2003 emissions were down 12 million tons since 2000, a 7.8 percent reduction (Sierra Club 2004; EPA 2004).

Benefits of the Clean Air Act from 1990 to 2020

The EPA develops periodic reports that estimate the benefits and costs of the Clean Air Act. The main goal of these reports is to provide Congress and the public with comprehensive, up-to-date, peer-reviewed information on the Clean Air Act's social benefits and costs, including improvements in human health, welfare, and ecological resources, as well as the impact of the act's provisions on the U.S. economy. This report is the result of *The Benefits and Costs of the Clean Air Act—Second Prospective Study from 1990 to 2020* (EPA 2011).

The CAAA of 1990 augmented the significant progress made in improving the nation's air quality through the original Clean Air Act of 1970 and its 1977 amendments. The amendments built on the existing structure of the original Clean Air Act, but went beyond those requirements to tighten and clarify implementation goals and timing, increase the stringency of some federal requirements, revamp the hazardous air pollutant regulatory program, refine and streamline permitting requirements, and introduce new programs for the control of acid rain and stratospheric ozone depleters.

The main purpose of this report was to document the costs and benefits of the 1990 CAAA provisions incremental to those costs and benefits achieved from implementing the original 1970 Clean Air Act and the 1977 amendments. The analysis estimates the costs and benefits of reducing emissions of air pollutants by comparing a "with-CAAA" scenario that reflects expected or likely future measures implemented under the CAAA with a "without-CAAA" scenario that freezes the scope and stringency of emission controls at the levels that existed prior to implementing the CAAA.

There are six basic steps undertaken to complete this analysis:

1. air pollutant emissions modeling
2. compliance cost estimation
3. ambient air quality modeling
4. health and environmental effects estimation
5. economic valuation of these effects
6. results aggregation and uncertainty characterization

The results of the analysis make it abundantly clear that the benefits of the CAAA exceed its costs by a wide margin, making the CAAA a good investment for the nation. The report estimates that the annual dollar value of benefits of air quality improvements will be quite substantial, and will grow over time as emission control programs take full effect, reaching a level of approximately $2.0 trillion in 2020.

These benefits will be achieved as a result of CAAA-related programs and regulatory compliance actions, estimated to cost approximately $65 billion in 2020. Most of these benefits (about 85%) are attributable to reductions in premature mortality associated with reductions in ambient particulate matter; as a result, researchers estimate that cleaner air will, by 2020, prevent 230,000 cases of premature mortality in that year. The remaining benefits are roughly equally divided among three categories of human health and environmental improvement: (1) preventing premature mortality associated with ozone exposure; (2) preventing morbidity, including acute myocardial infarctions and chronic bronchitis; and (3) improving the quality of ecological resources and other aspects of the environment, the largest component of which is improved visibility.

The wide margin between estimated benefits and costs and the results of an uncertainty analysis suggest that it is extremely unlikely that the monetized benefits of the CAAA over the 1990 to 2020 period reasonably could be less than its costs, under any alternative set of assumptions conceived (EPA 2011).

Environmental and Human Effects

Toxic Air Pollutants

Most toxic air pollutants originate from manmade sources that include mobile sources such as cars, trucks, and construction equipment; stationary sources such as factories, refineries, and power plants; and indoor sources such as some building materials and cleaning solvents. Some air toxics are also released from natural sources that include volcanic eruptions and forest fires (EPA 1991; EPA 2005a).

The Clean Air Act of 1990 identifies 188 air toxics from industrial sources (EPA 2005a). The EPA has identified 21 pollutants as mobile source air toxics, including benzene (a known human carcinogen), formaldehyde, acetaldehyde, 1,3-butadiene, and diesel particulate matter.

In addition, in 1999 the EPA listed 33 urban hazardous air pollutants that pose the greatest threats to public health in urban areas. The list of HAPs considered emissions from major, area, and mobile sources, including acetaldehyde, ethylene oxide, acrolein, formaldehyde, acrylonitrile, hexachlorobenzene, arsenic compounds, hydrazine, benzene, lead compounds, beryllium compounds, manganese compounds, 1,3-butadiene, mercury compounds, cadmium compounds, methylene chloride, carbon tetrachloride, nickel compounds, chloroform, polychlorinated biphenyls (PCBs), chromium compounds, coke oven emissions, polycyclic organic matter (POM), quinoline, dioxin, 1,1,2,2-tetrachloroethane, ethylene dibromide, vinyl chloride, propylene dichloride, perchloroethylene, trichloroethylene, 1,3-dichloropropene, and ethylene dichloride (EPA 2004b).

People who are exposed to toxic air pollutants at sufficient concentrations and for sufficient durations may be at increased risk of developing cancer or experiencing other serious health effects. Depending on which air toxics an individual is exposed to, these health effects can include damage to the immune system, as well as neurological, reproductive (e.g., reduced fertility), developmental, and respiratory problems. A growing body of evidence indicates that some air toxics (e.g., DDT, dioxins, and mercury) may disturb hormonal (or endocrine) systems. In some cases, this happens by pollutants either mimicking or blocking the action of natural hormones. Health effects associated with endocrine disruption include breast cancer, reduced male fertility, and birth defects. In addition to the hazards of being exposed to air toxics, there are also risks associated with the deposition of toxic pollutants onto soils or surface waters. These pollutants, through plants and animals, are magnified as they work their way up the food chain. Like humans, animals may experience health problems because of air toxic exposure.

The following is a summary of common air pollutants, their major sources, and their environmental and health effects (Koren and Bisesi 1995; EPA 2005a):

1. Ozone: ground-level ozone is the principal component of smog
   Source: chemical reaction of pollutants; VOCs and NO_x
   Environmental effects: ozone can damage plants and trees; smog can reduce visibility
   Health effects: breathing problems, reduced lung function, asthma, eye irritation, stuffy nose, reduced resistance to colds and other infections, may speed up aging of lung tissue
2. Volatile organic compounds (VOCs): the EPA does not list VOCs as criteria air pollutants
   Source: VOCs are released from burning fuel (for example, gasoline, oil, wood, coal, natural gas), solvents, paints, glues, and other products used at work and at home; cars are a significant source of VOCs that include such chemicals as benzene, toluene, methylene chloride, and methyl chloroform
   Environmental effects: in addition to ozone (smog) effects, some VOCs (such as ethylene and formaldehyde) may harm plants
   Health effects: in addition to ozone (smog) effects, many VOCs can cause serious health problems, including cancer
3. Nitrogen dioxide (one of the NO_x)
   Source: burning of gasoline, natural gas, coal, oil, and so on; cars are a significant source of NO_2
   Environmental effects: nitrogen dioxide is an ingredient of acid rain (acid aerosols), which can damage trees and lakes and reduce visibility
   Health effects: lung damage, illnesses of the respiratory system
4. Carbon monoxide (CO)
   Source: burning of gasoline, natural gas, coal, oil, and so on
   Health effects: reduces ability of blood to bring oxygen to body cells and tissues (cells and tissues need oxygen to work); carbon monoxide may be particularly hazardous to people who have heart or circulatory (blood vessel) problems or who have damaged lungs or breathing passages
5. Particulate matter (PM-10); (dust, smoke, soot)
   Source: burning wood, diesel, and other fuels; industrial plants; agriculture (plowing, burning off fields); unpaved roads
   Environmental effects: particulates are the main source of visibility-reducing haze
   Health effects: nose and throat irritation, lung damage, bronchitis, early death
6. Sulfur dioxide
   Source: burning of coal and oil, especially high-sulfur coal from the eastern United States; industrial processes (paper, metals)
   Environmental effects: SO_2 is an ingredient in acid rain (acid aerosols) that damage trees and lakes and reduce visibility
   Health effects: breathing problems; possible permanent damage to lungs
7. Lead
   Source: leaded gasoline (being phased out), paint (houses, cars), smelters (metal refineries); manufacture of lead storage batteries
   Environmental effects: can harm wildlife
   Health effects: brain and other nervous-system damage (children are at special risk); some lead-containing chemicals cause cancer in animals; lead also causes digestive and other health problems

Toxic pollutants in the air, or deposited on soils or surface waters, can have a number of environmental effects. The EPA *Health Effects Notebook* concluded that deposited air toxics contribute to birth defects, reproductive failure, and disease in animals. Persistent toxic air pollutants are of particular concern in aquatic ecosystems because the pollutants accumulate in sediments and may biomagnify in tissues of animals at the top of the food chain to concentrations many times higher than the original concentration in the water or air. Toxic pollutants that mimic hormones also pose a threat to the environment. In some wildlife (e.g., birds, shellfish, fish, and mammals), exposures to pollutants such as DDT, dioxins, and mercury have been associated with decreased fertility, decreased hatching success, damaged reproductive organs, and altered immune systems.

The primary source of information used by the EPA to develop these findings is its Integrated Risk Information System (IRIS) (EPA 2007), a database that summarizes available toxicity data and contains EPA's assessment of the data; it also contains secondary sources, such as EPA's Health Assessment Documents, Drinking Water Criteria Documents, Health Effects Assessment Summary Tables (HEAST), and the Agency for Toxic Substances and Disease Registry (ATSDR) Toxicological Profiles (CDC 2007). In addition, databases such as the Hazardous Substances Data Bank (HSDB), which contains summaries of peer-reviewed literature (NLM n.d.) and the Registry of Toxic Effects of Chemical Substances (RTECS) (CDC n.d.), which lists toxic effects of chemicals (and which is not peer reviewed), were used.

The EPA has developed a National-Scale Air Toxics Assessment (EPA 1999), a nationwide analysis of air toxics. It uses computer modeling of the 1996 National Emission Inventory (NEI) air toxics data as the basis for developing health-risk estimates for 33 toxic air pollutants (a subset of the Clean Air Act's list of 188 air toxics plus diesel PM). The national-scale assessment is intended to provide state, local, tribal, and other agencies with a better understanding of the risks of inhalation exposure to toxic air pollutants from outdoor sources. It will help the EPA and states prioritize data and research needs to better assess risk in the future, and it will also provide a baseline to help measure future trends in estimated health risks.

Three air toxics (formaldehyde, chromium, and benzene) appear to pose the greatest nationwide carcinogenic risk. The EPA generates maps showing the distribution of relative cancer risk across the continental United States, with 20 percent of counties containing almost three-fourths of the U.S. population at high risk. This map does not include the potential risk from diesel exhaust emissions, because existing health data are not sufficient to develop a numerical estimate of cancer risk for this pollutant. However, exposure to diesel exhaust is widespread, and the EPA has concluded that diesel exhaust is a likely human carcinogen and ranks with other substances that the national-scale assessment suggests pose the greatest relative risk. One air toxic, acrolein, is estimated to pose the highest potential nationwide risk for significant, chronic, and adverse effects on health after cancer.

This technical assessment represents an important step toward characterizing air toxics nationwide. It is designed to help identify general patterns in air toxics exposure and risk across the country, and it is not recommended as a tool to characterize or compare risk at local levels (e.g., to compare risks from one part of a city to another). More localized assessments, including monitoring and modeling, can be obtained from local radio and TV weather reports of daily air quality levels and air pollution forecasts in the area, as well as from newspapers and online sources, including the EPA (www.epa.gov/airnow/) and the American Lung Association (2000). Many of these online sites provide ambient air quality data on a state-by-state basis throughout the United Sates, including:

- outdoor air quality
- outdoor air pollutants
- children and ozone air pollution fact sheet
- air toxics
- carbon monoxide
- lead
- outdoor air pollution fact sheet
- ozone
- nitrogen dioxide
- particulate matter
- sulfur dioxide
- particle pollution fact sheet
- ozone fact sheet
- diesel exhaust and air pollution

- the air quality index
- Clean Air Week®: American Lung Association® Survey, and Air Quality Index Backgrounder
- air quality index fact sheet
- selected key studies on particulate matter and health

Acid Rain

Acid rain causes acidification of lakes and streams and contributes to the damage of trees and sensitive forest soils. In addition, acid rain accelerates the decay of building materials and paints, including irreplaceable buildings, statues, and sculptures that are part of our nation's cultural heritage. Prior to falling to the earth, SO_2 and NO_x gases and their particulate matter derivatives, sulfates and nitrates, degrade visibility and public health.

The Acid Rain Program confers significant benefits on the nation. Reducing SO_2 and NO_x will significantly improve many acidified lakes and streams so that they can once again support fish life. Visibility will improve, allowing for increased enjoyment of scenic vistas across our country, particularly in national parks. Stress to forests that populate mountain ridges from Maine to Georgia will be reduced. Deterioration of our historic buildings and monuments will be slowed. Most importantly, reductions in SO_2 and NO_x will reduce fine particulate matter (sulfates, nitrates) and ground-level ozone (smog), improving public health (EPA 2004a).

Greenhouse Effect

Gaseous components in the atmosphere, generated from such sources as fossil-fuel combustion from electrical power plants and emissions from automobiles, when combined with sunlight, create what is known as the "greenhouse effect." Since the 1860s, with the increase in fossil-fuel combustion for power and industrialization, emissions from these sources of greenhouse gases have contributed to significant levels of CO_2, NO_x, and methane. Table 3 shows average emission values in 1998 compared to pre-1750 levels. Emissions from these sources and from natural sources, such as volcanic activity and deforestation, have over time contributed to the warming of the earth (Sierra Club 2004). The pre-1750 values are based on scientists piecing together a picture of the earth's climate dating back decades to millions of years by analyzing a number of surrogate, or "proxy," measures of climate such as ice cores, boreholes, tree rings, glacier lengths, pollen remains, and ocean sediments; they have also done so by studying changes in the earth's orbit around the sun (NRC 2006, Wikipedia 2005a)

According to the NASA Astrobiology Institute (2005), most of the energy from the earth that affects weather comes from the sun. The planet and its atmosphere absorb and reflect some of the energy. The absorbed energy tends to produce warming, and the reflection or radiation of energy allows the planet to cool. The balance between absorbed and radiated energy determines the average temperature. The radiation balance can be altered by factors such as the intensity of solar energy, reflection of energy by clouds or gases, absorption of energy by various gases or surfaces, and emission of heat by various materials. A balance is continually found based on sunlight, depth, and density of atmospheric areas with various amounts of gases, clouds, and aerosols, and where seasons alter the ground cover. The planet is warmer than it would be in the absence of the atmosphere. Emissions of greenhouse gases tend to dissipate over time. These gases can be reabsorbed from the atmosphere through a series of natural physical and biological processes that include photosynthesis, oceanic activity, and climatic changes. The destruction of the ozone has been recognized as a phenomenon affecting global climate, arguably due to anthropogenic activities.

TABLE 3

Comparison of Average Emissions of Carbon Dioxide, Methane, and Nitrous Oxide—1750 to 1998

Gas	Current (1998) Amount by Volume	Increase Over Preindustrial (1750)	Percentage Increase
Carbon dioxide	365 ppm	87 ppm	31%
Methane	1745 ppb	1045 ppb	150%
Nitrous oxide	314 ppb	44 ppb	16%

(Adapted from Wikipedia 2005b)

Some scientists believe that climactic change due to rising temperatures is a natural progression that follows the cycle of earth's evolution. As with many fields of scientific study, there are uncertainties associated with the science of climate change. This does not imply that scientists do not have confidence in many aspects of climate science. Some aspects are known with virtual certainty, because they are based on well-known physical laws and on documented trends. Current understanding of many other aspects of climate change ranges from *likely* to *uncertain*. In short, a number of scientific analyses indicate, but cannot prove, that rising levels of greenhouse gases in the atmosphere are contributing to climate change, as some theories assert. In the coming decades, scientists anticipate that as atmospheric concentrations of greenhouse gases continue to rise, average global temperatures and sea levels will continue to rise as a result, and precipitation patterns will change (EPA 2006b).

Increased global industrialization has created international concerns, such as the potential effects of global warming associated with emissions and such as changes in the distribution of endemic diseases as concluded by the National Research Council (NRC 2006). The understanding of the relationship betweem weather/climate and human health is in its infancy, and the health consequences of climate change are still poorly understood. Worldwide concerns have, however, resulted in multinational policies such as the Montreal Protocol (UNEP 2000). The Montreal Protocol is an international policy for broad-based cooperation in the phase-out of Class 1 CFCs and Class 2 HCFCs over a scheduled period. The policy is an effort to eliminate chlorinated and fluorinated chemical compounds that contribute to the depletion of stratospheric ozone. The United States signed the Montreal Protocol of CFCs in 1988, with the anticipation of the signatory concurrence of over 59 countries by 1989. The United States further set a goal to eliminate the five CFCs under the protocol by 2030.

CONTROL TECHNOLOGIES AND METHODS

Today most of the air pollution in the United States is directly related to combustion of fuels for transportation, production of electricity, and manufacturing. As discussed in previous sections of this chapter, air pollution is a global concern. Recognizing the complexity of reducing or preventing air pollution, this section briefly discusses advantages and disadvantages of using different types of air pollution control equipment for major pollutants linked to stationary sources. The major air pollutants are particulates, sulfur dioxide, carbon monoxide, nitrogen oxides, and volatile organic compounds. Mathematics and engineering formulae are only introduced in this section to support or clarify concepts. A detailed discussion of the engineering design, operations, maintenance, and selection of air pollution control equipment is beyond the scope of this chapter. Recommended readings may be found in Appendix A at the end of this chapter.

Air pollution control can be achieved using isolation, substitution, treatment, or prevention techniques. Treatment is by far the technique most frequently used. Prevention is the preferred method. It is best achieved through proper planning, proper equipment maintenance, and adequate placement of various industrial sources. In general, air pollution is reduced by using many of the techniques known today, and specific controls are available for most industries.

Basic Science

Understanding and knowledge of some key scientific concepts are essential for determining the best control and preventions solutions for air pollution. Hence, this section will briefly introduce vital concepts of the atmosphere, gas law, concentration measurements in gases, material and energy balances, characteristics and behavior of particles, and engineering economics as they pertain to air pollution. Only frequently used formulae will be identified and discussed; a full discussion of these topics is beyond the scope of this chapter. The information in this section is extracted from the textbook, *Basic Physical Chemistry for the Atmospheric Sciences*, by Peter V. Hobbs (2000).

The Atmosphere

Air under dry ambient conditions consists of a number of gases, including nitrogen (78%), oxygen (21%), carbon dioxide (0.03%), and less than 1% of argon, neon, helium, crypton, and xenon. Oxygen oxidizes other substances by serving as an electron acceptor that bonds with them. Air also contains varying amounts of water vapor and a variety of natural and artificial pollutants. Dispersal of air pollutants is based on the stability of the air, thermal and mechanical turbulence, mixing depths, inversion, wind direction, wind speed, time of day, season, weather, land topography, and local obstructions that cause crosscurrents.

The rate that air temperature decreases as altitude increases is called the adiabatic lapse rate, theoretically 5.4°F for every thousand feet in dry air. Therefore, if air is permitted to rise without any heat exchange because of its environment, as the pressure decreases, the air expands and cools, and vice versa. However, the actual air temperature often changes with altitude at a higher rate than the theoretical rate. When such a situation exists, the air is said to be unstable, and warm surface air rises rapidly. This instability is good because it creates an up-and-down mixing of air currents that dilutes air pollutants.

Thermoturbulence is the rapid mixing of hot and cold air. The mixing depth of the air usually extends several thousand feet during the daylight hours of the summer and a few hundred feet during the winter, when the sun contributes less heat. At night, the air close to the earth is cooled by contact with it, but the air higher up stays relatively warm. This causes a minimal level of mixing, thereby concentrating the pollutants close to the surface of the earth. Winds at the surface and at higher elevations are important factors in determining the rate at which concentrations of pollutants can be dispersed. Note that the upward dispersion of pollutants is more effective than horizontal dispersion. Whenever the temperature at higher altitudes is greater than at the lower altitude, a temperature inversion is created that forms a "lid" and prevents vertical mixing (Fleagle and Businger 1980).

Weather has an effect on the degree of pollution in the air and the interaction of pollutants. Rain or snow will precipitate pollutants, making air cleaner but causing surface pollution. Fog, the condensation of water vapors in the air, contains aerosols (tiny suspended solid or liquid particles), but smog is a combination of smoke or chemicals and fog. As aerosols cool, the moisture in the air adheres to them. Fog can convert harmful gases, such as sulfur dioxide and nitrogen dioxide, into even more harmful chemicals, such as sulfuric acid, nitric oxide, and atomic oxygen (which reacts with oxygen molecules and other constituents of air emissions to form a variety of products, including ozone). Ozone is harmful and associated with highly complex, undesirable reactions in the atmosphere.

The Gas Law

Recall the gas law for an ideal gas

$$PV = nRT \qquad (2)$$

where P is the absolute pressure (atm), V is the volume (in liters), n is the number of moles (gmol), R is the ideal gas law constant equal to 0.08206 L-atm/gmol-K, and T is the absolute temperature (in degrees Kelvin). Note that in air pollution calculations, normal temperature of 25°C (298°K) and pressure of one atmosphere are used instead of the standard values of 0°C (273°K) and one atmosphere. Hence the volume per gram mole (V/n) is equal to 24.45 L/gmol, instead of the standard 22.4 L. The standard gas law equations are applicable for ideal gases, but air is not composed of ideal gases.

The gas law can be rewritten in terms of the mass density $(\rho)g/L$

$$\rho = M/V = P(MW)/RT \qquad (3)$$

where M is the mass of the sample (g) and MW the molecular weight of the gas (g/gmol).

Concentration Measurements in Gases

Common units used in air pollution to quantify concentration are parts per million (ppm) = (volume of pollutant/total volume of gas mixture) × 10^6, and micrograms per cubic meter ($\mu g/m^3$).

From the gas law, the concentration of a pollutant as a fraction of the total gas volume is expressed as

$$C_{ppm} = 10^6 V_p / V_t \qquad (4)$$

where V_p is the volume of the pollutant and V_t is the total volume.

Converting from volume (ppm) to mass ($\mu g/m^3$),

$$C_{(\mu g/m^3)} = 1000\, C_{ppm}\, MW_p/24.45 \quad (5)$$

where MW_p is the molecular weight of the pollutant.

Material and Energy Balances

The law of conservation of mass and energy is the basis for material and energy balance calculations, which can be expressed as:

$$\text{Accumulation} = \text{Input} - \text{Output} + \text{net generation} \quad (6)$$

For steady-state operation, all operating parameters are time-independent, and accumulation is equal to zero. In selecting and sizing most air pollution control equipment, steady-state conditions are assumed. Some exceptions to this generalization are encountered in the design of direct-fired dryers, incinerators, and adsorbers. It is necessary to define the system and its boundaries in such a way as to make maximum use of the information available on the system. To achieve this, draw a sketch of the process and then identify and label all entering and existing streams, performing material and energy balance calculations. Note that the pollution control engineer will be better equipped to perform the calculations. Because minimizing the use of energy is critical, a basic understanding of energy fundamentals is a prerequisite for good design. See the suggested reading for additional textbooks on this subject. For steady flow systems, the enthalpy (H) of a substance is a physical property and a function of the conditions at a point; hence, absolute enthalpy (H) is given as

$$H = U + PV \quad (7)$$

where U is the internal energy of the fluid per unit mass and PV is as previously defined. Note that absolute enthalpies are not used, but rather a difference in enthalpy between a desired point and a standard reference point; thus, reference to change in enthalpy (ΔH) is used in calculations.

$$\Delta H = H_a - H_b \quad (8)$$

where the subscripts a and b denote desired and standard points, respectively.

In performing energy calculations, absolute enthalpies are not used, but rather difference in enthalpies between a desired and a standard reference point. For example, enthalpy for steam and water can be found in standard steam tables.

CHARACTERISTICS AND BEHAVIOR OF PARTICLES

Polluting particles are composed of a variety of artificial and natural substances of varying sizes in different states. Collectively, they are called particulates and are often divided into smoke, fumes, dust, mist, and particles. Extracted from Lapple (1961), the following are some technical definitions for the various particulates:

- Smoke is both solid and liquid particles under 1 micron (μm) in diameter—usually less than 0.05 μm in diameter.
- Fumes are solid particles under 1 μm in diameter that are formed as vapors condense or as chemical reactions take place. Fumes are emitted by many industrial processes, including smelting and refining, both of which generate metallic oxide fumes.
- Solid particles are more than 1 μm in diameter and are generally referred to as dust. Dust may be formed from solid organic or inorganic matter by natural attrition or through innumerable industrial and agricultural processes when a parent material is reduced in size through some mechanical process, such as crushing, drilling, grinding, or friction.
- Mist is made up of liquid particles up to 100 μm in diameter. It is released industrially in such operations as spraying, splashing, foaming, and impregnating, or is formed by the condensation of vapor in the atmosphere or by the effect of sunlight on automobile exhaust. As mist evaporates, a more concentrated liquid aerosol or mist is formed.

Particulate size and, to a lesser degree, chemical state influence its divisions and behavior. For example, larger particulates (5–30 μm), when inhaled, tend to affect the upper nasal airways through inertia, but smaller particulates are deposited in the lungs. Through diffusion or Brownian movement, particles 0.1–1 μm in size tend to accumulate in the alveolar region. These particulates may cause localized irritation or lung disease or may be absorbed into the circulatory system, ultimately causing systemic problems. When particulates are emitted into the air, their properties and effects may change. These changes can result in detrimental effects. For example, the particles in the emission may break up, forming very small aerosols (from 0.001 to 0.1 μm in diameter) that act as nuclei on which vapor condenses relatively easily. This is the case with the formation of fogs, ground mists, and rain.

Particulates must be separated from a fluid as part of a pollution control system. So considering a particle in motion relative to a fluid, either the particle or the fluid or both can be moving relative to an absolute frame of reference. The fluid exerts an opposing force on the particle, termed *drag force*. Separating particles from the fluid will require external forces, causing impaction, interception, or diffusion. These forces must be greater than the drag force. Applying, for example, Stokes' law, Cunningham's correction to Stokes' law, Newton's law of turbulent flow, the laws of transitional flow, and the drag coefficient, the settling velocity of particles can be determined—a necessary parameter for selecting pollution control devices. Discussion of these topics is beyond the scope of this chapter but is covered in college physics textbooks and the air pollution design textbooks cited in the references and recommended readings.

Engineering Economics

In this section, some key concepts such as depreciation, optimization, incremental rate of return, and payout period will be briefly defined. These terms are frequently used in the financial analysis of alternatives. See the recommended readings for books on this subject.

There are several financial techniques and tools that range in sophistication from simple payback (investment/annual net savings) or rate of return (average annual net savings/total investment) to more accurate calculations, such as net present value (NPV) or internal rate of return (IRR), which take into account the time value of money. Regardless of which calculations are used, the most important part of a financial analysis is the estimation of project costs and benefits.

Only those incremental costs associated with the alternative should be included when determining the financial ramifications of the investment on the company. In other words, include only those costs that arise from an alternative and would not exist if the alternative were not pursued. These costs are generally dominated by direct costs, such as engineering fees, equipment purchases, supplies, contractor fees, costs of off-site training for employees, lost production resulting from disruption of production during project installation and learning curve, and ongoing maintenance of new equipment. Costs that do not change as the result of an investment decision are irrelevant to the decision. For example, overhead costs that may be allocated to an alternative, but which would exist regardless of the alternative, should not be included in a financial analysis because they are not incremental costs.

It is difficult to accurately estimate total benefits resulting from installation of air pollution control equipment. However, it is a critical step in the corporate capital-investment decision-making process to estimate all costs and benefits related to a proposed investment before the investment is made. Enhanced corporate image is one benefit that a company will probably not attempt to quantify, but it will still be taken into account qualitatively when making decisions with environmental benefits.

Return on Investment

Because return on investment (ROI) is a concept that determines viability in equipment purchase, maintenance, and replacement, these factors should be considered:

- ROI speaks the business language of safety.
- ROI illustrates a measure of profitability.
- ROI provides a consistent accounting method.

- ROI justifies equipment and program resource expenditures.
- ROI determines needs that go beyond operations and allow for payback potential.

To calculate the time value of money for pollution control equipment, assess the projected costs and savings associated with the equipment. The equipment must fit the requirements. Other tangible elements of the equipment need to be be defined. Benefits that derive from the use of equipment in terms of operational efficiency and savings should be communicated to management to secure support. NOTE: This calculation is drawn from Mr. David Pais' presentation to the American Society of Safety Engineers Greater San Jose Chapter meeting, February 8, 2011, and a college course in Engineering Economics.

Depreciation

Pollution control equipment decreases in value with time. This decrease in value is a noncash cost. Assuming straight-line depreciation (normal practice), the asset value after n years in service is equal to

$$V_n = V_i - d_n \text{ or } V_i(1-f)^n \tag{9}$$

where V is the value in dollars, d is the annual depreciation in dollars, f is the fixed percentage factor; subscripts n and i are years in service and initial value, respectively. Factoring in salvage average (s) the annual depreciation is equal to $(V_i - V_s)/n$ (Sepulveda et al. 1990).

The following is a simple example. In 2000, companies X and Y bought identical cyclone spray chambers that cost $150,000 each. In both applications, the service life was estimated to be five years with zero salvage value. The corporate income tax rate for both companies was 50 percent. Company X used straight-line depreciation and Company Y used the modified accelerated cost recovery system (MACRS method). How much more money did Company Y save over the first three years of service based on its depreciation procedure?

Solution:

Depreciation claimed by Company X:
$150,000/5 \times 3 = $90,000$

Depreciation claimed by Company Y:

From the MACRS tables, the depreciation in the first three years totals 76% of the initial cost.

$150,000 \times 0.76 = $114,000$

Because the corporate tax rate for each company is 50%, Company Y saved

$0.50 \times (\$114,000 - \$90,000) = \$12,000.$

Note that as a practical matter, most companies use the most advantageous method of depreciation allowed by law for tax purposes, whereas engineers typically use straight-line depreciation for evaluation of alternative cases.

Optimization

Optimization can be broadly defined as the determination of a highest or lowest quantifiable parameter over a range. Thus a problem can be maximized for profit or minimized for loss.

Minimization is the act of finding the numerically lowest point in a given function, or in a particular range of a given function.

The following is a simple example. Select the best replacement fabric bag from three different types that are available for the fabric filter, given the estimated total cost (capital and operating) per square yard and the manufacturer's rated pressure drop for each after 1000 cubic feet of dust-laden air has been filtered, as shown in Table 4.

Select the best system based on the optimum criterion stating that the best system is the one with the lowest total cost per pressure drop. Based on this criterion, option A is the best, because cost per pressure drop is the least. Note carefully in using this technique that the process design that provides the lowest total cost may differ from the one that provides the best operating efficiency.

TABLE 4

Type	Cost	Pressure Drop (psi)
A	$350	1.5
B	$360	0.9
C	$370	0.92

Incremental Rate of Return on Investments

The incremental rate of return on investment can be defined as the annual profit from incremental investment divided by incremental investment. In this technique, alternatives are selected based on profit and the least total investment.

The following is a simple example. A company invited bids for supplying a cyclone to control dust from its operations. The lowest bid on a cyclone that would meet all control requirements is for a carbon-steel cyclone with an installed cost of $50,000. The cyclone has a service life of five years. A second bid received is for a stainless-steel cyclone at an installed cost of $80,000 and guaranteed for ten years, which is projected to lower maintenance costs by $2000 per year. Both cyclones are estimated to have zero salvage value. If the company currently receives a 10 percent return before taxes on all investments, which cyclone should be purchased?

Solution:

Depreciation on carbon-steel cyclone = $50,000/5 = $10,000 per year

Depreciation on stainless-steel cyclone = $80,000/10 = $8000 per year

Total yearly savings with stainless-steel cyclone = ($10,000 − $8,000) + 2000 = $4000 per year

Incremental investment = $80,000 − 50,000 = $30,000

Incremental rate of return on investment = $4000/$30,000 × 100 = 13.3%

As the incremental return exceeds company requirements, the higher bid should be accepted. Note that, in this case, even if the incremental return did not appear to be acceptably high, further consideration must be given to the stainless-steel cyclone because, presumably, a second carbon-steel cyclone would need to be purchased after five years.

Payout Period

Payout period is a measure of profitability in terms of length of time required to recover the fixed capital investment. It can be defined as

$$\frac{\text{Fixed capital expenditure}}{(\text{average annual profit} + \text{average annual depreciation})}$$

Most companies assume that depreciation is linear over a fixed number of years, as allowed by governmental regulations.

Air Pollution Control Devices

In principle, air pollutants are controlled at the source or diluted after emission into the atmosphere. Source pollution control is accomplished by preventing the pollutant from forming. This can be achieved by changing existing industrial operations through modification or replacement of raw materials, fuels, equipment, or production methods; developing new products or processes that minimize air pollution problems; developing equipment that destroys, alters, or traps pollutants; and destroying, masking, or counteracting odorous materials.

Control of Particulates

Particulates are emitted in the gases or smoke from smokestacks. Koren and Bisesi (1995) concluded that a considerable quantity of particles could be removed from gas streams by applying the following principles:

1. Sufficiently reducing the velocity of the gas to allow the particles to settle by gravity (for example, a settling chamber)
2. Suddenly changing the direction of the gas flow to cause the particles to flow straight ahead because of inertia (for example, a cyclone or louver collector)
3. Filtering of dust-laden gas (for example, bag-house collectors)
4. Electrostatically charging particles to cause the charged particles to be attracted to objects with opposite charge (as in electrostatic precipitators)

Applying these principles, different styles and types of particulate control equipment can be developed. The major types are mechanical separators, such as gravity settlers, cyclones, fabric filters, electrostatic precipitators, and wet scrubbers. The following is a brief description of the operating principles of the above-mentioned control equipment. Examples and illustrations are available on the Internet that can aid in the understanding of the description and operations.

A *gravity settler* is a large chamber in which gas speed is slowed, allowing particles to settle.

A *cyclone* causes the entire gas stream to flow in a spiral pattern inside a tube. Affected by centrifugal force, the larger particles move outward and collide with the wall of the tube, falling down to the bottom of the cyclone, where they are removed. The cleaned gas flows out of the top of the cyclone. It is important to prevent moisture condensation within the tubes or cyclone area. Multi-tube cyclones are more efficient than the single-tube cyclones and may be used for final particulate collection. The efficiency of the multi-tube cyclones depends mainly on the velocity of the gas coming in, the diameter and length of the individual tubes, and the range of the particle size in the gas stream. Higher inlet gas velocities, smaller tube diameters, and longer tube lengths increase particle removal efficiency and resistance to gas flow. The major advantages of cyclones are low capital cost, ability to operate at high temperatures, and low maintenance requirements; the major disadvantages are low efficiencies and high operating costs.

A *fabric filter*, typically called a *bag-house* collector, operates on the same principle as a vacuum cleaner. Air carrying dust particles is forced through a cloth bag. As the air passes through the fabric, the dust accumulates on the cloth, providing a cleaned air stream. The dust is periodically removed from the cloth by shaking or by reversing the airflow. At times, the inert gas is pretreated or precleaned before it comes to the fabric filter. It is important to prevent moisture condensation within the bag-house or the filter area, which can otherwise cause collected particles to plug the bags. The collection efficiency of fabric filters is dependent upon the character of the fabrics used, the particle size distribution, and the porosity of the dust cake. Particulate matter removal efficiencies of greater than 99.9 percent are achieved in a variety of applications of the fabric filters known as HEPA filters, which are high-efficiency particulate air filters. The major advantages of fabric filters are high collection efficiencies and the ability to operate on a wide variety of dust types in a wide range of volumetric flow rates. The major disadvantages are required large floor areas, the inability to operate in moist environments, the potential of harm through high temperatures or corrosive chemicals, and the potential for fire or explosion.

An *electrostatic precipitator* (ESP) applies electrical force to separate particles from the gas stream. A high voltage drop is established between electrodes, and particles passing through the resulting electrical field acquire a charge. The charged particles are attracted to and collected on an oppositely charged plate, and the cleaned gas flows through the device. Periodically, the plates are cleaned by rapping to shake off the layers of accumulated dust, which is collected in hoppers at the bottom of the device. ESPs are used in a variety of industries and operations, such as the aluminum, pulp and paper, cement, gypsum, iron, and steel industries. They are also used in sulfuric acid recovery; asphalt blowing stills; phosphoric acid production; tar and oil recovery from waste, fuel, or gases; phosphate rock crushing; and coal-fired boiler operations. The collection efficiency of an electrostatic precipitate is dependent on the characteristics of the particulates: their size and electrical resistivity and the amount of collection electrode-plate surface area used. Particle-removal efficiencies of more than 99.9 percent have been achieved in some of these processes. The major advantages of ESPs are very high efficiencies, the ability to handle large volumes with low pressure drop, the dry collection of valuable materials or wet collection of fumes and mists, low operating costs (except at high efficiencies), and the potential for use in a wide range of gas temperatures. Major disadvantages are high capital costs, high space requirements; the inability to control gaseous emissions, inflexibility in operating conditions, and low efficiency for particles with high electrical resistivity.

A *wet scrubber* applies the principles of impaction and interception of dust particles through droplets of water. The heavier water droplets are easily separated from the gas by gravity. The solid particles can then be independently separated from the water, or the water can be otherwise treated before reuse or discharge.

Wet scrubbers are also used for the abatement of acid fumes generated from heated acid baths. In some cases, chemical treatment of the wet-scrubbing media is needed to adjust the pH level and optimize abatement efficiencies. A wet scrubber is a collection device that uses an aqueous stream or slurry to remove particulate matter and gaseous pollutants. Scrubbers are classified by energy consumption in terms of gas-phase pressure drop. Performance of typical wet scrubbers is affected by gas velocity, liquid-to-gas ratio, particle-size distribution, and inlet gas particulate-matter concentration. The gas-phase pressure drop is usually the major factor affecting the removal of the particulates. Wet scrubbers are best used for the collection of hygroscopic and corrosive submicron particles, such as those found in the phosphate fertilizer and in the lime, asphalt, and metal industries. The major advantages of wet scrubbers are their abilities to handle mists and flammable and explosive dusts, to cool hot gases, to provide gas absorption and dust collection in a single unit, and to neutralize corrosive gases and dusts. Their major disadvantages are that effluent liquids can present water pollution problems, their high potential for corrosion, the possible contamination of collected particulates (thus rendered unrecyclable), the necessity of protecting them from freezing, and the expense of disposing of waste sludge.

Each particulate air pollution control problem is unique and can only be resolved through engineered solutions. Note that cost efficiency is critical in designing a system; the following are broad generalities for identifying possible air pollution control alternatives. The overall collection efficiency of a system composed of two or more devices in series is not the sum or product of the efficiencies of each device. It is the total mass collected as a fraction of the total mass entering the first device. Mechanical collectors are typically much less expensive and moderately efficient than other types of equipment. They are better used for large particle removal than for fine dust and are often used as precleaners, especially when dust loading is high. Fabric filters tend to be costly and have very high efficiencies but are usually limited to dry, low-temperature conditions, although able to handle many different types of dust. Electrostatic precipitators are costly, relatively inflexible to changes in process operating conditions, and they can handle very large volumetric flow rates at low pressure drops while achieving very high efficiencies. Wet scrubbers can be very costly to operate because of high pressure drops but can achieve high efficiencies. One of their major advantages is that some gaseous pollutants can be removed simultaneously with the particulates, but they also produce a wet sludge that can present additional disposal problems.

Control of Gases

Carbon monoxide and nitrogen oxides (NO_x) are controlled by process modifications that include combustion control through proper use of temperature, oxygen, time, turbulence, and catalysis; absorption of gases by use of water or other liquids; adsorption of gases on activated carbon, silica gel, lithium chloride, and activated alumina; and controlled stack emission. With proper selection of adsorbing or adsorption material, and contact time between the material and vapor-laden exhaust stream, high collection efficiency can be achieved.

Flue Gas Desulfurization

Sulfur oxide emissions are controlled by flue gas desulfurization scrubbing systems. The two major systems are wet-scrubbing and spray-drying systems. The wet flue gas-desulfurization scrubbing process includes lime and limestone, nonregenerable sodium alkali, dual alkali, magnesium oxide, and Wellman–Lord. A major disadvantage is the large quantities of waste generated.

Control of Volatile Organic Compounds

Volatile organic compound (VOC) control systems rely upon the concept of chemical reaction. When the reaction involves organic hydrocarbons, the process is called oxidation. In the VOC oxidation process, heat and oxygen are added to the hydrocarbons to create the oxidation reaction. One of the most used oxidation methods for air pollution, as opposed to bulk liquids or solids, is incineration, specifically termed vapor incineration, or thermal oxidizers, or afterburners. Some VOC thermal abatement devices are optimized with pre-heaters or heat exchangers to improve fuel efficiency. In some cases, the heat generated can be used for operation of other equipment, such as water boilers, and so on. Note that vapor incinerators can sometimes be used successfully for air polluted with small particles of combustible solids or liquids, as well as for odor control. The process design of a vapor incinerator requires determining a temperature of operation along with a desired residence time and then sizing the device with the proper flow velocity. Controlling temperature, turbulence, and time are the key elements for achieving high process efficiency. Alternatives to incineration are recovery of the vapors, and liquid absorption coupled with either recovery or chemical oxidation. Some volatile organic compounds can also be abated through the use of carbon absorption systems.

Selection of the proper piece of equipment depends on such factors as mode of operation (continuous or intermittent), oxygen content, and the concentration of the VOC (Hemsath and Susey 1972). One of the drawbacks of thermal oxidation of VOCs is the generation of other pollutants such as nitrogen oxides (NO_x). This should be considered in the selection of abatement devices. Proper selection and proper sizing are very important when trying to minimize the overall cost of the incineration option. For this reason, it is desirable to keep the volume of the stream to be treated as low as possible. However, most insurance regulations limit the maximum VOC concentration in such streams to 25 percent of the lower explosive limit (LEL) of the VOC. Even so, many process streams encountered in industry have concentrations of 5 percent or less of the LEL. If the process stream could be concentrated from 5 percent up to 25 percent of the LEL (for instance, by reducing the flow rate of dilution air), the total volume to be incinerated would drop by 80 percent. Hence, the process exhaust stream must be characterized to determine the most appropriate VOC control technology available to best suit the application. The first step in characterizing the exhaust stream is to establish the current operating parameters, such as volumetric flow, volatile organic compound loading, and any other inorganic contaminants that might exist. The following is a list of considerations for determining the best cost-effective VOC control system:

- initial capital cost for the VOC system
- annual operating cost for VOC system
- annual maintenance cost for VOC system
- reliability of equipment vs. plant requirements for process run time
- the system's capture efficiency
- required destruction-rate efficiency for compliance with regulations
- flexibility for future operation of the plant's process

Innovative Air Pollution Control Devices

The number of innovative air pollution control devices is increasing sharply. The following are five examples identified by Koren and Bisesi (1995):

1. Vaporsep™ Membrane Process
   This device was developed by Membrane Technology and Research, Inc., and uses synthetic polymer membranes to remove organic vapors from contaminated air streams. The process generates a clean air stream and a liquid organic stream for reuse or disposal. Air laden with organic vapor reaches one side of a membrane 10 or 100 times more permeable to the organic compound than to the air. The membrane separates the gas into two streams: a permeate stream containing most of the organic vapor and a clean residual air stream. The organic vapor is condensed and removed as a liquid; the purified air stream may be vented or recycled. It can treat most air streams containing flammable or nonflammable halogenated and nonhalogenated organic compounds, including chlorinated hydrocarbons, chlorofluorocarbons (CFC), and fuel hydrocarbons.
2. TiO_2 Photocatalytic Air Treatment
   This device was developed by Matrix Photocatalytic Inc. It uses a titanium dioxide (TiO_2) photocatalytic air treatment technology to remove and destroy volatile and semi-

volatile organic compounds from airstreams. The technology is an ambient temperature, solid-state process in which contaminated air flows through a fixed TiO_2 catalyst bed activated by light. Typically, destruction of organic contaminants occurs in fractions of a second. The TiO_2 photocatalytic air-treatment technology can effectively treat dry or moist air. The technique has been demonstrated to purify streams directly, thus eliminating the need for condensation. Systems treating 100 cubic feet per minute of exhaust air have been successfully tested on vapor-extraction operations, air-stripper emissions, steam from desorption processes, and VOC emissions from manufacturing facilities.

3. Bio-scrubber

   This device was developed by the Aluminum Company of America. It uses a bioscrubber to digest hazardous organic emissions from soil, water, and air decontamination processes. The bioscrubber consists of a filter with an activated carbon medium that supports microbial growth. This unique medium, with increased microbial population and enhanced bioactivity, converts diluted organics into carbon dioxide, water, and other nonhazardous compounds. The filter provides biomass removal, nutrient supplement, and moisture addition. The technique is especially suited to treating streams that contain aromatic solvents, such as benzene, toluene, xylene, alcohols, ketones, hydrocarbons, and others.

4. Acoustic Barrier Particulate Separation

   Developed by General Atomics, Nuclear Remediation Technologies Division, acousic barrier particulate separation separates particulates in a high-temperature gas flow. The separator directs an acoustic waveform against the gas flow, causing particulates to move opposite the flow. Eventually, the particulates drift to the wall of the separator, where they aggregate and precipitate into a collection hopper. The acoustic barrier separator differs from other separators in that it combines both high-efficiency and high-temperature capabilities. It can treat off-gas streams from thermal desorption, pyrolysis, and incineration of soil, sediment, sludge, and other solid wastes. It is a high-temperature, high-throughput process with high-removal efficiency for fine dust and fly ash.

5. Reactor/Filter System

   This device was developed by the Energy and Environmental Research Corporation. It is designed to treat gaseous and entrained particulate matter emissions from the primary thermal treatment of sludge, soils, and sediments. It is used to remove entrained particulates, volatile toxic metals, and condensed-phase organics present in high temperature (800–1000°C) gas streams.

Best Practices

The practices in air pollution control are very diverse and technologically challenging, requiring specialized knowledge and skills. For the safety professional with the responsibility of environmental compliance, five key themes are recommended for adopting the best practices:

1. Using an integrated approach and the best technology available
2. Performing a comprehensive financial analysis
3. Continuously conducting surveillance and evaluations
4. Developing comprehensive air pollution control programs
5. Capturing and destroying fugitive emissions

An Integrated Approach

The EPA reports that since 1990 technology-based emission standards for industrial and combustion sources have proven extremely successful in reducing emissions of air toxics. The following two examples developed by the American Council for an Energy-Efficient Economy (ACEEE 1997) illustrate how industries implement projects; they also illustrate overall corporate strategies that profit from the synergies of energy efficiency, pollution prevention, process efficiency, and increased productivity. Note that the U.S. Department of Energy collaborates with U.S. industry to implement energy-efficiency demonstration projects in operating plants. At the end of each collaborative project, an assessment is conducted, and the results published if qualified as a best practice (DOE 2005).

These two projects developed many best practices and equipment, clearly underscoring the fact that air pollution prevention best practices must be identified in relationship to productivity, investment, and energy efficiencies. Below are two examples extracted from the DOE document on best practices.

EXAMPLE 1

Bowater, Inc., manufactures market pulp, newsprint, and coated magazine paper. During the processing of green wood chips (half water and half fiber), the water is converted to steam as the fibers are separated, processed, and pumped to paper machines to be converted to paper stock. By converting steam into energy, the company captured the energy lost in this low-pressure steam it vented from its seven thermomechanical pulping (TMP) refiner lines. The company installed two mechanical vapor recompression (MVR) heat pumps that efficiently converted the 19 psig steam at 250°F to 57 psig steam at 470°F. The converted steam was used to power the drying stage of the paper-production operations. The MVR compressor also had a turndown of 50 percent, allowing it to adapt to changing amounts of steam, which optimized energy use.

The major achievements cited in the DOE report were:

1. Annual energy savings of $1 million paid back the $1.5 million investment in 1.5 years.
2. About 200 gallons of turpentine (a TMP byproduct) is recovered daily for resale, reducing atmospheric emissions and providing additional income.
3. By preventing steam from escaping, 100 gallons of water per minute is saved, saving about $144 per day.
4. Controlling the steam vapor once it is released into the atmosphere reduces the plant's noise level.

EXAMPLE 2

Cominco America, Inc., produces ammonia for fertilizer, which uses water and gas fuel to generate steam. Process condensate is generated as wastewater, which is managed by a holding pond and injection wells. Cominco retained an engineering consultant, M.W. Kellogg Co., to reengineer its ammonia plant to reduce fuel and make up water consumption.

Fuel consumption was reduced by replacing existing plant parts with newer material that improved heat transfer. Convection-section and heating-coil modules were replaced with more efficient units that reduced heat and improved heat transfer, which reduced NO_x emissions and fuel consumption. The ammonia-converter reactor was modified with new equipment to reduce steam consumption. These new designs not only reduced fuel consumption but also increased productivity. Major achievements cited in the DOE report were:

1. Natural gas consumption declined 22 percent (1 billion cubic feet per year), saving over $1.7 million per year.
2. NO_x emissions declined 35 percent.
3. Average annual water usage for steam production was reduced by more than 110 million gallons, saving $65,000 per year.
4. Additional savings came from reduced disposal costs of wastewater into injection wells.
5. $16 million in capital costs were recovered in approximately six years.

Financial Analysis

The financial analysis of an efficiency project is the basis for making the investment decision. Hence, considering the cost of alternative control methods and technologies using a quantitative technique such as incremental analysis to determine the best choice is essential. Incremental analysis is a very simple method for determining the best rate of return on investment (ROI), and ensures that each increment of investment will provide an acceptable return. Cooper and

Alley (2002) suggested the following procedure for comparing alternatives:

1. Select the acceptable unit with the lowest installed cost as the base case and designate it as, say, "Alternative 1."
2. Designate higher-cost alternatives in order of increasing cost and designate them with distinguishing names.
3. Calculate the incremental rate of return on investment (ROI) between Alternative 1 and the next higher-cost identified alternative. If the ROI is acceptable, Alternative 2 now becomes the base case. If the ROI is not acceptable, Alternative 1 remains the base case and Alternative 2 is discarded.
4. Calculate the ROI between the next alternative and the base case. If the ROI is acceptable, Alternative 3 becomes the new base case. Again, if the ROI is unacceptable, Alternative 3 is discarded.
5. Continue this process until all alternatives are evaluated.

Surveillance and Evaluation

The EPA recommends that inspections and evaluations of emissions be conducted regularly to determine the level of air quality, the level of pollutants, and adherence to the established air quality standards. It is important when conducting the detailed survey to ensure that the site selection for sampling is made in such a way that it reflects the entire network design, that it is a representative sample consistent with objectives, and that the sampler considers the meteorological and topographical restraints as well as the sampling schedules. Sampling must be collected accurately and without contamination by skilled and trained individuals. Analysis and evaluation of the sample must be accurate, and the data-handling and evaluation systems must be accurate and consistent. The initial major step in surveillance and evaluation is proper planning. Planning is the advance thinking and organizing of a sequence of actions needed to accomplish the proposed objectives and to communicate the information to other individuals.

The planning of the survey must include the selection of the site for sampling, the sampling equipment to be used, the actual sample collection, the sample analysis, data processing, data evaluation, and comprehensive report writing.

The major objectives for monitoring air pollution include:

- providing an early warning system for potential health effects
- assessing air quality against standards
- tracking air pollution trends and specific polluters

Monitoring may also be required as part of the equipment permit requirements (EPA 1997).

Air Pollution Control Programs

A good program must include legal authority to institute and carry out a pollution control program and a continuing air quality monitoring program, to establish an emission-source inventory and continuously update it, to develop air quality goals and standards based on air quality criteria, to inculcate a thorough understanding of local meteorological conditions and their relationship to the movement of air pollutants, to make land-use planning decisions based on air quality control and other environmental factors, to develop good public information and educational programs, to train available personnel in the use of monitoring equipment, samplers, and laboratory analysis of pollutants, to implement air-use plans for existing industries, to approve plans for new industries, and to identify polluters and use enforcement techniques when needed to achieve compliance.

The management of air resources to protect the health and welfare of people must be carried out through the joint efforts of local, state, and federal agencies, the industry, and the population at large.

Fugitive Emissions

Process fugitive emissions come from a process or piece of equipment away from the main vent or stack. The fumes escape from valves, pumps, compressors, access ports, and feed or discharge ports of a process. Control techniques include leak detection and repair programs to seal the leaks. Further, the use of sophisticated pump seals, as well as valve and valve seals, can reduce emissions. Control techniques for organic or inorganic vapor emissions from area fugitive sources such as lagoons and ponds are very difficult to implement. The best approach is to reduce sharply the hazardous pollutant before it goes to the lagoon or pond and becomes a hazardous air pollutant.

Conclusions

The information related to air pollution presented in this chapter is intended to increase awareness of the problem and of the need for prevention and control. It also identified regulatory and compliance issues related to controlling and preventing air pollution associated with industrial operations. The chapter provided basic information for assisting, evaluating, and selecting air pollution control equipment and systems and guidelines for evaluating air-pollution control systems and programs. Most air pollution is directly related to combustion of fuels for transportation, production of electricity, and manufacturing, all reflections of the social demands of the way we live. Air pollution is a global concern that creates a need for international strategies and agreements. Toxic air pollutants may cause cancer or other serious health problems, as well as adverse environmental and ecological effects. Hence, air pollutants must be controlled at the source or diluted before being emitted into the atmosphere. Preventing pollutants from forming is the preferred method.

Challenges associated with the control of air pollution over the coming decades are complex and are likely to require mitigation strategies. These strategies not only require the understanding of the dispersion and interaction of multiple pollutants over national and international airsheds but also of the effects on human health and ecosystem conditions that arise from simultaneous exposure to multiple pollutants. Designing air pollution control systems and selecting the best air pollution control equipment requires engineering knowledge, which may be beyond the grasp of many safety professionals and is also beyond the scope of one chapter. However, an understanding of basic technological concepts and terms is essential for ensuring pollution control, productivity, investment, and energy efficiency.

Acknowledgment

I gratefully recognize the contributions from Moira McCue, MS, Adjunct Instructor of ESH, University of Connecticut, in the writing of this chapter.

References

American Council for an Energy-Efficient Economy. 1997. *The Integrated Approach: Case Studies* (retrieved October 23, 2005). www.aceee.org/p2/p2cases.htm

American Lung Association. 2000. *Outdoor Air Quality* (retrieved October 6, 2005). www.lungusa.org/site/apps

American Meteorological Society (AMS). 2002. Legislation: *A Look at Air Pollution Laws and Their Amendments* (retrieved October 22, 2005). www.ametsoc.org/sloan/cleanair/cleanairlegisl.html

Centers for Disease Control (CDC). Agency for Toxic Substances and Disease Registry (ATSDR). 2007. *Toxicological Profile Information Sheet.* www.astdr.cdc.gov/toxprof.html

_____. National Institute for Occupational Health and Safety (NIOSH). *Registry of Toxic Effects of Chemical Substances (RTECS).* www.cdc.gov/niosh.rtecs/default.html

Cooper, D., and F. Alley. 2002. *Air Pollution Control—A Design Approach.* 3d ed. Illinois: Waveland Press.

Department of Energy (DOE) Office Pollution Prevention. 2005. *Best Practices* (retrieved November 21, 2005). www.hss.energy.gov

_____. Office of Health, Safety and Security (OHSS). 1996. *Environmental Policy and Guidance: Clean Air Act.* (January 25) (retrieved October 18, 2005). www.eh.doe.gov/oepa/workshop/envlawsregs256/caa.ppt

Environmental Protection Agency (EPA). 2005a. *About Air Toxics, Health and Ecological Effects.* (retrieved October 18, 2005). www.epa.gov/air/toxicair/newtoxics.html

_____. 2005b. *Acid Rain* (retrieved November 18, 2005). www.epa.gov/airmarkets/index.html

_____. 1991. EPA 450/3-90-022, *Air Pollution and Health Risk.* (retrieved October 23, 2005). www.epa.gov/oar/oaqps/air_risc/3_90_022.html

_____. 1955. Air Pollution Control Act (APCA). P.L. 84-159. Washington, D.C.: EPA.

_____. 1967. Air Quality Act. P.L. 90–148. Washington, D.C.: EPA.

_____. 1999. *Air Toxics: National-Scale Air Toxics Assessment* (retrieved November 29, 2007). www.epa.gov/ttn/atw/nata/1999

———. 1963. *Clean Air Act of 1963 (CAA 1963)*. P.L. 88-206. Washington, D.C.: EPA

———. 1970a. *Clean Air Act of 1970 (CAA 1970)*. P.L. 91-604. 7401 et seq. Washington, D.C.: EPA

———. 1990a. *Clean Air Act Amendments of 1990 (CAAA)*. P.L. 101-549. Washington, D.C.: EPA

———. 2005c. *Clear Skies Act of 2005*. S.B. 131 (107th Congress). Washington, D.C.: EPA.

———. 2006. *Climate Change*. (retrieved November 15, 2006). www.epa.gov/climatechange/index.html

———. 2000. EPA-453/R-00-005, *Deposition of Air Pollutants to the Great Waters—3rd Report to Congress*. www.epa.gov/oar/oaqps/gr8water

———. 2004a. *EPA Acid Rain Program* (retrieved October 22, 2005). www.epa.gov/airmarkets/arp/index.html

———. 2004b. *Air Data*. (retrieved October 18, 2005). www.epa.gov/airmarkets/acidrain

———. 1997. *EPA Announces National Strategy for Toxic Air Pollutants* (retrieved October 22, 2005). www.epa.gov/history/topics/caa70/16.htm

———. 2005c. *EPA Clean Air Act*. (retrieved October 20, 2005). www.epa.gov/history/topics/caa70

———. 1971. *EPA History: Hearing Set on Automobile Pollution Control* (retrieved October 21, 2005). www.epa.gov/history/topics/caa70/05.htm

———. 1970b. *National Environmental Policy Act (NEPA)*. P.L. 91-90, 42 U.S.C. 4347. Washington, D.C.: EPA

———. Technology Transfer Network. 2006. *Air Toxics: List of 33 Urban Air Toxics*. (retrieved November 3, 2006). www.epa.gov/ttn/atw/urban/list33.html

———. 2011. *The Benefits and Costs of the Clean Air Act—Second Prospective Study from 1990 to 2020* (retrieved April 27, 2011). www.epa.gov/sect812/prospective 2-2.html

Fleagle, R. G., and J. A. Businger. 1980. *An Introduction to Atmospheric Physics*. 2d ed. New York: Academic Press.

Hemsath, K. H., and P. E. Susey. 1972. "Fume Incineration in Theory and Practice." Paper presented at the 71st National Meeting of the American Institute of Chemical Engineers, Dallas, TX, February 20–23.

Hobbs, P. V. 2000. *Basic Physical Chemistry for the Atmospheric Sciences*. Cambridge, UK: Cambridge University Press.

The Institute of Clean Air Companies (ICAC).2004. *Viewpoint on Hazardous Air Pollutants* (retrieved October 23, 2005). www.icac.com/i4a/pages/index.cfm?pageid=3397

International Labour Office (ILO). 1993. *Encyclopaedia of Occupational Health and Safety, Volume I, A-K*. 3d ed. Geneva, Switzerland: ILO. (AUTHOR: Review 1998 edition of this and revise accordingly.)

Kanarek, M. 2004. *History of the Air Pollution Problem* (retrieved October 19, 2005). www.admin.pophealth.wisc.edu/marty/phs502

Koren, Herman. 2003. *Handbook of Environmental Health and Safety Principles, Volume II*. 2d ed. Chelsea, MI: Lewis Publishers.

Koren, H., and M. Bisesi. 1995. *Handbook of Environmental Health and Safety, Volumes I and II*. 3d ed. Boca Raton, FL: Lewis Publishers.

Lapple, C. E. 1961. "Characteristics of Particles and Particle Dispersoids." *Stanford Research Institute Journal* 5:94.

Montague, P. 1999. *The Waning Days of Risk Assessment* (retrieved October 17, 2005). www.rachel.org/bulletin/index.cfm?St=2

National Aeronautics and Space Administration (NASA). *Astrobiology Institute, Ames Research Center*. (2005) (retrieved October 4, 2005). www.nai.arc.nasa.gov

National Library of Medicine (NLM). Toxocology Data Network (TOXNET). *Hazardous Substances Data Bank*. www.toxnet.nlm.nih.gov

National Oceanic and Atmospheric Administration (NOOA). 2002. *Fact Sheet: President Announces Clear Skies and Global Climate Changes* (retrieved October 20, 2005). www.whitehouse.gov/news/releases/2002/02/20020214.html

National Research Council (NRC). 2006. *Surface Temperature Reconstructions for the Last 2,000 Years*. Washington, D.C.: National Academy Press.

Sepulveda, J. A. et al. 1990. *Schaum's Outline Series Theory and Problems of Engineering Economics*. New York: McGraw-Hill.

Sierra Club. 2004. *Air Pollution Facts. Clean Air Resources*. (retrieved October 17, 2005). www.sierraclub.org/cleanair/factsheets

United Nations Environmental Programme (UNEP), Ozone Secretariat. 2000. *The Montreal Protocol on Substances that Deplete the Ozone Layer*. Nairobi, Kenya: UNEP. (retrieved November 28, 2007). www.unep.org/OZONE/pdfs/MontrealProtocol 2000.pdf

West, L. 2005. *About: Environmental Issues. Should the United States Ratify the Kyoto Protocol?* (retrieved October 19, 2005). www.environment.about.com/od/kyotoprotocol/i/kyotoprotocol.htm

Western Houston Association Issues. 2003. *EPA Reports on Clean Air Act* (retrieved October 21, 2005). www.westhouston.org/epa_report.htm

Wikipedia. 2005a. *Greenhouse Gas*. (retrieved October 19, 2005). www.en.wikipedia.org/wiki/Greenhouse_gas

———. 2005b. *Image: Global Carbon Emission by Type*. (retrieved October 19, 2005).www.en.wikipedia.org/wiki/Image:Global_Carbon_Emission_by_Type.png

Wooley, D. R. February 2000. *A Guide to the Clean Air Act for the Renewable Energy Community* (retrieved October 20, 2005). www.repp.org/repp_pubs/articles/issuebr15

APPENDIX: RECOMMENDED READING

Cengel, Y. A., and M. A. Boles. 2008. *Thermodynamics: An Engineering Approach with Student Resources DVD.* 6th ed. Boston: McGraw-Hill Higher Education.

Cheremisinoff, N. P. 2002. *Handbook of Air Pollution, Prevention and Control.* Boston: Butterworth-Heineman.

De Nevers, N. 2000. *Air Pollution Control Engineering.* 2d ed. Boston: McGraw-Hill.

Licht, W. 1988. *Air Pollution Control Engineering: Basic Calculations for Particulate Collection.* 2d ed. New York: Decker.

Moran, M .J., and H. N. Shapiro. 2000. *Fundamentals of Engineering Thermodynamics.* 4th ed. New York: Wiley.

Mycock, J. C., J. D. McKenna, and L. Theodore. 1995. *Handbook of Air Pollution Control Engineering and Technology.* Boca Raton, FL: CRC Press.

Newnan, D. G., T. G. Eschenbach, and J. P. Lavelle. 2004. *Engineering Economic Analysis.* 9th ed. New York: Oxford Univ. Press.

Park, C. S. 2004. *Fundamentals of Engineering Economics.* Upper Saddle River, NJ: Pearson/Prentice Hall.

Park, C. S., and G. P. Sharp-Bette. 1990. *Advanced Engineering Economics.* New York: Wiley.

Schnelle Jr., K. B., and C. A. Brown. 2002. *Air Pollution Control Technology Handbook.* Boca Raton, FL: CRC Press.

Stern, A. C., ed. 1976. *Air Pollution. Volume 7, Supplement to Measurements, Monitoring, Surveillance, and Engineering Control.* 3d ed. New York: Academic Press.

_____. 1976. *Measurements, Monitoring, Surveillance, and Engineering Control.* New York: Academic Press.

Smith, J. M., H. C. Van Ness, and M. Abbott. 2005. *Introduction to Chemical Engineering Thermodynamics.* 7th ed. Boston: McGraw-Hill.

Sullivan, W. G., E. M. Wicks, and J. Luxhoj. 2006. *Engineering Economy.* 13th ed. Upper Saddle River, NJ: Pearson/Prentice Hall.

Van Ness, H. C. 1983. *Understanding Thermodynamics.* New York: Dover.

Wang, L. K., N. C. Pereira, Y. Tse-Hung, and K. H. Li, eds. 2005. *Advanced Air and Noise Pollution Control.* Totowa, NJ: Humana Press.

_____. 2004. *Air Pollution Control Engineering.* Totowa, NJ: Humana Press.

White, J. A., M. H. Agee, and K. E. Case. 1998. *Principles of Engineering Economic Analysis.* 4th ed. New York: Wiley.

Water and Wastewater

Judy Freeman

2

LEARNING OBJECTIVES

- Recognize the federal laws that govern water and understand the difference between the Safe Drinking Water Act (SDWA) and the Clean Water Act (CWA).

- Examine the wastewater discharge permit system and know the difference between the permits for direct dischargers and indirect dischargers.

- Understand the basic parameters of the pretreatment system.

- Understand the basic concepts of sampling and analysis.

- Consider how current wetlands management rulings might impact industry.

- Be exposed to a number of wastewater treatment technologies.

THE MAJORITY OF AMERICANS living and working in cities get their water from municipal water supplies derived from surface water sources. Thus, the responsibility for providing safe drinking water to employees and clean process water for operations is not an issue for most environmental health and safety (EHS) managers in the United States, unless they are located in rural areas. How that water is used inside the facility and the quality of the water as it leaves in the form of waste, however, is the ultimate responsibility of the EHS manager.

In rural areas there are fewer people, but more water sources. Most workplaces that draw drinking water and process water from groundwater wells are subject to regulations. For these, the quality of water coming into the workplace, as well as that going out, must be assessed, maintained, and controlled by EHS personnel.

WATER-QUALITY REGULATORY ISSUES

In general, the quality of the water coming into the facility is ruled by the Safe Drinking Water Act (SDWA 1974), and the quality of the water going out is ruled by the Clean Water Act (CWA 1956). Both laws have something to say about how water is used in the facility. In most states, the laws are enforced at the state level. This means that state law may well be stricter than federal law.

Most people in the United States get their water from surface water sources managed by community water systems. Thus, the regulatory demands of the SDWA 1974 are beyond their control and responsibility.

However, where the water for a facility does not qualify as a community water system, the owner or individual responsible for that water source has the responsibility to maintain it according to SDWA regulations (SDWA 1986; SDWA 1996). The act covers water sources—primarily groundwater wells but also streams, ponds, and lakes—that meet the definition of "a public water system that is not a community water system and that regularly serves at least 25 of the same persons over 6 months per year" (SDWA 1974). States may independently impose restrictions on noncommunity water systems or stricter regulations on community water systems than those of the SDWA.

The SDWA addresses the quality of water in the public water supply. As noted, "public" here does not necessarily mean owned by the public, but rather used by it. The objective of the SDWA is to protect public water supplies from harmful contaminants by requiring the suppliers of water to achieve established standards (SDWA 1974).

Originally passed in 1974 and amended in 1986 and 1996, the SDWA controls community public water systems, defined as those which provide water to the public for human consumption and have at least 15 service connections or serve at least 25 individuals for at least 60 days a year. A community water system may include private sources (SDWA 1974; SDWA 1986; SDWA 1996). The SDWA does not have jurisdiction over nonpublic water supplies, which may include private residential wells, and individual schools, churches, motels, and some commercial or industrial facilities where use might be described as more incidental. A workplace where employees routinely use water for drinking and washing would probably not qualify as incidental use.

An EHS manager with responsibility for a plant should ensure that such sources fall within acceptable limits. Further, operators of facilities whose operations could impact the quality of a drinking water aquifer over which they reside must take precautions to avoid allowing chemical releases that will damage this resource. Such operations controls include:

- adequate containment of chemical storage should catastrophic failure occur
- knowledge of any aboveground or underground chemical/petroleum storage tanks that are on site. What is their content? age? condition?
- knowledge of the particular aquifer that feeds the facility, and what other pollutants may have been or are contaminating the common resource

In addition to establishing standards and treatment requirements for drinking water, the SDWA controls underground injection of waste and protects groundwater. It covers:

- improperly disposed-of chemicals
- animal waste
- pesticides
- human waste
- wastes injected underground
- naturally occurring contamination

EHS directors have the responsibility for ensuring that both water taken into the plant and wastewater discharged from the plant are within regulation. Underground injection of wastewater is highly regulated and should be contemplated carefully, if at all. The risk of potential contamination of a groundwater or surface water source should be understood.

States are granted *primacy*, or the authority to implement the SDWA by establishing water-quality standards that are at least as stringent as those imposed by the Environmental Protection Agency (EPA). Their role is then to enforce the law by providing oversight to the operations of water systems.

The SDWA directs the EPA to set water-quality levels for both man-made and naturally occurring contaminants based on health-related science. Currently, the EPA has standards set for 90 chemical, microbiological, radiological, and physical contaminants in drinking water. These are listed on the EPA's Web site, which may be found in the reference section at the end of this chapter.

National Primary Drinking Water Regulations (NPDWR) (EPA 1975) and National Secondary Drinking Water Regulations (NSDWRs) (EPA 2007) both are established, but only NPDWRs are enforceable; secondary levels are for guidance only.

NPDWRs establish maximum contaminant levels (MCLs) for certain specific drinking water contaminants. Other constituents are controlled using specific required treatment techniques in order to achieve the established standards (EPA 1975). NSDWRs address aesthetic values in a water supply, such as color, odor, taste, or turbidity. They must be considered for guidance only, because their values are not enforceable (EPA 2007).

Maximum contaminant level goals (MCLGs), based on the most stringent standards that would limit potential health effects, are established as goals rather than enforceable limits (EPA 1975). MCLs are required to be set as close to MCLGs as feasible. Decisions regarding feasibility take the cost of best available treatment technology into account when establishing limits.

The SDWA amendments (1986) resulted in the establishment of 83 contaminant levels, and the 1996 amendments added 20 more (see Table 1).

The 10 percent of Americans whose water comes from private wells (individual wells serving fewer than 25 persons) are not required to be protected by these federal standards. People with private wells are responsible for making sure that their own drinking water is safe. Some states do set standards for private wells, so well owners should check their state requirements. The EPA recommends testing water *at least* once per year to see if it meets federal and state standards (EPA 2006b).

Environmental health and safety directors of facilities that draw water from nonpublic water systems must be aware of the limits of their particular states. Further, in order to protect the health of their employees or the public who may use their facility, regular testing and compliance with the standards of the act are recommended.

TABLE 1

Regulated Chemicals under SDWA

Organics

Benzene	Di(2-ethylhexyl)adipate
Carbon tetrachloride	Di(2-ethylhexyl)phthalate
Chlorobenzene	Dibromochloropropane (DBCP)
1,2-Dichlorobenzene	Dinoseb \4\
1,4-Dichlorobenzene	Diquat
1,2-Dichloroethane	Endothall
cis-Dichloroethylene	Endrin
trans-Dichloroethylene	Ethylene dibromide (EDB)
Dichloromethane	Glyphosate
1,2-Dichloropropane	Heptachlor
Ethylbenzene	Heptachlor epoxide
Styrene	Hexachlorobenzene
Tetrachloroethylene	Hexachlorocyclopentadiene
1,1,1-Trichloroethane	Lindane
Trichloroethylene	Methoxychlor
Toluene	Oxamyl
1,2,4-Trichlorobenzene	PCBs \3\ (as decachlorobiphenyl)
1,1-Dichloroethylene	PCBs \3\ (as Aroclors)
1,1,2-Trichloroethane	Pentachlorophenol
Vinyl chloride	Picloram \4\
Xylenes (total)	Simazine \2\
2,3,7,8-TCDD (dioxin)	Toxaphene
2,4-D \4\	Total trihalomethanes
2,4,5-TP \4\ (Silvex)	
Alachlor \2\	
Atrazine \2\	
Benzo(α)pyrene	
Carbofuran	
Chlordane	
Dalapon	

Inorganics

Antimony	Nitrate
Arsenic	Nitrite
Asbestos	Selenium
Barium	Thallium
Beryllium	Coliform
Cadmium	Turbidity
Chromium	
Cyanide	
Mercury	
Nickel	

Water Sampling

Where a company manages a private water source, routine sampling is recommended as a minimum and may be mandated by state law. This requires sampling of the water source, whether surface water or groundwater. Additionally, where chemical releases from spills or leaking underground storage-tank incidents are suspected of contaminating groundwater, whether a water source or not, groundwater sampling is required to make that determination.

Equipment required for sampling groundwater from an established monitoring well includes a water-level indicator, a bailer, a rope, and possibly a pump. Equipment used to test water quality in the field includes a thermometer, a pH meter, and a conductivity meter. Turbidity meters, dissolved oxygen meters, and oxygen reduction potential (ORP) meters are also used.

Measurements in the field are used not only to test the targeted parameters, but also to determine the stability of the water. If meter readings fluctuate from one reading to the next, the water has not yet stabilized and samples should not be drawn until the readings are consistent.

Sampling protocol is to move from clean wells to the dirty ones and from up-gradient to down-gradient to minimize the chance of cross-contamination. Bailing water from the well should be performed with care to minimize both turbulence and volatilization of chemicals. The bailer should be tied securely to the rope so it does not slip off and remain in the well. Pumps may be used to retrieve water where flow is less generous, and to conduct well development.

Upon completion of the drilling and construction of a well, well development must occur to remove foreign matter, including sediments from the well walls and water that may have been used in drilling. The well must be purged prior to sampling to ensure that the water being sampled is representative of the aquifer. Samples must be taken according to EPA protocol and must be refrigerated immediately. A chain of custody must be maintained (Bodger 2003).

WASTEWATER

The objective of the Clean Water Act (CWA 1977) is to restore and maintain the integrity of the nation's waters. Specific goals of the act, established to achieve this objective, are to eliminate discharge of pollutants; to make water quality fishable and swimmable; and to reach zero discharge, that is, to eliminate any discharge of toxic pollutants in toxic amounts. The target dates set for these goals were passed in the mid-1980s, but even though compliance has not been reached, the goals remain the same.

When the CWA took effect, only 33 percent of the nation's waters were fishable and swimmable; 460,000 acres of wetlands were lost annually. Soil erosion into lakes and rivers was estimated at 2.25 billion tons. Phosphorus and nitrogen levels were high. Only 85 million people were served by sewage treatment (Cox 2000).

Since that time, approximately 60–65 percent of the nation's waterways are fishable/swimmable. The amount of wetland reduction has decreased to about 70,000 to 90,000 acres annually. Soil erosion is down to 1.5 billion tons. Phosphorus and nitrogen levels are reduced, and 173 million people are served by sewage treatment.

Legislative History

The first U.S. water legislation was the Rivers and Harbors Act (1894), which prohibited unauthorized obstruction or alteration of the nation's waters. This was followed by the Refuse Act (1899), which prohibited discharge of refuse that would affect the course, location, condition, or physical capacity of navigable waters. It mandated comprehensive programs to reduce pollution in interstate waters.

The Water Pollution Control Act (WPCA 1948) serves as the regulatory framework upon which subsequent laws have been developed. Under the Federal Water Pollution Control Act (FWPCA 1956), water-quality standards were based on desired uses of receiving waters: drinking water, recreation, navigation, body contact, and fishing. The Clean Water Restoration Act (CWRA) of 1965 was the first to require states to set standards for interstate waters that would be used to determine actual pollution levels. These laws were generally ineffective because of political, technical, and legal weaknesses, designated uses designed to attract industry, lack of information on effects of industrial discharges, and inadequate consideration of aquatic ecosystems (CWRA 1965).

With the 1972 amendments, the CWA incorporated the philosophy that no one has the right to pollute. The only acceptable reason for water pollution might be the limits of control technologies. For the first time, nationally uniform industrial limits were established. It was also this law that established the system of National Pollutant Discharge Elimination

System (NPDES) permits. Also for the first time, secondary treatment was required for publicly owned treatment works (POTWs). The act established a construction grants program to upgrade community sewage treatment systems. The act also established a watershed management system, which covers the country's river basins and regions. Enforcement authority was vested in the administrator of the EPA.

Previous versions of the CWA had focused primarily on conventional pollutants such as biological oxygen demand and suspended solids, but the 1977 amendments expanded the EPA's program to focus on control of toxic substances and required promulgation of pretreatment standards for 65 priority pollutants in (now) 34 industrial categories. Technology-based controls were imposed on industry with the standard set at the best practicable control technology (BPT) currently available. By 1983, the EPA had raised the bar again to a standard of compliance representing the best available technology (BAT) economically achievable. The 1987 amendments established a program aimed at focusing on the improvement of waterways that were expected to remain polluted even after the most stringent technology-based requirements were met. Particular attention was to be given to areas such as Chesapeake Bay and the Great Lakes. Furthermore, the 1987 law imposed additional regulations on stormwater.

How the System Works

The Clean Water Act (CWA 1977) regulates industry in two ways. Direct dischargers (or point sources of pollution) are required to secure a NPDES permit (EPA 2006a). Indirect dischargers—those discharging into a sewer leading to a publicly owned treatment works (POTW)—are required to meet another set of pollution limits on their wastewater (EPA 1982). In order to meet these limits, these industries must pretreat their wastes before discharging them into the sewers. They may also be required to have a permit from the POTW, which, in turn, has its own NPDES permit for its treated effluent. A regulated facility may have an NPDES permit, a POTW permit, or both.

Direct Dischargers

Primarily, the CWA limits discharges into the nation's waterways through the act's NPDES system. Under the NPDES permit program, every point-source facility is required to obtain an NPDES permit from the EPA or state agency (whichever has primacy in that state). A point source is one that discharges directly into the waterway.

NPDES permits allow industrial facilities to discharge a specified volume of wastewater, containing specified pollutants, from a specified outfall.

NPDES permit applications are required for process and nonprocess wastewater, and the requirements are slightly different for each, as well as for all other miscellaneous categories of entities regulated by these permits.

Other limits are also generally set in the permit, such as volume, duration, visual appearance, pH, temperature, sampling and reporting protocols, and frequency. Regulated waste streams requiring a NPDES permit include industrial process waters, noncontact cooling water, boiler blowdown, and stormwater runoff.

Pollution limits in the NPDES permit are based on multiple requirements, with the most stringent requirements imposed in most cases. They incorporate federal effluent guidelines and toxic standards, state effluent standards, and, potentially, water-quality-based limits. The list of priority pollutants must be considered, as well as categorical standards. Limits may be stated in terms of the volume of a pollutant in the waste stream or as a concentration of the pollutant—or, as is usually the case, as both.

Indirect Dischargers

Indirect dischargers, those discharging into the local POTW (sewage treatment plant), are also required to achieve technology-based effluent limits and minimum treatment requirements. Known as the pretreatment program, industrial users (IUs) discharging into the sanitary sewer system account for about 80 percent of the nation's wastewater flow (EPA 1982). Permits are issued by the POTW.

The POTW has its own NPDES permit, and its treatment of incoming wastewater provides one basis for its effluent limits under that permit. IUs are prohibited from any discharges to the POTW that may cause a *pass-through* or *interference* violation. A pass-through, either by itself or in combination with other wastewater with which it commingles in the treatment plant, is a violation of the POTW's NPDES permit. Interference inhibits or disrupts the POTW's treatment process. Also of concern is the solid waste left after treatment has occurred—sludge, the disposal of which is also regulated. Substances that alter the sludge and render the POTW unable to dispose of it by reuse are in violation.

Certain industries are targeted as categorical dischargers and as such are subject to the categorical pretreatment standards, which establish set effluent limits for them (see Table 2). The effluent limits are based on technology-based limits analogous to BAT.

TABLE 2

Regulated Chemicals under Pretreatment Standards

1. Acenaphthene
2. Acrolein
3. Acrylonitrile
4. Aldrin/Dieldrin
5. Antimony and compounds
6. Arsenic and compounds
7. Asbestos
8. Benzene
9. Benzidine
10. Beryllium and compounds
11. Cadmium and compounds
12. Carbon tetrachloride
13. Chlordane (technical mixture and metabolites)
14. Chlorinated benzenes (other than di-chlorobenzenes)
15. Chlorinated ethanes (including 1,2-di-chloroethane, 1,1,1-trichloroethane, and hexachloroethane)
16. Chloroalkyl ethers (chloroethyl and mixed ethers)
17. Chlorinated naphthalene
18. Chlorinated phenols (other than those listed elsewhere; includes trichlorophenols and chlorinated cresols)
19. Chloroform
20. 2-Chlorophenol
21. Chromium and compounds
22. Copper and compounds
23. Cyanides
24. DDT and metabolites
25. Dichlorobenzenes (1,2-, 1,3-, and 1,4-di-chlorobenzenes)
26. Dichlorobenzidine
27. Dichloroethylenes (1,1- and 1,2-dichloroethylene)
28. 2,4-Dichlorophenol
29. Dichloropropane and dichloropropene
30. 2,4-Dimethylphenol
31. Dinitrotoluene
32. Diphenylhydrazine
33. Endosulfan and metabolites
34. Endrin and metabolites
35. Ethylbenzene
36. Fluoranthene
37. Haloethers (other than those listed elsewhere; includes chlorophenylphenyl ethers, bromophenylphenyl ether, bis(dichloroisopropyl) ether, bis(chloroethoxy) methane, and polychlorinated diphenyl ethers)
38. Halomethanes (other than those listed elsewhere; includes methylene chloride, methylchloride, methylbromide, bromoform, and dichlorobromomethane)
39. Heptachlor and metabolites
40. Hexachlorobutadiene
41. Hexachlorocyclohexane
42. Hexachlorocyclopentadiene
43. Isophorone
44. Lead and compounds
45. Mercury and compounds
46. Naphthalene
47. Nickel and compounds
48. Nitrobenzene
49. Nitrophenols (including 2,4-dinitrophenol and dinitrocresol)
50. Nitrosamines
51. Pentachlorophenol
52. Phenol
53. Phthalate esters
54. Polychlorinated biphenyls (PCBs)
55. Polynuclear aromatic hydrocarbons (including benzanthracenes, benzopyrenes, benzofluoranthene, chrysenes, dibenz-anthracenes, and indenopyrenes)
56. Selenium and compounds
57. Silver and compounds
58. 2,3,7,8-Tetrachlorodibenzo-*p*-dioxin (TCDD)
59. Tetrachloroethylene
60. Thallium and compounds
61. Toluene
62. Toxaphene
63. Trichloroethylene
64. Vinyl chloride
65. Zinc and compounds

(*Source:* EPA 2007)

These limits may be reduced where the POTW demonstrates the capacity to treat and remove named pollutants. The POTW can also set more stringent local limits for problem pollutants and to achieve the POTW's program objectives: specifically, its compliance with its own permit limits under NPDES and sludge disposal regulations.

Limits into the POTW are established so that the POTW can maintain its own NPDES permit, can keep the POTW system operating effectively, and can meet its sludge disposal limits.

The list of regulated chemicals provided derives from EPA's Model Pretreatment Ordinance. Each municipality that operates a POTW will have its own ordinance, which may be more stringent than that of the federal government.

The Industry's Relationship with the POTW

Industry is prohibited from discharging anything into the system that will affect operations of the POTW. These systems aerate wastes in an aerobic digestion process, which uses bacteria to convert waste. Many chemicals, in sufficiently large quantities, can kill off these beneficial bacteria and cause the sewage treatment plant a costly and painful restart.

The POTW will also set local limits based on the technology they have in place to treat a facility's discharge. Any chemical that cannot be removed by the POTW, passing through the system, is prohibited to be discharged. A facility is also prohibited from discharging into a POTW a waste stream containing chemicals that the POTW *can* remove, but which will end up in the sludge, if that discharge will cause the POTW to be in violation of its federal sludge disposal requirements. Local POTW discharge limits must be at least as stringent as the federal rules and must take into account the capabilities of the local POTW to eliminate the toxic contaminates present in the waste.

It may be worth noting here that there is no black box that makes waste disappear. It can be converted to other forms, and the most toxic elements can be removed and disposed of in other ways, but what goes into the system comes out of the system in one way or another. Aerating volatile organic compounds in a sewage treatment plant may take them from a liquid form to an aerosol or a gas, but in that case they simply become air pollution instead of water pollution.

If a company has an NPDES permit, or a permit to discharge into the local POTW, it will likely be required to perform sampling and analysis for conventional pollutants—biochemical oxygen demand (BOD), total suspended solids (nonfilterable) (TSS), pH, fecal coliform, oil and grease—as well as for categorical standards for that particular industry and compliance standards for anything else the POTW believes it might expect to be in the waste stream that they do not want to have to deal with. Some of these are regulated as user charge items and some as compliance items.

The POTW has a responsibility under the Section 204(b)(1)(A) of the Clean Water Act, as a condition of receiving federal funding for wastewater treatment works, to charge each recipient of waste treatment services its proportionate share of the costs of operation and maintenance of waste treatment services provided to it. User charges are not compliance items but rather cover the costs of volume and pollution loading the POTW can remove, such as BODs, chemical oxygen demands (CODs), and TSSs.

Compliance items are those that are either categorical standards or items that cause the POTW problems. These include limits on heavy metals, pH, extreme temperatures, sulfide compounds, and a number of other organic and inorganic compounds.

Over the years that these laws have been enforced, most industrial dischargers have come to understand what it takes to stay out of trouble with the local POTW (for example, maintaining an efficient wastewater treatment system, reporting within deadlines, and maintaining good communication with inspectors). However, as in any process, errors occur. When compliance excursions occur, those responsible in the plant must take responsibility and fix the problem. Failure to do so will usually result in problems with the POTW that are worse than the one that was ignored.

Permit Applications

Permits may be required from the EPA (state or federal, in the case of direct dischargers) or from the local POTW (for dischargers into the local sewer system). Specifics of these applications differ, but both processes have common elements.

Applications will contain detailed information, including:

- outfall location with drawings
- average flows and treatment, intermittent flows, and maximum production capacity
- current upgrade activities
- effluent characteristics

The process of effluent characterization requires a baseline monitoring of at least the following:

- biological oxygen demand (BOD)
- chemical oxygen demand (COD)
- total organic carbon (TOC)
- total suspended solids (TSS)
- ammonia (N)
- temperature (summer and winter)
- pH

Other effluent characterization, including quantitative data, may be required for each specified pollutant from each outfall containing wastewater. Specified pollutants are likely to include:

- processes in specific industry categories
- organic toxic pollutants
- specified pesticides
- toxic metals
- cyanide
- total phenols
- any other Appendix D parameter that the applicant might have reason to discharge from any outfall

Waivers from particular requirements of an application are available from the EPA Regional Administrator for individual point sources, particular industries, or targeted pollutants under certain circumstances.

Examples of discharge permit applications may be found on the EPA's Web site (EPA 2010).

Permit Conditions

Most of the authority under the Clean Water Act is allocated to state agencies (with strong oversight from the federal EPA). States set water-quality standards—subject to federal approval—for waterways based on their use. The EPA can assume authority where state standards are deemed inadequate. It is important to keep in mind that the EPA has broad discretionary authority to impose a variety of restrictions on facilities as it deems appropriate.

Permit Limit Framework

The EPA's effluent limits are based on the levels of compliance the EPA has determined can be achieved at various levels of treatment technology. Technology-based treatment requirements set the minimum level of control that must be imposed in a permit.

When the rules under the CWA were first promulgated, all dischargers were responsible for achieving the best practicable control technology (BPT) currently available. After 1983, compliance was based on the best available technology (BAT) economically achievable. A less stringent standard of best conventional pollutant-control technology (BCT) applies to conventional pollutants (biological oxygen demand, total suspended solids, fecal coliform, pH, and oil and grease). None of these standards apply to new sources, which must meet an even higher standard of best available demonstrated control technology. In general, these limits are set to reflect the levels that, in the EPA's assessment, an industry could achieve with the specified levels of pollution control in place. To reiterate, while the limits are based on the technology, compliance is going to be determined by what comes out of the plant as effluent. BPT standards are established by surveying particular industries to identify the better-run facilities and mirror their achievements.

At the BAT level, maximum feasible pollution reduction should be achieved. These standards are based upon a number of factors beyond choosing the technology that provides the maximum pollution removal, including energy usage, other environmental impacts, and cost. The standards are required to be economically achievable. The BCT category was developed in order to impose a cost-reasonableness standard on conventional pollutants.

An effluent limit is set based upon the maximum allowance of a pollutant without exceeding the standard for the receiving waters. Permit limitations based on chronic health effects are defined as 4-hour averages; acute health effects are defined as 1-hour or 24-hour limitations. A dilution factor is calculated based upon the proposed pollution load and the rate of flow of the receiving stream.

The CWA has anti-backsliding provisions in order to assure continuous improvement of the nation's waterways. This means that new and renewing permits cannot be issued or reissued with lower limits. States establish a total maximum daily load (TMDL), the maximum allowable pollution load for a specific waterway in order to try to achieve water-quality standards.

Toxicity-based limitations are also used. Whole effluent toxicity (WET) imposes requirements for sampling and monitoring the effluent. Effluent toxicity tests involve exposing selected species of aquatic life to the proposed concentrations of effluent to determine the consequences of short- and long-term exposures.

Effluent Limits

As noted, these discharge standards are technology-based; that is, the EPA establishes effluent guidelines that incorporate discharge limits for specific types of industries (see Table 3). Categorical dischargers will be subject to the specific limits of their industry sector. Other local limits are particular to a specific POTW and their ability to treat the wastes from their service sector.

In addition to chemical sampling, the permittee may be required to maintain limits on water volumes, temperature, and pH, as well as on chemical constituency.

The EPA has issued effluent guidelines for over 50 industrial categories (see Table 4).

Sampling and Monitoring

Permit conditions for either direct or indirect discharge will likely require routine sampling and monitoring of wastewater discharges in order to comply with the permit. Samples must be representative of the monitored activity. How the sample is taken, whether it is a grab or a composite, and the frequency and duration of sampling are all regulated. Monitoring records are required to be maintained for 5 years (or longer where required by 40 CFR 503). These records must be provided to the EPA as required and upon request.

Sampling Safety

Safe work practices must be maintained during sampling procedures. If sampling requires entering a manhole, confined space regulations must be followed (29 CFR 1910.146). All potential confined space atmospheres should be tested and appropriate ventilation

TABLE 3

Industrial Categories	
Dairy products processing	Mineral mining and processing
Grain mills	Centralized waste treatment
Canned and preserved fruits and vegetables processing	Metal products and machinery
	Pharmaceutical manufacturing
Canned and preserved seafood processing	Ore mining and dressing
	Transportation equipment cleaning
Sugar processing	Paving and roofing materials (tars and asphalt)
Textile mills	
Cement manufacturing	Waste combustors
Concentrated animal feeding operations (Cafo)	Landfills
	Paint formulating
Electroplating	Ink formulating
Organic chemicals, plastics, and synthetic fibers	Concentrated aquatic animal production
Inorganic chemicals manufacturing	Gum and wood chemicals manufacturing
Soap and detergent manufacturing	
Fertilizer manufacturing	Pesticide chemicals
Petroleum refining	Explosives manufacturing
Iron and steel manufacturing	Carbon black manufacturing
Nonferrous metals manufacturing	Photographic
Phosphate manufacturing	Hospital
Steam electric power generating	Battery manufacturing
Ferroalloy manufacturing	Plastics molding and forming
Leather tanning and finishing	Metal molding and casting
Glass manufacturing	Coil coating
Asbestos manufacturing	Porcelain enameling
Rubber manufacturing	Aluminum forming
Timber products processing	Copper forming
Pulp, paper, and paperboard	Electrical and electronic components
Meat and poultry products	
Metal finishing	Nonferrous metals forming and metal powders
Coal mining	
Oil and gas extraction	

(*Source*: California State University 1996)

TABLE 4

Effluent Characteristics from Various Industries

Industry	Effluent Characteristics
Automotive	Oil and grease, phenols, metals, BOD, COD, acids, toxic organics
Bakery	Fats, oil and grease
Batteries	Acids, metals
Chemicals, organic	Toxic organics, BOD, COD, acids, metals
Chemicals, inorganic	Acids, metals, TDS, ammonia, phosphate
Electrical and electronics	Metals, acids, SS, toxic organics, fluoride
Electroplating and metal finishing	Acids, metals, cyanide, toxic organics
Foods	BOD, COD, SS, alkalies, oil and grease
Leather tanning and finishing	BOD, SS, chromium, oil and grease, sulfide, fecal coliforms
Metals (primary metals, smelting, and refining)	Acids, metals, BOD, COD, SS, phenols, cyanide, sulfide, ammonia
Mining	Acids, metals
Paints	BOD, COD, SS, toxic organics, copper, lead, mercury
Petroleum	Oil and grease, BOD, COD, acids and alkalies, metals, sulfide, ammonia, phenols, mercaptans, heat
Pharmaceuticals	BOD, metals
Plastics and synthetics	BOD, COD, SS, toxic organics
Power generation (utilities)	Heat, oils, SS, TDS, metals, chlorine, PCBs
Pulp and paper	Acids, alkalies, BOD, COD, wood preservatives
Rubber	BOD, SS, oil and grease
Textiles	COD, chromium, phenol, sulfide, dyes
Wood products	SS, oil and grease, BOD, COD, wood preservatives

(*Source*: California State University 1996)

employed, as necessary, prior to entry. Personal protection equipment (PPE) appropriate to the specific risks of the company must be worn and must include safety shoes, gloves, eye protection, and respiratory protection where required.

There are hazards that are unique to each industry, which should be known, understood, and addressed prior to conducting sampling activities at that facility. It is not possible to list all of these hazards, which may be as diverse as high-voltage electricity in metal finishing shops to slips, trips, and falls.

Sampling generally means end-of-pipe sampling, but routine monitoring of system operations is also required (California State University 1996). Flow and pH charts, flow-meter calibrations, temperature, conductivity, lower explosive limit (LEL), and oxidation reduction potential are all possible sampling protocols that may be required.

Odor detection can also alleviate problem areas or even emergency response situations. Organic material can accumulate in waste treatment lines and release hydrogen sulfide into the atmosphere. The odor of rotten eggs should act as a trigger to test for the presence of hydrogen sulfide gas, which is the most common toxic gas encountered while sampling wastewater. Although its strong odor is readily identified, olfactory fatigue occurs at high concentrations and at continuous low concentrations. For this reason, odor is not a reliable indicator of hydrogen sulfide's presence and may not provide adequate warning of hazardous concentrations (CDC/ATSDR 2011). The recommended exposure limit (REL) of the National Institute of Occupational Safety and Health (NIOSH) for hydrogen sulfide is 10 ppm (CDC 1994); the immediately dangerous to life and health (IDLH) limit is 100 ppm (NIOSH 1997).

Other gases that may be of concern in sampling include hydrogen cyanide, having a threshold limit value (TLV) of 10 ppm (NIOSH 1997). Hydrogen cyanide gas can be generated when discharged from improperly treated metal-finishing wastewater and then combined with acidic wastewater in the system. Exposure to cyanide gas can be fatal. Chlorine gas can be encountered in a wastewater treatment system that uses it for cyanide destruction. The NIOSH limit for chlorine is 0.5 ppm (NIOSH 1997).

Other chemicals that may be encountered in sampling activities include corrosives, solvents and flammable materials, poisonous and toxic chemicals, and infectious agents.

Sampling Protocol

Samples may be collected as *composites* or *grab samples*. Composites are defined as "a collection of individual samples obtained at regular intervals, usually every one or two hours during a 24-hour time span. Each individual sample is combined with the others in proportion to the rate of flow when the sample was collected. Equal volume, individual samples also may be collected at intervals after a specific volume of flow passes the sampling point or after equal time intervals and still be referred to as a composite sample. The resulting mixture (composite sample) forms a representative sample and is analyzed to determine the average conditions during the entire sampling period" (California State University 1996).

Composites may be flow-weighted averages or time-weighted averages (TWAs). Grab samples are collected as single samples taken all at one time. A composite is a number of flow-weighted (taken from discharges of equal flow) or time-weighted (taken from discharges at equal time intervals) grab samples. Composites are more representative than grab samples.

Sampling for total toxic organics must be conducted with care to minimize volatilization of the chemicals; such samples should be refrigerated and immediately transported to the laboratory.

Where baseline monitoring reflects pollutants present only in traces, infrequent sampling may be sufficient. Where pollutants are discharged near limits, more frequent sampling may be required to avoid violations.

Sampling should be representative of operations. Where operations fluctuate either seasonally or cyclically (over the course of a week or a month), samples should be collected to reflect those fluctuations.

Samples should be analyzed by a certified laboratory qualified to conduct the necessary tests using U.S. EPA–approved methods. Appropriate containers, properly labeled and preserved, must be used. A chain of custody must be maintained.

Treatment

Each facility must design its own wastewater treatment system to address its own physical layout and permit limits. For a more thorough discussion of wastewater treatment, see the "Applied Scientific and Engineering Principles" section.

Inspection

The permittee must allow access to authorized representatives of the EPA (including the POTW) to review records; inspect facilities, equipment, and operations; and sample and monitor for any substance (40 CFR 122.41(i)). POTWs will generally perform routine inspection of each significant industrial user at least once annually, including sampling for constituents listed in the permit.

Receptionists and security guards should be trained to handle unannounced visits, to request identification, and to notify EHS staff promptly. Note that, if the individual normally responsible for escorting inspectors is not available, the inspector still has the right to inspect the facility. The facility should be prepared to supply a back-up escort. Denial of access is a permit violation.

The inspector may wish to review records, including logs of flow measurements, pH, flow-meter calibrations, process upsets, MSDSs, and liquid waste hauler's manifests to gain additional knowledge of the plant's operation. A facility inspection will generally at least include inspection of the company's outfall(s), but a complete facility tour may be requested.

Should violations be found in the POTW's sampling, the company may be issued a citation for a violation. Additional sampling and monitoring may be required until the company has shown compliance.

Reporting

A facility is required to notify the EPA or its authorized representative of:

- any planned physical alterations or additions to the permitted facility if the changes might prompt the EPA to reassess the facility as a new source or if the change will have significant impact on the nature or quantities of the pollutants discharged
- any incidents of noncompliance

Each reporting agency will have its own set of requirements.

Enforcement

As with all other aspects of regulatory compliance, an EHS director must be aware of aspects of law that may be industry- or region-specific.

Either the EPA or, where appropriate, the state agency or local POTW can enforce against Clean Water Act violations. Facilities that experience violations will be required to increase sampling, monitoring, and reporting activities until the facility has demonstrated to the permitting agency its return to compliance. Criminal and civil penalties may be sought and fines of at least $1000 per day for each violation may be imposed for any negligent or intentional violation.

Environmental law is complex and confusing. When there is doubt about the law, the company's attorney should always be consulted. It should be remembered that environmental liability may "pierce the corporate veil." That means that an EHS director, company officer, or board member may be personally liable for information appearing above his or her signature, or for actions taken by company personnel. Further, the Clean Water Act is enforceable not only for wanton acts, but for negligence; lack of knowledge about the law is not a defense.

OTHER WATER REGULATIONS
The Oil Pollution Act

The Oil Pollution Act (OPA), Section 311 of the Clean Water Act, prohibits discharge of oil or hazardous substances into navigable waterways (OPA 1990). Congress passed OPA in August 1990, partially in response to the *Exxon Valdez* spill in 1989.

The law was based on damage that was caused by one cargo-hold load of oil in the 1989 spill. This assumption grossly underestimated the potential for release into the waters of the United States, as was experienced in the Gulf of Mexico following the explosion of the Deepwater Horizon oil-drilling platform on April 20, 2010, and subsequent release of an estimated 4.9 million barrels of oil before the well was capped on July 15, 2010. As of June 2011, the impact assessment and investigation of this incident is ongoing, but it is clear that the incident overwhelmed the environmental health and safety systems in place at the time. The social, political, and legislative response to this disaster will inform how future catastrophic releases are addressed (Freeman 2011).

It is in the best interests of all stakeholders that a thorough and scientific analysis be conducted to enhance decisions regarding continued efforts to improve the environment in the Gulf region, and future legislation and regulatory rulemaking regarding how such incidents are addressed.

One of the components of this law relates to spill control, listing 300 substances considered hazardous when spilled. Exceeding threshold limits for these substances must prompt a call to the National Response Center.

Spill Control

A spill prevention, control, and countermeasure plan (SPCC) is required at sites where petroleum products exceed the designated minimum quantities (1320 gallons above ground; 42,000 below ground; 660 gallons in a single aboveground tank) The plan must cover the facility components that are specifically designed to control spills—both on-site control measures and off-site clean-up measures. The plan must be updated every 3 years (EPA 2002a). A facility response plan is required of "any non-transportation-related on-shore facility that, because of its location, could reasonably be expected to cause substantial harm to the environment by discharging oil into or on the navigable waters or adjoining shorelines" (EPA 2002a).

Spills that are discharged to the local POTW in excess of reportable limits require that the POTW be notified so that it can take evasive action. This is a self-reporting system, and failure to notify can result in civil or criminal penalties.

Components of the SPCC Plan

A spill prevention, control, and countermeasure (SPCC) plan must be carefully thought out, prepared in accordance with good engineering practices, and have full approval of management at a level necessary to commit the necessary resources. Where the potential exists for equipment failure to result in a spill event, the plan should include a prediction of direction and rate of flow and the total quantity of oil that could result.

Containment sufficient to handle predictable spills should be provided. Such containment could include dikes, berms, or retaining walls; curbing; culverts, gutters, or other drainage facilities; wiers or booms; spill diversion ponds; retention ponds; and sorbent materials. Where facilities are located off shore, containment may also include sumps and storage tanks.

The plan should also address controls and monitoring for:

- facility drainage
- bulk storage tanks, underground storage tanks, aboveground storage tanks
- material transfer and pumping operations
- tank-car and tank-truck loading and unloading

Oil production, pipelines, and drilling facilities have their own specific rules.

Inspections must be made and records kept in accordance with the facility's own plans. Security, consisting of fencing and gates, must be present. Valves must be locked. Lighting must be appropriate for night on-site facility response. Personnel must be trained to operate equipment in such ways as to prevent discharges, and plans to do so should be reviewed. Each facility should have a designated person accountable for oil-spill prevention.

The plan must be amended whenever there is a change in facility design, construction, or operation that materially affects the facility's potential for discharge of oil. Amendments must be made within six months of such changes.

APPLIED SCIENTIFIC AND ENGINEERING PRINCIPLES

Although the regulatory framework dictates standards for water quality for consumption and effluent limits for discharge, how those values are maintained from withdrawal to discharge is a function of wastewater management engineering.

Before population growth and industrial development began to overtax natural systems, streams, rivers, wetlands, ponds, and lakes had more capability for eliminating contamination. Wetlands still provide more benefits than just serving as important habitats for wildlife; they contribute water storage to reduce flood risk and are a natural buffer to pollution.

Wetlands Management

The Clean Water Act addresses the maintenance of the nation's wetlands. This is important for flood-control issues as well as for a healthy environment. This section on wetlands management is added here, however, not only to recall the importance of wetlands in environmental management but also to point out the potential difficulties in constructing on wetland properties.

The definition of a protected wetland has undergone a legal shift as a result of a series of Supreme Court cases. In 2001, the Supreme Court heard *Solid Waste Agency of Northern Cook County v. Army Corps of Engineers*. In this case, the solid waste agency had petitioned for the construction of a landfill. In the period between the application for the landfill and the court case which followed, the unused property, which had previously been a quarry, became a wetland and home to a rookery and endangered species birds.

The Army Corps of Engineers declined the permit and based their jurisdiction on the definitions of "waters of the United States" under the Clean Water Act. The Supreme Court reversed the 6th Circuit Court, which had upheld the Corps' jurisdiction in the case, taking the position that isolated wetlands did not constitute navigable waters as defined in the Clean Water Act.

Decisions handed down on June 16, 2006, in *Rapanos v. United States* and *Carabell v. United States* left many unanswered questions as to what is a protected wetland under the law. The question comes down to what is considered "navigable waters," and whether wetlands are adjacent to or connected to navigable waters. In *Rapanos*, the connection was remote, consisting of a series of about 20 miles of ditches and canals through which the water from the wetlands had to meander before reaching navigable waters. In *Carabell*, the wetland in question was adjacent to a ditch that eventually emptied into navigable waters, but there was no direct connection, and a berm separated the ditch from the wetlands.

The Court split three ways in its findings, with no majority achieved. Four justices sided with one opinion, which would have severely limited the Corps' jurisdiction over wetlands. A dissenting opinion would have upheld the Corps' jurisdiction. One justice wrote a solitary opinion that "waters of the United States" includes not only navigable waters, but also nonnavigable waters that have a "significant nexus" to navigable waters. Such a nexus might include wetlands, which "either alone or in combination with similarly situated lands in the region, significantly affect the chemical, physical, and biological integrity of other covered waters more readily understood as 'navigable.'" This decision, because it mediates between the two sides, will be the one that stands. The result, then, is that the Corps must determine whether a "significant nexus" exists on a "case-by-case basis." Thus, the Corps might be said to have jurisdiction over the two cases heard, but because this standard was not applied, the cases were remanded to the lower court (Murphy 2006).

Wastewater Management

The first step in wastewater management is an understanding of the character of, and the water and wastes in, the water being discharged. As with other wastes, prevention is the first line of defense. That includes reducing the amount of water going through the system, as well as the volume of waste materials it contains. Waste reduction options include product reformulation, product substitution (replacing toxic materials with those that are less so), process redesign, process control, and waste concentration.

Waste recovery technologies that operate on a closed-loop system to reuse water and product in the system are often more cost effective and environmentally sound than end-of-pipe treatment technologies. Where waste products are of no use to producers, most state EPAs provide waste recycling services that find users for many waste products.

Housekeeping measures that minimize spillage, check for leaks, and make minor process changes can help to keep costs under control. Further management of wastewater depends upon the volume of water flow and concentration of waste materials in the flow.

Consideration must be given to total, average, and peak flows, for which there will likely be permit limits. Total flows are used to calculate user charges. The average daily flow is often used to size a waste treatment system for optimal efficiency. Peak flow is used to size pumps, pipes, and flow metering devices, and should be reflected in the company's waste treatment capacity (California State University 1996).

Wastewater is classified by its chemical, physical, and microbial characteristics. Chemical characteristics include organics (BOD, COD), heavy metals and inorganics, cyanide, toxics, oil and grease, and pH. Physical characteristics include solids (settleable, suspended, colloidal, and dissolved), odor, temperature, and color. Microbial characteristics include bacteria, particularly pathogens (California State University 1996).

Wastewater Treatment

Treatment options must be designed to correspond with the flow, composition, and effluent limits of the waste stream, which is unique to each individual company.

Waste treatment technologies may be grouped into five categories:

1. physical treatment
2. chemical treatment
3. biological treatment
4. land treatment
5. thermal treatment.

The following discussions of waste treatment technologies have been adapted by Michael C. Lee, Richard G. Wilson, and Douglas K. Garfield (California State University 1996). This series of manuals provides a very detailed overview of wastewater treatment operations for the reader seeking more thorough knowledge.

The waste treatment operator at a facility needs a thorough knowledge of the waste stream, the specific technology and operation of the waste treatment operation in use to handle it, and what to do when the system does not work as it should. While it may be useful in considering what additional technologies might enhance a company's current waste treatment system, it is not necessary for a waste treatment operator to have the knowledge of how every type of waste treatment system works in order to be an effective employee. The following provides many of the highlights.

Physical Treatment

Physical treatment includes those processes that separate waste stream constituents or change their form without altering their chemical structure. These processes include equalization, screening, filtration, evaporation, distillation, adsorption, and stripping.

Equalization is performed in a tank, a sump, a basin, or an elongated pipe, and might be used to mix rather than separate constituents in order to neutralize them by mixing acid and basic materials, or by releasing materials slowly that might otherwise cause a shock to the system if released all at once.

Screening removes large particles from the waste stream. This may be accomplished with a rotating drum that is coated with a screen medium through which the water passes. Solids are scraped off the filter as it rotates. A vibrating or stationary screen is tilted so that solids fall off one side.

In a *sedimentation* system, suspended solids are removed by a clarifier, which is a holding tank or basin that allows gravitational settling to occur. Often, a series of baffles and weirs direct the water flow, separate the liquids from the solids, and contribute to the collection and thickening of the settled solids. A *flocculant* (lime, aluminum sulfate, or ferrous chloride) is introduced at the inlet to agglomerate the solid particles so that they can settle faster. Material collected from the settling operation is often still very wet, so additional sludge dewatering must be incorporated at the end. Such systems generate sludge that must then be disposed of.

Flotation is a process for removing solids and oil and grease by introducing air bubbles to the discharge to induce floating. This method is particularly useful for lighter materials that do not lend themselves to sedimentation methods.

Filtration separates liquids and solids by using various types of filtration media. Filters are used to achieve a greater level of separation in the wastewater following clarification or to further dry solids that have been removed from a clarifier.

Evaporation heats a waste solution or slurry in order to condense and concentrate wastewater solutions. Although an expensive alternative, it can be used to concentrate and recycle rinse waters and to recover valuable constituents.

Distillation is used primarily in oil refineries and chemical plants to separate organic liquids at different boiling points.

Adsorption separates constituents by passing them through a filtration medium—usually activated carbon, which has a large surface area per unit of mass. Organic contaminants are removed by adsorbing (clinging) to the surface of the carbon granules. It is effective with dilute concentrations of organic contaminants (solvents, pesticides, PCBs, and phenols), especially nonbiodegradable organics, and some inorganic contaminants, such as cyanide and chromium.

Stripping removes volatile components of wastewater through treatment with a stripping fluid using steam or air.

Reverse osmosis removes or recovers dissolved organic and inorganic materials, particularly soluble metals and most total organic carbon. The process involves pressure filtration through a semipermeable membrane at a pressure greater than the natural osmotic pressure caused by the dissolved materials in the wastewater. It is often used for ultrafiltration to achieve high purity of water.

Solvent extraction is used to remove organic substances through the use of an immiscible solvent (one that normally forms a separate phase) with the waste stream. Added to the wastewater, it combines with the organics and is then extracted through a series of mixing and settling operations. In addition, it is often used in removing phenol from coke industry waste and toxic dyes.

Chemical Treatment

Chemical treatments alter the chemical structure of the constituents to remove them from the waste stream prior to discharge to render the resultant solution less hazardous. These are normally easy to implement but result in sludges.

Neutralization is used to adjust the pH of wastewater by adding acids or bases to produce a neutral solution. Sulfuric and hydrochloric acids are commonly used for neutralization of alkaline streams, and sodium hydroxide (caustic soda), calcium hydroxide (hydrated lime), calcium oxide (quicklime), calcium carbonate (limestone), sodium bicarbonate (soda ash), and ammonia are used to neutralize acids.

Precipitation removes soluble compounds by forming an insoluble precipitate through the addition of a chemical. When lime or caustic soda is added to metal-bearing wastewater, hydroxide precipitates form. The resulting material is removed as a solid. Precipitation is used in the iron, steel, and copper industries to remove metals from pickling wastewater, in metal finishing to remove spent metals from rinse water, and in the inorganic chemical industry in a number of applications.

Ion exchange is accomplished with ion-exchange resin beads composed of synthetic molecular weight polyelectrolytes that are insoluble in water. These beads contain a loosely held ion in their structure that can be exchanged for another ion of the same charge. Cationic resins generally exchange hydrogen ions (H^+) for other positive ions such as metal ions, and anionic resins exchange hydroxyl ions (OH^-) for negative ions such as carbonate. These resins can be designed to be very selective in the ions they remove so that systems can be tailored to a specific application. The liquid is passed through a fixed bed of natural or synthetic resin. One type of ion contained in the water is adsorbed onto an insoluble solid material and replaced by an equivalent quantity of another ion of the same charge. Inorganic material in the solution attaches to the resin and moves from the solution to the resin bed. This technology is effective in handling cyanide and chromium waste streams and in separating metals from mixed metal waste streams. It makes the most sense when metal-bearing waste streams are of high value. However, its disadvantages include its cost, the need to treat regenerate solutions, the need to prefilter prior to ion exchange, the downtime required for regeneration, and upper concentration limits beyond which the process is not feasible.

Oxidation/reduction refers to processes that involve the exchange of electrons to convert toxic compounds into simpler, less toxic chemicals. Common applications of oxidation include conversion of cyanide to cyanate (and then to nitrogen gas and carbon dioxide) and conversion of sulfide to sulfate or elemental sulfur in a two-step process: first, cyanide to cyanate at a pH of 10 to 11; and, second, cyanate to nitrogen at a pH of 8.5. Common reduction applications include the conversion of hexavalent chromium to trivalent chromium. Trivalent chromium precipitates out and can be removed as a solid at a pH of 8 to 8.5, while hexavalent is soluble in water over a wide range of pH levels.

Dechlorination strips chlorine atoms from highly chlorinated toxic compounds, such as PCBs and chlorinated pesticides, producing nontoxic residue.

Biological Treatment

The biological treatment of wastewater involves processes that decompose organic wastes through a variety of methods. These technologies do not usually add microbes but rather encourage the growth and use of the microbes that are already there in order to achieve consumption of a contaminant. There are *designer bacteria* that can be added to a waste stream to handle its particular constituency. In addition to the organic wastes that this technology can address, nitrogen and sulfur compounds can benefit from its application. However, this technology uses living organisms that can die if not properly cared for through feeding and watering.

In *stabilization ponds*, wastes are allowed to decompose biologically over a long period of time. These ponds may be aerobic, aerobic–anaerobic, or anaerobic. In an aerobic pond, bacteria and algae biodegrade the wastes.

Aerated lagoons treat waste on a flow-through basis using the same biological processes that are used by activated sludge systems. This technology has a long retention time while organic matter decomposes. It has been used to treat wastewaters from petroleum, textile, and refinery wastes but is not recommended for waste having high solids or metal content, or for mixed organic wastes.

Activated sludge converts organic matter in a waste stream to carbon dioxide and simpler organics under organic conditions. The technology has been successfully applied to refinery, petrochemical, and other biodegradable organic wastewaters.

Trickling filters consist of a bed of rock or synthetic material with attached bacteria. As wastes are trickled through, the bacteria decompose them.

Anaerobic digestion metabolizes organic matter in the absence of free or dissolved oxygen. The process provides a high degree of waste stabilization with a low production of biological sludges. The end products of this process are methane gas, carbon dioxide, and microbial cell mass. It has traditionally been used for treatment of municipal wastewater sludges. Additional discussion of anaerobic treatment technologies and the potential for energy recovery may be found in the "Best Practices" section.

Land Treatment

In a land-farm treatment scenario, waste, soil, climate, and biological activity all interact to degrade, immobilize, or deactivate waste constituents. Waste may be applied on or into the soil and regularly tilled to enhance biological degradation or left to evaporate and degrade biologically. Waste biosludges, tank-bottom sludges, separator sludge, emulsion solids, and cooling-tower sludges are all appropriate targets, as long as they are biodegradable and organic. Oily wastes from petroleum refinery operations treat waste in this manner. Again, this technology depends upon living organisms. Extreme temperature fluctuations or toxic content in the waste can interfere with this biological activity and render the site useless. Odors and air pollution from volatilization of some chemicals may also be a problem.

Thermal Treatment

Thermal technologies apply temperatures above 300°F/150°C to reduce the volume and break down toxic components of wastes into simpler, less toxic forms. It is applicable for a wide variety of wastes. Energy may be recovered in the process. Thermal treatment can occur in the presence of oxygen (incineration) or in the absence of oxygen (pyrolysis).

The downside to thermal technologies, particularly for wastewaters, is the need for supplemental fuel. It has proven costly for treatment of sludges because they are wet. Air emissions are a concern with these technologies, and siting and permitting may be particularly difficult.

Example: Electroplating

The metal-finishing industry is representative of regulated water-using industries in many ways. Electroplaters are defined as "dischargers of pollutants in process wastewater resulting from the process in which ferrous or nonferrous base material is electroplated in copper, nickel, chrome, zinc, tin, lead, cadmium, iron, aluminum or any combination thereof" (EPA 1986). The category consists of plating, anodizing, metal coating, etching, electro-less plating, and printed circuit-board manufacture. An electroplating operation is a categorical discharger with established compliance sampling deadlines and limits.

In an electroplating operation, items are submerged in a series of baths to perform cleaning, etching, plating, and rinsing operations. Items may be cleaned to remove machine oil and dirt prior to plating, and in this stage solvents may be used. In etching operations, acid solutions are added to remove metal from certain areas of the item. In the plating operation, an electric current is run through the bath and the metal adheres to the item being plated. The item to be plated must be rinsed in clean water after

TABLE 5

Categorical Standards for Electroplaters			
Conventional pollutants			
Biochemical oxygen demand (BOD)		pH	
Total suspended solids (nonfilterable) (TSS)		Fecal coliform	
		Oil and grease	
Metals			
Total cyanide		Zinc	
Copper		Lead	
Nickel		Cadmium	
Chrome (total and hexavalent)		Total metals	
Total toxic organics			
Acenaphthene	1,2-Dichloropropane	N-Nitrosodi-n-propylamine	Vinyl chloride (chloroethylene)
Acrolein	1,3-Dichloropropylene	Pentachlorophenol	Aldrin
Acrylonitrile	(1,3-dichloropropene)	Phenol	Dieldrin
Benzene	2,4-Dimethylphenol	Bis(2-ethylhexyl) phthalate	Chlordane (technical mixture
Benzidine	2,4-Dinitrotoluene	Butyl benzyl phthalate	and metabolites)
Carbon tetrachloride	2,6-Dinitrotoluene	Di-n-butyl phthalate	4,4-DDT
(tetrachloromethane)	1,2-Diphenylhydrazine	Di-n-octyl phthalate	4,4-DDE (p,p'-DDX)
Chlorobenzene	Ethylbenzene	Diethyl phthalate	4,4-DDD (p,p'-TDE)
1,2,4-Trichlorobenzene	Fluoranthene	Dimethyl phthalate	Alpha-Endosulfan
Hexachlorobenzene	4-Chlorophenyl phenyl ether	1,2-Benzanthracene	Beta-Endosulfan
1,2-Dichloroethane	4-Bromophenyl phenyl ether	(benzo(a)anthracene)	Endosulfan sulfate
1,1,1-Trichloroethane	Bis (2-chloroisopropyl) ether	Benzo(a)pyrene (3,4-benzopyrene)	Endrin
Hexachloroethane	Bis (2-chloroethoxy) methane	3,4-Benzofluoranthene	Endrin aldehyde
1,1-Dichloroethane	Methylene chloride	(benzo(b)fluoranthene)	Heptachlor
1,1,2-Trichloroethane	(dichloromethane)	11,12-Benzofluoranthene	Heptachlor epoxide
1,1,2,2-Tetrachloroethane	Methyl chloride (chloromethane)	(benzo(k)fluoranthene)	(BHC-hexachlorocyclohexane)
Chloroethane	Methyl bromide (bromomethane)	Chrysene	Alpha-BHC
Bis(2-chloroethyl) ether	Bromoform (tribromomethane)	Acenaphthylene	Beta-BHC
2-Chloroethyl vinyl ether (mixed)	Dichlorobromomethane	Anthracene	Gamma-BHC
2-Chloronaphthalene	Chlorodibromomethane	1,12-Benzoperylene	Delta-BHC
2,4,6-Trichlorophenol	Hexachlorobutadiene	(benzo(ghi)perylene)	(PCB-polychlorinated biphenyls)
Parachlorometacresol	Hexachlorocyclopentadiene	Fluorene	PCB-1242 (Arochlor 1242)
Chloroform (trichloromethane)	Isophorone	Phenanthrene	PCB-1254 (Arochlor 1254)
2-Chlorophenol	Naphthalene	1,2,5,6-Dibenzanthracene	PCB-1221 (Arochlor 1221)
1,2-Dichlorobenzene	Nitrobenzene	(dibenzo(a,h)anthracene)	PCB-1232 (Arochlor 1232)
1,3-Dichlorobenzene	2-Nitrophenol	Indeno (1,2,3-cd) pyrene)	PCB-1248 (Arochlor 1248)
1,4-Dichlorobenzene	4-Nitrophenol	(2,3-o-phenylene pyrene)	PCB-1260 (Arochlor 1260)
3,3-Dichlorobenzidine	2,4-Dinitrophenol	Pyrene	PCB-1016 (Arochlor 1016)
1,1-Dichloroethylene	4,6-Dinitro-o-cresol	Tetrachloroethylene	Toxaphene
1,2-trans-Dichloroethylene	N-Nitrosodimethylamine	Toluene	2,3,7,8-Tetrachlorodibenzo-
2,4-Dichlorophenol	N-Nitrosodiphenylamine	Trichloroethylene	p-Dioxin (TCDD)

(*Source*: EPA 2011)

each step. The process requires large volumes of water that are eventually discharged as wastewater after the potency of the solution has been exhausted.

The list of contaminants that must be removed from electroplating-system wastewater prior to discharge represent many of the EPA's targeted chemicals, including cyanide, oil and grease, high pH, total toxic organics (TTOs), and metals such as copper, nickel, chrome, zinc, cadmium, lead, and iron. In lieu of TTO monitoring, the POTW may allow the IU to provide an affidavit certifying it has not discharged any TTOs since its last filing period (see Table 5).

Electroplaters are required to implement process controls and pretreatment technologies to achieve discharge limits. Conventional pretreatment technology for an electroplater consists of the addition of chemical reagents that react with soluble pollutants, followed by settling, resulting in the production of insoluble, metal-laden sludges. The wet sludge is dewatered or thickened and then disposed of in a landfill (Campbell and Glenn 1982). A determination must be made as to whether sludges constitute a hazardous waste; the material must be treated based on that determination.

Wastewater entering the treatment system at an electroplating shop will first be screened to remove large debris. Cyanide will be treated first—and separately to avoid mixture with other substances, which could prove more harmful. Hexavalent chrome, because of its toxicity, will be treated next.

Wastewater will move into primary treatment, or clarification, where solid matter will settle out or float to the surface for separation. Solids may be dissolved or suspended, and treatment protocols are different for each. Dissolved solids are those left after suspended solids have been filtered or settled out. Secondary or biological treatment will introduce beneficial bacteria that will eat the organic material remaining in the wastewater.

In larger, more complex facilities, the sludge will be sent for digestion and dewatering. Tertiary treatment is generally saved for municipal wastewater treatment facilities, and more sophisticated ones at that. However, as more cost-effective tools are sought in order to stay competitive, and as energy costs rise, biological treatments that capture energy may prove more cost effective for some wastes than traditional pipeline solutions.

Reverse osmosis has been used effectively in the electroplating industry to remove TOC, copper cyanide, zinc, and nickel. Reverse osmosis was discussed previously in the "Applied Science and Engineering Principles" section.

Electrolytic recovery, also known as *cementation*, is a process in which electrochemical reduction of metal ions at the cathode reduces those ions to elemental metal. This technology is generally used to pull metal ions from solution.

Other technologies, such as ion exchange, will remove metals for recycling. These are in use currently in certain plants and central recovery facilities. However, they are considered cost effective only for those metals of high recovery value.

PERFORMANCE MEASUREMENT AND BENCHMARKING

Discharge limits draw the line in the sand for industry. Over the line is bad; inside is good. But on either side of that simple equation are fluctuations in values that are the result of very specific conditions of operation. Perhaps pH goes down when temperature goes up. If bottles are left unstopped, chemicals volatize. A pump jams and leaves a tank full of grass clippings to create some serious odor. The hotter the sun, the lower the pH, the faster the chemicals in the bottle evaporate, and the quicker the neighbors complain about the smell.

Treatment performance ebbs and flows because of any number of factors. The job of the system operator is to know why the system ebbs and flows, what its potential ranges are, and how to keep operation within a range of tolerable limits.

Maintenance of an effective wastewater treatment facility requires vigilant oversight. If the system is sized appropriately and designed properly, and the operator is well trained on the system, it is left to the operator to maintain it and keep it functioning. Records of all treatment-system upsets should be maintained and excursions investigated. If the treatment system is undersized or poorly designed, changes must be made to bring the facility into compliance.

Statistical process control measures can be used to track system effectiveness and target points of concern. System effectiveness often follows a standard bell-curve distribution, peak performance occurring at a particular point when system chemicals are new, there is a storm event that dilutes process flows, or the plant is down for clean up. Monitoring the activities that coincide with poor performance can help to determine what changes must be made.

Overall system effectiveness can be further refined by tracking individual process lines, specific constituents, or a particular time of day when values tend to be higher. Often, by careful monitoring of such variables, a minor change in process flow can have a greater impact on compliance.

COST ANALYSIS AND BUDGETING

The goal of a waste management system is to use the most cost-effective combination of management options to handle waste streams within the confines of applicable regulations. Large capital expenditures are by no means the only way to achieve this (Campbell and Glenn 1982). The seemingly smallest and cheapest of acts can have monumental impact. Simple housekeeping practices can show immediate return in terms of cost control. How corn meal is washed down the drain during clean up in a tortilla factory, for instance, can mean a major dollar difference in user charge fees. Table 6 provides a listing of anticipated capital and operating costs for the installation or retrofitting of a water treatment system.

When waste treatment equipment must be purchased or retrofitted, major capital expenditures are often involved. The price will range (depending upon the size of the system and its functionality) from a small holding tank to capture and treat small quantities of material in the back of a shop to vast municipal waste treatment systems with many employees, but the purpose is the same.

It is wise to seek the counsel of a qualified wastewater treatment engineer. If treatment must be installed, the type of system, the cost of maintenance and operations, and the amount of waste that will require hauling will greatly affect long-term costs. Where a strategy means lower capital costs, perceived savings may be quickly offset by high operating and disposal costs. It is usually best, unless acting as a wastewater management engineer, to hire a company with the ability to handle the entire job in a turnkey fashion. Make sure the bid includes all components such as piping and installation. Beware of unexpected costs: for example, the excavation of the old system to find the contamination its operation left. It should also be noted that it is often more cost effective to plan for future growth than to retrofit systems every few years. Where new technologies are considered, it is prudent to lease equipment or require performance guarantees.

TABLE 6

Anticipated Costs of a Waste Treatment System Installation or Retrofit

Capital Costs	Operating Costs
Wastewater treatment system, engineering, and installation	Wastewater treatment chemicals
Trucks, as needed	Sludge hauling/transportation costs
	Sludge disposal costs
	POTW user charges
	Permit and license fees
	Fixed costs
	Sampling and analytical costs
	Utility costs

(*Source*: Freeman 2008)

The POTW will charge the company discharging into its system for the costs of treating its wastes. Thus, measures that minimize the amount of water used, and the contributions of BOD or COD, suspended solids, and other user charge items will have an effect on these costs. Wherever possible, waste minimization is always cheapest.

Various treatment technologies create sludges, which must be hauled away and disposed of. Costs of both transportation and disposal continue to increase. Some waste treatment systems require large amounts of electricity, costs of which will also escalate. Technologies that convert waste to energy are preferred for this reason, where feasible.

BEST PRACTICES

As the wastewater treatment industry matures, many of the practices outlined in this chapter have become commonplace in water-using industries. New and improved wastewater treatment technologies continue to be developed that provide new opportunities to minimize product loss and waste and to do so in a cost-effective manner.

Objective analysis of most of the nation's water suggests that point-source pollution is by and large under control.

However, emergency situations, such as the explosion in the Gulf of Mexico, can arise from circumstances not imagined nor adequately planned for. Development of technologies that allow drilling in deeper and more difficult places than ever before brings new responsibilities for minimizing impact to area waters. EHS directors who are involved with EHS operations that push boundaries must be aware and address their unique issues.

Further, nonpoint-source pollution continues to be a problem in the nation's waters. Nitrates and phosphorus from agricultural irrigation runoff, stormwater runoff from roads and into surface water, and leaks and spills into groundwater all usually occur without the benefit of sewage treatment systems. The EPA has established a number of regulations for the agricultural sector and continues to monitor the impact of these sources on water quality. The EPA has increased its scrutiny of the agricultural sector for its contributions to these environmental problems and continues to monitor the impact of these sources on water quality. How these problems are solved is currently beyond the control or direct concern of most EHS personnel at most industrial sites. However, it is incumbent upon every EHS manager to recognize his own company's potential for off-site contamination and to control for it.

The impact of Environmental Management Systems, ISO 14001, on wastewater treatment systems continues to increase, as is discussed in other chapters of this book.

There has been growing awareness of unmeasured and unregulated chemicals that flow through POTWs untreated. Among these are nanoparticles and endocrine disrupters, including the pharmaceuticals for human and animal hormones. These may be passed through the body or flushed down the toilet unused. They are not treated by the POTW, and there are no standards for municipal discharge. However, concerns do exist about the impact of these hormones on public health, and research has begun.

Issues related to sustainability, including old concepts of conservation and resource management—but with the addition of sustainable development and the incorporation of new technologies—is a burgeoning area of environmental management. Increased awareness of global climate-change issues, international energy demands, and environmental indicators that continue to decline worldwide are driving such changes.

On the forefront of these changes is the use of waste products as fuels in digester and gasification projects that mine our waste products for their resource value. Production of ethanol from waste cornhusk rinses may at this time be more expensive than refining oil drawn from the ground, but will likely not always be so. These are not new ideas, but they are being approached with new fervor.

Industry Innovation

Each industry brings its own contribution to the pollution loading in our waterways—and new solutions. When technical innovation reaches the marketplace, EHS concerns must be identified and addressed.

Automated process control of wastewater systems allows continuous monitoring to catch and correct fluctuations in wastewater discharge, engendering greater compliance, as well as cost containment, since chemicals are metered out only as needed.

CONCLUSION

Water is a nonrenewable resource that must be monitored and controlled to maintain a healthy environment. Federal, state, and municipal laws are in place to facilitate this. It is the responsibility of EHS staff to determine how its facility is impacting local water sources and to take the necessary steps to comply.

IMPORTANT TERMS

Aerobic: With oxygen

Anaerobic: Without oxygen

Anti-backsliding: A provision of the Clean Water Act whereby renewals of NPDES permits cannot be issued to dischargers using any limits but final limits, unless it can be shown that the process has undergone substantial change.

Average monthly (or weekly) discharge limitation: The highest allowable average of daily discharges over a calendar month (week), calculated as the sum of all daily discharges, divided by the total number of daily discharges measured during that month (week) (40 CFR 122.2).

Best available technology (BAT): The best technology, treatment technique, or other means available, taking cost into consideration. For the purpose of setting MCLs for synthetic organic chemicals, any BAT must be at least as effective as activated carbon (40 CFR 141.2).

Biological (or biochemical) oxygen demand (BOD): The quantification of the amount of dissolved oxygen needed to satisfy the metabolic rate of microorganisms living in aerobic conditions. Wastewater with a high loading of organic material will reduce oxygen levels in receiving waters, leading to eutrophic conditions. BOD testing will calculate the amount of decompostable material in wastewater by measuring the amount of oxygen (mg/L) used over a period of 5 days at 20°C.

Blowdown: The minimum discharge of recirculating water for the purpose of discharging materials contained in the water, further buildup of which would cause concentration in amounts exceeding limits established by best engineering practice (40 CFR 401.11).

Categorical pretreatment standards: Industry-specific wastewater discharge standards (40 CFR 403-471).

Chemical agent: That element, compound, or mixture that coagulates, disperses, dissolves, emulsifies, foams, neutralizes, precipitates, reduces, solubilizes, oxidizes, concentrates, congeals, entraps, fixes, makes the pollutant mass more rigid or viscous, or otherwise facilitates the mitigation of deleterious effects or the removal of the pollutant from the water. Chemical agents include biological additives, dispersants, sinking agents, miscellaneous oil-spill control agents, and burning agents, but do not include sorbents (40 CFR 300.5).

Coliform: A type of bacterium that is an indicator of possible pathogenic bacterial contamination.

Community water system: A public water system that serves at least 15 service connections used by year-round residents or regularly serves at least 25 year-round residents (40 CFR 141.2).

Conventional pollutant: The following comprise the list of conventional pollutants designated pursuant to section 304(a)(4) of the CWA: BOD, TSS, pH, fecal coliform, oil and grease.

Daily discharge: Discharge of any pollutant measured during a calendar day or any 24-hour period (40 CFR 122.2).

Direct discharge: Discharge of a pollutant (40 CFR 122.2).

Discharge: Any spilling, leaking, pumping, pouring, emitting, emptying, or dumping. This also means the addition of any pollutant to the waters of the United States. This includes addition of pollutants from surface runoff. It may also mean substantial threat of discharge. Discharge also refers to introduction of pollutants into a POTW from any nondomestic source of the act (40 CFR 112.2, 122.2, 300.5, 307(b), (c) or (d), and 403.3).

Disinfection: The process that inactivates pathogenic organisms in water by chemical oxidants or equivalent agents (40 CFR 141.2).

Effluent: Liquid waste, treated or untreated, from sewage or industrial process or treatment.

Effluent limitation: Any restriction imposed on the quantities, discharge rates, and concentrations of pollutants discharged from point sources into waters of the United States, contiguous zones, or the ocean (40 CFR 401.11).

Effluent standard: "Any effluent standard or limitation which may include a prohibition of any discharge, established or proposed to be established for any toxic pollutant under Section 307(a) of the Act" (40 CFR 122.2).

Filtration: A process for removing particulate matter from water by passage through porous media (40 CFR 141.2).

Finished water: Water that is introduced into the distribution system of a public water system and is intended for distribution and consumption without further treatment, except as necessary to maintain water quality in the distribution system (e.g., booster disinfection, addition, or corrosion control chemicals) (40 CFR 141.2).

Ground water: Water in a saturated zone or stratum beneath the surface of land or water (40 CFR 101.12).

Hazardous ranking system: The method used by the EPA to evaluate the relative potential of a hazardous substance release to cause health or safety problems, or ecological or environmental damage (40 CFR 300.5).

Indirect discharge: The introduction of pollutants into a POTW (40 CFR 403.3).

Indirect discharger: A nondomestic discharger introducing "pollutants" to a POTW (40 CFR 403.3).

Industrial user: A source of indirect discharge (40 CFR 403.3).

Inorganic waste: Waste material containing substances of mineral origin.

Interference: A discharge that inhibits or disrupts the POTW, its treatment processes or operations, or its sludge processes, use, or disposal, and therefore is a cause of a violation of the POTW's NPDES permit or the prevention of sewage-sludge use or disposal (40 CFR 403.3).

Local limits: Specific prohibitions or limits on pollutants or pollutant parameters developed by a POTW.

Maximum contaminant level (MCL): The maximum permissible level of a contaminant in water that is delivered to any user of a public water system. It is required to be as close to MCLG as possible (40 CFR 141).

Maximum contaminant level goals (MCLGs): The most stringent drinking water standards at which no known or anticipated adverse effect on the health of persons would occur, plus an adequate margin of safety. Maximum contaminant level goals are nonenforceable health goals (40 CFR 141).

National Pollution Discharge Elimination System (NPDES): The national program for issuing, modifying, revoking and reissuing, terminating, monitoring, and enforcing permits, and imposing and enforcing pretreatment requirements under sections 307, 402, 318, and 405 (40 CFR 122.2).

National pretreatment standard: Any regulation containing pollutant discharge limits promulgated in accordance with Section 307(b) & (c) of the Act.

Navigable waters: Waters of the United States.

New source: Any facility from which there is or may be a discharge of pollutants and the construction of which commenced after effluent standards were proposed for the discharges of its operation (40 CFR 307).

Noncommunity water systems: A public water system that is not a community water system. A noncommunity water system is either a "transient noncommunity water system (TWS)" or a "nontransient noncommunity water system (NTNCWS)" (40 CFR 141.2).

Noncontact cooling water: Water used for cooling that does not come into direct contact with any raw material, intermediate product, waste product, or finished product.

Nontransient noncommunity water systems (NTNCWS): A public water system that is not a community water system and that regularly serves at least 25 of the same persons over 6 months per year. Workplaces with over 25 employees will be thus classified (40 CFR 141.11).

Nonpoint sources: Pollution from diffuse sources, not a point source.

Oil: Oil of any kind in any form, including but not limited to petroleum, fuel oil, sludge, oil refuse, and oil mixed with wastes other than dredge spoil (40 CFR 112.2). The definition is slightly different under OPA, which specifies that the Act does not include petroleum, including crude oil or any fraction thereof, which is specifically listed and designated as a hazardous substance under CERCLA (40 CFR 311(a)(i)).

Organic waste: Waste material derived mainly from animal or plant sources, including petrochemical derivatives.

Pass through: A discharge which exits the POTW into waters of the United States in quantities or concentrations which, alone or in conjunction with a discharge from other sources, is a cause of a violation of the POTW's NPDES permit (40 CFR 403.3).

Pathogenic organisms: Bacteria or viruses that can cause disease.

Permit: An authorization, license or equivalent, and control document issued by the EPA or an approved state (40 CFR 122.2).

pH: Measurement of the acid–base condition of a liquid on a scale of 0 to 14, with 0 being the most acidic, 14 being the most basic, and 7 neutral.

Point source: Any discernible, confined, and discrete conveyance, including but not limited to any pipe, ditch, channel, tunnel, conduit, well, discrete fissure, container, rolling stock, animal feeding operation, landfill leachate collection system, vessel, or floating craft (40 CFR 122.2).

Pollutant: Any material that can contaminate water.

Pollution: Any man-made or man-induced alteration of the chemical, physical, biological, or radiological integrity of water (40 CFR 401.11).

Pretreatment: The reduction of the amount of pollutants, the elimination of pollutants, or the alteration of the nature of pollutant properties in wastewater prior to, or in lieu of, discharging or otherwise introducing such pollutants into a POTW (40 CFR 403.3).

Pretreatment standard: Any regulation containing pollution discharge limits promulgated by the EPA in accordance with Sections 307(b) and (c) of the Act that applies to industrial users of a publicly owned treatment works. It further means any state or local pretreatment requirement applicable to a discharge and which is incorporated into a POTW under Section 402 of the Act (40 CFR 117).

Primary treatment: Treatment by screening, sedimentation, and skimming adequate to remove biochemical oxygen-demanding material and suspended solids, and disinfection where appropriate.

Process wastewater: Any water that comes, during manufacturing or processing, into direct contact with or results from the production or use of any raw material, intermediate or final product, by-product, or waste (40 CFR 122.2).

Publicly owned treatment works: A facility owned by a state or municipality that includes any devices and systems used in the storage, treatment, recycling, and reclamation of municipal sewage or industrial wastes of a liquid nature (40 CFR 403.3).

Receiving water: The waters of the United States into which treated or untreated wastewater is discharged.

Secondary treatment: A wastewater treatment process that converts dissolved or suspended materials into a form more readily separated from the water being treated.

Sedimentation: A process for removal of solids before filtration by gravity or separation.

Septage: The liquid or solid material pumped from a septic tank, cesspool, or similar domestic sewage treatment system (40 CFR 122.2).

Septic: A condition produced by anaerobic bacteria that creates a heavy oxygen demand.

Sewage sludge: Any solid, semisolid, or liquid residue removed during the treatment of municipal wastewater or domestic sewage (40 CFR 122.2).

Significant industrial users: All categorical dischargers, plus companies discharging over 25,000 gallons per day or those whose discharge is of concern to the POTW.

Stabilize: To convert to a form that resists change.

Toxic pollutant: Any pollutant thus identified in the Act (40 CFR 122.2, 307, 405(4)).

Transient noncommunity water system (TWS): A noncommunity water system that does not regularly serve at least 25 of the same persons over six months per year (40 CFR 141.11).

Technology-based treatment requirements: The minimum level of control that must be imposed in a permit (40 CFR 125.3).

Variance: Any mechanism or provision that allows modification to or waiver of the generally applicable effluent limitation requirements or time deadlines of CWA (40 CFR 122.2).

Waters of the United States: All waters which are, were, or may be used in interstate or foreign commerce. These waters are specified as all waters that are subject to the ebb and flow of the tide. These include interstate waters such as wetlands and all other waters—including interstate lakes, rivers, streams, mudflats, sandflats, wetlands, sloughs, prairie potholes, wet meadows, playa lakes, and natural ponds—the use of which would or could affect interstate or foreign commerce. Specifically excludes cooling ponds operating as waste treatment systems (40 CFR 122.2).

Water-quality standards: "Provisions of the State or Federal law which consist of a designated use or uses for the waters of the United States and water quality criteria for such waters based upon such uses. Water quality standards are to protect the public health or welfare, enhance the quality of water and serve the purposes of the Act" (40 CFR 131.2)

Wetlands: Areas that are inundated or saturated by surface or groundwater at a frequency and duration sufficient to support a prevalence of vegetation typically adapted for life in saturated soil conditions (40 CFR 122.2).

REFERENCES

Agency for Toxic Substances and Diseases (ATSDR). 2011. *Toxic Substances Portal: Hygrogen Sulfide* (accessed May 31, 2011). www.astdr.cdc.com/mmg/mmg.asp?id+385&id=67

Bodger, K. 2003. *Fundamentals of Environmental Sampling.* Lanham, MD: Government Institutes.

California State University Sacramento, School of Engineering. 1996. *Pretreatment Facility Inspection.* 3d ed. Washington D.C.: U.S. Environmental Protection Agency.

Campbell, M. E., and W. M. Glenn. 1982. *Profit from Pollution Prevention, A Guide to Industrial Waste Reduction and Recycling.* Toronto, Ontario, Canada: Pollution Probe Foundation.

Cox, D. B. 2000. *Hazardous Materials Management Desk Reference.* New York: McGraw-Hill.

Environmental Protection Agency (EPA). 1975. 40 CFR 141.2. "National Primary Drinking Water Regulations; Definitions." Washington, D.C.: EPA.

———. 1982. 40 CFR, Subchapter N. "Effluent Guidelines and Standards." Parts 401–424. Washington, D.C.: EPA.

———. 1986. 40 CFR 413, *et seq.* "Electroplating Point Source Category." Washington, D.C.: EPA.

———. 2006a. 40 CFR 125. "Criteria and Standards for the National Pollutant Discharge Elimination System." Washington, D.C.: EPA.

———. 2006b. *Safe Drinking Water Act 30th Anniversary, Drinking Water Standards & Health Effects.* www.epa.gov/safewater/privatewells/index2.html

———. 2007. 40 CFR 143. "National Secondary Drinking Water Regulations." Washington, D.C.: EPA.

———. 2008. *Effluent Characteristics from Various Industries.* www.epa.gov/waterscience/guide/industry.html#exist

———. 2010. *NPDES Permit Program Basics.* www.cfpub.epa.gov/npdes/home.cfm?program_id=45

———. 2011. "Effluent Guidelines: Electroplating (40 CFR 413) (retrieved November 8, 2011). www.epa.gov/scitech/watertech/guide/eletroplating/index.cfm

Freeman, Judy. 2011. "What Oil?" *EnviroMentor*, vol. 10, no 2.

Murphy, J. 2006. *"Rapanos v. United States:* Wading Through Murky Waters." *National Wetlands Newsletter* 28(5):1, 16–19.

National Institute of Occupational Safety and Health (NIOSH). 1997. *NIOSH Pocket Guide to Chemical Hazards.* Washington, D.C.: Government Printing Office.

Occupational Health and Safety Administration (OSHA). 1994. *Documentation for Immediately Dangerous to Life and Health (IDHLs): Hydrogen Sulfide* (accessed May 31, 2011). www.cdc/niosh/idhl/7783064.html

———. 1998. 29 CFR 1910.146, *Permit-Required Confined Spaces.* Washington, D.C.: OSHA.

Rapanos v. United States. 2006. 547 US 715. 376 F3d 629 (No. 04-1034) and 391 F3d 704 (No. 04-1384). Vacated and remanded.

Solid Waste Agency of Northern Cook County v. Army Corps of Engineers. 2001. 531 US 159, 191 F3d 845. Reversed.

U.S. Congress. 1977. *Clean Water Act of 1977.* P.L. 95-217. Washington, D.C.: Government Printing Office.

———. 1965. *Clean Water Restoration Act.* P.L. 89-753. Washington, D.C.: Government Printing Office.

———. 1948. *Federal Water Pollution Control Act* (FWPCA). P.L. 80-845. Washington, D.C.: Government Printing Office.

———. 1972. *Federal Water Pollution Control Act of 1972.* P.L. 92-500. Washington, D.C.: Government Printing Office.

———. 1972. *Federal Water Pollution Control Act Amendments.* P.L. 92-500. Washington, D.C.: Government Printing Office.

———. 1990. *Oil Pollution Act* (OPA). P.L. 101-380. Washington, D.C.: Government Printing Office.

———. 1899. *Protection of Navigable Waters and of Harbor and River Improvements, Generally.* (Known as the *Refuse Act.*) P.L. 33-407, Chapter 9. Washington, D.C.: Government Printing Office.

———. 1894. *Rivers and Harbors Appropriation Act.* P.L. 33, Chapter 1, Section 1. Washington, D.C.: Government Printing Office.

———. 1974. *Safe Drinking Water Act (SDWA).* P.L. 93–523. Washington, D.C.: Government Printing Office.

———. 1986. *Safe Drinking Water Act Amendments.* P.L. 99-339. Washington, D.C.: Government Printing Office.

———. 1996. *Safe Drinking Water Act Amendments.* P.L. 104–182. Washington, D.C.: Government Printing Office.

———. 1956. *Water Pollution Control Act* (WPCA). (Known as the *Clean Water Act* (CWA)). P. L. 84-660. Washington, D.C.: Government Printing Office.

———. 1987. *Water Quality Act.* P.L .100-4. Washington, D.C.: Government Printing Office.

APPENDIX A: ABBREVIATIONS

BAT: Best available technology economically achievable
BCT: Best control technology
BPT: Best practicable control technology currently available
BOD: Biological (or biochemical) oxygen demand
CERCLA: Comprehensive Environmental Response, Compensation and Liability Act of 1980, as amended by the Superfund Amendments and Reauthorization Act of 1986
COD: Chemical oxygen demand
CWA: Clean Water Act
FWPCA: Federal Water Pollution Control Act
IDHL: Immediately dangerous to life and Health
IU: Industrial user
MCL: Maximum contaminant levels
MCLG : Maximum contaminant level goals
mg/L: Milligrams per liter
NPDWR: National Primary Drinking Water Regulations
NPDES: National Pollution Discharge Elimination System
NTNCWS: Nontransient noncommunity water systems
PPB: Parts per billion
PPM: Parts per million
pH: The value of a chemical's acidity/alkalinity
POTW: Publicly owned treatment works
RQ: Reportable quantity
SARA: Superfund Amendments and Reauthorization Act
SDWA: Safe Drinking Water Act
SDWR: National Secondary Drinking Water Regulations
SPCC: Spill prevention, control and countermeasure plan
TDS: Total dissolved solids
TMDL: Total maximum daily load
TOC: Total organic carbon
TSS: Total suspended solids
TTO: Total toxic organics
µg/kg: Micrograms per kilogram

APPENDIX B: RECOMMENDED READINGS

Envirolink. *Environmental Resources*. www.envirolink.org/index.html

Environmental Protection Agency (EPA). 1996. 40 CFR 110. "Discharge of Oil." Washington, D.C.: EPA.

_____. 2002. 40 CFR 112. "Oil Pollution Prevention." Washington, D.C.: EPA.

_____. 2007. 40 CFR 122.41(i). "Conditions Applicable to All Permits; Inspections and Entry." Washington, D.C.: EPA.

_____. 2007. 40 CFR 122.41(j). "Conditions Applicable to All Permits; Monitoring and Records." Washington, D.C.: EPA.

_____. 2007. *Clean Water Act* (Sept). www.epa.gov/r5water/cwa.html

_____. 2007. EPA 833-B-06-002, *Developing Your Stormwater Pollution Prevention Plan: A Guide for Industrial Operations* (accessed August 24, 2011). www.epa.gov/npdes/pubs/industrial/swppp_guide.pdf

_____. 2007. EPA 833-B-06-002, *EPA Model Pretreatment Ordinance* (January). www.epa.gov/npdes/pretreatment_model_suo.pdf

_____. 2008. *Clean Water Act—Analytical Test Methods*. www.epa.gov/waterscience/methods

_____. 2008. *Ground Water and Drinking Water*. www.epa.gov/safewater/index.html

_____. 2008. *Safe Drinking Water Act, Contaminants*. www.epa.gov/safewater/contaminants/index.html

_____. 2008. *Safe Drinking Water Act, Groundwater and Drinking Water.*" www.epa.gov/safewater/publicoutreach/index.html

_____. 2002. *A Strategy for National Clean Water Industrial Regulations, Effluent Limitations, Guidelines, Pretreatment Standards, and New Source Performance Standards* (November). www.epa.gov/guide/strategy/304mstrategy.pdf

_____. 2007. *Water Laws*. www.epa.gov/water/laws.html

_____. 2007. *Water Pollution Control Technologies*. www.epa.gov/waterscience/guide/p2/ch5.htm#1

_____. 2007. *Water Quality Standards*. www.epa.gov/waterscience/standards

_____. 2007. *Wetlands; Laws, Regulations, Treaties*. www.epa.gov/owow/wetlands/laws

Farnan, J., General Superintendent, Metropolitan Water Reclamation District of Greater Chicago (MWRDGC). 2006. "Transmittal Letter for Board Meeting" (April 7). www.mwrdgc.dst.il.us

U.S. Army Corps of Engineers. 33 CFR 320-326. *Corps of Engineers, Department of the Army, Department of Defense*. www.wetlands.com/regs

U.S. Department of Agriculture (USDA). 2003. *Agricultural Impacts on Water Quality*. www.ers.usda.gov/publications/arei/ah722/

U.S. Geological Survey (USGS). 2005. *Use of Water in the United States in 2000*. www.water.usgs.gov.circ/2004/circ1268

SOLID WASTE

3

William S. Fink

LEARNING OBJECTIVES

- Analyze the fatality statistics of the solid waste industry as presented by the Bureau of Labor Statistics, indicating why this industry is one of the most dangerous in the United States.

- Become familiar with the basic introduction to solid waste regulations from the U.S. Environmental Protection Agency (EPA), including the definition of solid waste, and how these regulations apply to various types of solid waste landfills.

- Learn about historic waste-handling procedures and current solid waste definitions.

- Recognize which items are necessary in developing a landfill safety plan.

- Identify the safety and health issues to be considered at waste management and recycling facilities.

SOLID WASTE collection and waste treatment and disposal at solid waste landfills are dangerous occupations. The 2009 Census of Fatal Occupational Injuries (CFOI) provided by the U.S. Department of Labor, Bureau of Labor Statistics, indicates that "refuse and recyclable material collectors" work in occupations rated among the top six most dangerous in the United States.

The Bureau of Labor Statistics (BLS) reports fatality data in the Census of Fatal Occupational Injuries according to the North American Industrial Classification System (NAICS) Codes by (1) total fatalities, (2) transportation incidents, (3) assaults or acts of violence, (4) contact with objects and equipment, (5) falls, (6) exposure to harmful substances or environments, and (7) fire and explosions. Fatalities are measured per 100,000 workers (BLS 2010).

An analysis of the CFOI data for the occupations in solid waste collection (NAICS 562111) for the years 2003 through 2009 is presented in the following seven subsections. (BLS 2003, 2004, 2005, 2006, 2007, 2008, 2009).

Table 1 lists the highest-ranking occupations (excluding mining) by fatalities incurred in 2009.

Total Fatalities

In the seven-year period from 2003 through 2009 a total of 515 fatalities occurred in Waste Management and Remediation (NAICS 562). This code includes Waste Collection (Solid Waste), Waste Treatment and Disposal, Hazardous Waste Treatment and Disposal, Solid Waste Landfill and Other Nonhazardous Waste Treatment and Disposal.

Within the NAICS 562 code, Solid Waste Collection (NAICS 562111) indicated a total of 240 fatalities, which occurred during that same 7-year period. Solid waste collection activities accounted for 46 percent of the total number of NAICS 562 labor-classification fatalities.

A review of the NAICS 562 (Waste Management and Remediation) fatality data indicates that in 2003 a total of 91 fatalities occurred. During the subsequent five years (2004 through 2008), an average of 76 fatalities occurred each year. In 2009 a total of 43 fatalities occurred—a 43 percent decrease from the past 5-year average. The 2009 data is encouraging and has dropped this industry down from fifth to sixth in the ranking of most dangerous occupations in the United States.

A review of the NAICS 562111 (Solid Waste Collection) total fatality data indicates that, during the 6-year period from 2003 through 2008, an average of 26 fatalities occurred each year. The 2009 total fatalities' figure of 15 is well below the past 6-year average of 26. This drop in total fatalities is encouraging.

Transportation Fatalities

Transportation-related fatalities in the census include highway, nonhighway, air, water, rail, and fatalities resulting from being struck by a vehicle.

In the Waste Management and Remediation code, transportation fatalities accounted for 59 percent (302) of the total over the 7-year period from 2003 to 2009. The average fatality rate is 43 per year for the seven years. In 2009, 28 fatalities occurred due to transportation incidents—a 39 percent decrease from the preceding 6-year fatality rate of 46.

Solid Waste Collection (NAICS 562111) transportation fatalities accounted for 70 percent (169) of the total over the same 7-year period. The average fatality rate is 24 per year for the seven years. In 2009, 15 fatalities occurred due to transportation incidents—a 44 percent decrease from the preceding 6-year fatality rate of 27.

Assaults or Acts of Violence

Three fatalities related to this category were reported in 2007 for Waste Management and Remediation. No fatalities occurred in the other years evaluated (2003–2006 and 2008–2009). In addition, no fatalities occurred in this category for Solid Waste Collection (NAICS 562111) in the years 2003 through 2009.

TABLE 1

Selected Occupations with High Fatality Rates per 100,000 Employed, 2009

Occupation	Fatality Rate per 100,000 Employed	Total Worker Fatalities
Fishermen (and related) workers	128.9	50
Logging workers	115.7	82
Aircraft pilots and flight engineers	72.4	90
Structural iron and steel workers	46.4	36
Farmers and ranchers	39.5	317
Refuse and recyclable material workers	36.8	31
Roofers	34.4	69
Electrical power-line installers and repairers	29.8	35
Drivers/sales workers and truck drivers	22.8	815
Taxi drivers and chauffers	19.3	69

Total Fatalities = 5,701
All worker fatality rate = 6

NOTE: In 2008, CFOI implemented a new methodology, using hours worked for fatality rate calculations rather than employment. For additional information on the fatality rate methodology changes, please see www.bls.gov/iif/oshnotice10.htm.
(*Source*: BLS 2009)

Contact with Objects and Equipment

Waste Management and Remediation reported a total of 120 fatalities (23%) in this category over the past seven years. The average fatality rate per year is 17. In 2009, 11 fatalities occurred due to contact with objects and equipment—a 39% decrease from the preceding 6-year fatality rate of 18.

Under the Solid Waste Collection code, a total of 51 fatalities (21%) was reported in this category over the past seven years. The average fatality rate per year is 7. In 2009, 5 fatalities occurred due to contact with objects and equipment—a figure slightly below the preceding 6-year fatality rate of 7.

Falls

Waste Management and Remediation reported a total of 21 fatalities (4%) in this category over the past seven years. The average fatality rate per year is 3.

Under the Solid Waste Collection code, no fatalities were reported in this category over the past seven years. Zero fatalities in this category is being achieved!

Exposure to Harmful Substance or Environments

Waste Management and Remediation reported a total of 41 fatalities (8%) in this category over the past seven years. The average fatality rate per year is 7. In 2009 no fatalities were reported in this category—the first year in the past seven in which zero fatalities in this category was achieved!

Under the Solid Waste Collection code, a total of 7 fatalities (3%) was reported in this category over the past seven years. The average fatality rate per year is 1. In the reporting years 2005 through 2009, no fatalities were reported in this category—zero fatalities in this category is being achieved!

Fires and Explosions

Waste Management and Remediation reported a total of 9 fatalities (2%) in this category over the past seven years. The average fatality rate per year is 1. From 2004 to 2007 and in 2009, no fatalities were reported in this category.

Solid Waste Collection reported no fatalities in this category over the past seven years. Zero fatalities in this category is being achieved!

INTRODUCTION TO SOLID WASTE REGULATIONS

The Solid Waste Disposal Act of 1965 (SWDA) was the first federal law that required environmentally sound methods for disposal of household, municipal, commercial, and industrial waste (SWDA 1965). This law was amended in 1970 by the Resource Conservation and Recovery Act of 1970 (RCRA 1976), which was the first nationwide recycling initiative. A definition of solid waste can be found in the Environmental Protection Agency (EPA) regulations (specifically, the RCRA statutes) that can be summarized as follows (RCRA 1985, amended 1987):

> A solid waste is any discarded material that is not excluded by 40 CFR 261.4(a), which addresses nineteen specific excluded materials, ranging from domestic sewage, industrial wastewater discharge, excluded scrap metals, mercury-free switches, shredded circuit boards, etc. Discarded materials may also be excluded by variance granted under 40 CFR 260.30 and 260.31.

Examples of solid wastes include discarded materials that are abandoned or recycled. Military munitions can be classified as solid wastes when meeting the criteria specified in 40 CFR 266.202. Materials are classified as solid waste if they are abandoned by being burned or incinerated; accumulated, stored, or treated (but not recycled) before or in lieu of being abandoned by disposal; or burned or incinerated. Materials are also solid wastes if they are recycled or accumulated, stored, or treated (before recycling) as specified in the regulations. The RCRA definitions are very complex and the regulations need to be studied closely to identify and classify particular waste streams (EPA 2000).

Methods for the management of solid wastes include landfilling, incineration, recycling, source reduction, and composting. Hazardous wastes and medical wastes must be managed separately from nonhazardous solid wastes. The EPA currently regulates the management of solid waste landfills (EPA 2006).

This rule is an important step in improving the safety of municipal landfills. It establishes comprehensive, protective standards for managing the nation's solid waste burden by specifying location provisions and design, operating, and closure requirements for municipal landfills.

By improving the safety of nearly 6000 municipal solid waste landfills, these regulations help to bolster public confidence in landfills as a component of a workable, integrated waste management system. In addition, the rule is an incentive for increasing source reduction and recycling nationwide.

The EPA establishes requirements for municipal solid waste landfills. It covers location restrictions, facility design and operations, groundwater monitoring, corrective action measures, and conditions for closing (including financial responsibility).

SOLID WASTE LANDFILLS

Modern landfills are well-engineered facilities that are located, designed, operated, and monitored in compliance with federal regulations. Solid waste landfills must be designed to protect the environment from contaminants that may be present in the solid waste stream. The landfill siting plan—which prevents the siting of landfills in environmentally sensitive areas—as well as on-site environmental monitoring systems that watch for any sign of groundwater contamination and for landfill off-gas provide additional safeguards. In addition, many new landfills collect potentially harmful landfill gas emissions and convert them into energy. Instead of allowing landfill gas (LFG) to escape into the air, it can be captured, converted, and used as an energy source. Using LFG helps to reduce odors and other hazards associated with LFG emissions and helps prevent methane from migrating into the atmosphere and contributing to local smog and global climate change. Landfill gas is extracted from landfills using a series of wells and a blower/flare (or vacuum) system. This system directs the collected gas to a central point where it can be processed and treated depending upon the ultimate use for the gas. From this point, the gas can be simply flared or used to generate electricity, replace fossil fuels in burned-off industrial and manufacturing operations, fuel greenhouse operations, or be upgraded to pipeline-quality gas (see Figure 1).

Landfill gas is the natural by-product of the decomposition of solid waste in landfills and is comprised primarily of carbon dioxide and methane. By preventing emissions of methane (a powerful greenhouse gas) through the development of landfill gas energy projects, the EPA Landfill Methane Outreach Program (LMOP) helps businesses, states, energy providers, and communities protect the environment and build a sustainable future (EPA 2008e). See Figure 2.

There are several types of solid waste landfills:

- municipal solid waste
- bioreactors
- construction and demolition debris
- industrial waste

Municipal Solid Waste Landfills

Municipal solid waste landfills (MSWLFs) receive household waste. MSWLFs can also receive nonhazardous sludge, industrial solid waste, and construction and demolition debris. All MSWLFs must comply with the federal regulations in 40 CFR Part 258 (Subtitle D of RCRA), or equivalent state regulations (EPA 2006). Federal MSWLF standards include:

- *Location restrictions*, ensuring that landfills are built in suitable geological areas away from faults, wetlands, flood plains, or other restricted areas.

  Suitable geological areas indicate areas meeting criteria acceptable to the EPA and state and local governments where the landfill will not adversely affect the surrounding environment because of depth to groundwater, stable soil conditions, and other relevant factors.

- *Composite liners requirements* that include a flexible membrane (geomembrane), overlaying two feet of compacted clay soil lining the bottom and sides of the landfill, protecting groundwater and the underlying soil from leachate releases.

- *Leachate collection and removal systems*, which sit on top of the composite liner, removing leachate from the landfill for treatment and disposal.

  Leachate is a liquid that has passed through or emerged from solid waste and contains soluble, suspended, or miscible materials removed from such waste. Leachate typically flows downward in the landfill but may also

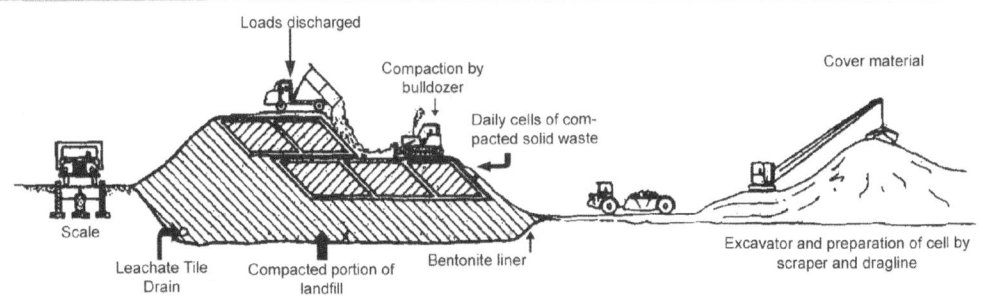

FIGURE 1. A modern municipal solid waste landfill (*Source:* EPA 2008e)

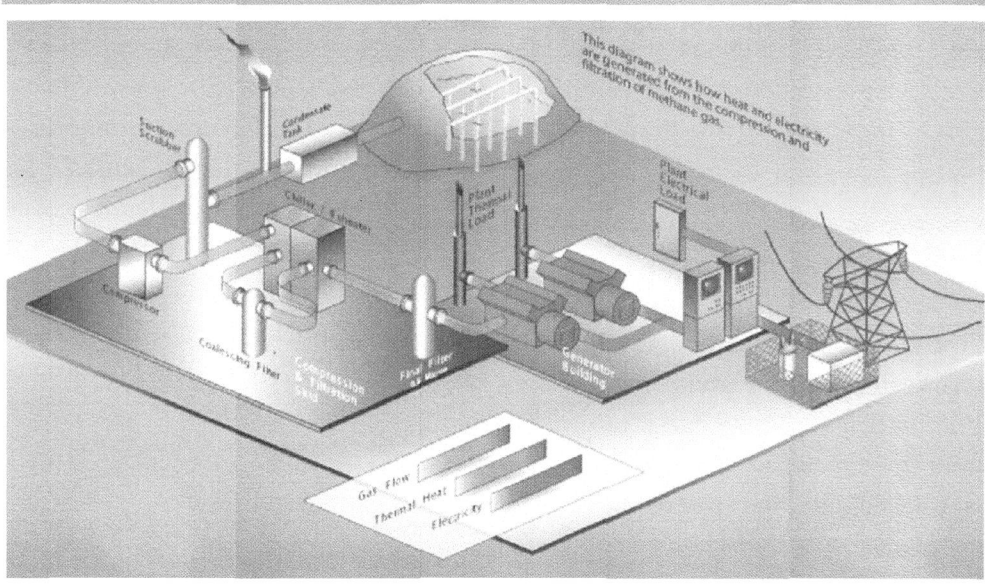

FIGURE 2. Example of a landfill gas-to-energy operation (*Source:* EPA 2008e)

flow laterally and escape through the side of the landfill.

A leachate collection system consists of pipes placed at the low areas of the landfill liner to collect leachate for storage and eventual treatment and discharge.

Leachate flow over the liner to the pipes is facilitated by placing a drainage blanket of soil or plastic netting over the liner. An alternative to collection pipes is a special configuration of geosynthetic materials that will hydraulically transmit leachate to collection points for removal.

Leachate will continue to be generated after the landfill is closed. The quantity should diminish if a good cover was placed over the landfill. Providing cover maintenance will also reduce leachate generation. The chemical composition will also change as the landfill becomes more biologically stabilized with pollutant concentrations slowly diminishing. Leachate collection and treatment generally will be necessary throughout the entire postclosure care period. Pumps and other leachate collection equipment must be operated and serviced. Every few years, leachate lines must be cleaned with sewer-cleaning equipment.

On-site leachate treatment facilities must be maintained and operated. Where leachate is transported off site, arrangements for trucking and treatment must be continued (EPA 1995).

- *Operating practices* include the following:
  - compacting and covering waste frequently (daily) with several inches of soil to help reduce odor
  - controlling disease vector populations (i.e., rodents, flies, mosquitoes)
  - controlling litter
  - protecting public health
  - controlling stormwater runoff and protecting surface water from pollutants
  - keeping out regulated hazardous waste
  - monitoring methane gas
  - restricting public access
  - keeping appropriate records
- *Groundwater monitoring requirements* require testing groundwater wells to determine whether waste materials have escaped from the landfill.
- *Closure and postclosure care requirements* include covering landfills and providing long-term care of closed landfills.
- *Corrective action provisions* control and clean up landfill releases to achieve groundwater protection standards.

- *Financial assurance* provides funding for environmental protection during and after landfill closure (i.e., closure and postclosure care).

Some materials may be banned from disposal in municipal solid waste landfills, including common household items such as paints, cleaners/chemicals, motor oil, batteries, and pesticides. Leftover portions of these products are called household hazardous waste (HHW). These products, if mishandled, can be dangerous to personal health and to the environment. Many municipal landfills have a household hazardous waste dropoff station for these materials. Homeowners may have options in local communities where municipalities set up HHW collection stations at fixed locations or have periodic HHW collection days. Services for collection may be contracted with licensed HW contractors. These HW contractors conduct collection from the public, segregate waste, test waste materials, and dispose of the waste (EPA 2008b).

Bioreactor Landfills

A bioreactor landfill operates to rapidly transform and degrade organic waste. The increase in waste degradation and stabilization is accomplished through the addition of liquid and air to enhance microbial processes. This bioreactor concept differs from the traditional *dry tomb* municipal landfill approach.

A bioreactor landfill is not just a single design and will correspond to the operational process invoked. There are three different general types of bioreactor landfill configurations:

1. *Aerobic:* In an aerobic bioreactor landfill, leachate is removed from the bottom layer, piped to liquid storage tanks, and recirculated into the landfill in a controlled manner. Air is injected into the waste mass using vertical or horizontal wells, promoting aerobic activity and accelerating waste stabilization.
2. *Anaerobic:* In an anaerobic bioreactor landfill, moisture is added to the waste mass in the form of recirculated leachate and other sources to obtain optimal moisture levels. Biodegradation occurs in the absence of oxygen (anaerobically) and produces landfill gas. Landfill gas—chiefly methane—can be captured to minimize greenhouse gas emissions and for use in energy projects.
3. *Hybrid (Aerobic–Anaerobic):* The hybrid bioreactor landfill accelerates waste degradation by employing a sequential aerobic–anaerobic treatment to rapidly degrade organics in the upper sections of the landfill and collect gas from lower sections. Operation as a hybrid results in the earlier onset of methanogenesis in comparison to aerobic landfills

The Solid Waste Association of North America (SWANA) has defined a bioreactor landfill as "any permitted Subtitle D landfill or landfill cell where liquid or air is injected in a controlled fashion into the waste mass in order to accelerate or enhance biostabilization of the waste" (EPA 2008c).

The bioreactor accelerates the decomposition and stabilization of waste. At minimum, leachate is injected into the bioreactor to stimulate the natural biodegradation process. Bioreactors often need other liquids, such as stormwater, wastewater, and wastewater treatment plant sludges to supplement leachate and enhance the microbiological process by purposeful control of the moisture content. This differs from a conventional landfill, which simply recirculates leachate for liquid management. Landfills that simply recirculate leachate may not necessarily operate as optimized bioreactors.

Moisture content is the single most important factor promoting the accelerated decomposition. The bioreactor technology relies on maintaining optimal moisture content near field capacity (approximately 35–65%) and adds liquids when necessary to maintain that percentage. The moisture content, combined with the biological action of naturally occurring microbes, decomposes the waste. The microbes can be either aerobic (requiring the presence of oxygen) or anaerobic (requiring a lack of oxygen). A side effect of the bioreactor is that it produces landfill gas (LFG), such as methane, in an anaerobic unit at an earlier stage in the landfill's life and at an overall much higher rate of generation than traditional landfills. Another type is the hybrid bioreactor landfill, which accelerates waste degradation by employing a sequential aerobic–anaerobic treatment to rapidly degrade organics in the upper sections of the landfill and collect gas from the lower sections. Operation as a hybrid results in the earlier onset of methanogenesis (creation of landfill gas) in comparison to aerobic landfills.

Decomposition and biological stabilization of the waste in a bioreactor landfill can occur much sooner than in a traditional dry tomb landfill, providing a potential decrease in long-term environmental risks and landfill operating and postclosure costs. Potential advantages of bioreactors include (EPA 2008a):

- decomposition and biological stabilization in years (versus decades in dry tombs)
- lower waste toxicity and mobility because of both aerobic and anaerobic conditions
- reduced leachate disposal costs
- a 15–30 percent gain in landfill space because of an increase in the density of the waste mass
- significantly increased generation of LFG, which, when captured, can be used to provide energy on site, or sold
- reduced postclosure care

The EPA indicates that municipal solid waste can be rapidly degraded and made less hazardous (because of the degradation of organics and the sequestration of inorganics) by enhancing and controlling the moisture within the landfill under aerobic or anaerobic conditions. Leachate quality in a bioreactor rapidly improves, leading to reduced leachate disposal costs. Landfill volume may also decrease as airspace is recovered, extending the operating life of the landfill.

LFG emitted by a bioreactor landfill consists primarily of methane and carbon dioxide, as well as lesser amounts of volatile organic chemicals and hazardous air pollutants. The EPA indicates that the operation of a bioreactor may generate LFG earlier in the process and at a higher rate than a traditional landfill. The bioreactor LFG is also generated over a shorter period of time, because the LFG emissions decline as the accelerated decomposition process depletes the source waste faster than in a traditional landfill. The net result appears to be that the bioreactor produces more LFG overall than the traditional landfill does (EPA 2008a).

Construction and Demolition (C&D) Debris Landfills

These landfills accept only C&D debris, such as concrete, asphalt, brick, wood, drywall, asphalt roofing shingles, metals, and some types of plastics generated during the construction and demolition of homes, commercial buildings, and other structures. C&D landfills are subject to less stringent standards than municipal solid waste landfills because of the relatively inert nature of C&D debris.

Reducing C&D Debris

C&D debris consists of the materials generated during the construction, renovation, and demolition of buildings, roads, and bridges. C&D debris often contains bulky, heavy materials that include:

- concrete
- wood (from buildings)
- asphalt (from roads and roofing shingles)
- gypsum (the main component of drywall)
- metals
- bricks
- glass
- plastics
- salvaged building components (doors, windows, and plumbing fixtures)
- trees, stumps, earth, and rock from clearing sites

Reducing and recycling C&D debris conserves landfill space, reduces the environmental impact of producing new materials, creates jobs, and can reduce overall building project expenses by avoiding purchase/disposal costs.

C&D debris reduction can be achieved through *green building* techniques. The EPA's Office of Solid Waste (OSW) supports projects to reduce, reuse, and recycle waste generated from building construction, renovation, deconstruction, and demolition (EPA 2007g).

These techniques for demolition debris reduction and recycling involve setting demolition materials recycling goals and incentives for demolition contractors. Examples include recycling building brick for landscaping use or marine reef building; harvesting building wood products for resale to specialty-use contractors and carpentry shops; cutting up metal building components for scrap recycling; and stripping copper and aluminum wiring for recycling. All buildings slated for demolition must have hazardous and toxic materials removed or abated prior to demolition. These materials include, but are not limited to, PCBs found in ballasts and transformers, fluorescent light fixture tubes due to mercury content, and asbestos-containing building materials. Process piping and vessels must be pumped, decontaminated, and decommissioned in accordance with federal and state regulations. It is possible to achieve 80–90 percent recycling of C&D debris through aggressive *green demolition* programs, thereby vastly reducing the amount of solid waste going to the municipal landfill.

Reducing the amount of C&D debris disposed of in landfills or combustion facilities provides numerous benefits.

- Less waste can lead to fewer disposal facilities, potentially reducing associated environmental issues, including methane gas emissions that contribute to global climate change.
- Reducing, reusing, and recycling C&D debris offsets the need to extract and consume virgin resources, which also reduces greenhouse gas emissions.
- Deconstruction and selective demolition methods divert large amounts of materials from disposal and provide business opportunities within the local community.
- Recovered materials can be donated to qualified 501(c)(3) charities, resulting in a tax benefit.

Industrial Waste Landfills

These landfills are designed for the management of nonhazardous industrial process wastes. Industrial waste consists of a wide variety of nonhazardous materials that result from the production of various goods and products. Industrial waste landfills are subject to the federal requirements in 40 CFR Part 257, Subparts A and B, as well as any state-specific regulations (EPA 2008d).

In order to properly characterize a waste material as nonhazardous or hazardous, the waste generator can use the following:

- *Process knowledge.* The generator should obtain a thorough understanding of the process generating the waste material, enabling proper characterization of the waste. This includes information on process flow diagrams or plans and all inputs and outputs, as well as characteristics such as the physical states of the waste, the volume produced, and its general composition. Trade organizations can be contacted; many industries have already conducted thorough testing to characterize waste over time. This information may be beneficial in evaluating similar processes. Other resources to utilize include chemical engineering designs and plans showing process input chemicals, expected primary and secondary output chemicals and products, material safety data sheets (MSDSs), manufacturer's literature, previous waste analysis, and preliminary test results.
- *Leachate Testing.* The intent of leachate and extraction testing is to estimate the leaching potential of constituents of concern to water sources. Estimating leaching potential allows for the accurate estimation of the quantity of chemicals that could potentially reach groundwater or surface water resources. This includes drinking water supply wells and waters used for recreation. The toxicity characteristic and leachate procedure (TCLP) and elements of a sampling and analytical plan are discussed in detail in several EPA publications (EPA 1996e; EPA 1996b; EPA 1998a; EPA 1996a; EPA 2002).

Historical Waste-Handling Procedures and Current Solid Waste Definitions

Backyard Burning

Burning trash in the open produces many pollutants, including:

- dioxins
- particle pollution
- polycyclic aromatic hydrocarbons
- volatile organic compounds
- carbon monoxide
- hexachlorobenzene
- ash

Many dangerous health conditions can be caused by inhaling or ingesting even small amounts of these pollutants. Small children, the elderly, or people with preexisting respiratory conditions can be especially vulnerable to some of these pollutants. For details on these human health concerns, refer to the EPA Web site (EPA 2007b).

Batteries and Consumer Electronics

Batteries of all shapes and sizes supply power to everyday electronics like toys and power tools, but they affect our world in many more ways. During a power outage, phone lines still operate because they are equipped with lead-acid batteries. Batteries help control back-up power fluctuations, run commuter trains, and provide back-up power for critical needs like hospitals and military operations. The versatility of batteries is reflected in their different sizes and shapes, but all batteries have two common elements that combine to create power—an electrolyte and a heavy metal.

Batteries contain heavy metals such as mercury, lead, cadmium, and nickel, which can contaminate the environment when batteries are improperly disposed of. When incinerated, certain metals might be released into the air or can concentrate in the ash produced by the combustion process. For more details, refer to the EPA Web site (EPA 2007c).

The use of electronic products has grown substantially over the past two decades, changing the speed at which we communicate, and how we obtain information and entertainment. Our growing reliance on electronics (such as computers, cell phones, televisions, gaming systems, and printers) is illustrated by some remarkable figures. According to the Consumer Electronics Association (CEA), Americans own approximately 24 electronic products per household (CEA 2008).

The EPA is working to educate consumers and others on why it is important to reuse and recycle electronics and what the options are for safe reuse and recycling of these products.

Increasingly, state and local governments, manufacturers, and retailers are providing more opportunities to recycle and reuse this equipment. Many computer, TV, and cell-phone manufacturers, as well as electronics retailers, offer some kind of take-back program or sponsor recycling events.

More than twenty states have enacted legislation to manage end-of-life electronics, and more are expected to follow suit.

Recently, steps were taken to significantly increase safe reuse and recycling of electronic equipment. Recyclers can now become certified in responsible recycling standards by demonstrating to an accredited, independent third party that they can, and do, meet available standards. The EPA encourages all recyclers of electronics to become certified and all consumers to choose recyclers that are certified (EPA 2011a).

Composting

Yard trimmings and food residuals together constitute 23 percent of the U.S. municipal solid waste stream. This is a large percentage of waste going to landfills that could become useful, environmentally beneficial compost instead.

Composting offers the obvious benefits of resource efficiency and the creation of a useful product from organic waste that would otherwise have been dumped in a landfill.

Compost can:

- suppress plant diseases and pests.
- reduce or eliminate the need for chemical fertilizers.
- promote higher yields of agricultural crops.
- facilitate reforestation, wetlands restoration, and habitat revitalization efforts by amending contaminated, compacted, and marginal soils.
- cost effectively remediate soils contaminated by hazardous waste.
- remove solids, oils, greases, and heavy metals from stormwater runoff.

- capture and destroy 99.6 percent of industrial volatile organic chemicals (VOCs) in contaminated air.
- provide cost savings of at least 50 percent over conventional soil, water, and air pollution remediation technologies, where applicable.

For more details on composting, refer to the EPA Web site (EPA 2007d).

Household Hazardous Waste

Leftover household products that contain corrosive, toxic, ignitable, or reactive ingredients are considered to be household hazardous waste (HHW). Products that contain potentially hazardous ingredients, such as paints, cleaners, oils, batteries, and pesticides, require special care in disposal.

HHW FACTS AND FIGURES

- The American population generates 1.6 million tons of HHW per year.
- The average home can accumulate as much as 100 pounds of HHW in its basement, garage, and storage closets.

During the 1980s, many communities started special collection days or permanent collection sites for handling HHW. In 1997, there were more than 3000 HHW permanent programs and collection events throughout the United States.

Improper disposal of household hazardous wastes can include pouring them down the drain, onto the ground, into storm sewers, or in some cases putting them out with the trash. The dangers of such disposal methods might not be immediately obvious, but improper disposal of these wastes can pollute the environment and pose a threat to human health. Many communities in the United States offer a variety of options for conveniently and safely managing HHW. For more information on which wastes at home are hazardous refer to Figure 3, which identifies common household products containing potentially hazardous ingredients (EPA 2008g).

These items may be found in garages, basements, or other storage spaces around the home.

Cleaning Products
- Oven cleaners
- Drain cleaners
- Wood and metal cleaners and polishes
- Toilet cleaners
- Tub, tile, and shower cleaners
- Bleach (laundry)
- Pool chemicals

Indoor Pesticides
- Ant sprays and baits
- Cockroach sprays and baits
- Flea repellents and shampoos
- Bug sprays
- Houseplant insecticides
- Moth repellents
- Mouse and rat poisons and baits

Automotive Products
- Motor oil
- Fuel additives
- Carburetor and fuel injection cleaners
- Air-conditioning refrigerants
- Starter fluids
- Automotive batteries
- Transmission and brake fluid
- Antifreeze

Workshop/Painting Supplies
- Adhesives and glues
- Furniture strippers
- Oil or enamel based paint
- Stains and finishes
- Paint thinners and turpentine
- Paint strippers and removers
- Photographic chemicals
- Fixatives and other solvents

Lawn and Garden Products
- Herbicides
- Insecticides
- Fungicides/wood preservatives

Miscellaneous
- Batteries
- Mercury thermostats or thermometers
- Fluorescent light bulbs
- Driveway sealer

Other Flammable/ Combustible Products
- Propane tanks and other compressed gas cylinders
- Kerosene
- Home heating oil
- Diesel fuel
- Gas/oil mix
- Lighter fluid

FIGURE 3. Common household items containing potentially hazardous ingredients (*Source:* EPA 2008g)

REGULATED MEDICAL WASTE

Medical and infectious waste or *regulated medical waste* is generally defined under state regulations. This waste stream is often described as any solid waste that is generated in the diagnosis, treatment, or immunization of human beings or animals, in research pertaining thereto, or in the production or testing of biologicals, including, but not limited to:

- blood-soaked bandages
- culture dishes and other glassware
- discarded surgical gloves (after surgery)
- discarded surgical instruments (scalpels)

- needles (used to give shots or draw blood)
- cultures, stocks, and swabs (used to inoculate cultures)
- removed body organs (tonsils, appendices, limbs, and so on)
- lancets (the little blades doctors use to prick fingers to get drops of blood)

For example, the state of Wisconsin defines medical waste as infectious waste and items that may be mixed with infectious waste, in order to call attention to the noninfectious items that should be recycled instead. Pharmaceuticals, mercury thermometers and medical supplies are not considered medical waste under this definition unless they are mixed with infectious waste (WisDNR 2011).

Medical wastes generally fall into one of four categories—infectious, hazardous, radioactive, and other general wastes from healthcare and medical facilities. Infectious, hazardous, and radioactive wastes represent only a small portion of all medical waste generated each year but garner the greatest amount of concern. The vast majority of medical waste is very similar to wastes generated in households and offices across the country.

The EPA defines infectious waste as a waste that contains pathogens with sufficient virulence and quantity that exposure to the waste by a suspectible host could result in an infectious disease (EPA 1995; EPA 2007f).

Currently, more than 90 percent of potentially infectious medical waste is incinerated (see Figure 4).

Treatment by incineration, and disposal of the resultant ash in a landfill, is an attractive option for managing medical waste. A major benefit of incineration is the destruction of pathogens (disease-causing agents) in the high temperatures of medical waste incinerators (MWIs).

Medical waste is burned in incineration units under controlled conditions to yield ash and combustion gases. The combustion process is a complex combination of chemical reactions that involve the rapid oxidation of organic substances in the waste and in auxiliary fuels. The goal of the process is to achieve complete combustion of the organic materials and destruction of pathogens in the waste while minimizing the formation and release of undesirable pollutants. How well the process approaches complete combustion is determined by temperature, time, turbulence, and mixture with oxygen.

Each organic substance in medical waste has a characteristic minimum ignition temperature that must be attained or exceeded, in the presence of oxygen, for combustion to occur. Above that ignition temperature, heat is generated at a sufficient rate to sustain combustion. Wastes containing high levels of moisture, however, require additional supplemental heat input. A waste constituent should stay in the high-temperature region of the MWI for a duration exceeding the time required for it to completely combust. Because the combustion reaction rate increases with increasing temperature, a shorter residence time is required for combustion at higher temperatures (assuming the presence of good combustion conditions). Adequate oxygen supplies and turbulence sufficient to promote the mixing of organic materials and oxygen are also essential for efficient combustion. Inadequate mixing of

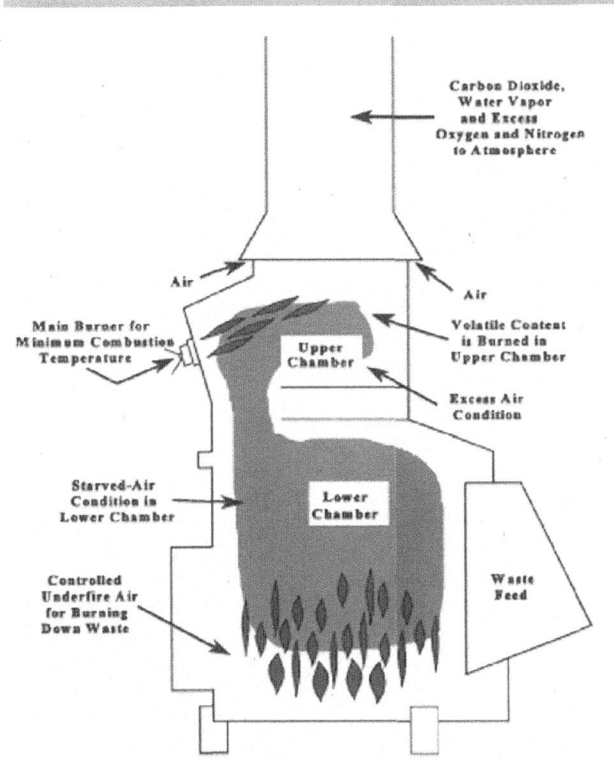

FIGURE 4. Example of a controlled-air incinerator (*Source:* EPA 1993)

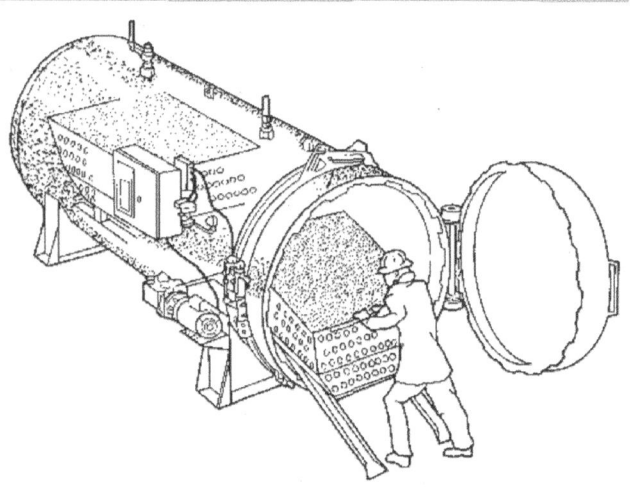

FIGURE 5. Example of an autoclave
(*Source:* OTA 1990)

combustible gases and air can result in emissions of incomplete combustion products. Turbulence within the primary chamber helps to break down the ash layer formed around burning particles of waste and expose the waste material to the high temperatures and combustion air. Bed turbulence is needed to maintain the combustion process and the elevated temperatures throughout the bed (EPA 1994).

The EPA promulgated regulations governing the emissions from medical waste incinerators (MWIs) (EPA 2007a). These regulations include:

- Stringent air emissions guidelines for states to use in developing plans to reduce air pollution from medical waste incinerators built on or before June 20, 1996.
- Final air emission standards for medical waste incinerators built after June 20, 1996.

These guidelines and standards will substantially reduce MWI emissions. The EPA estimates that mercury emission will decline by 94 percent, particulate matter by 90 percent, hydrogen chloride by 98 percent, and dioxin by 95 percent (EPA 2007f).

One anticipated result of the MWI standards and guidelines is the exploration of the use of alternative technologies for treating medical waste. Because of the high cost of compliance with the MWI standards, the EPA expects that few healthcare facilities will be likely to install new MWIs and that many facilities are likely to discontinue use of existing MWIs. (The EPA expects that operation of 50 to 80 percent of the 2400 existing MWIs could be discontinued.) As an alternative to MWIs, facilities are likely to switch to other methods of waste disposal such as off-site commercial disposal or on-site disinfection technologies. Some potential alternative treatment technologies include thermal treatment (e.g., microwave technologies), steam sterilization (e.g., autoclaving; see Figure 5), electropyrolysis, and other chemical and mechanical systems (EPA 2007f).

Municipal Solid Waste (MSW)
Basic Facts

MSW—more commonly known as trash or garbage—consists of everyday items such as product packaging, grass clippings, furniture, clothing, bottles, food scraps, newspapers, appliances, paint, and batteries.

In 2009, U.S. residents, businesses, and institutions produced more than 243 million tons of MSW (before recycling), approximately 4.3 pounds of waste per person per day (EPA 2011b).

Figure 6 depicts the percentage by which different materials contribute to the municipal solid waste stream.

Several MSW management practices, such as source reduction, recycling, and composting, prevent or divert materials from the waste stream. Source reduction involves altering the design, manufacture, or use of products and materials to reduce the amount and toxicity of what gets thrown away. Recycling diverts

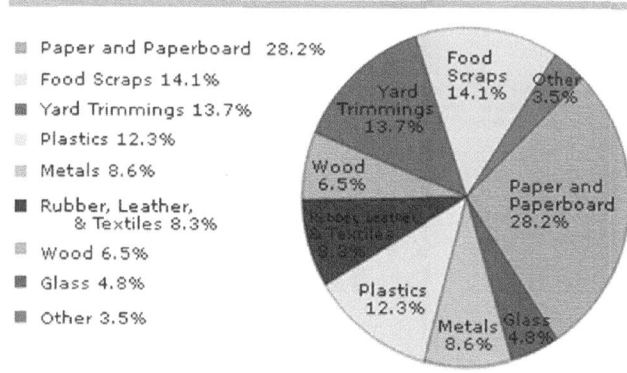

FIGURE 6. Total MSW generation (by material), 2009 (*Source:* EPA May 2011)

items, such as paper, glass, plastic, and metals, from the waste stream. These materials are sorted, collected, and processed and then manufactured, sold, and bought as new products. Composting decomposes organic waste, such as food scraps and yard trimmings, with microorganisms (mainly bacteria and fungi), producing a humus-like substance.

Other practices address those materials that require disposal. Landfills are engineered areas where waste is placed into the land. Landfills usually have liner systems and other safeguards to prevent groundwater contamination. Combustion is another MSW practice that has helped reduce the amount of landfill space needed. Combustion facilities burn MSW at a high temperature, reducing waste volume and generating electricity.

What to Compost		
• Animal manure	• Eggshells	• Nut shells
• Cardboard rolls	• Fireplace ashes	• Sawdust
• Clean paper	• Fruits and vegetables	• Shredded newspaper
• Coffee grounds and filters	• Grass clippings	• Tea bags
• Cotton rags	• Hair and fur	• Wood chips
• Dryer and vacuum cleaner lint	• Hay and straw	• Wool rags
	• Houseplants	• Yard trimmings
	• Leaves	

What Not to Compost
Black walnut tree leaves or twigs—release substances that might be harmful to plants.
Coal or charcoal ash—might contain substances harmful to plants.
Dairy products (e.g., butter, egg yolks, milk, sour cream, yogurt)—create odor problems and attract pests such as rodents and flies.
Diseased or insect-ridden plants—may transfer diseases or insects to healthy plants.
Fats, grease, lard, and oils—create odor problems and attract pests such as rodents and flies.
Meat or fish bones and scraps—create odor problems and attract pests such as rodents and flies.
Pet wastes (e.g., dog or cat feces, soiled cat litter)—might contain parasites, bacteria, germs, pathogens, and viruses harmful to humans.
Yard trimmings treated with chemical pesticides—might kill beneficial composting organisms.

FIGURE 7. Example of a type of source-reduction composting (*Source:* EPA 2007d)

Solid Waste Hierarchy

The EPA has ranked the most environmentally sound strategies for MSW. Source reduction (including reuse) is the most preferred method, followed by recycling and composting, and, lastly, disposal in combustion facilities and landfills.

Currently, in the United States, 30 percent of solid waste is recovered and recycled or composted, 14 percent is burned at combustion facilities, and the remaining 56 percent is disposed of in landfills.

Source Reduction (Waste Prevention)

Source reduction can be a successful method of reducing waste generation. Practices such as grass cycling, backyard composting (see Figure 7), two-sided copying of paper, and transport packaging reduction by industry have yielded substantial benefits through source reduction.

Source reduction has many environmental benefits. It prevents emissions of many greenhouse gases, reduces pollutants, saves energy, conserves resources, and reduces the need for new landfills and combustors.

Recycling

Recycling, including composting, diverted 72 million tons of material away from disposal in 2003, up from 15 million tons in 1980, when the recycle rate was just 10% and 90% of MSW was being recycled (EPA 2008f).

Typical materials that are recycled include batteries, recycled at a rate of 93 percent, paper and paperboard (48 percent), and yard trimmings (56 percent). These materials and others may be recycled through deposit systems, curbside programs, drop-off centers, and buy-back programs (EPA 2008f).

Recycling prevents the emission of many greenhouse gases and water pollutants, saves energy, supplies valuable raw materials to industry, creates jobs, stimulates the development of greener technologies, conserves resources for the future, and reduces the need for new landfills and combustors.

Recycling also helps reduce greenhouse gas emissions that affect the global climate. In 1996, solid waste recycling in the United States prevented the release of 33 million tons of carbon into the air—roughly the amount emitted annually by 25 million cars (EPA 2008f).

Combustion/Incineration

Burning MSW can generate energy while reducing the amount of waste by up to 90 percent in volume and 75 percent in weight.

The EPA's Office of Air and Radiation is primarily responsible for regulating combustors because air emissions as a result of combustion pose the greatest environmental concern.

In 2001, in the United States, there were 97 combustors with energy recovery with the capacity to burn up to 95,000 tons of MSW per day (EPA 2008f).

Landfills

Under the Resource Conservation and Recovery Act (RCRA), landfills that accept MSW are primarily regulated by state, tribal, and local governments. The EPA has established national standards that these landfills must meet in order to operate. Municipal landfills can, however, accept household hazardous waste.

The number of landfills in the United States is steadily decreasing—from 8000 in 1988 to 1767 in 2002. The capacity, however, has remained relatively constant. New landfills are much larger than those of the past (EPA 2008f).

Resource Conservation and Recovery Act of 1976 (RCRA)

The RCRA was enacted by Congress in 1976 and amended in 1984. The Act's primary goal is to protect human health and the environment from the potential hazards of waste disposal. In addition, RCRA is an integral source-reduction mechanism; the law calls for conservation of energy and natural resources, reduction in waste generated, and environmentally sound waste-management practices (EPA 1976).

Environmental Terms, Abbreviations, and Acronyms

The EPA provides a glossary that defines in nontechnical language some commonly used environmental terms appearing in EPA publications and materials. It also explains abbreviations and acronyms used throughout the EPA.

Recommended Sources for MSW Information

Municipal Solid Waste in the United States: 2005 Facts and Figures describes the national MSW stream based on data collected between 1960 and 2005. It includes information on MSW generation, recovery, and discard quantities; per capita generation and discard rates; and the residential and commercial portions of MSW generation (EPA 2008f).

The Decision-Maker's Guide to Solid Waste Management, Volume II, contains technical and economic information to assist solid waste management practitioners in planning, managing, and operating MSW programs and facilities. It also includes suggestions for best practices when planning or evaluating waste and recycling collection systems, landfill and combustion issues, source reduction and composting programs, and public education (EPA 1995).

Scrap Tires

There are at least 275 million scrap tires in stockpiles in the United States. In addition, approximately 290 million scrap tires were generated in 2003.

Markets now exist for about 80 percent of scrap tires—up from 17 percent in 1990. The states have played a major role in tackling this problem by regulating the hauling, processing, and storage of scrap tires and by working with industry to recycle and beneficially use scrap tires by developing markets for the collected scrap tires.

The three largest scrap-tire markets are tire-derived fuel, civil engineering applications, and ground-rubber applications/rubberized asphalt.

Several industries use tires as fuel, including the cement industry, the pulp and paper industry, electric utilities, industrial/institutional boilers, and dedicated tire-to-energy facilities.

Examples of civil engineering applications include: subgrade fill and embankments, backfill for walls and bridge abutments, subgrade insulation for roads, landfills, and septic system drain fields.

Examples of ground-rubber/rubberized asphalt applications include asphalt rubber and athletic and recreational applications, such as ground cover under playground equipment, running track material, and sports and playing fields. Other applications include molded rubber products (carpet underlay, flooring material, dock bumpers, patio decks, railroad-crossing blocks, livestock mats, roof walkway pads, rubber tiles and bricks, movable speed bumps), new tire manufacturing, brake pads and shoes, additives to injection-molded and injection-extruded plastics, automotive parts, agricultural and horticultural applications or soil amendments, and horse-arena flooring (EPA 2007e).

Oil

Oil keeps cars, lawnmowers, and many other machines running smoothly, but once it is used it must be discarded properly to keep from contaminating the environment. Recycling used oil is becoming the preferred way of handling it to protect the environment and conserve natural resources.

Used oils, such as engine lubrication oil, hydraulic fluids, and gear oils used in cars, bikes, or lawnmowers can pollute the environment if not disposed of properly. Used oil must be recycled or disposed of properly by local waste management authorities or automotive repair shops. Used oil filters pose similar waste concerns. If properly drained, they can be safely recycled or disposed of.

Benefits of Recycling Used Oil and Oil Filters

Recycling used oil keeps it from polluting soil and water.

Motor oil does not wear out—it just gets dirty—so recycling it saves a valuable resource.

Less energy is required to produce a gallon of re-refined base stock than a base stock from crude oil.

Used oil can be re-refined into lubricants, processed into fuel oils, and used as raw materials for the refining and petrochemical industries. Used oil filters contain reusable scrap metal that steel producers can use as scrap feed.

To recycle used oil, processors and refiners remove water, insolubles, dirt, heavy metals, nitrogen, chlorine, and oxygenated compounds from oil drained from automobiles or other machines. The resulting product, called *re-refined* oil, must meet the same stringent refining, compounding, and performance standards as virgin oil for use in automotive, heavy-duty diesel, and other internal combustion engines, and hydraulic fluids and gear oils. Extensive laboratory testing and field studies conclude that re-refined oil is equivalent to virgin oil; it passes all prescribed tests and, in some situations, even outperforms virgin oil.

The same consumers and businesses that use regular oil also can use re-refined oil, because re-refining simply reconditions used oil into new, high-quality lubricating oil. Any vehicle maintenance facilities, automobile owners, and other machinery maintenance operations that use oil also can use re-refined oil. In some cases, fleet maintenance facilities that use large volumes of oil arrange to reuse the same oil that they send to be re-refined—a true closed recycling loop.

DEVELOPING A LANDFILL SAFETY PLAN

Compactors, bulldozers, and other heavy equipment pose many hazards. They require safety awareness on the part of operators and a planned approach to safety. Federal and state safety and health rules and regulations must be followed. Frequent safety training and frequent safety inspections of job-site materials and equipment are required.

The following items should be considered when developing a landfill safety plan:

- site-specific accident prevention procedures
- methods to limit exposure to disease and pollutants
- regular equipment and operations inspections
- list of safety rules for operations of site equipment
- personal protective equipment
- emergency notification procedures
- confined-space-entry procedures

The landfill safety plan should emphasize:

- identification of lines of responsibility and authority
- regular inspections and audits of health and safety operations
- becoming the basis for open safety discussions with all employees, chiefly through daily and weekly tailgate safety meetings

- a positive management attitude toward safety and health in order to instill a positive safety culture among employees

The landfill safety plan needs to address all safety and health issues that will arise in the facility-required solid waste program.

A special waste management plan must include procedures for special waste acceptance; record keeping; and waste characterization, handling, storage, and disposal.

The plan should contain:

- an analysis of special waste management alternatives
- a rationale for the proposed disposal alternative
- the physical and chemical characteristic of each waste
- the proposed (EPA- and state-approved) procedures for waste sampling, testing, and analysis
- an evaluation of whether the waste is compatible with the landfill (or other impoundment) liner and leachate management system
- procedures to document and record daily and annual waste quantities (weight or volume), waste sources, and generating processes
- potential hazards associated with some wastes that may require special handling for disposal (see Figure 8).

Potential Hazard	Example Waste
Personnel safety	Asbestos
Odor and vector problems	Large dead animals
Excessive leachate generation	Sewage sludge
Excessive settlement in landfill	Yard debris
Puncturing or tearing of landfill liner	Construction and demolition debris
Fire hazards	Tire chips
Increasing toxicity of landfill toxic materials	Clean-up materials contaminated with leachate

FIGURE 8. Special handling for toxic material disposal (*Source:* Oregon DEQ u.d.)

Special handling and training is required for asbestos waste materials. Consideration for specialized worker training, medical surveillance, state licensing, monitoring, postings, PPE, respiratory protection, and written safety plans that include spill response and emergency notification must be taken.

Sewage sludge also requires special handling and trained workers. Consideration for specialized worker training, monitoring, postings, PPE, respiratory protection, and written safety plans that include spill response and emergency notification must be taken.

An example of protective measures to safeguard against hazards presented by sewage exposure includes:

- the use of nitrile gloves to avoid hand contact with raw sewage and sewage-contaminated soils, piping, equipment and other materials
- the use of eye and or face protection to prevent splashes of sewage from contacting the open eye
- the use of respiratory protection as necessary
- the use of protective coveralls to prevent contamination of work clothing from gross sewage contamination
- the use of antibacterial soap and water for hand cleaning prior to breaks and at the end of work shifts
- the use of vigorous hand-cleaning practices to remove surface contamination from hands, fingernails, and face prior to eating, using tobacco products, applying cosmetics, using the restroom, and leaving the work site
- providing an eyewash station in the event of splash contamination of the eyes
- providing a full-body shower in the event of gross sewage contamination from a splash event on work clothes.

Toxic and hazardous contaminated materials require highly specialized handling and trained personnel. The Occupational Safety and Health Administration (OSHA) hazardous waste operations and emergency response (HAZWOPER) regulations found in 29 CFR 1910.120, require a training program, contingency plan, and provisions for preparedness and prevention.

Waste Management and Recycling Facilities—Safety and Health Issues

Waste transfer stations are facilities where municipal solid waste is unloaded from collection vehicles and briefly held while it is reloaded onto larger long-distance transport vehicles for shipment to landfills or other treatment or disposal facilities. By combining the loads of several individual waste collection trucks into a single shipment, communities can save money on the labor and operating costs of transporting the waste to a distant disposal site. They can also reduce the total number of vehicular trips to and from the disposal site. Although waste transfer stations help reduce the impacts of trucks traveling to and from the disposal site, they can cause an increase in traffic in the immediate area where they are located. If not properly sited, designed, and operated, they can cause problems for residents living near them (EPA 2001).

Facility Safety Considerations

Traffic: Important design and operating features:

- Select sites that have direct access to truck routes, highways, and rail or barge terminals.
- Provide adequate space within the facility so customers waiting to use the transfer station do not block public roadways or impact nearby residences or businesses.
- Designate haul routes to and from transfer stations that avoid congested areas, residential areas, business districts, schools, hospitals, and other sensitive areas.
- Designate safe intersections with public roads.

Noise: Heavy truck traffic and operating heavy-duty facility equipment (e.g., conveyors and front-end loaders) are primary sources of noise from transfer stations. Design and operating practices that reduce noise include:

- confining noisy activities within buildings or other enclosures as much as possible
- using landscaping, sound barriers, and earth berms to absorb exterior noise
- arranging site so traffic flows are not adjacent to properties that are sensitive to noise
- providing set-back distances, called buffer zones, to separate noisy activities from adjacent land uses
- conducting activities that generate maximum noise during the day
- providing hearing protection devices (HPDs) to operating staff

Odor: Garbage (food waste and grass) has a high potential for odor. Proper facility design can significantly reduce odor problems. Doorways should be carefully positioned, in consideration of neighbors. The waste transfer building can be equipped with filtered exhaust fans and rooftop exhaust vents.

Odor reduction operating procedures can include:

- "first-in/first-out" waste-handling practices that keep waste on site for short periods of time
- removing waste from the tipping floor or pit by the end of each day to allow for sweeping down and washing down
- "Good-housekeeping" measures that include regular cleaning and disinfecting of surfaces and equipment that comes into regular contact with waste
- water misting and deodorizing systems

Rodents and Birds: Rodents and birds can be a nuisance and a potential health concern at waste transfer stations. A few basic design and operational elements can control them.

- Good-housekeeping practices mean a simple and effective means of minimizing their presence and include:
  - removing all waste deliveries to the facility by the end of each day and cleaning the receiving floor daily
  - receiving waste only within an enclosed structure and otherwise preventing litter, to reduce the presence of birds
  - baiting and trapping rodents if problems persist in the vicinity

Litter: Stray pieces of waste may become litter in and around the waste transfer facility.

Measures to reduce litter include:

- positioning the main transfer building so that predominant winds are less likely to blow through the building and carry litter off site
- installing perimeter landscaping and fencing to reduce wind speeds and to trap litter
- ensuring that tarps on open-top trucks are secure
- providing skirting around loading chutes
- removing litter frequently to reduce the opportunity for it to travel off site
- patrolling nearby access roads to control litter from truck traffic

Exposure to Potentially Hazardous Equipment

Potentially hazardous equipment includes anything with moving parts, including conveyor belts, push blades, balers, and compactors. Facility operators need to develop an employee equipment-orientation program and establish safety programs to minimize the risk of injury from station equipment. A program to effectively control hazardous energy (lockout/tagout) that uses locks and tags to prevent equipment from operating while being serviced will aid in minimizing hazards in the transfer station. Transfer station operators must implement and strictly enforce rules that require children and pets to stay within vehicles at all times. Posting signs and applying bright-colored paint or tape to hazards will alert customers to potential dangers.

Personal Protective Equipment (PPE)

Transfer station workers coming in close contact with heavy equipment, machinery, and waste material should wear appropriate PPE. PPE should include hard hats, protective eyewear, dust masks, protective gloves, and steel-toed boots. When working in close proximity to loud machinery and heavy equipment, hearing protection devices must be used as well. Each facility must conduct a PPE hazard assessment, and all workers must be trained in the use, care, and limitations of assigned PPE.

Exposure to Extreme Temperatures

Facilities located in areas of extreme weather must account for potential impacts to employees from prolonged exposure to extreme heat or cold. Heat exhaustion and heat stroke are addressed with proper facility operations, including good ventilation inside buildings, access to water and shade, and periodic breaks. Cold stress is addressed by proper clothing, shelter from wind and precipitation, and access to warming areas. Extreme temperatures should not pose problems for customers, whose exposure times are much briefer than those of facility workers.

Traffic

Controlled, safe traffic flow in and around the facility is critical to ensuring customer and employee safety. Ideally, a transfer station is designed so that traffic from large waste-collecting vehicles is kept separate from self-haulers, who typically use cars and pickup trucks. Facility designers should consider:

- Traffic flow that may be directed in a one-way loop through the main transfer facility and around the entire site.
- Facilities with one-way traffic have buildings (and sometimes entire sites) with separate entrances and exits.
- Transfer trailers are difficult to maneuver, require gentle slopes and adequate turning radius. It is ideal that trailers need not back up.
- Building sites should be arranged to minimize road intersections and the need for vehicles to back up or make sharp turns.
- Space should be provided for incoming traffic to line up when tipping traffic is backed up. Sufficient space should be located after the scale house and before the tipping area to prevent backing up onto public roads.
- Easily understood and highly visible signs, pavement markings, and directions from transfer station staff should be set up to indicate proper traffic flow.
- Bright lighting, both artificial and natural, should be provided inside buildings. Using

light-colored interior finishes that are easy to keep clean is very helpful. When entering a building on a bright day, a driver's eyes need time to adjust to the darker interior. This adjustment period can be dangerous. Good interior lighting and light-colored surfaces can reduce the contrast and shorten adjustment time.
- An area for self-haulers should be provided to unload separately from large trucks. Typically, self-haulers must manually unload the back of a pickup truck, car, or trailer. This process takes longer than the automated dumping of commercial waste-collection vehicles and potentially exposes the driver to other traffic. It is often a good idea to have a staff member assist the public with unloading activities.
- Staff members should be required to wear brightly colored safety vests.
- Back-up alarms should be installed on all moving facility equipment and personnel trained in proper facility equipment operations safety. Back-up alarms must be maintained on moving facility equipment in working condition at all times. Cameras and monitors can be installed as an added precaution.
- Too much reliability should not be placed on reversing alarms. They may be a useful additional safeguard when segregating pedestrians from vehicle movements, but eliminating unnecessary reversing cannot adequately control risks. They cannot be heard by everyone, and on a busy, noisy site they can become part of the background noise or cause confusion when more than one vehicle is operating in reverse. The environmental impact of the noise and operating times may have to be considered.
- For good all-round vision when reversing, closed-circuit television (CCTV), or mirrors, or a mix of both, should be fitted to vehicles; the use of mirrors or CCTV alone may be insufficient. They should be checked at least daily and maintained in good working order. The reliability and quality of CCTV is now high and the costs of fitting and maintenance are low. CCTV can pay for itself within a few months by reducing vehicle and property damage. All subsequent savings add to the company's profits.

Safe Vehicles

When attempting to make vehicles safer, the methods used must be evaluated in terms of their fitness for the purpose intended:

- Safety specifications of vehicles used on site are essential. Vehicle capabilities and site conditions have to be consistent with the tasks performed. A full risk assessment will be required to ensure that the task can be done safely. Stability and ground clearance of vehicles should be adequate for site conditions and tasks.
- Vehicles should be provided with suitable means of access and egress, including cab access for routine tasks.
- Reversing is a high-risk activity. The site should be laid out so as to eliminate or minimize the need to reverse wherever possible. Wherever reversing is required, all-around vision is essential wherever achievable. Closed circuit TV (CCTV), additional rear view mirrors and reversing (or back-up) alarms (or a combination of them) may be required as part of the controls in place to reduce the risks of reversing.
- Many operators are now purchasing new vehicles with CCTV fitted and are retrofitting existing vehicles based on risk assessments. They are also finding that the damage reduction and increased productivity achievable by fitting CCTV is a worthwhile return on investment.
- Roll-over protection (ROPs) should be provided to protect the driver in the event of vehicle rollover. This protection is also required for smaller mobile vehicles that may be used on site (e.g., dumpers, tractors, and so on).
- Falling-object protection (FOPs) should be consistent with the risks. Particular attention should be paid to loading tasks.
- For some tasks the vehicle cab may not be sufficient to protect a driver unless it has been

specially reinforced. You should consider the adverse effects of providing extra reinforcement and the potential for obscuring rear vision, especially through rear windscreens. Examples include the loading/unloading of some metal scrap and demolition debris and the use of heavy prybars and shovels in the vicinity of the cab.

- Seatbelts save lives. Fitting seatbelts and enforcing their use can dramatically reduce injuries and fatalities in overturns and collisions. Brightly colored, high-visibility seatbelts can help ensure use.
- Seatbelt design is important in the avoidance of back and other musculoskeletal problems. Their correct adjustment should be part of operator training.
- Body props should be provided on tipper vehicles. Using body and door props should be part of site rules. Their use should be monitored and enforced.
- *Outside-of-cab* controls pose specific risks, potentially exposing drivers to other moving vehicles. External controls are not advised for tipping vehicles with a risk of fallover. Many vehicles with external controls are designed for one-person operation, with the operator in a safe position when at the controls. Others in the area may not be as well protected and should be kept clear.
- Other safety equipment may be required as determined by risk assessments, such as *impact grills* on plant windscreens, door props/clasps, and so on. They should be part of the risk-assessment and plant-specification process.
- Vehicle maintenance, regularly carried out to a good standard, is essential. It ensures that the safety features are working and can help in reducing noise and vibration.
- Many companies have instituted plans to ensure that
  - all new vehicles are fitted with auto-sheeting (or auto-tarping) equipment
  - existing vehicles are part of a retrofitting plan based on risk assessment.
- Some companies are revising their contracts with waste haulers to ensure that only auto-sheeted (or auto-tarped) vehicles will be permitted on site.

Containers

When considering containers for a facility, design and safety features are important:

- Container types and designs of door-locking mechanisms should be selected to be appropriate for the task. Violent door release has caused amputations and other serious injuries. Loads can move or settle and pressurize the door. Damage to containers can lead to doors being sprung, presenting the same risks.
- Use of ratchet and remote door-opening devices can reduce the risks associated with sprung and/or pressurized doors. Safe systems to work or deal with sprung or pressurized doors need to be in place. Containers should be of good construction, free from patent defect and constructed to appropriate standards.
- Containers' general integrity and the condition of their doors, hinges, opening mechanisms, lifting lugs, and other points are safety-critical. Drivers should visually inspect them regularly. A formal defect reporting system is expected for containers. Quarantine areas for defective containers at transport-operation sites will assist in ensuring that drivers do not use damaged containers by mistake.

Maintenance, Daily Checks, and Defect Reporting

Daily and weekly vehicle checks should be carried out for defects. They should include brakes, lights, tires, steering, and all-around vision. Keep a record of these checks. DOT-required inspections need to be programmed and carried out. They should include:

- Defect reporting, which is essential.
- Scheduled maintenance that should be carried out according to manufacturers' specifications.

- Keeping maintenance and legally required test records on site.

More regular maintenance schedules may be required, depending upon the activities carried out and the environment a vehicle may work in.

Visitors and Customer Vehicles

Customer vehicle design and condition is a valid safety concern for site operators. On landfill sites, vehicle design can affect the safety of tipping operations. Ultimately, site operators may choose not to allow unacceptable vehicle types on their sites. The risks posed by tipping vehicles (such as fallover) need to be controlled. All vehicles with obviously unsafe defects should be brought to the attention of the driver and the employer. Close cooperation and communication with customers on vehicle types can reduce the risks.

Spotters

Guiding vehicles through the use of spotters on the ground is a very high-risk activity. Actions to eliminate their use should be evaluated and implemented when reasonably practicable by improving site layout or traffic control and driver vision aids. In situations where spotters must be utilized:

- They should be adequately trained.
- They should wear ANSI Type-III reflective high-visibility vests (at minimum) and be visible at all times during vehicle movements.
- They must be provided with effective radio communication devices in order to communicate with one another and with drivers (as needed).
- Employees and visiting drivers must understand and obey their instructions.
- The system must be enforced to ensure compliance.

Falls

Accidental falls are another concern for facility employees and customers, especially in facilities with pits or direct-dump designs where the drop at the edge of the tipping area might be 5 to 15 feet deep. Facilities with flat tipping areas offer greater safety in terms of reducing the height of falls, but they present their own hazards. These include standing and walking on loading floors that are slick from recent waste materials and being close to station operating equipment that removes waste materials after each load is dumped. A number of safety measures should be considered to reduce the risk of slips, trips, and falls:

- For direct gravity loading of containers by the public, a moderate grade separation will reduce the fall distance. For example, some facilities place roll-off boxes 8 feet below grade to facilitate easy loading of waste into the container (so the top of the roll-off box is even with the surrounding ground). This scenario, however, creates an 8-foot fall into an empty roll-off box. Alternatively, the roll-off box can be set about 5 feet below grade with the sides extending 3 feet above the floor. This height allows for relatively easy lifting over the box's edge yet is high enough to reduce the chance of accidental falls.
- For pit-type operations, the pit end can be tapered to accommodate commercial unloading at the deep end (typically 8–12 feet) and public unloading at the shallow end (3–6 feet).
- Safety barriers can be placed around the pit edges at the end of the day or during cleaning periods to prevent falls. The barriers can be removed during normal waste-loading operations.
- Substantial wheel stops can be placed to stop vehicles from backing into pits or bins.
- Locating wheel stops a good distance from the edge of the unloading zone keeps self-haul customers from finding themselves dangerously close to the edge of the bin pit during unloading or dangerously close to an operating zone for station equipment.
- To prevent falls caused by slipping, floors should be cleaned on a regular basis and treated with a nonskid flooring material.
- Designers need to provide a sufficient slope in floors and pavements so they drain readily and

eliminate standing water. This is especially crucial in cold climates where icing can cause an additional fall hazard. Because of transfer stations' large size and volume, and because of the constant flow of vehicles, it is impractical to design and operate them as heated facilities.

- Use of colored floor coatings (such as bright red or yellow) in special hazard zones (including the area immediately next to a pit) can give customers a strong visual cue.
- Designing unloading stalls for self-haul customers with a generous width (at least 12 feet when possible) maximizes the separation between unloading operations and reduces the likelihood of injury from activity in the next stall. For commercial customers, stall widths of at least 15 feet are needed to provide a similar safety cushion. This is particularly necessary where self-haul and commercial stalls are located side by side.
- If backing movements are required, design the facility so vehicles back in from the driver's side (i.e., left to right) to increase visibility.

Noise

Unloading areas can have high noise levels due to the stations operating equipment, the unloading operation and waste movement, and customers vehicles. Back-up safety alarms and beepers required on most commercial vehicles and operating equipment can also be particularly loud. The noise levels also might cause customers not to hear instructions or warnings or the noise from an unseen approaching hazard.

Designers have limited options for dealing with the noise problem. The principal way to reduce the effects of high-decibel noise in enclosed tipping areas is to apply a sound-absorbing finish over some ceiling and wall surface areas. Typically, spray-on acoustical coatings are used, but these finishes tend to collect dust, dirt, and grime and are hard to keep clean and bright. Using a rubber shoe on the bottom of waste-moving equipment buckets and blades and avoiding use of track-type equipment that produces high mechanical noise can also limit noise exposure. These approaches, however, can affect the transfer system's operational efficiency. Regardless of which approaches are employed, transfer station employees exposed to high levels of noise for prolonged periods of time should use hearing protection devices such as earplugs or ear muffs to prevent hearing loss.

Air Quality

Tipping areas often have localized air-quality problems (dust and odor) that constitute a safety and health hazard. Dust in particular can be troublesome, especially where dry, dusty commercial loads (e.g., C&D wastes) are tipped. Prolonged exposure to air emissions from waste and motor-vehicle emissions in the building pose another potential health threat to facility employees. Facility air-quality issues can be addressed through a number of design and operational practices. These might include:

- Water-based dust-suppression (misting or spraying) systems used to knock down dust. Different types of systems are available that typically involve a piping system with an array of nozzles aimed to deliver a fine spray to the area where dust is likely to be generated (e.g., over the surge pit). These systems typically are actuated by the station staff on demand when dust is generated.
- Dust-suppression systems can operate using only water or they can have an injection system that mixes odor-neutralizing compounds (usually naturally occurring organic extracts) with the water. These dual-purpose systems effectively control both dust and odors. Water-based dust-suppression systems, however, can have adverse economic impacts. The additional moisture added to the waste increases the weight of the outbound loads, potentially reducing truck capacity and increasing costs.
- Hand-held hoses can be used to wet down waste where it is being moved or processed,

typically in a pit. Designers need to consider using conventional reel-mount hoses for this purpose.
- Ventilation systems can control air quality inside enclosed transfer buildings. Although the high roofs and large floor areas common in transfer stations put unique demands on ventilation systems, it is still possible through engineering techniques to create air velocities needed to entrain dust particles. One approach is to concentrate system fans and air-removal equipment above the dustiest and most odor-prone area, creating a positive air flow from cleaner areas. Often, the air-handling equipment is designed with multiple-speed fans and separate fan units that can be activated during high-dust or high-odor events. Filtering and scrubbing exhaust air from transfer stations is also possible.
- Respiratory protection may be necessary if employees' direct exposure to harmful emissions from vehicles and waste at the facility is not sufficiently minimized.

Hazardous Waste and Materials

Although MSW is generally nonhazardous, some potentially hazardous materials such as pesticides, bleach, and solvents could be delivered to transfer stations. Facility operators should ensure that employees are properly trained to identify and handle these materials. Some stations have a separate household hazardous waste (HHW) receiving and handling area. If the transfer station operates a program that manages HHW, the material is often collected by appointment only, during designated hours, or during special single- or multiple-day events.

All transfer stations must be equipped to handle the occasional occurrence of hazardous waste, real or suspected, mined with other wastes. Personal protective equipment (PPE), such as goggles, gloves, protective full-body coveralls, and respirators should be on hand and easily accessible to employees. Because staff or customers might inadvertently come into contact with a hazardous substance, it is also good practice and often required by code, to have dedicated emergency eyewash stations and deluge shower stations in the operating area. These stations must comply with the American National Standard Institute/International Safety Equipment Association (ANSI/ISEA) Standard Z358-1 2004, *Emergency Eyewash and Shower Equipment* (ANSI/ISEA 2004).

The transfer station's operating plan should outline detailed procedures to guide station personnel in identifying and managing these types of wastes. Many stations have a secure area with primary and secondary barriers near the main tipping area where suspect wastes can be placed for evaluation and analysis. Public education efforts can reduce the likelihood of hazardous materials showing up in the solid waste stream.

Ergonomics

Improper body position, repetitive motion, and repeated or continuous exertion of force contribute to injuries. Both employers and employees should receive ergonomics training to reduce the likelihood of injury. Such training provides guidance on minimizing repetitive motions and heavy lifting and using proper body motions to perform tasks. As of May 2011, there are no federal ergonomics standards. A few states have such standards under their job safety and health programs. The Occupational Safety and Health Administration (OSHA) lists states with such programs and provides links to a number of these states' Web sites (OSHA 2007).

Transport

Vehicle movements cause deaths and some of the most serious accidents in the waste industry. The aim is to ensure the following:

- safe sites
- safe vehicles
- safe working routines
- safe workers

	Yes	No
Site Safety		
Segregation of people, vehicles, and mobile plant to prevent collisions?		
Enforced speed limits?		
Clear site layout for visiting drivers?		
Adequate vehicle clearance of overhead power lines?		
Site roads designed and maintained for vehicle traffic (no potholes, no steep grades, no tight turns for large vehicles, and so on)?		
Blind corners eliminated at road intersections?		
Mirrors and warning signs placed at blind corners that cannot be eliminated?		
One-way traffic implemented as necessary to eliminate collisions and reversing of vehicles?		
Traffic safety, flagging, and other control systems in place at transfer stations and landfill access sites?		
Vehicle and Equipment Safety		
Vehicles equipped with driver visibility systems, such as mirrors and CCTV camera systems?		
100% enforcement of driver seat-belt use?		
Daily safety inspection by operators of all vehicles (documented and kept on file)?		
Daily safety inspections of forklifts, skidsteers, containers, doors, chains, hooks, lifting equipment, and so on (documented and kept on file)?		
System Safety		
Dumping/discharging restricted to specified areas?		
Dumping/discharging areas equipped with restraints to prevent vehicles and personnel from falling into pits?		
Adequate clearance provided from other vehicles and obstructions during dumping activities?		
Minimum of one vehicle length maintained between vehicles?		
No obstructions within swing radius of dump truck?		
Staging area for vehicles to allow safe tarping and untarping of loads?		
Safe access for work performed under waste containers?		
Safe Workers		
Drivers outside cabs and ground support personnel wearing ANSI Type-II reflective high-visibility vests?		
Traffic-control personnel and vehicle spotters wearing ANSI Type-III reflective high-visibility vests?		
Safety training and supervision provided for all workers on site?		
Safety Compliance Agreement form signed by workers, indicating that they understand the hazards and will comply with all elements safety and health rules part of the training?		
Safety enforcement procedures adequate for ensuring compliance with site safety and health rules?		

FIGURE 9. Site safety checklist for a waste transfer facility (*Source:* EPA 2001)

Figure 9 contains a brief checklist for sites. The list does not aim to cover everything, but it may help identify areas needing improvement at a particular site.

Major Causes of Slips and Trips

Figure 10 contains a brief checklist of some of the major causes of slips and trips at waste management sites. It does not aim to cover risks in refuse collection, where special and sometimes different risks arise.

Conclusion

The objective of this chapter on solid waste safety was not meant to be all-encompassing but to serve as an introduction to the history, regulatory background, and hazards of a complex and dangerous occupation that serves an important purpose in our society: solid waste management. The occupation of solid waste collection (specifically refuse and recyclable material efforts) sustains the fifth-highest fatality rate in the

Potential Safety and Health Hazard	Recommended Response and Controls
Dumping of wet and dry materials outside of designated areas	Implement spill response protocols. Attempt to clear away materials as soon as practicable using spill response and clean-up materials, such as absorbents for liquids and grease. Cordon area off using barriers and signs to prevent vehicles and untrained personnel from interfering with activities. Determine how and why spill occurred through a root-cause analysis and enact a prevention plan to mitigate future events.
Waste piles on floors	Restrict access to these areas. Determine methods for preventing workers from walking over the waste piles.
Trailing water hoses and electrical cords	Electrical outlets and water sources may need to be relocated to minimize the need for trailing cords and hoses. Equipment must be positioned to avoid pedestrian routes. Restrict pedestrian access. Use suitable covers for pipes and cables.
Office rugs and mats, linoleum, tiles, other flooring surfaces	Ensure that flooring surfaces are secure and have no edges that can contribute to trips and falls. Select suitable flooring surfaces. Practice good maintenance.
Slippery surfaces	Minimize pedestrian traffic in these areas. Select suitable nonslip surface treatments to prevent slips, trips, and falls.
Transition areas from wet to dry floor surfaces	Provide door mats and foot scrapers as necessary to prevent water and mud from being tracked onto dry floors. Provide areas to change into clean, dry footwear. Post warning signs as appropriate.
Poor lighting	Improve lighting levels. Change bulbs as necessary. Keep bulbs clean.
Floor-level transition areas	Improve lighting levels. Add high-visibility tread and floor markings. Post warning signs as appropriate.
Unsafe footwear	ANSI-approved steel-toe footwear is recommended.

FIGURE 10. Major causes of slips and trips at waste management sites (*Source:* EPA 2001)

country, making it important for this occupation (and all solid waste management occupations) to become the subject of efforts to protect the safety and health of all workers within this industry. Lessons learned should be used to assist in the development and improvement of safety programs for these operations. After introducing the solid waste management regulations of the United States, the definitions surrounding landfill types, various waste-stream categories, and recycling and disposal methods, this chapter dealt with safety and health hazard identification at landfills; landfill safety plans; and identification of safety and health issues at waste management, waste transfer, and waste recycling facilities, attempting to pass on the insights necessary to improve safety and health in future solid waste management endeavors.

REFERENCES

American National Standards Institute and International Safety Equipment Association (ANSI/ISEA). 2004. ANSI Z358.1 2004, *Emergency Eyewash and Shower Equipment*. Arlington, VA: ISEA.

Bureau of Labor Statistics (BLS). 2003, 2004, 2005, 2006, 2007, 2008, 2009. *Census of Fatal Occupational Injuries (CFOI) – Current and Revised Data for 2003, 2004, 2005, 2006, 2007, 2008, 2009*. Table A-1. Fatal and Occupational Injuries by Industry and Event or Exposure.

Bureau of Labor Statistics, U.S. Department of Labor, Economic News Release, USDL 09-0979, National Census of Fatal Occupational Injuries in 2008 (retrieved September 02, 2010). www.bls.gov/news.release/archives/cfoi_08202009.htm

Consumer Electronics Association (CEA). 2008. *Market Research Report: Trends in CE Reuse, Recycle and Removal*. Arlington, VA: CEA.

Environmental Protection Agency (EPA). 1965. Solid Waste Disposal Act of 1965. P.L. 89-272, Title II. Washington, D.C: EPA.

_____. 1970. Resource Recovery Act of 1970. P.L. 91-512, 84 Stat. 1227. Washington, D.C.: EPA.

_____. 1976. Resource Recovery and Conservation Act of 1976. 42 USC 6901.6992k. Washington, D.C.: EPA.

_____. 1993. AP 42, *Air Pollutant Emission Factors*, Volume I: Stationary Point and Area Sources. Vol I. Emission Factors. Chapter 2, "Medical Waste Incineration" (July 1993; reformatted January 1995) (retrieved January 28, 2008). www.epa.gov/ttn/chief/ap42/ch02/final/c02s03.pdf

_____. 1994a. EPA-453/R-94-043a, *Medical Waste Incinerators—Background Information for Proposed Standards and Guidelines: Process Description Report for New and Existing Facilities* (July). Washington, D.C.: EPA

_____. 1994b. EPA QA/G4, *Guidance for the Data Quality Objectives Process*. Washington, D.C.: EPA.

_____. 1995. EPA 530-R-95-023, *Decision Maker's Guide to Solid Waste Management*, vol. II, chapter 9, "Land Disposal." Washington, D.C.: EPA.

_____. 1996a. EAP QA/G9, *Guidance for the Data Quality Assessment: Practical Methods for Data Analysis*. QA 96 Version. Washington, D.C: EPA

_____. 1996e. SW-846, *Test Methods for Evaluating Solid Waste, Physical/Chemical Methods* (retrieved January 28, 2008). www.epa.gov/sw-846/sw846.htm

_____. 2000. 40 CFR Part 261.2, *Definition of Solid Waste*. Washington, D.C.: EPA.

_____. 2001. EPA 530-D-005, *Waste Transfer Stations: A Manual for Decision-Making* (Draft) (February) (retrieved January 28, 2008). www.epa.gov/garbage/pubs/r02002.pdf

_____. 2002. EPA/240/R-02/009, *Guidance on Quality Assurance Project Plans*. Washington, D.C.: EPA.

_____. 2006. 40 CFR Part 258, *Criteria for Municipal Waste Landfills*. Washington, D.C.: EPA.

_____. 2007a. *Air and Radiation Regulations*. Mid-Atlantic Regulations and Plans. Hospital/Medical/Infectious Waste Incinerators. Undated (retrieved January 28, 2008). www.epa.gov/reg3artd/airregulations/ap22/incin2.htm

_____. 2007b. *Backyard Burning; Human Health* (retrieved January 28, 2008). www.epa.gov/garbage/backyard/health.htm

_____. 2007c. *Batteries* (retrieved January 28, 2008). www.epa.gov/epr/products/batteries.htm

_____. 2007d. *Composting* (retrieved January 28, 2008). www.epa.gov/epaoswer/non-hw/composting/index.htm

_____. 2007e. *Markets/Uses; Scrap Tires* (retrieved January 28, 2008). www.epa.gov/epaoswer/non-hw/muncpl/tires/markets.htm

_____. 2007f. *Medical Waste* (retrieved January 28, 2008). www.epa.gov/epaoswer/other/medical/#one

_____. 2007g. *Reducing C&D Materials* (retrieved January 28, 2007). www.epa.gov/epaoswer/non-hw/debris-new/reducing.htm

_____. 2008a. *Bioreactors* (retrieved January 28, 2008). www.epa.gov/epaoswer/non-hw/muncpl/landfill/bioreactors.htm#2

_____. 2008b. *Household Hazardous Waste* (retrieved January 28, 2007). www.epa.gov/msw/hhw.htm

_____. 2008c. *EPA Municipal Solid Waste; Bioreactors* (retrieved January 28, 2008). www.epa.gov/garbage/landfill/bioreactors.htm#1

_____. 2008d. *Landfills/Land Disposal* (retrieved January 28, 2008). www.epa.gov/epaoswer/non-hw/muncpl/landfill/landfills.htm

_____. 2008e. *Landfill Methane Outreach Program* (retrieved January 28, 2008). www.epa.gov/outreach/lmop/index.htm

_____. 2008f. *Municipal Solid Waste. Basic Information* (retrieved January 28, 2008). www.epa.gov/msw/facts.htm

_____. 2011a. *Wastes – Resource Conservation – Common Wastes & Materials – eCycling* (retrieved May 16, 2011). www.epa.gov/epawaste/conserve/materials/eccling/index.htm

_____. 2011b. *Municipal Solid Waste: Basic Information* (retrieved May 16, 2011). www.epa.gov/msw/facts.htm

Occupational Health and Safety Administration (OSHA) 2007, *Safety and Health Topics: Ergonomics* (retrieved January 28, 2008). www.osha.gov/SLTC/ergonomics/index.html

Office of Technology Assessment (OTA). 1990. *Finding the Rx for Managing Medical Wastes*. Washington, D.C.: U.S. Government Printing Office.

Oregon Department of Environmental Quality (DEQ). Undated. *Land Quality – Solid Waste: Safe Disposal;*

Solid Waste Landfill Guidance Document; Section 9 – Landfill Operations. Salem, OR: Oregon DEQ (retrieved January 28, 2008). www.deq.state.or.us/lq/sw/disposal/landfillguidance.htm

Sales, John. 1986. EPA530-SW-86-014, *Guide for Infectious Waste Management*. Washington, D.C.: EPA.

Wisconsin Department of Natural Resources (WisDNR). 2009. *Medical and Infectious Waste; Material Description* (retrieved April 27, 2011). dnr.wi.gov/org/aw/wm/medinf/

4

Hazardous Waste

Salvatore Caccavale, Barry R. Weissman,
Thomas S. Butler, Jr., and Judy Freeman

LEARNING OBJECTIVES

- Recognize the criteria for identifying the characteristics of hazardous waste and for listing hazardous waste as defined in RCRA, Title 40 §261.

- Recognize and understand the definition of a solid waste as defined in §261.2.

- Recognize and understand the definition of a hazardous waste as defined in §261.3.

- Recognize the characteristic of ignitability as defined in §261.21.

- Recognize the characteristic of corrosivity as defined in §261.22.

- Recognize the characteristic of reactivity as defined in §261.23.

- Recognize the characteristic of toxicity as defined in §261.24.

- Recognize other regulations that require compliance when dealing with chemicals as discussed in Title 40 of the *Code of Federal Regulations*.

THE ADVENT OF the Industrial Revolution in the late 1800s and early 1900s saw the birth of many innovative products that are now taken for granted in the twenty-first century. Cellular phones, new types of clothing, power tools, sports equipment, and new forms of transportation have all made our lives easier.

The flip side to these miraculous achievements is the increased generation of waste. Today, consumer product companies are trying to minimize waste by offering many different types of reusable packaging. Recycling has taken on a larger role in society, with many states and communities implementing mandatory programs to reduce the amount of solid waste placed in landfills.

In the early days of the Industrial Revolution there were no treatment, storage, or disposal facilities (TSDFs) to manage and/or destroy hazardous waste. Companies were not even required to determine if the waste generated at the end of the production line was categorized as hazardous. Typically a big hole was dug somewhere on the industrial site for the deposit of production waste. When that hole was filled, it was capped off and another hole was dug. Fortunately, some companies had the environmental insight to install liners, either natural (clay) or man-made (plastic or cloth), at their dumping grounds in an attempt to catch the leachate.

For years industries claimed they did not realize that what they were putting into the ground would have any effects on the environment. The growing influence of the environmental disciplines in the mid-1960s led society to realize what a mistake that approach was. Even today, abandoned industrial sites and misused landfills are still being cleaned up through the Environmental Protection Agency's (EPA's) "Superfund" program (SARA 1986).

Industry was not the only culprit, however; mom-and-pop shops, farmers, dry-cleaning operations, and other types of small businesses also played a role in polluting the environment.

The management of hazardous waste is a broad and complex subject. The purposes of this chapter are to present an overview of the hazardous waste regulatory system in the United States; to explain the process of hazardous waste determination, primarily through the application of the provisions of the Resource Conservation and Recovery Act (RCRA 1976); and to give a brief overview of other regulatory requirements applicable when dealing with chemicals. This chapter is not intended to be a definitive treatment of the U.S. hazardous waste regulatory system, but it should provide a reference for safety, health, and environmental professionals who may not have extensive background or experience in hazardous waste, allowing them to approach the topic and helping them obtain additional hazardous waste information.

It should be noted that under federal legislation, each state is permitted to establish its own regulatory system for hazardous waste as long as the state's regulatory system is at least as effective as the federal requirements (EPA 2009a). EHS professionals should review all applicable state and local hazardous waste regulations as appropriate (EPA 2010a-e).

In order to reflect this process, the following discussions of environmental laws are organized in chronological order rather than by subject matter. The balance of this chapter is organized by subject sections to facilitate their use as guidelines.

Resource Conservation and Recovery Act (RCRA)

In the early 1970s, Love Canal, a housing development built over a capped industrial dumpsite in suburban Niagara Falls, New York, was exposed by the media, and the story took the public by surprise. Concern that such a development could happen in "our backyard" led to public demand for legislation that would ensure the proper management of industrial wastes (for details, see Appendix C).

In 1965, Congress had passed the Solid Waste Disposal Act (SWDA 1965) for the purpose of improving solid waste disposal methods. SWDA has been amended several times, most significantly and largely as a result of the exposure of Love Canal, by the Resource Conservation and Recovery Act (RCRA 1976) and later by the Hazardous and Solid Waste Amendments (HSWA 1984). These acts collectively are known as RCRA.

RCRA was designed to establish a national program to protect the natural resources of the United States from the improper handling and storage of hazardous wastes. Congress gave the task of tracking this regulation to the Environmental Protection Agency (EPA). The codified RCRA regulations can be found in Title 40 of the *Code of Federal Regulations* (CFR), Parts 240 through 282.

The main components of RCRA include:

1. identification of hazardous waste
2. manifest tracking "cradle-to-grave"
3. operating standards for generators, transporters, and treatment, storage, and disposal facilities
4. a permit system for TSDFs
5. state authorization to assist in implementing the program

The current goals set forth by RCRA are to:

- protect human health and the environment from the potential hazards of waste disposal
- conserve energy and natural resources
- reduce the amount of hazardous waste generated
- ensure wastes are managed in an environmentally sound manner
- prevent future problems caused by irresponsible waste management
- clean up releases of hazardous waste in a timely, flexible, and protective manner

To achieve these goals three distinct yet interrelated sections (called subtitles) were created under RCRA. Other subtitles can be found in RCRA, but the three discussed in this chapter are the most significant (RCRA 1976).

- **Subtitle C:** Establishes a system for controlling hazardous waste from the time of generation until ultimate disposal.

- **Subtitle D:** Establishes a system for controlling solid (primarily nonhazardous) waste, such as household waste.
- **Subtitle I:** Established by HSWA, regulates toxic substances and petroleum products stored in underground tanks.

Another important section is the Land Disposal Restriction (LDR) (EPA 2010c). One of the major impacts HSWA had on the implementation of the RCRA program was the restriction of land disposal for certain wastes. These land disposal restrictions are commonly referred to as *land ban*, and the hazardous wastes affected are called *restricted wastes*. The EPA banned land disposal for certain hazardous wastes that can migrate through soil and pollute groundwater. Hazardous wastes covered by the land ban include: liquid metals; free cyanides; dioxin-containing wastes; and discarded chemical products, like xylene, formic acid, and methyl alcohol. The ban also prohibits land disposal of diesel fuel, hydrochloric acid, and used solvents without proper treatment or certification of limited recycling operations.

Although RCRA creates a framework for the proper management of hazardous and nonhazardous solid wastes, it does not address hazardous waste problems encountered at inactive or abandoned sites or those resulting from spills that require an emergency response. These issues are addressed by the Comprehensive Environmental Response, Compensation and Liability Act (CERCLA 1980), otherwise known as Superfund.

Subtitle C: Hazardous Waste Management

Subtitle C establishes a comprehensive "cradle-to-grave" program for regulating hazardous waste from generation through proper disposal or destruction. Generators of hazardous waste are the first link in this "cradle-to-grave" chain. Those creating more than 100 kilograms (220 lb) of hazardous waste, or 1 kilogram (2.2 lb) of acutely hazardous waste a month, must comply with all generator requirements under Subtitle C.

Subtitle D: State or Regional Solid Waste Plans

The SWDA established grant programs for the development of solid waste plans by states and/or interstate agencies (SWDA 1965). Subsequent amendments to the SWDA have substantially increased the EPA's involvement in solid waste management. However, the Subtitle D (EPA 2010a) program continues to be implemented by state and local governments.

The term *solid waste* used in Subtitle D refers almost exclusively to nonhazardous solid waste. The primary objectives of Subtitle D are to encourage environmentally sound solid waste management practices, maximize the reuse of valuable recoverable resources, and foster resource conservation.

Subtitle I: Regulation of Underground Storage Tanks

Congress enacted Subtitle I to control and prevent leaks from underground storage tanks (USTs). The UST program broke new ground for RCRA; for the first time, the RCRA program applied to products as well as wastes. Specifically, Subtitle I regulates underground tanks storing regulated substances, including petroleum products (e.g., gasoline and crude oil) and Superfund-defined hazardous substances (EPA 1994). Tanks storing hazardous waste, however, are regulated under Subtitle C.

Comprehensive Environmental Response, Compensation, and Liability ACT (CERCLA)

The Resource Conservation and Recovery Act (RCRA 1976) addresses the generation, handling and disposal of waste, but the Comprehensive Environmental Response, Compensation, and Liability Act (CERCLA 1980), also known as Superfund, addresses sites that have been contaminated by hazardous materials. The authority under CERCLA to respond directly to releases or threatened releases of hazardous substances that may endanger human health and the environment is held by the federal government and is not shared with the states. CERCLA established prohibitions and requirements concerning closed and abandoned hazardous waste sites, provided for liability of persons responsible for releases of hazardous waste at these sites, and established a trust fund to provide for clean up when no responsible party could be identified (EPA 2007b).

CERCLA was significantly amended by the Superfund Amendments and Reauthorization Act (SARA 1986) and again as the Small Business Liability Relief and Brownfields Revitalization Act (2001), both of which will be discussed later.

Used Oil Recycling Act

The Used Oil Recycling Act of 1980 was established to encourage the safe reuse of used oil and to discourage improper burning or disposal. Used oil not subject to the hazardous waste rules must be managed according to the requirements of 40 CFR 279 (EPA 2006d). There are also requirements pertaining to used oil processors, transporters, marketers, and burners for energy recovery. Some state environmental agencies (e.g., California, Massachusetts) classify used oils as hazardous wastes. Companies should check with their respective states to ensure compliance. Used oil must be sent to a reputable oil recycling company.

Used oil, if it is recycled or reclaimed, does not have to be managed as a hazardous waste if it meets specific conditions, such as:

- It includes any oil that has been refined from crude oil or any other synthetic oil that has been contaminated by physical or chemical impurities.
- It is not mixed with any listed hazardous waste.
- It contains less than 1000 ppm total halogens.
- It does not exhibit a hazardous waste characteristic (EPA 2006d).

Note: The proper federal terminology for labels and/or markings on containers and tanks is "Used Oil."

The Superfund Amendments and Reauthorization Act (SARA) Amendments

The Superfund Amendments and Reauthorization Act (SARA 1986) amended the Comprehensive Environmental Response, Compensation, and Liability Act (CERCLA) on October 17, 1986. SARA reflected the EPA's experience in administering the complex Superfund program during its first six years and made important changes and additions to the program.

SARA changes:
- stressed the importance of permanent remedies and innovative treatment technologies in cleaning up hazardous waste sites
- required Superfund actions to consider the standards and requirements found in other state and federal environmental laws and regulations
- provided new enforcement authorities and settlement tools
- increased state involvement in every phase of the Superfund program
- increased the focus on human health problems posed by hazardous waste sites
- encouraged greater citizen participation in making decisions on how sites should be cleaned up
- increased the size of the trust fund from $1.6 billion to $8.5 billion

SARA also required the EPA to revise the Hazard Ranking System (HRS) (EPA 2007c) to ensure that it accurately assessed the relative degree of risk to human health and the environment posed by uncontrolled hazardous waste sites that may be placed on the National Priorities List (NPL) (EPA 2007e).

Oil Pollution Act (OPA)

The purpose of the Oil Pollution Act (OPA 1990) was to consolidate oil-spill response systems and laws and to establish liability and financial responsibility requirements. It was enacted in response to rising public concern following the *Exxon Valdez* incident. "[O]n March 24, 1989, the Exxon Valdez oil tanker departed the Valdez oil terminal and struck Bligh Reef in Prince William Sound, spilling an estimated 10.8 million gallons of crude oil. . . . Only 7 of 26 monitored species and resources have recovered to prespill health and abundance" (Prince William Soundkeeper 1989).

Title III of SARA, Emergency Planning & Community Right to Know Act (EPCRA)

"In 1984 a deadly cloud of methyl isocyanate killed thousands of people in Bhopal, India. Shortly thereafter, there was a serious chemical release at a sister plant in West Virginia. These incidents underscored demands by industrial workers and communities in several states for information on hazardous materials. Public interest and environmental organizations around the country accelerated demands for information on toxic chemicals being released 'beyond the fence line'—outside of the facility" (EPA 2007i). EPCRA reporting provides vital information for emergency response personnel regarding chemical hazards in the community. EPCRA requires each state to appoint a State Emergency Response Commission (SERC) and Local Emergency Planning Committees (LEPCs) for each district; it is these entities who are responsible for compiling the information gleaned through this process and for planning for emergency eventualities.

Facilities required to maintain Material Safety Data Sheets (MSDSs) per OSHA's Hazard Communications Standard (OSHA 1994) must file with the SERC, LEPC, and local fire department and either provide copies or a list of their MSDSs.

To provide the necessary information to the various governmental agencies concerning those chemicals that a company releases into the environment (the air, land, and waters of the country), the company is required to complete an annual toxic release inventory (TRI) (EPA 2007i).

Inventory reporting is required for a specified list of chemicals (EPA 2011a).

Chemical releases exceeding specific threshold limits must also be reported. Lists of those chemicals may be found at the same Web site. The EPA has also compiled a list of all chemicals covered by name under these regulations into a single list and published them as the Title III List of Lists (EPA 2011a).

APPLIED SCIENTIFIC AND ENGINEERING PRINCIPLES IN ENVIRONMENTAL MANAGEMENT

Working within the framework of environmental law requires the diligent application of standards established within each regulation. The purpose of this section is to provide specific guidelines that the EHS manager can apply to operations that will assist in company compliance with these laws.

Waste Management

Those involved in the generation, handling, or disposal of hazardous wastes must comply with RCRA's "cradle-to-grave" control system. The first step in understanding how to comply with a regulation is to read not only the regulation but also the preamble to that regulation from the Final Federal Register Notice for that regulation. Unfortunately, RCRA was promulgated in 1976, before the Internet and the electronic publishing of the Federal Register.

There are many other guides that can also help generators sort through the system, including the EPA's *Managing Your Hazardous Waste: A Guide for Small Businesses* (EPA 2001a).

Registration

The initial step in beginning to determine what if any waste materials are hazardous begins with registering a facility as a hazardous waste generator. The EPA requires the completion of Form 8700-12 (EPA 2009).

Once the form has been completed and submitted, the EPA will issues an EPA Identification number consisting of three letters and nine digits. This number is unique to a particular property. If a location has never been a hazardous waste generator, it will be issued a new number. If, however, a property has already been registered, the EPA will reissue that number. This helps to preserve the history of waste generation on that site in the event of the site's abandonment and subsequent labeling as a superfund site.

Identification/Determination of Solid Waste

In order to determine regulatory requirements for disposal, wastes must first be classified as solid wastes. If they meet requirements for a solid waste, it must then be determined whether they are also a hazardous waste.

A waste classified as a solid waste nevertheless puts municipalities and waste management entities subject to a myriad of disposal regulations under RCRA. *Solid waste* is defined as any discarded material including garbage; refuse; sludge from a wastewater treatment plant, water supply treatment plant, or air pollution control facility; and other discarded material, including

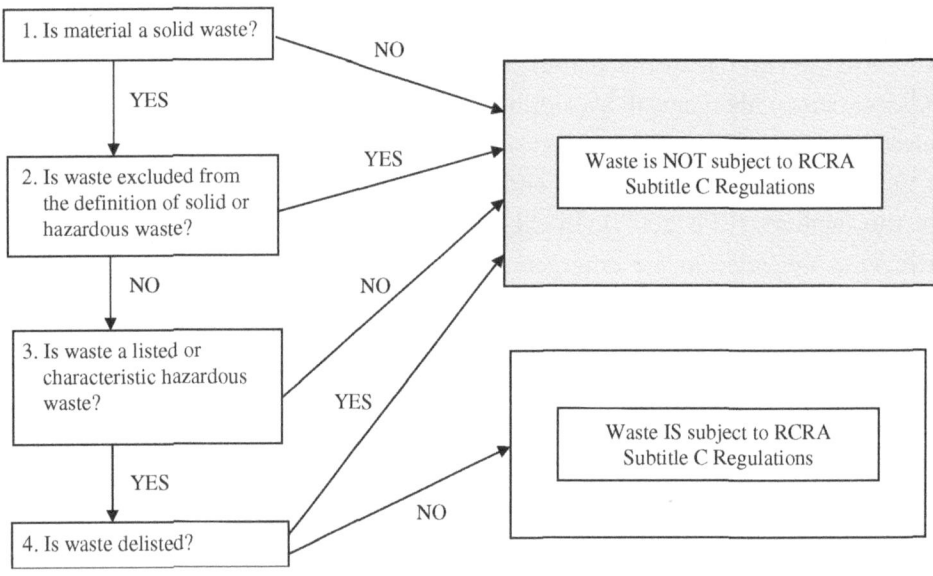

FIGURE 1. Hazardous waste identification process (*Source:* EPA 2006b)

solid, liquid, semisolid, or contained gaseous material resulting from industrial, commercial, mining, or agricultural operations or from community activities (40 CFR 261.2) (EPA 2010f).

Any discarded material is a solid waste, provided that no statutory exclusion applies. These exclusions include:

- domestic sewage or waste passing through a publicly owned treatment works (POTW)
- industrial discharges as defined under the Clean Water Act
- irrigation return flow
- nuclear material, nuclear source, or special nuclear or byproduct material, as defined under the Atomic Energy Act (1954)
- mining wastes that do not leave mines
- industrial scrap metal being recycled

A material is discarded if it is:

- abandoned
- recycled, including land applied, burned for energy, or reclaimed
- inherently waste-like
- military munitions

Hazardous Waste Determination

Once a material is determined to be a solid waste, it must then be determined whether it is also a hazardous waste (see Figure 1). Certain materials are exempt by definition, including (40 CFR 261.4) (EPA 2010f):

- household waste, including that of hotels and other residential properties, but excluding incinerator ash
- agricultural wastes used as fertilizer
- arsenic-treated wood wastes generated by those who use such wood for its intended purpose
- petroleum-contaminated material failing the toxic characteristic leaching procedure (discussed elsewhere) and which may be subject to corrective action provisions for underground storage tanks (USTs) under RCRA
- used chlorofluorocarbons (CFCs) totally enclosed in heat transfer equipment and which may be reclaimed (40 CFR 260.20 and 260.22) (EPA 2009b)
- uranium wastes

Special Wastes

Some exempted wastes are classified as special wastes. At the time RCRA was written, those wastes designated as special wastes were considered of sufficient concern to warrant further investigation. Each of these special wastes has its own regulatory requirements, but none is considered hazardous under RCRA (EPA 2007h):

- mining wastes returned to the mine site
- utility wastes from fossil fuel combustion

- oil and natural gas exploration, or drilling mud and water
- wastes from the extraction, beneficiation, or processing of ores and minerals
- uranium wastes
- cement kiln dust wastes

Listed Wastes

If a waste is not excluded, exempted, or classified as a special waste, it could be a hazardous waste. Four series of hazardous waste codes list such materials (EPA 2010f):

- F-listed wastes come from general processes such as cleaning, degreasing, metal finishing, and manufacturing.
- K-listed wastes come from specific industrial processes and are grouped by industrial category, such as petroleum refining or metal manufacturing, and include wastewater treatment sludges (40 CFR 261.32).
- P-listed wastes include discarded commercial chemical products more toxic than U-listed wastes, include pesticides and pharmaceuticals, and are considered to be acute hazardous wastes (40 CFR 261.33(e)).
- U-listed wastes include old, off-specification, or discarded commercial products (40 CFR 261.33(f)).

Some of these wastes are considered "acutely hazardous" because of their inherently hazardous characteristics and will be discussed elsewhere.

Characteristic Wastes (40 CFR 261.3) (EPA 2010f)

Wastes can be hazardous if they exhibit (40 CFR 261.20–261.24):

- ignitability
- corrosivity
- reactivity
- toxicity

Ignitability (40 CFR 261.21)—D001 (EPA 2010f)

A waste is considered ignitable if it is:

- a liquid having a flashpoint of < 140°F (60°C) (ASTM closed-cup method)
- a nonliquid with the capacity for spontaneous combustion
- a DOT-listed ignitable compressed gas
- a DOT-listed oxidizer

Included in this classification are solvents, paints, and degreasers.

Corrosivity (40 CFR 261.22)—D002 (EPA 2010f)

A waste is considered corrosive if it is:

- aqueous, having a pH ≤ 2 or ≥ 12.5
- a liquid that corrodes steel at a rate greater than 6.35 mm yearly

Among other chemicals, this category includes rust removers, acid or alkaline cleaning fluids, and battery acid.

Reactivity (40 CFR 261.23)—D003 (EPA 2010f)

A waste is considered reactive if it:

- is unstable and readily undergoes violent change
- reacts violently with water
- forms potentially explosive mixtures with water
- generates toxic gases, vapors, or fumes when mixed with water
- is a cyanide- or sulfide-containing waste that can release toxic gases, vapors, or fumes between pHs of 2 and 12.5
- is capable of detonation or explosion when struck or heated
- is capable of detonation or explosive decomposition or reaction at standard temperature and pressure
- is a DOT-listed explosive

Cyanides and sulfide-bearing wastes are included in this classification.

Toxicity (40 CFR 261.24) (EPA 2010f)

A waste is considered toxic when the Toxic Characteristic Leaching Procedure (TCLP) produces leachate with one or more of the toxic constituents listed by the EPA in concentrations above permissible limits, as listed in Table 1 of 40 CFR 261.24 (EPA 2010f). To determine whether a waste is toxic, it is subjected to the Toxic Characteristic Leaching Procedure (TCLP). The TCLP is an analytical protocol simulating the leaching of toxic constituents in a landfill.

Land Disposal Restriction (LDR) (EPA 2010c)

Once it has been determined that a hazardous waste has been generated, the next question is, "Does the waste have a LDR?" The EPA has identified wastes that are prohibited from land disposal unless they meet specific treatment standards.

The LDR program has three main components: the disposal prohibition, the dilution prohibition, and the storage prohibition. This series of prohibitions restrict how wastes subject to LDR requirements are handled. According to 40 CFR 268.2, "Land disposal means placement in or on the land, except in a corrective action unit, and includes, but is not limited to, placement in a landfill, surface impoundment, waste pile, injection well, land treatment facility, salt dome foundation, salt bed formation, underground mine or cave, or placement in a concrete vault or bunker intended for disposal purposes" (EPA 2010c).

The *disposal prohibition* forbids the dumping of hazardous waste in land that has not been adequately treated to reduce the threat to human health and the environment. The criteria that hazardous wastes must meet before being disposed of are known as treatment standards. These treatment standards (EPA 2010c) can be either concentration levels for hazardous constituents that the waste must meet or treatment technologies that must be performed on the waste before its disposal is permitted.

The *dilution prohibition* bans the addition of soil or water to waste, for example, in order to reduce the concentrations of hazardous constituents and can prohibit ineffective or inappropriate treatment methods.

The *storage prohibition* prevents the indefinite storage of untreated wastes for reasons other than the accumulation of quantities necessary for effective treatment or disposal.

The full listing of wastes that are prohibited from land disposal can be found in 40 CFR 268.20 to 268.39 (EPA 2010c). Some waste examples that are restricted from land disposal include:

- solvent wastes, as specified in 40 CFR 261.31 (F001, F002, F003, F004 and F005) (EPA 2010f)
- dioxin-containing wastes, as specified in 40 CFR 261.31 (F020, F021, F022, F023, F026, F027 and F028) (EPA 2010f)
- the "California list" wastes, as specified in 40 CFR 268.32 (EPA 2010c)
- RCRA-listed wastes, as specified in 40 CFR 268.33–268.35 (EPA 2010c)

The initial generator of the hazardous waste is responsibile for determining whether the waste meets the applicable standards and for communicating the LDR status of the waste in writing to downstream treatment, storage, or disposal facilities. Specific LDR documentation and record-keeping requirements apply to generators and to treatment, storage, or disposal facilities.

The basic steps for generators to comply with LDRs are:

- Determine the significant LDR waste code(s) for the waste at the initial point of generation of the waste.
- Determine all treatment standards applicable to the waste, based on the significant waste code(s).
- Determine whether the waste meets the applicable standards.
- Notify the designated TSDF in writing if the waste does not meet the applicable standards, or certify if it does meet all applicable standards.
- Keep copies of all notifications, certifications, and any supporting documentation used to make any of the above determinations. Retain records for at least five years.

Most hazardous waste transporters and/or brokers have developed a standardized LDR certification form that must be reviewed, signed, and sent with the shipment. A copy should be retained in their files.

Determination of Generator Category

RCRA classifies hazardous waste handlers as generators, transporters, or disposal facilities. Transportation and disposal of hazardous waste is beyond the scope of this section, except as pertaining to generators.

The first step in the classification process is to audit the facility and develop a list of all wastes generated (hazardous and nonhazardous) and the approximate monthly and annual amounts from production areas, maintenance shops, laboratories, loading/unloading docks, and wastewater treatment plants. This list should be reviewed with the company or facility management team to obtain agreement with the inventory. This list can also be used in the company or facility pollution prevention program to reduce or eliminate these waste streams.

The next step is to meet with someone within the organization, such as the corporate RCRA specialist, or with a representative from the hazardous waste disposal company, to determine whether the identified wastes should be considered hazardous or not. Samples are taken and sent to a laboratory for analysis. Waste profiles are then developed to accurately describe each waste stream. According to Caccavale, most hazardous waste disposal companies have developed a standardized waste profile sheet, to gather as much information as possible on the waste from the generator prior to sending waste to its final destination. It is important that the information on the initial waste profile is accurate and that future shipments of the same waste stream remain within that range. The implications of sending incompatible wastes to an incinerator or fuel blender could be harmful to their personnel and equipment.

Developing a waste profile sheet is similar to developing a material safety data sheet (MSDS) for products. Information requested on the profile will include:

- general facility information
- waste description
- process or source that generates the waste
- physical properties, such as physical state; number of phases; viscosity; color; odor; boiling, flash, and melting points; pH; specific gravity; vapor pressure; total organic carbon; and btus per pound
- waste composition
- constituents
- regulatory status
- DOT information
- transportation requirements
- sample status
- special waste-handling instructions

Testing the waste to determine whether it is hazardous should be done by a certified laboratory that can handle the RCRA waste analytical methodologies (TCLP). EPA SW-846 outlines the testing methods for solid wastes (EPA 2008d). Someone in the organization should be familiar with these laboratory methodologies and conduct an audit of the lab facility. If this option is not available, other businesses in the area or trade associations should be contacted for referrals.

Once generators have determined whether wastes are excluded, listed, or hazardous by examining their characteristics (40 CFR 261) (EPA 2010f), they must then determine how they are regulated based upon the amount of waste generated each month. There are three classifications, between which a company can jump on a monthly basis. However, it is best practice for a company to determine what the highest volume of hazardous waste is that it may generate, preparing accordingly. If a company exceeds the threshold for the next largest classification, it must be in full compliance with the requirements of that classification on the day it enters that classification.

The classifications are as follows:

- Conditionally Exempt Small-Quantity Generators (CESQGs) produce less than 100 kg of total hazardous waste *and* less than 1 kg of acutely hazardous waste monthly.
- Small-Quantity Generators (SQGs) produce more than 100 kg but less than 1000 kg of total hazardous waste *and* less than 1 kg of acutely hazardous waste monthly.
- Large-Quantity Generators (LQGs) produce equal to or greater than 1000 kg of total hazardous waste or equal to or more than 1 kg of acutely hazardous waste monthly.

(Conversion: 2.2 lb = 1 kg)

Note: Acute hazardous wastes are defined in §261.5(e)(1) as wastes listed in §§261.30(d) or 261.33(e) (EPA 2010f).

The amount of all hazardous wastes that have accumulated on site, been sent off site for treatment, or been treated on site should be measured. A generator's classification can change month to month. These weights may be estimated as long as the estimation is conservative. When in doubt, the higher category should always be chosen.

TABLE 1

Summary of Requirements for Hazardous Waste Generators

	CESQG	SQG	LQG
Quantity Limits	≤100 kg/month ≤1 kg/month of acute hazardous waste ≤100 kg/month of acute spill residue or soil §§261.5(a) and (e)	Between 100–1000 kg/month §262.34(d)	≥1000 kg/month >1 kg/month of acute hazardous waste >100 kg/month of acute spill residue or soil Part 262 and §261.5(e)
EPA ID Number	Not required §261.5	Required §262.12	Required §262.12
On-Site Accumulation Quantity	≤1000 kg ≤1 kg acute ≤100 kg of acute spill residue or soil §§261.5(f)(2) and (g)(2)	≤6000 kg §262.34(d)(1)	No limit
Accumulation Time Limits	None §261.5	≤180 days or ≤270 days (if greater than 200 miles) §§262.34(d)(2) and (3)	≤ 90 days §262.34(a)
Storage Requirements	None §261.5	Basic requirements with technical standards for tanks or containers §§262.34(d)(2) and (3)	Full compliance for management of tanks, containers, drip pads, or containment buildings §262.34(a)
Sent To	State approved or RCRA permitted/interim status facility §§261.5(f)(3) and (g)(3)	RCRA permitted/interim status facility §262.20(b)	RCRA permitted/interim status facility §262.20(b)
Manifest	Not required §261.5	Required §262.20	Required §262.20
Biennial Report	Not required §261.5	Not required §262.44	Required §262.41
Personnel Training	Not required §261.5	Basic training required §262.34(d)(5)(iii)	Required §262.34(a)(4)
Contingency Plan	Not required §261.5	Basic plan §262.34(d)(5)(i)	Full plan required §262.34(a)(4)
Emergency Procedures	Not required §261.5	Required §262.34(d)(5)(iv)	Full plan required §262.34(a)(4)
DOT Transport Requirements	Yes (if required by DOT)	Yes §§262.30-262.33	Yes §§262.30-262.33

(*Source*: EPA 2005a)

Table 1 is a summary of the hazardous waste generator requirements.

Some states may require or recommend that a CESQG have an ID number.

Useful guides for measuring liquid wastes with a density approximately that of water follow:

- Slightly more than half of a 55-gallon drum (30 gallons) weighs about 220 pounds.
- Slightly less than 6 drums (300 gallons) weighs 2200 pounds.
- The number of gallons in a container × 8.34 × the density of the liquid waste = the number of pounds of waste in the container.

Requirements for Conditionally Exempt Small-Quantity Generators (CESQGs)

If waste is shipped off site and is not treated or recycled on site, it must be sent to a state- or federally regulated hazardous waste management treatment, storage, or disposal facility, or to a facility that will reuse, recycle, or treat it, and which is permitted, licensed, or registered by the state to handle that waste.

Use caution when adopting this category. Check whether the host state has more stringent requirements on this classification than the federal regulations. It is also important to make sure that all transporters and waste sites are properly permitted, and it is prudent to make a call to the state to verify permit status, as well as to document the call.

Unlike other hazardous waste generators, conditionally exempt small-quantity generators (CESQGs) are not required to notify the EPA of their activities and, as seen in Table 1, are not required to obtain an EPA ID number. However, some transporters will not accept any wastes without an ID number. Several states recommend that CESQGs obtain an ID number and will issue one in the same form as the EPA ID number (three letters and nine digits) so that CESQG wastes may be transported without problem.

Any company that feels it fits into the CESQG category should be very careful not to generate more than the various quantities of waste in a single month, moving it into a different category of generator where it is subject to additional requirements, as shown in Table 1 and as described below.

Requirements for Small-Quantity Generators (SQGs) and Large-Quantity Generators (LQGs)

EPA Identification Number

Form 8700-12 and its instructions can be downloaded from the EPA Web site (EPA 2009a).

Notification, Monitoring, and Tracking

Both small- and large-quantity generators must notify the EPA of their activities, as mentioned above, using Form 8700-12 (EPA 2009a). When the waste is shipped off site, the EPA ID number is required for the manifest.

Proper Packing, Packaging, Marking, Labeling, and Shipping

Generators are required to follow all Department of Transportation (DOT) regulations for the preparation and shipping of wastes. Vehicles used to ship wastes may need to be placarded in accordance with DOT regulations.

Selection of Shipping and Disposal Facilities

Waste generators are responsible to select an approved treatment, storage, and disposal facility (TSDF) that can properly handle the wastes shipped to it. The TSDF will have an EPA ID Number and sufficient insurance to handle all materials received for the life of the facility as well as for a period of time afterwards. The TSDF may recommend a transporter or may include a transportation division that is approved to move the wastes. All wastes must meet DOT requirements for shipping and must be manifested and tracked.

Chemical Analysis

Generators are responsible for properly identifying and classifying wastes. To ensure that this is correct, a TSDF may require that the analysis of the waste material be provided prior to shipment in order to safely handle the material.

A small-quantity generator (SQG) and a large-quantity generator (LQG) should develop a written general waste plan under 40 CFR 265.13 (EPA 2010b) to ensure that they can provide sufficient information about their wastes to any TSDF or governmental agency that may request it. The general waste analysis plan should follow the requirements in §265.13, and the generator may want to include, at a minimum, the eight points found in 40 CFR 264.13(b) (EPA 2010b).

Manifesting System

The *manifest* is the tracking document behind the entire RCRA "cradle-to-grave" concept. It is the official DOT shipping document, which tracks the hazardous waste shipment from the time it is loaded on the hazardous waste transporter's vehicle until the waste is disposed of (incinerated, fuel blended, made part of a landfill, recycled, and so on). The manifest carries with it legal liability for the person who signs the document from the facility.

Distribution of the manifest copies is important as well to ensure all applicable parties have received their respective copy in a timely fashion. The federal regulations were revised on September 5, 2006, so that the same Uniform Hazardous Waste Manifest form is now used for all shipments throughout the United States; individual states no longer have their own manifests. The manifest will consist of at least six copies, which will provide the generator, each transporter, and the owner or operator of the designated TSDF facility with one copy for their records. When the hazardous waste shipment has been accepted at the TSDF, one signed manifest copy is then returned to the generator, while another is sent to the state environmental agency (if applicable). Generators must check with individual state agencies to determine whether a copy of the completed manifest is required (EPA 2005c).

The generator must designate on the manifest one facility that is permitted to handle the waste described. The generator can also designate one alternate facility in the event that an emergency prevents delivery of the waste. If the transporter cannot deliver the waste to the primary or alternate facility, the generator should designate another facility or instruct the transporter to return the waste to the originating facility.

The generator must: (1) sign the manifest certification by hand, (2) obtain the handwritten signature of the initial transporter and date of acceptance on the manifest, and (3) retain three copies. The generator keeps one copy, one copy is forwarded to the generator's state agency, and one copy is forwarded to the hazardous waste destination state agency (only if applicable). The generator must then give the transporter the remaining copies of the signed manifest.

The dates next to the signatures are critical. There are limitations governing how long a waste can be in transit. If a generator does not receive a signed, completed manifest from the TSDF within 35 days of shipment, the generator must track the waste. If the waste is not found in 45 days for a large-quantity generator, or 60 days for a small quantity generator, an exception report must be provided to either the EPA or the state agency. Some states have more stringent requirements. As a rule of thumb, some type of file should be compiled that flags a waste shipment manifest not sent back to you within a certain timeframe (for example 20 days). This will enable the generator to call either the transporter or the TSDF to determine the delay.

Sometimes, TSDFs reject shipments because the manifest does not have the correct paperwork attached. For example, virtually all liquid hazardous wastes are banned from landfills until they are rendered nonhazardous. If such materials are being disposed of, a land ban certificate must be attached to the manifest.

A TSDF could reject a waste stream if a sample of the waste analyzed upon arrival at the TSDF does not meet the specifications of the waste profile agreed to prior to shipment of the waste. This can cause the TSDF treatment and/or catastrophic problems, such as fires or explosions.

The key to completing the manifest is understanding the DOT regulations for proper shipping names (DOT 2011). Most hazardous waste transportation company representatives can assist generators in filling out the manifest prior to shipment. This information is gathered from the waste profile already on record with the waste disposal company.

An important resource used in completing the manifest is the Pipeline and Hazardous Materials Safety Administration's *Emergency Response Guidebook* (ERG) (PHMSA 2008). Each hazardous material shipped across the highways and railroads in North America is affixed with a United Nations (UN) or North America (NA) number. These numbers are located on the DOT class placards on the sides of railcars and trucks (e.g., methyl ethyl ketone (MEK) is UN1193, sulfuric acid is UN1830).

On the manifest, the ERG guide number for each hazardous waste in the shipment can be referenced in Section 15, Special Handling Instructions, or a copy of each applicable ERG guide page may be attached to the manifest prior to shipment.

The manifest also requires the generator to provide a 24-hour emergency response number of a person knowledgeable about the waste. This means someone within the organization must be available to provide technical information in the event of an emergency scenario.

Accumulating Waste On Site

When discussing accumulation requirements at a facility, understanding which hazardous waste generator classification a facility falls into is very important. If your facility is classified as a CESQG [less than or equal to 100 kg (220 lb) of hazardous waste per month], there are no accumulation time requirements. If a facility is classified as a SQG [greater than 100 kg and less than or equal to 1000 kg (2200 lb) of hazardous waste per month], hazardous waste may be accumulated on site for 180 days or less without a permit, or up to 270 days if the hazardous waste must be transported, stored, or treated at a distance of 200 miles or more.

For an LQG, a generator may accumulate hazardous waste on site for 90 days or less without a permit or without having interim status, provided that:

- the waste is placed in containers and the generator complies with 40 CFR 265 Subpart I (Use and Management of Containers), or the waste is placed in tanks and the generator complies with Subpart J (Tank Systems) (EPA 2010b)
- the date upon which each period of accumulation begins is clearly marked and visible for inspection on each container
- while being accumulated on site, each container and tank is labeled or marked clearly with the words, *hazardous waste*
- the generator complies with the requirements for owners and operators in 40 CFR 265 Subparts C and D (Preparedness and Prevention, Contingency Plan and Emergency Procedures) and Part 265.16 (Personnel Training) (EPA 2010b).

An extension can be filed with the Regional EPA Administrator if the waste cannot be removed from a facility within 90 days for situations such as an unforeseen emergency or uncontrollable circumstances. However, these extensions (usually for 30 days) are judged on a case-by-case basis. A facility may have multiple less-than-90-day accumulation areas as long as it can maintain the areas and has the manpower to conduct inspections. The accumulation area(s) must be:

- located in an area with limited access
- clearly identified with posted signs and warning placards
- away from floor drains, furnaces, or open flames
- not be subject to extreme temperature changes

The regulations focus on ensuring that:

- containers are labeled properly
- incompatible wastes are separated
- the accumulation area has secondary containment
- the accumulation area is inspected
- written emergency procedures are up to date
- fire control and emergency response equipment is readily available
- site personnel involved in any aspect of handling the hazardous waste are trained
- arrangements for emergency response activities have been made with local authorities

Safe Handling of Hazardous Waste

If a facility is going to be handling hazardous waste, moving it is a high priority. Whether small containers of waste are transferred to larger containers, a large container is moved around a worksite and transferred to another location, or containers are moved to on-site storage, there are several things to consider.

The first consideration is personal protective equipment (PPE). What type of PPE is necessary depends on the potential danger from exposure to moving the hazardous waste. A company's respective safety and industrial hygiene personnel should be consulted to ensure proper PPE is selected. Personnel also need to be properly trained to wear the appropriate PPE.

Splashes are probably the most common form of hazardous waste exposure. When opening a drum, the small bung should always be opened first and unscrewed slowly. If there is any pressure in the drum, it should be vented while the cap is still partially threaded into the lid. A funnel should always be used when pouring from one container to another, and the containers must be grounded and/or bonded.

Two common types of containers used in hazardous waste storage are 55-gallon drums and five-gallon cans. Some of these cans are self-closing to prevent spills should they tip over and self-venting to prevent dangerous buildup of explosive vapors. Self-venting cans are required by law for certain flammable substances (EPA 2010b).

If small waste containers are being moved, a cart that has the capacity for secondary containment should be used. If one of the containers were to spill, the liquid would spill into the cart and not on the ground or onto a person.

Prior to moving a 55-gallon drum, both bung caps should be checked to make sure they are tight. The drum should always be checked for rust, dents, and/or leaks, especially if the drum has been sitting out in the elements for a period of time. If there is any evidence of damage to the drum, it should not be moved; the appropriate personnel within the company should be consulted to determine what needs to be done. To move a 55-gallon drum any distance, either a drum dolly with some type of restraint or a forklift should be used.

Falling drums are one of the most common causes of injuries. The drum might land on or pin an employee; if it ruptures, the employee can be exposed to the contents of the drum. If a drum starts to fall, the employee should let it go.

Vapor or particulate releases are another concern when handling hazardous waste. These releases can harm an employee in several ways. Inhalation of poisonous hazardous waste can irritate the eyes, nose, mouth, or lungs. Many vapors are flammable, so there is the potential of fire or explosion. Some vapors have the ability to corrode pipes, sprinkler heads, or equipment. The areas where people work with hazardous wastes, specifically transfers, should have adequate ventilation and/or an exhaust system that draws airborne contaminants away from workers and out of the area. For certain types of waste, respiratory protection may be required.

Another hazard is the mixture of incompatible wastes, which must not be done; this is called *segregation and separation*. A reaction could result if incompatible wastes are mixed. Some chemicals, such as acids, and any waste containing sulfide may become explosive when mixed together. Hazardous wastes should never be mixed together unless they are compatible. In addition, the container must be compatible with its contents.

Finally, the importance of grounding and bonding should be recognized. All stored metal containers should be properly grounded. The *storage* container is to be grounded while the *receiving* container (usually a 1- to 5-gallon container) is to be bonded to the storage container using bonding straps or cables to eliminate the potential generation of a static discharge. This concept also applies to the transfer of liquid waste materials between plastic containers to reduce the potential of static electricity.

Labeling and Marking (EPA 2010d)

Prior to transporting and offering hazardous waste for transportation off site, the generator must label each package (box, drum, and so on) in accordance with the applicable Department of Transportation regulations on packaging materials (DOT 2011). These labels reflect the DOT hazard classes (e.g., corrosive, flammable liquid, oxidizer, and organic peroxide).

Also prior to shipping, the generator must mark each container of 110 gallons or less with the following words and information displayed in accordance with the requirements of 49 CFR 172.304 (DOT 2011) or their state's labeling requirement:

> HAZARDOUS WASTE – Federal Law Prohibits Improper Disposal. If found contact the nearest police or public safety authority or the U.S. Environmental Protection Agency. Generator's name and address. Manifest document number.

These standardized hazardous waste labels (commonly yellow in color, although not required) can be purchased and even customized with the company's name, address, and telephone number.

Personnel Training Plan

Generators of hazardous wastes must ensure that all wastes are under the control of trained personnel. These regulations are found in multiple places, beginning with 40 CFR 262.34(a)(1)(i) (EPA 2010f), and then 40 CFR 265.16 (EPA 2010b), which states that the minimum training program will include:

1. Procedures for using, inspecting, repairing, and replacing facility emergency and monitoring equipment

2. Key parameters for automatic waste feed cut-off systems
3. Communications or alarm systems
4. Response to fires or explosions
5. Response to groundwater contamination incidents
6. Shutdown of operations

This training must be provided within six months of an employee's assignment to handle hazardous wastes, and such an employee must not work unsupervised if untrained. Employees must be retrained annually, and the training records of current employees must be kept for the life of the facility or for three years after the employees leave the company.

The company is required to maintain these training records along with:

1. The job title for each position at the facility related to hazardous waste management and the name of the employee filling each job.
2. A written job description for each hazardous waste position.
3. A written description of the type and amount of both introductory and continuing training that will be given to each hazardous waste employee.
4. Records documenting the training or job experience required of the hazardous waste employees of the company.

Preparedness and Prevention—Contingency Plan

LQGs are required to have a contingency plan describing preparations emergencies at the facility. The contingency plan must conform to the requirements listed at 40 CFR 265.50 (EPA 2010b). In addition, copies of the plan are to be submitted to local emergency agencies and to hospitals that could respond to or be affected by the activation of the plan.

SQGs are not required to have as complete a plan as are LQG facilities but should have trained personnel able to respond in an emergency. However, if the facility becomes a LQG because of excessive waste generation some month, it will need a complete plan. It is recommended that every generator, regardless of size, have a complete contingency plan.

CESQGs are not required to have a plan, but, again, it is recommended.

If the facility has an emergency plan as required under 29 CFR 1910.38 (OSHA 1980) or some other regulation, it only needs to include the additional information required by the hazardous waste regulations for a combination plan that covers all requirements. Having one coordinated plan will make it easier for plant personnel to understand their tasks when they respond to an emergency.

Waste Minimization

Every time a company representative signs a hazardous waste manifest, he or she certifies that, in addition to the hazardous wastes being properly packaged, packed, marked, and labeled according to the Department of Transportation regulations at 49 CFR, a program is in place to minimize the amount of wastes generated.

Waste minimization has been used successfully by industry for many years to reduce the volume and toxicity of waste streams, producing cost savings for materials and waste disposal. The EPA proposes incorporating a tiered approach to waste management (see Figure 2).

The EPA says that its waste minimization program has the following goals:

1. Complete elimination of, or substitution for, priority chemicals, wherever possible.
2. Minimizing the amount of priority chemicals used whenever elimination or substitution is not possible.
3. Maximizing recycling whenever elimination, substitution, or minimization is not possible, creating closed-loop materials management systems that eliminate or constrict release pathways.
4. Promoting cradle-to-cradle waste management instead of cradle-to-grave waste management.
5. Increasing cooperative efforts between the EPA, states, and regulated communities through partnership programs.

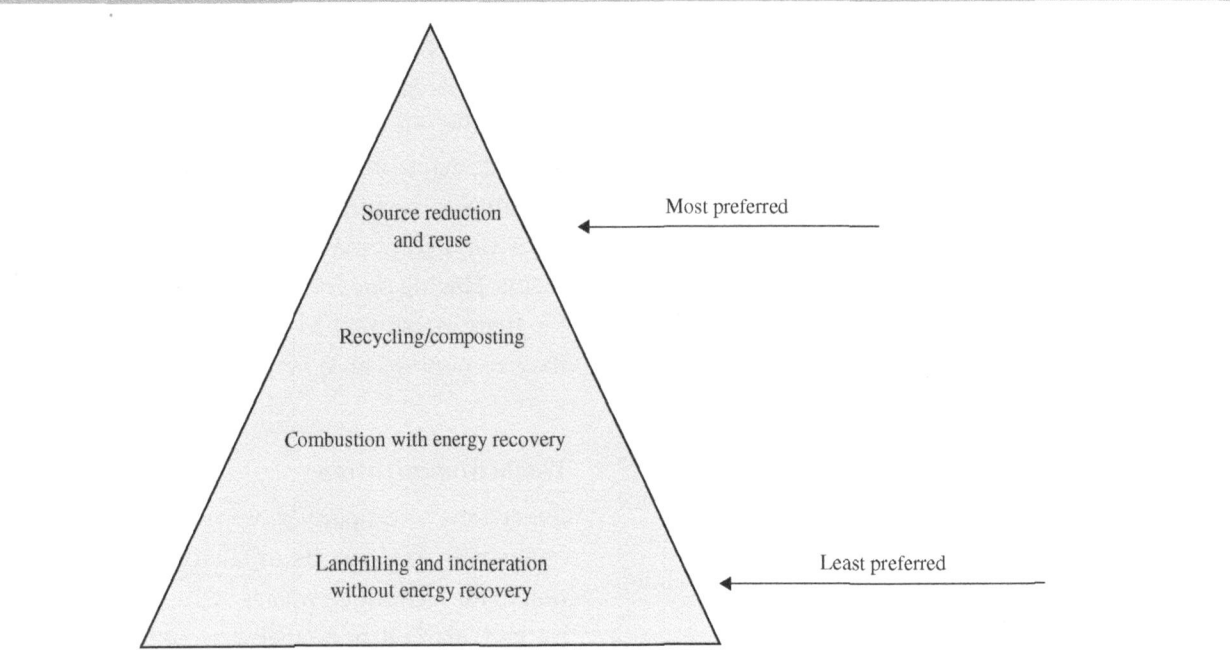

FIGURE 2. Solid waste management hierarchy (*Source*: EPA 2008b)

It thus makes very good sense for any company generating hazardous wastes to also adopt those goals, training its employees to work toward their implementation.

In addition, other simple waste minimization strategies that a company can implement include:

- segregating hazardous waste streams from nonhazardous waste streams
- recycling and reusing raw materials and extracting water and raw material from rinses, solvent tanks, and spent chemicals
- replacing toxic materials, products, or processes with less toxic alternatives
- controlling leaks and spills

Suppose, for example, that a company has been using methylene chloride as a paint stripper for the past thirty-five years, since the company's founding. Methylene chloride is an excellent paint stripper. However, it is now known that it is a human carcinogen, mutagen, and tumorigen. Because it is chlorinated, it has a low heat value (btus), which means that disposal costs are very high and that there are land ban restrictions upon its disposal. With a little research, the company finds and switches to one of several commercial paint strippers on the market that are both environmentally friendly and either slightly toxic or nontoxic, a paint stripper so safe that employees may use it without wearing personal protective equipment. Thus the company has minimized its waste by eliminating a highly toxic material and replacing it with a less toxic material. The company's waste is now classified as industrial waste instead of hazardous waste, saving the company money.

Record Keeping

Hazardous waste generators are required to maintain records to identify the quantities, composition, and disposition of hazardous waste generated. Required reports include:

- a contingency plan—keep a current version
- emergency agreements with local authorities—keep a current version
- land disposal restrictions—keep for five years
- manifests—keep for three years
- manifest exception reports (40 CFR 262.40 (b))—keep for three years (EPA 2010f)
- personnel training documentation (40 CFR 262.34 (c) & (d))—keep for three years after employee termination or separation of employment (EPA 2010f)

- waste analyses/test results (or other bases used for hazardous waste determination) (40 CFR 262.34 (c))—keep until facility closure (EPA 2010d)

Requirements Specific to Large-Quantity Generators

Large-quantity generators (LQGs) may accumulate unlimited amounts of hazardous wastes on site, but they may store those wastes for no longer than 90 days from the date of initial storage, unless the LQG is a permitted storage facility. LQGs must abide by all other requirements listed above and must also submit a report on even-numbered years that includes:

- the generator's EPA ID number
- the EPA ID numbers for each transporter and designated facility used
- the quantity and nature of hazardous waste generated
- efforts to reduce volume and toxicity of waste
- changes in volume and toxicity of waste achieved

The biennial report is to be submitted on EPA Forms 8700-13 A/B (EPA 2007a).

Requirements Specific to Acutely Hazardous Waste

Acutely hazardous wastes are defined as wastes listed in §§261.31, 261.32, or 261.33(e); in §§262.34(c)(1) and other sections of the regulations, only those wastes in §§261.33(e) are considered acutely hazardous (40 CFR 261.5(e)(1)) (EPA 2010f). These wastes are considered acutely hazardous because of their inherently hazardous characteristics. Such waste contains chemicals dangerous enough to pose a threat to human health and the environment even when properly managed. These wastes are fatal to humans and animals even in low doses.

When any company generates more than 1 kg of acutely hazardous waste per calendar month, that company is a considered a large-quantity generator and must manage its wastes according to LQG requirements.

Medical Wastes

Medical wastes are generally managed by the states, but federal laws do exist that control emissions from incinerators and for treatment. Medical wastes were addressed in 42 U.S.C. 82, Subchapter X, as the Medical Waste Tracking Act of 1988, which was promulgated as a response to medical wastes that washed ashore (MWTA 1988). The Act, which expired after two years, called for demonstration projects for shipment and disposal of medical wastes in several east coast and Great Lakes states. After the demonstrations, the EPA made recommendations to Congress regarding additional steps needed for management of medical wastes. State laws and regulations should be referred to for specifics on the handling of medical wastes.

Universal Wastes

The category of universal wastes was finalized in the Federal Register in May 1995 by the EPA in order to encourage the recycling of certain potentially hazardous items generated in large quantities in the nonhazardous waste stream. Such wastes, including batteries, items containing mercury, certain pesticides, and certain light bulbs are found routinely in maintenance operations (40 CFR 273) (EPA 2005b).

Companies that generate universal wastes are broken down into two categories: small-quantity and large-quantity handlers of universal wastes. There are also universal waste transporters and universal waste destination facilities, but those are outside the scope of this chapter.

Small-Quantity Handler of Universal Waste (SQHUW)–Subpart B

Generators in the small-quantity category must stay below 5000 kg of all universal waste categories combined at their location at any time. They are required to manage their universal wastes in ways that prevent releases to the environment; in case of release, they must immediately respond and initiate clean up (RCRA 1976).

Large-Quantity Handler of Universal Waste (LQHUW)–Subpart C

LQHUWs are those companies that exceed the 5000 kg of all universal waste categories and will remain large-quantity handlers for the balance of the year. They must comply with all requirements that the SQHUW has to comply with, must have an EPA ID number, and must keep records of materials generated.

Requirements for All Handlers

Both large and small universal waste handlers must train their employees in basic waste handling and emergency response procedures.

Waste containers must be labeled in any one of the following ways (whichever makes sense) and with the date the material first became a waste or when it was received from another facility:

- Universal Waste *(name of material—lamps, batteries, oil, and so on)*
- Waste *(name of material—lamps, batteries, oil, and so on)*
- Used *(name of material—lamps, batteries, oil, and so on)*

Universal wastes may be allowed to accumulate for up to one year in order to collect sufficient volume for recycling and may be transported using any vehicle or transport company. If the SQHUW or LQHUW transports the universal wastes with a company vehicle, it becomes a Universal Waste Transporter and must comply with all regulations applying to transporters. SQHUWs may ship universal wastes off-site without manifests or recordkeeping. LQHUWs must develop a recordkeeping method, track all wastes shipped off-site and maintain those records for three years.

All items must be stored in containers and handled in such ways as to prevent release into the environment. In case of release, clean-up materials are considered a hazardous waste and must be stored and shipped as such.

Recycling of Hazardous Wastes (40 CFR 266, Subparts C & F)

The goal of these regulations is to ensure that hazardous wastes are handled properly for disposal. If wastes are recycled or reused instead of disposed of, the goal of these regulations is met.

However, there may be times when materials that could be recycled are "used in a manner that constitutes disposal" if applied to the land. The EPA is aware of those materials and the disposer must follow the generators regulations for the disposition of those materials (40 CFR 266, Subpart C). Certain precious metals, such as gold, silver, and platinum, are of significant value and not willingly discarded. The EPA recognizes this and allows those companies involved in the handling of these metals flexibility in doing so. These companies must have an EPA ID number and must follow the regulations concerning generators and transporters. They are required to use manifests and to note any discrepancies on manifests. If they store such materials on-site, records must be kept that show that the material is being recycled and not accumulated for speculation (40 CFR 266 Subpart F) (EPA 2010e). State environmental agencies should be consulted for any additional requirements for this type of recycling.

Achieving Excellence in Pollution Prevention

According to the Pollution Prevention Act of 1990, the following characteristics are repeatedly found in companies that achieve excellence in pollution prevention:

- *Top-level support and commitment:* A clear commitment to pollution prevention by senior management is exhibited through policy, communications, and resources.
- *Proactive management:* Management is proactive rather than reactive. Actions are taken in advance to prevent pollution.
- *Interdisciplinary management:* A wide variety of people in the company are exposed to the ideas and techniques of pollution prevention. Companies integrate the research, engineering, and production staffs into the pollution prevention programs, increasing understanding and commitment all the way from the design staff to the sales force.
- *Corporate policies that integrate environmental issues:* Specific statements regarding environmental issues are incorporated into the company's goals and policies. These are

often stated in a positive rather than a negative way (i.e., "Company policies should improve the environment," rather than "Company policies should not harm the environment").

- *Pollution prevention "champion":* Companies that excel in pollution prevention often have one or two key individuals who support and drive the programs. The champion believes in the program and pushes for its implementation.
- *High degree of employee awareness and training:* Thorough training of employees is essential in pollution prevention. Numerous examples exist where companies failed to prevent pollution simply because employees were not trained properly.
- *Strong environmental auditing program:* Frequent assessments of pollution prevention include: top-down, self-assessment, and third-party audits. These audits evaluate existing pollution prevention controls and measure pollution releases and reductions.

There are many examples of how a company can minimize its waste: equipment or technology modifications, reformulation or redesign of products, substitution of raw materials, improvements in housekeeping, and maintenance and inventory control systems. The best method should be chosen for each company; commitment should be obtained from management; and as many people as possible should be involved. Waste minimization, source reduction, pollution prevention—whatever the company uses to describe the reduction of hazardous and solid wastes—will not only benefit the company's bottom line, but also keep the environment healthy for generations to come.

Selecting a Hazardous Waste Transporter and a Treatment, Storage, and Disposal Facility (TSDF)

While reviewing the finer details of both good hazardous waste transporters and treatment, storage, and disposal facilities (TSDFs), the key word to remember is *liability*. Whether the waste generated is sitting on company property, in transit to the TSDF, sitting at a transfer station in the middle of nowhere or at the TSDF, the liability of the waste rests with the generator. Hazardous waste transporters will provide all kinds of guarantees, but the bottom line is that when an emergency response occurs involving a company's hazardous waste in the middle of the night in a rural area, someone in that organization must be ready to mitigate the situation, either with manpower or cash flow.

Transporters

Since hazardous waste transporters move regulated wastes on public roads and highways, rails and waterways, they are regulated not only by RCRA but also by the Department of Transportation (DOT). To avoid regulatory discrepancies, the hazardous waste transporter regulations were developed jointly by EPA and DOT. Although these regulations are integrated, they are not located in the same part of the CFR. DOT's Hazardous Materials Transportation Act regulations are found in the 49 CFR Parts 171–179 (EPA 2011b), while the RCRA Subtitle C transporter requirements are located in 40 CFR Part 263 (EPA 2010d).

Transporter regulations only apply to off-site transportation of hazardous waste. The regulations do not apply to on-site transportation of hazardous waste within a facility's property or boundary.

Prior to selecting a hazardous waste transporter, a waste-generating company must look for dependability, reliability, regulatory knowledge, and a good transportation track record.

The company can select either a TSDF with transportation capabilities or a waste broker who will subcontract transportation services. Such a determination should be based on the type and amount of waste streams the company generates.

Once the selection of hazardous waste transportation companies has been narrowed down to two or three that suit the company's needs, the state environmental agency should be contacted to confirm that the transporters are licensed in the state and to learn their compliance records, such as any filed or pending notices of violations (NOVs) in both EPA and DOT. The transporters' DOT numbers should be requested and each company's driving safety and inspection records should be reviewed online at the Comprehensive Safety Analysis 2010 System of the Federal

Motor Safety Analysis Administration (FMCSA) (DOT 2010).

Another avenue to pursue if the company is a multi-site organization, is to check with other facilities within the organization that may have used the transporter to determine if they are dependable. Finally, the company should always request and check the transporter's references.

Under the Superfund (CERCLA) regulation, if the transporter spills the hazardous waste in transit, the company that generated the waste will incur the financial responsibility toward the clean-up operation. The company is not released of any liability during the shipment phase, despite any statements the transporter may make (CERCLA 1980).

Information that a company should request from any transporter includes:

- EPA identification number
- DOT number
- TSDFs where the transporter is permitted to transport the waste streams
- waste destination, such as a transfer station (if so, where and for how long)
- waste pickup scheduling lead time
- regulatory background, such as assistance with completion of waste profiles, manifests, and land-ban forms
- on-site services, such as labeling, marking of containers, overpacking (if necessary), and lab-packing
- training competencies of on-site technicians and drivers
- emergency response capabilities
- pricing

Transfer Facilities

Transporters accepting hazardous waste from a generator or another transporter may need to hold waste temporarily during the normal course of transportation. A *transfer facility* is defined as any transportation-related facility, such as a loading dock, parking area, storage area, or other similar area where shipments are held during the normal course of transportation. A transporter may hold waste at a transfer facility for up to 10 days. Transfer facilities are usually used by transporters as a cost-saving measure to maximize trailer capacity on runs to different TSDFs.

TSDFs

Once the waste transporter has been selected, a decision must be made as to where to send the waste. The final disposition of the waste will determine the selection of a type of TSDF. Incineration, fuels blending, recycling, land-filling, and Class I injection wells are the most common options. Pricing will play a part in this decision, but liability must be factored into the decision. Some TSDFs have transportation services available, which make prices competitive. This may be the best option for a company that has consistent waste streams. If a company produces a variety of waste streams, they may need to go to different types of TSDFs, in which case a waste broker may be the best solution.

Waste minimization, or producing less waste, is the best way to protect the environment and reduce liability risk. However, once waste is produced, the EPA recommends recycling as the next best method for managing wastes. Recycling offers the advantages of avoiding disposal costs and protecting the environment. But if mismanaged, recycling can release hazardous waste into the environment. RCRA, therefore, exclusively regulates wastes destined for recycling.

Recycling includes burning wastes for energy, which must destroy at least 99.99 percent of the waste, which in turn minimizes the risk of future liability. The destruction efficiency is based on the type of incineration unit, temperature, and the type of waste burned. Recycling usually derives a useful product from wastes, plus recycling may preserve natural resources, such as coal and fossil fuels used in the incineration process. Depending upon the material, recycling may be less expensive (EPA 2010f).

Incineration and fuel blending have become popular disposal or treatment options as the EPA continues to tighten regulations governing landfills, and as future liabilities associated with buried wastes increase.

Land disposal of waste has the highest potential liability risk, and many consider it the method of last resort. The EPA's land disposal restriction (LDR) program prohibits placing untreated waste in land-based disposal or treatment units. Hazardous waste destined for land disposal must be pretreated to specified safe levels to reduce its risk to the environment.

The advantage of incineration and fuel blending is that both are forms of thermal destruction that break down hazardous components of the waste to an efficiency of 99.9999 percent. The volume and weight of the waste are reduced to a fraction of their original state (referred to as *ash content*).

The major advantage of these disposal methods is that many toxins are destroyed rather than merely contained; thus, the risk to the environment and the generator are limited. While thermal destruction generally costs more than disposal in a landfill, increasing costs and limited availability of landfills are closing the gap.

There is a difference between fuel blending and incineration. In the United States, there are approximately 80 to 90 cement kilns in operation, about 25 of which burn waste-derived fuel (or blended fuel). Fuel is fed into the lower hot end of the kiln where gas temperatures can reach 3500° F. As waste-derived fuels burn in the kiln, organic compounds are destroyed and inorganic compounds recombine with raw materials that are incorporated into gypsum used by ready-mix concrete makers.

Typically, *fuel blending* is the least expensive, most efficient form of incineration and has the least impact on the environment. Waste is converted into fuels with complete thermal destruction of organic waste. This waste-to-energy conversion preserves natural energy resources while destroying waste. *Incineration*, on the other hand, uses virgin fuels, such as coal, to fire the incinerator, which burns at temperatures ranging from 1000–2500° F. Because fuel blending uses wastes as energy, it is significantly less expensive than incineration.

Wastes that are high in btu (British thermal unit) value and have low residual ash content are prime candidates for fuel blending. These values are important in the incineration process because the higher the btu value, the more efficiently wastes will burn and convert to energy. For example, absorbents are most commonly used in daily maintenance to absorb oil leaks and spills; however, not all absorbents used for this purpose are good candidates for fuel blending. Clay pellets, a low-grade absorbent frequently used in industry, are unacceptable for fuel blending because of their 100 percent ash-content remainder and low btu value.

Wastes sent for incineration and/or fuel blending operations used for btu value keep that unit operational. Thus, the higher the btu value of a hazardous waste stream, the more likely the incinerator or fuel blending facility will accept the waste.

Auditing the TSDF

Prior to sending waste to a TSDF, a company should develop a methodology for ensuring that the waste is in good hands for final disposal. Whether a TSDF facility audit is performed by someone within the waste-generating company or is contracted out, an audit of the TSDF is necessary for company liability purposes.

Most TSDFs are not that large and can usually be audited in a day or two. Much of the regulatory paper review can be done prior to the audit. Most TSDF facilities schedule audits certain days of the week and/or times of the month to maintain the least amount of interruption to their production schedule. The TSDF or waste broker representative can arrange an audit. With competition in the hazardous waste services field at its highest, most TSDFs have already developed a preliminary audit package for the auditor to review. The waste management facility evaluation document should include the following sections:

- *Facility history:* How many years in operation, EPA identification number
- *Processing capabilities:* Services available on site, waste types accepted and not accepted at the facility, hours of operation, weekly processing capacity
- *Storage practices and capacities:* Permitted waste storage capacity, truck unloading area, drum storage area, signs of leakage or deterioration, signs of growing backlog of wastes, air emission controls
- *Laboratory capabilities and waste stream qualifications:* On-site laboratory and capabilities, prequalification of waste streams

- *Receiving and loading practices:* Testing of waste deliveries prior to unloading each truck, notification to the generator or transporter of a rejection
- *Waste released by or shipment from the facility*: Any visible air emissions, detectable odors, control of storm water runoff from contained areas, wastes or by-products shipped from the facility for off-site disposal or use as a fuel (tank bottoms, leachate, and so on)
- *Regulatory compliance:* RCRA Part B permit in order; inspections from regulatory agencies (citations, corrective actions, compliance schedule met); employee training program; facility's financial capability to handle environmental impairment liability; security system; description of surrounding area (residential, industrial, wooded); groundwater monitoring and leachate control programs; record keeping
- *Other facilities:* Company-owned or -operated
- *Summary:* Concerns, comments, and observations

Although it is difficult and time-consuming to conduct an audit, it is probably in the best interest of the company to send an auditor familiar with both the environmental and safety regulations. The length of time between audits is determined by how well the audit goes; a three-year interval is a good rule of thumb; less than three years would be necessary in cases of regulatory intervention of the TSDF, or poor management practice.

Regulations Governing TSDFs

Any person who treats, stores, or disposes of hazardous waste is operating a TSDF. There are requirements established under the RCRA regulation for TSDFs (EPA 2010b and 2010f).

A TSDF needs to obtain approval to operate from the EPA or authorized state agency. There is a two-step approval process before a facility can be classified as a permitted TSDF. The "Part A" or *interim status permit* requires a facility to obtain an EPA ID number and submit summary information to the agency(s), which includes design, construction, operation, and maintenance of a facility. A TSDF may operate under a "Part A" permit until the "Part B" application is either approved or denied.

The "Part B" permit allows a TSDF to accept, store, treat, and dispose of hazardous waste with the following requirements:

- waste analysis plan for incoming shipments
- security measures
- documented inspection program for malfunctions, operator errors, and discharges
- personnel training
- handling storage of ignitable, reactive, and incompatible wastes
- preparedness for and prevention of emergencies and releases
- written contingency plan and emergency procedures
- written operating records, manifest records, and biennial reports of facility activities
- groundwater protection for land disposal facilities
- closure plan and post-closure plan and use
- financial information regarding closure, post-closure, accidents, and bankruptcy

TSDFs must be built in locations away from natural disasters (floods, hurricanes, earthquakes, and so on). The facility must also be able to:

- accept wastes in accordance with manifest rules
- manage containers in accordance with container rules
- manage tanks in accordance with tank rules
- manage other units in accordance with applicable technical standards (surface impoundments, landfills, incinerators, and so on)
- control, monitor, and document volatile organic air emissions (fugitive emissions)
- comply with land disposal restrictions (where applicable)
- maintain adequate insurance during operating and adequate funding for closure and beyond (post-closure)

Some TSDFs provide their own transportation services; however, most do not and subcontract with licensed hazardous waste haulers. Even though the hazardous waste has shipped under the "cradle-to-grave" concept, the waste-generating company is liable for the hazardous waste shipment until official disposal of the waste. The transporter's terminal and TSDF should be audited by company personnel (including cement kilns), or by third-party auditor prior to sending waste off site. It is a worthwhile investment.

Companies or facilities do not have to apply for a RCRA permit if they fall under one of the following specific exemptions:

- generators that accumulate hazardous waste on site for less than 90 days
- generators that produce less than 100 kg (220 lb) of hazardous waste in a calendar month, which is treated, stored or disposed of accordingly
- owners or operators of totally enclosed treatment facilities; for example, a hazardous waste treatment facility directly connected to an industrial production process constructed and operated to prevent the release of hazardous waste into the environment during treatment (e.g., a pipe in which waste acid is neutralized)
- transporters that store manifested shipments of hazardous waste for 10 days or less in permitted containers at a transfer facility

These are the federal RCRA requirements; companies should check with their respective states for more stringent state requirements.

Hazardous Waste Combustion

Combustion in boilers, industrial furnaces, or incinerators can ultimately dispose of hazardous wastes. Thermal destruction is used to destroy not only toxic materials such as dioxins or polychlorinated biphenyls but also organics and nonhazardous trash or municipal wastes—but the methods differ significantly.

Hazardous waste combustors, such as boilers or industrial furnaces, use the waste as a fuel additive for such things as rotary kilns, blast furnaces, smelters, reactors, or calciners used in the manufacturing of cement or lime. The inclusion of the hazardous waste provides an increase in heat value (btus) thus lowering the amount of fuel required. To ensure that these units remain environmentally compliant, the waste gas mixture is put through precipitators, bag filters, and/or scrubbers to ensure that what's coming out of the stack is as clean as practical. The material going into these units is covered by 40 CFR 266 (EPA 2010e), and the materials coming out of the stacks are governed by air regulations at 40 CFR 60.

An incinerator is a special type of combustion unit that uses very high temperatures to completely destroy solids or liquids.

Hazardous waste incinerators must be permitted under regulations covered in 40 CFR 264 and 265 covering TSDFs. Wastes must be analyzed to ensure that they are allowable under the facility's permit. Strict performance, operating, monitoring, record keeping, and inspection requirements must be maintained.

Information on the EPA's research on combustion and incineration and diagrams of related equipment are available at the EPA Web site (EPA 2007d and 2006a).

Underground Storage Tanks (USTs)

The Solid Waste Disposal Act was amended in 1984 to regulate underground storage tanks (USTs). Specifically, the law covers USTs and related piping that have been used to store petroleum or hazardous materials, imposing minimum standards for performance and operation to minimize potential for leakage. The requirements include:

- spill protection, such as a catchment basin to contain spills from delivery hoses
- overfill protection, such as automatic shut-off valves when the tank is 95 percent full
- corrosion protection, such as tank construction with noncorrodible material, corrosion-resistant coating, or steel-clad with a thick layer of noncorrodible material
- financial requirements and the ability to pay for clean-up costs and environmental effects

Existing tanks can be brought into compliance by the addition of cathodic protection (such as the technology used in home water heaters in which a sacrificial anode attracts the electrical charge that causes corrosion), interior lining, or both. Piping, too, must meet standards requiring cathodic protection and a corrosion-resistant coating, or an encasement of noncorrodible material for piping systems.

Leak-detection requirements apply to new petroleum and hazardous substance UST systems. Because leaks from hazardous substances are more difficult to detect than are those from petroleum tanks, the resulting requirements are more stringent and mandate secondary containment systems and monitoring devices. Federal law does not cover heating oil tanks, although some state jurisdictions do.

Regulations can be found in 40 CFR 280–284 that address all UST systems. Existing systems installed before 1988 were required to meet standards for spill, overfill, and corrosion protection, or to be removed prior to December 22, 1998. Systems installed today must be in full compliance with 40 CFR 280.20—Performance Standards.

Proper closure and removal of a UST requires the following prior to removal:

- notification of the regulatory authority at least 30 days beforehand
- determination of releases from the UST and contamination of surrounding soils or groundwater
- emptying and proper disposal of tank contents in accordance with confined-space protocols

Some tanks can be filled with inert material (sand, stone, or concrete) rather than removed. However, local and state regulations vary in allowing this.

Regulatory Enforcement

The EPA or authorized state has three enforcement options under RCRA:

- administrative sanctions or penalties
- civil penalties
- criminal penalties

Administrative sanctions or penalties are nonjudicial enforcement actions taken by either the EPA or the state. There are two types: informal actions and administrative orders (i.e., compliance orders and corrective action orders). The maximum penalty is $25,000 per day of noncompliance for each violation.

Civil penalties involve a formal lawsuit against a person who has failed to comply with some statutory/regulatory requirement or administrative order. There are four types of civil penalties: compliance action, corrective action, monitoring and analysis, and imminent hazard. The maximum penalty is the same; $25,000 per day of noncompliance for each violation.

Criminal penalties are incurred by knowingly committing any of the following seven criminal acts under RCRA Section 3008:

1. Transporting waste to a nonpermitted facility.
2. Treating, storing, or disposing of waste without a permit.
3. Omitting information/false statement in any application, label, manifest, record, report, permit, or compliance document.
4. Not complying with record-keeping and reporting requirements.
5. Transporting without a manifest.
6. Exporting waste without the consent of receiving country.
7. Action resulting in imminent danger.

The maximum penalties are:

- $50,000 per day of violation and 2 years in prison
- $100,000 per day and 4 years in prison (for repeat offenses)
- $250,000 per day and 15 years in prison for an individual or $1 million for an organization (applicable to #7 only).

The seventh criminal act is the knowing transportation, treatment, storage, disposal, or export of any hazardous waste in such a way that another person is placed in imminent danger of death or serious bodily injury. This act carried a possible penalty of up to $250,000 or 15 years in prison for an individual or a $1 million fine for corporate entities (EPA 2008b).

Repeat offenses not only apply if a repeat offense has occurred in the same facility, but such offenses that occur in company facilities at different locations or states can be construed as repeat offenses, carrying the heavier fine and prison sentence. Therefore, if one facility in an organization is cited for a RCRA violation that carries a "fine and time," there should be a mechanism in place to communicate the violation to the rest of the company.

Property Transfers

CERCLA (Comprehensive Environmental Response, Compensation and Liability Act of 1980) establishes liability for clean up of sites that present a threat to human health and the environment because of the presence of hazardous substances and places the responsibility and liability for clean-up costs on those responsible for the contamination.

Liability and responsibility for clean up is established for a facility where a release or threatened release of a hazardous substance "causes the incurrence of response costs." The *potentially responsible party* (PRP) is either the current or prior owner/operator, the "arranger" (for disposal or treatment of hazardous substances at a facility), or the "transporter" (of hazardous substances to the facility). Liability can be transferred whether the property is acquired by land contract, deed, easement or lease of the property on which hazardous substances are placed.

The Superfund Amendments and Reauthorization Act (SARA 1986) established an innocent landowner defense by which a potentially responsible party (PRP) of a contaminated facility is not held liable if the PRP acquires ownership after disposal or placement of hazardous substances on the property, did not know and had no reason to know the property was contaminated, exercised due care, and took reasonable precautions.

Reasonable Precautions

A prospective purchaser of a commercial property should ensure that he or she is covered by the innocent landowner defense by performing or having performed an investigation of the history of the property. The history should show what chemicals were used on site, how they were disposed of (whether on site or off site), and what types of products and processes occurred on site. These reasonable precautions have been formalized by the American Society for Testing and Materials (now ASTM International) as published in its standard, E1527, "Environmental Site Assessments: Phase I Environmental Site Assessment Process." This standard is the guide most consultants follow in performing a due diligence investigation on property to be acquired (ASTM 2005).

Phase I Environmental Site Assessment

The purpose of the Phase I Environmental Site Assessment is to provide "all appropriate inquiry" (AAI) into potential liabilities in the purchase of properties with potential environmental risks in order to qualify for an "innocent landowner defense" under SARA, under which "all appropriate inquiry" is not clearly defined (SARA 1986).

Industry standards were amended by the Small Business Liability Relief and Brownfields Revitalization Act (P.L. 107-118), which was enacted in January 2002 and took effect in November 2006. The purpose of the amendments was to relieve small businesses of the cost of environmental remediation and to encourage the development of Brownfield sites. Brownfield sites are defined by this law as "real property, the expansion, redevelopment, or reuse of which may be complicated by the presence or potential presence of a hazardous substance, pollutant, or contaminant." Certain legal exclusions apply.

The effects of these regulations on environmental professionals include changes in the due diligence process and new definitions of AAI. ASTM E1527 has also been revised to incorporate changes in the law, and ASTM E1527-05 is now considered the standard of care (ASTM 2005).

The EPA has developed several guidance documents regarding the amendments. Although there are many common elements between the 2000 and the 2005 ASTM standard that incorporates AAI, there are also significant changes.

For example, under the ASTM Standard, an *environmental professional* is defined as an individual with training and experience sufficient to conduct the assessment and provide the required opinion and conclusions. Note that some states require those doing site assessments to be licensed. Under the new amendments, specific qualifications of training and experience are for the first time delineated in describing environmental professionals (a minimum of five years' experience and a Bachelor's degree in a related program). Greater responsibility is also imposed upon environmental professionals in determining what to do with contamination once it is discovered. The uniqueness of each site is also recognized, and greater emphasis is placed upon judgment than upon standardization.

Under both protocols, the process of conducting a Phase I Environmental Site Assessment begins with a review of current and historical public records regarding the site. These may include building permits, Sanborn maps (described below), topographical maps, aerial photographs, and commercially available databases that map registered tanks, leaking underground storage tank incidents, RCRA generators, disposal facilities, and so forth. Sources of information may also include the federal EPA, state environmental offices, local or regional publicly owned treatment works (POTWs), offices of the States' Fire Marshalls, municipal water sources, commercial waste transporters, and local government (city and county) departments of buildings, public health, engineering and planning, fire protection, and waste. Histories and previous use records are also included for adjoining sites, which may have an environmental impact on the site in question.

Building permits often identify previous business uses, tank installation, or even the installation of monitoring wells, and so on. Often the exact dates of tank installation will be available from either local code officials or from state environmental offices.

Sanborn maps or other historical fire protection maps, used for insurance purposes, are a source of information regarding previous uses of the property. They are often particularly good sources of information regarding underground storage tanks. (Look for small circles initialed GT, which indicate gasoline tanks.) These maps are published about every decade and can reveal old tanks that may have been subsequently removed. According to copyright law, these maps must be purchased if they are to be included in a report.

Topological maps will help determine the direction of flow of a potential plume of contamination or whether a particular site is upstream from a source of drinking water.

Aerial photographs, also taken every decade, can show the use of a site. A site undeveloped 40 years ago might have been a gas station 30 years ago and a shopping center 20 years ago.

Research is followed by a site visit in which key personnel are interviewed and the site examined for signs of environmental issues that might not have surfaced in the research.

The final report contains observations and conclusions related to the apparent environmental conditions of the site and includes a description of the site conditions encountered, notations of records reviewed, and commentary regarding possible environmental effects.

A report written in accordance with generally accepted professional standards should not be construed as a guarantee or warranty of the potential liability associated with environmental conditions or effects on the site.

Please note that many companies offer Phase I assessments or provide historical information about environmental issues on site. Site-specific and customer-detailed Phase I assessments may be purchased from many vendors.

Should environmental or other issues be noted, a Phase II investigation may be recommended.

Phase II Environmental Site Investigations

The function of a Phase I investigation is to identify potential issues, but a Phase II investigation looks at a suspected site to verify the presence of environmental conditions that have negatively impacted a property. Specific geological and analytical chemistry data will be sought.

In the case of surface or subsurface soil contamination, soil borings are conducted around a tank or in the vicinity of a spill. The number of borings depends upon the size of the tank or the area of the spill.

A magnetic survey may be conducted to determine the presence or location of a tank. Samples are taken on the surface or every two feet until the desired depth is reached. A photoionization detector (PID) will screen the sample in the field for the presence of volatile organic contamination. After field screening, samples are collected.

Samples indicating the highest volatile contamination are then analyzed with gas chromatography/mass spectroscopy using the EPA Method 8260, volatile organics protocol, and the EPA Method 8270, semi-volatile organics protocol, or are analyzed for specific constituents, such as RCRA metals, PCBs, and so on, using atomic absorption or inductively coupled plasma spectroscopy.

Monitoring wells may be installed if the contaminant zone is suspected of affecting groundwater. Suspect building materials may be analyzed for asbestos, lead, and mold.

Corrective Action to Clean Up Hazardous Waste Contamination

Where releases of hazardous wastes cause contamination of soil and groundwater, the EPA requires remediation to restore the land and water to acceptable limits. RCRA permits are withheld until such incidents have been adequately addressed. This process is sometimes known as Phase III.

Remediation

If contamination is found, a determination is made based on the impact of the contamination on the site. Risk-Based Corrective Action (RBCA) has been implemented in every state. This allows the state to establish limits of contamination for specific chemicals or for contamination that has a limited threat to human health and the environment (either because of naturally occurring geology or engineered barriers) to remain *in situ*.

Often, if a plume of contamination has spread, additional samples must be taken in order to determine how deep or how far contamination has spread. Recommendations are then made communicating whether the site requires remediation.

A remediation plan will be guided by state RBCA measures. Remediation may involve digging up contaminated soil and transporting it to a landfill. A "pump-and-treat" operation may be installed to remediate contaminated groundwater. More and more frequently, strategies involving biological oxidation or degradation are being employed. Levels of contamination may be further mitigated by the use of engineering controls or administrative work practices.

Engineering Controls and Administrative Work Practices

In remedial activities, engineering controls might include the use of a cap on a site to discourage further attenuation of contamination. Administrative controls may be used, such as an agreement with the local authority to leave contamination under a street in such a way as to negligibly affect human health and the environment.

Construction Workplan

In cases in which hazardous waste must be remediated, the permit will require a construction workplan documenting the overall management strategy, construction quality-assurance procedures, and a schedule for constructing the corrective measure.

The elements required in a construction workplan using a project management approach must describe organization; lines of communication; qualifications of key personnel; the project schedule; the construction quality assurance/quality control program; waste management procedures; any sampling and monitoring activities that may be needed; a quality assurance project plan (QAPP) to ensure that all information, data, and resulting decisions are technically sound, statistically valid, and properly documented; construction contingency procedures for notification of the agency of unforeseen changes, problems, or emergencies; evaluation, documentation, and management procedures of analytical data and results; and a cost estimate and financial assurance section. Financial assurance mechanisms are used to assure the implementing agency that the project has adequate financial resources to implement and sustain the corrective measure.

The construction workplan must include a cost estimate describing construction, operation, and maintenance costs, and specifying the financial mechanism that will be used. The financial assurance mechanism is covered in 40 CFR 265.143 (EPA 2010b).

All monitoring procedures, sampling, field measurements, and sample analysis performed during these activities must be documented. Approved quality assurance, quality control, and chain-of-custody procedures must be used. Guidance may be found in the *EPA Requirements for Quality Assurance Project Plans* (EPA 2001b).

Construction safety procedures will be specified in a separate health and safety plan.

Construction Completion Report

A construction completion (CC) report documenting how the completed project is consistent with the final plans and specifications will include the synopsis of the corrective measure, design criteria, and certification that the corrective measure was constructed in accordance with the final plans and specifications; an explanation and description of any modifications to the final plans and specifications and why these were necessary; the results of any operational testing or monitoring, indicating how initial operation of the corrective measure compares to the design criteria; a summary of significant activities that occurred during construction, including a discussion of problems encountered and how they were addressed; a summary of any inspection findings (including copies of key inspection documents listed in appendices); "as built" drawings or photographs; and a schedule indicating when any treatment systems will begin full-scale operation (EPA 1994).

Monitoring Plans

Monitoring plans are covered in 40 CFR 268.6, and examples are given on the EPA Web site (EPA 2010c).

BENCHMARKS AND PERFORMANCE APPRAISAL CRITERIA IN ENVIRONMENTAL MANAGEMENT

With the myriad aspects of environmental management, operating within permitted limits is the critical benchmarking criteria.

Compliance Defines the Baseline

The movement away from traditional compliance models of environmental management to environmental management systems (EMS) does not change the requirements of management and staff to maintain operations within permitted limits. A model that measures, tracks, and encourages improvements in operations still holds compliance more important than all other elements.

ISO 14001 incorporates measuring and monitoring requirements, and not merely for permit compliance. The EMS extends to documenting such elements of an EHS program as what is tested, when it is tested, and how it is sampled and tested. Key to the EMS process is the establishment of performance tracking and monitoring for improvement. These monitoring criteria are also modeled in the EMS.

For some operations, benchmarking this compliance framework becomes very straightforward. If a waste does not meet certain threshold levels, it will not be disposed of in a designated landfill. Other environmental operations require more tweaking to stay compliant, such as wastewater treatment systems.

Benchmarking a UST Operation

More often than not, current UST operation requires routine monitoring activities, such as tightness testing and leak detection. Many times, monitoring test wells are installed alongside UST cavities to allow for routine groundwater testing.

Environmental Site Assessments

The environmental site assessment, investigation, and remediation process on contaminated properties involves benchmarking activities at every step. From identifying potential issues in Phase I to investigating the actual presence and perhaps extent of contamination in Phase II to the development of remedial strategies, the EHS professional is responding to available data from previous assessments to chart the course for each next step. In determining the impact of contamination, the EHS manager must determine what is contaminating the property and at what concentrations, where on the property the release occurred and how far and how deep it has migrated, whether it has impacted groundwater or nearby surface waters, and whether it has migrated to neighboring sites or public ways. Both field-screening measures [photoionization detectors (PIDs) or flame ionization detectors (FIDs)] and laboratory analyses are used.

Risk-Based Corrective Action (RBCA)

Risk-based corrective action is a streamlined approach in which exposure and risk-assessment practices are integrated with traditional components of the corrective action process to ensure that appropriate and cost-effective remedies are selected and that limited resources are properly allocated.

Risk-based corrective action measures allow contamination under certain threshold limits to remain *in situ*. Each state has its own rules, which may be more stringent than federal regulations. Sampling and analysis will extend into the remedial period. Where soil is taken, sampling assures that what is left is below the state's clean-up objectives. Soil removed must be tested to determine disposal criteria.

Where other clean-up strategies are used, the soil treated must be tested to ensure that it complies with the state's clean-up objectives.

Often, the state will allow contamination to remain with the imposition of engineering controls or administrative work practices. Among these may be ongoing sampling and monitoring activities. For example, there may be a requirement to monitor groundwater for a specified period of time to assure that no further contamination occurs.

COST ANALYSIS AND BUDGETING

Potential Areas of Loss from Hazardous Waste

The conventional economic wisdom associated with hazardous waste operations is that prevention of the generation and associated costs of collection, transportation, treatment, storage, and disposal of hazardous waste is the economically prudent as well as the environmentally sensitive course of action. In addition, the expensive potential financial and criminal penalties associated with infractions of hazardous waste laws and regulations encourage a prudent course of action in compliance. This section examines the potential exposure to economic loss associated with the treatment, storage, and disposal of hazardous waste.

To fully determine the cost of waste disposal requires that a company determine both the fixed and variable cost of the product from inception to final delivery—or, in other words, the life-cycle cost of the product. Every product manufactured in any country of the world has a myriad of costs associated with its development, manufacture, storage prior to sale, and sales and delivery. Several countries (for example, Germany) have also imposed a cost of disposal of packaging materials and a cost of disposal of the product when it no longer serves it purpose. To undertake such a complete analysis is outside the scope of this chapter, but certain practices will be informative to discuss.

Initial design is where life-cycle cost savings begin. It is the designer who will determine what materials will be used in the product and how to best recycle either the product or its components once the product's life is spent.

Manufacturing can look at cost savings by ensuring that employees have the training and tools necessary to do their jobs properly and correctly the first time. Once materials have been found to be of no use in the process, they are a waste—either a nonregulated waste, a solid waste, or a hazardous waste. Regardless, there is a cost for disposal of such materials.

EHS is usually looked upon as a cost center. However, it can become a profit center by back-charging each department for the disposal of their waste materials. This provides a very important step. Rather than spread the cost of waste disposal over the fixed costs of the company, it places the costs of disposal where it should be—onto the product or the department that generated those wastes so that the actual cost of the product or of that department can be calculated.

Cost-Benefit Analysis

The application of cost-benefit analysis to hazardous waste operations can effectively identify economic solutions to the control of generation of hazardous waste and resulting costs of collection, transportation, treatment, storage, and disposal. The methodology of cost-benefit analysis is available from a number of sources: An excellent step-by-step explanation of the cost-benefit process is contained in the *Cost Analysis for Pollution Prevention* (Washington State 2005).

BEST PRACTICES IN ENVIRONMENTAL MANAGEMENT

The emphasis of environmental management is shifting from traditional "command and control" compliance to management systems. EMS are being implemented by corporations operating globally—often in multiple locations.

In the United States and in many other parts of the world, public pressure and regulatory requirements have given companies the incentive to implement pollution-prevention and sustainability measures.

As previously discussed, going beyond compliance, such as material substitutions and process changes, to achieve waste reduction and developing sustainability programs are measures that exceed the mandates of waste minimization under RCRA.

But beyond well-known and well-practiced strategies to achieve compliance in any given situation, EHS managers are being challenged to think strategically about their operations in order to meet the growing demand for a sustainable economy.

Green construction, using Leadership in Energy and Environmental Design (LEED) from the United States Green Building Council (www.usbgc.org), helps to maximize energy conservation and adaptive reuse, alternative energy from biofuels, and a myriad of other technologies that have moved beyond the demonstration phase to a level where viable models are being replicated worldwide. City governments are fostering this initiative as a way of reducing wastes and increasing renewable resources.

Waste Management

Waste management is a natural partner in such initiatives. For example, when the waste from one operation can be used as fuel for another and those operations colocated to minimize transportation, significant energy savings can be achieved.

The solid waste hierarchy represents baseline environmental management. It prioritizes waste management practices to encourage the use of source reduction, recycling, and reuse. These practices have less impact on the environment than incineration and landfilling. The waste disposal options that are chosen as best practices are those that maximize waste diversion into other processes, have lower harmful emissions, and have the best safety record. An incineration technology that produces energy would be considered preferable to one that does not.

Recent developments in gasification and digestion technologies show promise for producing energy with no emissions. Although landfilling and deep-well injection are generally considered less desirable than other forms of waste disposal, a landfill that collects methane is considered superior to one that does not.

Waste exchanges operate in virtually every state. They distribute catalogues of wastes that are available for use as raw materials by other companies. The Southern Waste Information eXchange (SWIX) (www.swix.ws) and the California Materials Exchange (CalMAX) (www.calrecycle.ca.gov/CalMax) are examples, or just do an internet search on the term "materials exchange."

Remediation Technology Development

Technologies continue to emerge that address contamination remaining on properties. *In situ flushing* is accomplished by injecting an aqueous solution into a contaminated soil or groundwater zone and then extracting and treating the elutriate. Phytotechnology uses various plants to extract contaminants from soil and water. Other treatment technologies, including activated carbon treatment, air stripping, bioremediation, oxidation, fracturing, natural attenuation, vapor extraction, air sparging, solvent extraction, and vitrification are addressed on the EPA's Web site (EPA 2008c).

SUMMARY/CONCLUSION

Hazardous waste management involves a complex legal structure and technical competence in many disciplines. An EHS manager must have knowledge and understanding of the waste streams generated by an operation, as well as of their permitting, monitoring, and reporting requirements, and the measures that must be taken in the event of release. Many guidelines are available, for which a number of references have been cited. When questions remain, remember that an entire industry is available to provide technical assistance on the management of hazardous waste or the clean up of sites where improper handling has occurred. Care should be taken in hiring hazardous waste consultants, brokers, laboratories, transporters, or disposal firms who must be verified to be properly permitted, licensed, and insured.

References

American Society for Testing and Materials (ASTM). 2005. ASTM Standard E1527-05, *Environmental Site Assessments: Phase I Environmental Site Assessment Process*. West Conshohocken, PA: ASTM.

Atomic Energy Act of 1954. P.L. 83-703, 42 U.S.C. §2011 *et seq*. www.nrc.gov/reading-rm/doc-collections/nuregs/staff/sr0980/ml22200075-vol1.pdf#pagemode=bookmarks&page=14

Comprehensive Environmental Response, Compensation and Liability Act of 1980 (CERCLA or Superfund). 42 U.S.C. §9601 *et seq*. www.epa/gov/superfund/policy/remedy/pdfs/cercla/pdf

Department of Transportation (DOT). 2010. *Comprehensive Safety Analysis 2010* (retrieved July 28, 2010). www.csa2010.fmcsa.dot.gov

Environmental Protection Agency (EPA). 1994. OSWER Directive 9902.3-2A, "RCRA Corrective Action Plan (Final)" (May). www.epa.gov.wastes/hazard/corrective action/resources/guidamce/gen_ca/rcracap/pdf

_____. 1995. 40 CFR 280, "Technical Standards and Corrective Action Requirements for Owners and Operators of Underground Storage Tanks (UST)" (retrieved July 29, 2011). ecfr.gpoaccess.gov/cgi/t/text/text=idx?c=ecfr&sid=a91168e9620c9d76056cd1efaaa8cb&rgn=div5&view=text&node=40.27.0.1.1.10&idno+40

_____. 2001a. EPA 530-K-01-005, *Managing Your Hazardous Waste: A Guide for Small Businesses* (December). www.epa.gov/wastes/hazard/generation/sgg/k01005.txt

_____. 2001b. EPA QA/R-5. *Requirements for Quality Assurance Project Plans for Environmental Data Operations* (March). www.epa.gov/quality/qs-docs/r5-final.pdf

_____. 2002. EPA-K-02-027, *25 Years of RCRA: Building on Our Past To Protect Our Future* (April). www.epa.gov/wastes/inforesources/pubs/k02027.pdf

_____. 2005a. *RCRA, Superfund and EPCRA Call Center Training Module: Introduction to Generators*. (September). www.epa.gov/wastes/inforesources/pubs/hotline/training/trans.pdf

_____. 2005b. 40 CFR 273. "Standards for Universal Waste Management." ecfr.gpoaccess.gov/cgi/t/text/text-idx?c=ecfr+3796b14b055e3c42d8adb6d1371f51b&rgn=div5&view=text&node=40:26.0.1.1.4&idno=40

_____. 2005c. Form 8700-22, "Uniform Hazardous Waste Manifest" (June). www.epa.gov/wastes/hazard/transportation/manifest/pdf/manfst-cn.pdf

_____. 2006a. *Hazardous Waste Incineration*. www.epa.gov/wastes/hazard/testmethods/sw846/pdfs/chap13/pdf

_____. 2006b. *RCRA Orientation Manual, 2006*, www.epa.gov/epawaste/inforesources/pubs/orientat/rom.pdf

_____. 2007a. "National Biennial RCRA Hazardous Waste Report." www.epa.gov/osw/inforesources/data/biennialreport/

_____. 2007b. *CERCLA Overview*. www.epa.gov/superfund/policy/cercla.htm

_____. 2007c. *Introduction to the Hazard Ranking System (HRS)*. www.epa.gov/superfund/programs/npl_hrs/hrsint.htm

_____. 2007d. *Municipal Waste Combustion*. www.epa.gov/wastes/nonhaz/municipal/index.htm

_____. 2007e. "National Priorities List (NPL)." www.epa.gov/superfund/sites/npl/index.htm

_____. 2007f. *RCRA Online*. www.epa.gov/rcraonline

_____. 2007g. 40 CFR 721, "Significant New Uses of Chemical Substances." ecfr.gpoaccess.gov/cgi/t/text/text-idx?c=ecfr&sid=ef220cad185d504c5471c4a11a9858cd&rgn=div5&view=text&node=40:30.0.1.1.10&idno=40

_____. 2007h. *Special Wastes*. www.epa.gov/wastes/nonhaz/industrial/special/

_____. 2007i. "What is the Toxics Release Inventory (TRI) Program? www.epa.gov/tri/whatis.htm

_____. 2008a. 20 CFR 172, "Environmental Use Permits" (retrieved August 1, 2011). ecfr.gpoaccess.gov/cgi/t/text/text-idx?c=ecfr&sid=f4702581cd85b2176341a134acdf3b812&rgn=div&view=text&node=40.0.1.1.22&idno=40

_____. 2008b. *Frequent Questions About Recycling and Waste Management*. www.epa.gov/epawaste/nonhaz/municipal/index.html#1

_____. 2008c. *Remediation; Phytotechnology Project Profiles*. www.epa.gov/superfund/remedytech/remed.htm#tech

_____. 2008d. SW-846, *Test Methods for Evaluating Solid Waste, Physical/Chemical Methods*. www.epa.gov/epawaste/hazard/testmethods/se846/index.htm

_____. 2008e. *Orientation Manual*, Section III: RCRA Subtitle C--Managing Hazardous Waste, Chapter 10, "Engorcement of Hazardous Waste," III134-III135 (retrieved August 1, 2011). www.epa.gov/wastes/inforesources/pubs/orientat/rom310.pdf

_____. 2009. Notification of RCRA Subtitle C Activity, Instruction and Form. EPA Form 8700-12, "Notification of Regulated Waste Activity" (July). www.epa.gov/wastes/inforesources/data/form8700/8700-12.pdf

———. 2010a. 40 CFR 255, "Identification of Regions and Agencies for Solid Waste Management" (retrieved July 29, 2011). ecfr.gpraccess.cgi.t.text.text=if?c=ecfr&sid=a119b70g22c16a8ce1b48a1661919d19&rgn=div5&view=text& node=40.25.0.1.4.3&idno=40

———. 2010b. 40 CFR 265, "Interim Standards for Owners and Operators of Hazardous Waste Treatment, Storage, and Disposal Facilities" (retrieved August 1, 2011). ecfr.gpoaccess.gov/cgi/t/text/text=idx?c=ecfr&sid=f470258cd85b176341acdf3b812&rgn=div5&view=text and node 40-26.0.1.1&idno=40

———. 2010c. 40 CFR 268, "Land Disposal Restrictions." ecfr.gpoaccess.gov/cgi/t/text/text-idx?c=ecfr&sid=a91168e96200c6976065cd1ef4aaa8bc&rgn=div5&view=text&node=40:26.0.1.1.3&idno=40

———. 2010d. 40 CFR 263, "Standards Applicable to Transportation of Hazardous Waste." ecfr.gpoaccess.gov/cgi/t/text/text-idx?c+ecfr&sid=379b614b055e3c42d8adb6d1371f51b&rgn=div5&view=text&node=40:26.0.1.1.4&idno=40

———. 2010e. 40 CFR 266, "Standards for the Management of Specific Hazardous Wastes and Specific Types of Hazardous Waste Management Facilities" ecft.gpoaccess.gov/cgi/t/text/text=idx?sid=9f676a5375d650278f4362b9732e22&c=ecfr&pl=ecftbrowse/Title40cfrv27_20.tpl

———. 2010f. 40 CFR 261, "Identification and Listing of Hazardous Waste" gpoaccess.gov/cgi/t/text/text_idx?c=ecfr&sid=a060ffb5c961de457c26bb1368f&rgn=div8&view=text&node=40:26.0.1.1.1&idno=40

———. 2011. EPA 550-B-10-001, "List of Lists; Consolidated List of Chemicals Subject to the Emergency Planning and Community Right to Know Act (EPCRA) and Section 112(r) of the Clean Air Act" (July). (retrieved September 13, 2011) www.epa.gov/oem/docs/chem/list_of_lists_revised_7_26_11.pdf

Esty, Daniel C., Marc Levy, Tanja Srebotnjak, and Alexander de Sherbinin. 2005. *2005 Environmental Sustainability Index: Benchmarking National Environmental Stewardship*. New Haven, CT: Yale Center for Environmental Law & Policy. www.yale.edu/esi/ESI2005_Main_Report.pdf

Federal Facility Compliance Act of 1992. P. L. 102-386. www.epa.gov/fedfac/documents/ffc92.htm

Hazardous and Solid Waste Amendments of 1984 (HSWA), Pub. L. 98-616, 98 Stat. 3221 (November 8). www.cq.com/graphics/sal/98/sal98-616.pdf

Medical Waste Tracking Act of 1988 (MWTA). 42 U.S.C. 82, Subchapter X. www.epa.gov/epawaste/nonhaz/industrial/medical/tracking.htm

National Environmental Policy Act of 1969 (NEPA). P. L. 91-190, 42 U.S.C. 4321-4347. www.nepa.gov/nepa/regs/nepa/nepaeqia.htm

Occupational Health and Safety Administration (OSHA). 1978. 29 CFR 1910.1025, "Occupational Safety and Health Standards; Lead." ecfr.gpoaccess.gov/cgi/t/text/text-idx?c=ecfr&sid= 07658e28ffa5a495eae41c01c6ec0f2e&rgn=div5&view=text&node=29:6.1.1.1.1&idno=29#29:6.1.1.1.1.1.22

———. 1980. 29 CFR 1910.38, "Emergency Action Plans." www.osha.gov/pls/oshweb/owadisp.show_document?table+STANDARDS&p_id=9726

———. 1986. 29 CFR 1926.1101, "Toxic and Hazardous Substances; Asbestos." www.osha..gov/pls/oshaweb/owadisp.show_documents?p_tables+STANDARDS&p_id=10862

———. 1993. 29 CFR 1926.62, "Health and Environmental Controls; Lead." www.osha,giv/SLTC/lead/construction.html

———. 1994. 29 CFR 1910.1200, "Hazardous Communications." www.osha.gov/oshaweb/owadisp.show_document?p_table=STANDARDS&p_id=10099

———. 1996. 29 CFR 1910.120, "Hazardous Waste Operations and Emergency Response (HAZWOPER)." www.osha.gov/pls/oshaweb/owadisp.show_document?p_table=STANDARD&p_id=9765

Peart, Karen & Dave DeFusco. 2005. "Finland Tops Environmental Scorecard at World Economic Forum in Davos." Yale Press Release (January 26). www.yale.edu/opa/newsr/05-01-26-02.all.html

Pipeline and Hazardous Materials Safety Administration. 2008. *Emergency Response Guide* (retrieved August 1, 2011). www.phmsa.dot.gov/statisfiles/PHMSA/DownloadableFile/Files/erg2008_eng.pdf

Prince William Soundkeeper. 1989. "*Exxon Valdez* Oil Spill." www.pws.wildapricot.org/Default.aspx?pageid+553853

Resource Conservation and Recovery Act (RCRA) of 1976. 42 U.S.C. §6901 *et seq.* frwebgate.access.gpo.gov/cgi-bin/usc.cgi?ACTION=BROWSE&TITLE=42USCC82

Small Business Liability Relief and Brownfields Revitalization Act. 2002. P.L. 107-118. www.osha.gov/fdsys/pkg/PLAW-107pub118/pdf/PLAW-107pub118.pdf

Solid Waste Disposal Act. 1965. P.L. 89 - 272, 79 Stat. 997, as added (October 20, 1965). epw.senate.gov/rcra.pdf

Superfund Amendments and Reauthorization Act of 1986 (SARA). frwebgate.access.gpo.gov/cgi/-bin/usc.cgi?ACTION=BROWSE&TITLE=42USCC103

Toxic Substances Control Act of 1976 (TSCA), P.L. 94-469, 15 U.S.C. §2601 *et seq.* www.epa.gov/lawsregs/laws/tsca.htm

Washington State Department of Ecology. 2005. Publication No 95-400, *Cost Analysis for Pollution Prevention* (Revised April). ecy.wa.gov/pubs/95400.pdf

APPENDIX A: ACRONYMS AND ABBREVIATIONS

ASTM: American Society for Testing and Materials
CAA: Clean Air Act
CAMU: Corrective Action Management Unit
CERCLA: Comprehensive Environmental Response, Compensation, and Liability Act
CERCLIS: Comprehensive Environmental Response, Compensation, and Liability Information System
CESQG: Conditionally Exempt Small Quantity Generator
CFC: Chlorofluorocarbon
CFR: *Code of Federal Regulations*
DOT: Department of Transportation
EPA ID number: Environmental Protection Agency Identification Number
EPCRA: Emergency Planning and Community Right-to-Know Act
HAZWOPER: Hazardous Waste Operations and Emergency Response Worker Protection Standard
HRS: Hazard Ranking System
HSWA: Hazardous and Solid Waste Amendments
kg: kilogram
lb: pound
LDR: Land Disposal Restrictions
LQG: Large-Quantity Generator
LUST: Leaking Underground Storage Tank
NCP: National Oil and Hazardous Substances Pollution Contingency Plan
NESHAP: National Emission Standards for Hazardous Air Pollutants
NPDES: National Pollutant Discharge Elimination System
NPL: National Priorities List
OPA: Oil Pollution Act
OSHA: Occupational Safety and Health Act
OSWER: Office of Solid Waste and Emergency Response
PCB: Polychlorinated Biphenyl
POTW: Publicly Owned Treatment Works
ppm: parts per million
PRP: Potentially Responsible Party
RBCA: Risk-Based Corrective Action
RBDM: Risk-Based Decision-Making
RCRA: Resource Conservation and Recovery Act
RCRIS: Resource Conservation and Recovery Act Information System
SARA: Superfund Amendments and Reauthorization Act
SPCC: Spill Prevention, Control, and Countermeasures
SQG: Small-Quantity Generator
SWDA: Solid Waste Disposal Act
SWMU: Solid Waste Management Unit
TCLP: Toxicity Characteristic Leaching Procedure
TSCA: Toxic Substances Control Act
TSDF: Treatment, Storage, and Disposal Facility
UST: Underground Storage Tank

APPENDIX B: RCRA AND SOLID WASTE RESOURCES

HOTLINES

Emergency Planning Community Right-to-Know Hotline CERCLA (SARA, Title III) 8:30 AM–7:30 PM ET	1-800-424-9346
EPA Hotline (Region V)	1-800-621-8431
EPA RCRA, Superfund, Hazardous Waste Hotline Office of Solid Waste and Emergency Response 8:30 AM–7:30 PM ET	1-800-424-9346
National Response Center/Coast Guard Command (Report spills, chemical releases, radiological incidents)	1-800-424-8802
Solid Waste Assistance Program	1-800-677-9424

ORGANIZATIONS

Environmental Protection Agency (EPA)
1200 Pennsylvania, NW
Washington, DC 20460   1-202-260-2090

EPA Web Site   www.epa.gov

EPA Region 1	(Boston, Massachusetts)	1-617-918-1111
EPA Region 2	(New York, New York)	1-212-637-3000
EPA Region 3	(Philadelphia, Pennsylvania)	1-215-814-5000
EPA Region 4	(Atlanta, Georgia)	1-404-562-9900

EPA Region 5 (Chicago, Illinois)   1-312-353-2000
EPA Region 6 (Dallas, Texas)   1-214-665-6444
EPA Region 7 (Kansas City, Kansas)   1-913-551-7003
EPA Region 8 (Denver, Colorado)   1-303-312-6312
EPA Region 9 (San Francisco, California)   1-415-947-8000
EPA Region 10 (Seattle, Washington)   1-206-553-1200

Public Information Center
401 M Street SW
Washington, DC 20460   1-202-260-7751

This EPA subsidiary maintains a wide selection of publications on major environmental topics. The materials distributed by PIC are nontechnical, and have been prepared as sources of general environmental information for the public.

RCRA Docket Information Center (RIC)
U.S. Environmental Protection Agency
RCRA Docket Information Center (5305W)
401 M Street, SW.
Washington, DC 20460   1-703-603-9230

Holds and provides public access to all regulatory materials on solid waste and distributes technical and nontechnical information on solid waste.

U.S. Government Printing Office
Superintendent of Documents
Post Office Box 371954
Pittsburgh, PA 15250-7954   1-202-512-1800

More than 15,000 books, pamphlets, posters, periodicals, subscription services, and other government publications are available for purchase from the Superintendent of Documents.

U.S. Department of Labor
Occupational Safety and Health Administration
200 Constitution Avenue, N.W.   1-202-693-2000
Washington, D.C. 20210   www.osha.gov

U.S. Department of Transportation
Hazardous Material Information Center   1-800-467-4922
Department of Energy – EH&S Home Page   www.tis.eh.doe.gov
Environmental Industry Web Site   www.enviroindustry.com

PROFESSIONAL SOCIETIES/ASSOCIATIONS and PRIVATE AGENCIES

Alliance of Hazardous Materials Professionals (AHMP)
Post Office Box 1216
Rockville, Maryland 20849   1-800-437-0137
Home Page   www.achmm.org

Established in 1985, the AHMP is a nonprofit membership organization dedicated to fostering professional development through continuing education, peer group interaction, the exchange of ideas, and information relating to hazardous materials management.

Air and Waste Management Association
1 Gateway Center, 3rd Floor
420 Fort Duquesne Boulevard
Pittsburgh, Pennsylvania 15222   1-412-232-3444
Home Page   www.awma.org

The Air and Waste Management Association is a nonprofit technical, scientific and educational organization with more than 14,000 members in 65 countries. Founded in 1907, the Association provides a forum where all viewpoints of an environmental issue (technical, scientific, economic, social, political, and risk assessment) receive consideration.

American Society of Safety Engineers
Environmental Practice Specialty
1800 East Oakton Street
Des Plaines, Illinois 60018-2187   1-847-699-2929
Home Page   www.ASSE.org

The ASSE Environmental Practice Specialty targets members with formal education and experience in safety management, engineering, chemistry, health, physics, toxicology, management, and training.

Environmental Document Service
Ben Franklin Station
Post Office Box 7167
Washington, DC 20044   1-800-424-9068

A document service providing copies of environmental legislation, legal decisions and court filings, EPA rules, Superfund plans, and policy statements and directives.

Environmental Hazards Management Institute
10 Newmarket Road
Post Office Box 932
Durham, North Carolina 03824   1-603-868-1496

A nonprofit environmental consulting corporation specializing in environmental and regulatory education and compliance assistance. Publishes the *Household Hazardous Waste Wheel*.

National Recycling Coalition, Inc.
1325 G Street NW, Ste. 1025
Washington, DC 20005   1-202-347-0450

Washington, DC-based association whose members distill, blend, recover, or recycle used chemicals and other hazardous and nonhazardous wastes.

APPENDIX C: LOVE CANAL—AN ENVIRONMENTAL TRAGEDY

Love Canal was originally meant to be a dream community. Instead, it is one of the most appalling U.S. environmental tragedies.

The vision of Love Canal belonged to the man for whom the three-block tract of the eastern edge of Niagara Falls, New York, was named: William T. Love. He thought that, by digging a short canal between the upper and lower Niagara River, inexpensive power could be generated to fuel the industry and homes there, and it would become a model city.

By 1910, the dream was shattered, and all that was left to commemorate Love's hope was a partial ditch where construction on the canal had begun. In the 1920s the canal was turned into a municipal and industrial dumpsite. In 1953, the Hooker Chemical Company, then owners and operators of the property, covered the canal with earth and sold it to the city for one dollar. It was a bad buy. In the late 1950s, about 100 homes and a school were built at the site. It wasn't Love's model city, but it was a solid working-class community, at least for a short while. On August 1, 1978, the lead paragraph of a story in the *New York Times* read:

> In an article prepared for the February 1978 EPA Journal, EPA Administrator for Region 2 Eckardt C. Beck wrote, regarding chemical dumpsites in general, that "even though some of these landfills have been closed down, they may stand like ticking time bombs." Just months later, Love Canal exploded. The explosion was triggered by a record amount of rainfall. Shortly thereafter the leaching began.

Twenty-five years after the Hooker Chemical Company stopped using the Love Canal as an industrial dump, 82 compounds, 11 of them suspected carcinogens, had been percolating upward through the soil and leached their contents into the backyards and basements of 100 homes and a public school built on the banks of the canal. Unusually high amounts of birth defects and miscarriages, as well as high white blood cell counts in the population, forced the New York State Health Department to respond and inquire about what was happening.

On August 7, 1978, then New York Governor Hugh Carey announced to the residents of the Canal that the state government would purchase the homes affected by the chemicals. State figures showed more than 200 homes were purchased, and all families were moved from the contaminated land.

On that same day, President Jimmy Carter approved emergency financial aid for the Love Canal area (the first emergency funds ever to be approved for a non-natural disaster).

Hazardous Material Spills and Response

5

George and Cherie Walton

LEARNING OBJECTIVES

- Identify the three federal agencies that regulate some aspect of hazardous material spills and releases and understand the basic roles of each.

- Gain an awareness of the various types of federal, public, private, and community sources of information and other assets.

- Know what types and sizes of spills or releases must be reported and to whom they must be reported.

- Gain a basic understanding of terms and concepts that relate to hazardous materials.

- Be able to perform a hazard assessment, and then develop and implement a site-specific emergency response plan.

- Understand federal hazardous materials training requirements.

- Learn the terms used in planning for and conducting responses to hazardous material spills or releases.

THE THREE PRIMARY agencies at the federal level that promulgate and enforce laws and regulations relating to spills and releases of hazardous materials are the U.S. Department of Transportation (DOT), the Environmental Protection Agency (EPA), and the Occupational Safety and Health Administration (OSHA). Because these regulations tend to intertwine and overlap, it is important to gain a general understanding of the role of each agency. The information that follows consists of significantly condensed overviews of the regulations. Complete information can be found in the appropriate section of the Code of Federal Regulations (CFR), published by the Government Printing Office.

Individual states have the right to promulgate and enforce standards that are stricter than the federal rules, except in the case of DOT regulations. According to 49 CFR 171.1(f), states may not impose provisions that are substantially different from any hazardous materials transportation law, regulation, or directive issued by the Secretary of Homeland Security.

In general, OSHA regulations apply to the safety and health of workers involved in spill clean up; EPA regulations apply to protection of the environment during and after the spill (including treatment and disposal of waste products and residues); and DOT regulations apply to the transportation of hazardous materials and waste resulting from the spill. As previously stated, agency regulations tend to overlap at times. For example, parts of DOT regulations are incorporated into EPA regulations and vice versa, and OSHA promulgated and enforces the *Hazardous Waste Operations and Emergency Response* (HAZWOPER) standard under a mandate from EPA. The resolution of any spill or release is likely to be governed by more than one federal agency as well as state and local agencies.

DEPARTMENT OF TRANSPORTATION

The mission of DOT as stated on its Web site at www.dot.gov/mission.htm is to "Serve the United States by ensuring a fast, safe, efficient, accessible and convenient transportation system that meets our vital national interests and enhances the quality of life of the American people, today and into the future."

DOT is composed of thirteen departments, nine of which are major modal, multimodal, and/or intermodal agencies. Of these agencies, the Pipeline and Hazardous Materials Safety Administration (PHMSA) provides many transportation-related safety and research services. Within PHMSA the Office of Hazardous Materials Safety is responsible for most of the regulations concerning the packaging and transportation of hazardous materials and hazardous waste in commerce.

DOT divides hazardous materials into hazard classes and divisions. A hazard class is a single-digit number—3 or 8, for example. Some hazard classes are further divided into divisions. Gases, for example, may be flammable, nonflammable, or toxic (poisonous, or pose an inhalation hazard). The general hazard class for all gases is 2. Specific hazards within the class are listed in specific divisions: flammable gases are in division 2.1; nonflammable gases are in division 2.2; and toxic, poisonous, or inhalation gases are in division 2.3.

Gases and liquids that pose an acute inhalation hazard are assigned to a Hazard Zone. In 49 CFR 171.8, "Definitions and Abbreviations," DOT defines "Hazard Zone" as one of four levels of hazard (Hazard Zones A through D) assigned to gases, as specified in 49 CFR 173.116(a), and one of two levels of hazards (Hazard Zones A and B) assigned to liquids that are poisonous by inhalation, outlined in 49 CFR 173.133(a). As specified in 49 CFR 173.133(a), the hazard zone is based on the LC_{50} value for acute inhalation toxicity of gases and vapors.

Federal Hazardous Materials Transportation Law

The hazardous materials transported in the United States are regulated by the U.S. Department of Transportation. The primary purposes of these regulations are to provide regulatory and enforcement authority to DOT to protect against the inherent risks during the transportation of hazardous materials in commerce. The Hazardous Materials Regulations (HMR) can be found in section 49 of the Code of Federal Regulations, Parts 171–178, which is generally written as 49 CFR 171–178.

The Hazardous Materials Transportation–Uniform Safety Act (HMT–USA) was enacted by Congress in 1990 to clarify conflicting state, local, and federal regulations. Additionally, this statute provides for the regulation of the transportation of radioactive materials and provides criteria for the issuance of federal permits to motor carriers of hazardous materials.

Transportation Security

Hazardous material shipments are very vulnerable when in transit. Without adequate security, tens of thousands of pounds of hazardous materials are accessible to unscrupulous individuals and groups. Some potential security risks include the theft or hijacking of vehicles carrying hazardous materials, tampering with valves on trucks or valves at tank farms, tampering with railroad equipment and cars, and tampering with other bulk transportation equipment. Additionally, forged shipping papers and fraudulent shipments of hazardous materials can put these materials in the wrong hands.

Written transportation security plans are required for organizations that offer or transport hazardous materials in commerce. The Department of Transportation's Pipeline and Hazardous Materials Safety Administration's *Hazardous Materials: Risk-Based Adjustment of Transportation Security Plan Requirements*, effective October 1, 2010, expands the requirement for shippers to prepare security plans. The current requirements for security plans include all placarded shipments as well as a "large bulk quantity" of hazardous materials. A *large bulk quantity* is any amount greater than 3000 kilograms (6614 pounds) of solids or 3000 liters (792 gallons) for liquids or gases in a single packaging, such as a cargo-tank motor vehicle, portable tank, tank car, or other bulk container.

DOT requires transportation security awareness training for all hazmat employees and in-depth security training for employees of an employer that is required to have a transportation security plan. General hazardous material training requirements are listed at 49 CFR 172.704. Detailed security training requirements are listed at 49 CFR 172.704 (a)(4) and (5) and 172.800.

DOT also requires that shippers of hazardous materials provide a 24-hour emergency telephone number on shipping papers (49 CFR 172.201(d)), so that in the event of an accident involving hazardous materials, 24-hour help is available. A helpful resource available from DOT is the *Emergency Response Guidebook*, which is designed to aid responders to hazardous material releases.

ENVIRONMENTAL PROTECTION AGENCY

The mission of the EPA, as shown at www.epa.gov, is to protect human health and the environment. EPA is a vast organization with many agencies that directly or indirectly oversee the management of hazardous material spills and releases. Of the federal agencies, EPA was the first to formalize emergency planning requirements. It is the controlling agency for most spills on land. Several branches of the EPA have separate spill prevention and reporting requirements for those facilities that manufacture or use certain chemicals. Some of the major laws and regulations are discussed below.

The Comprehensive Environmental Response, Compensation, and Liability Act (CERCLA)

CERCLA, commonly known as Superfund, was signed into law by Congress in 1980. This law imposed a tax on the petroleum and chemical industries that went into a trust fund for cleaning up abandoned or uncontrolled hazardous waste sites. CERCLA also gave the federal government authority to respond directly to releases or threatened releases of hazardous substances that may endanger human health or the environment and to provide for legal and financial liability of those responsible for releases of hazardous waste at these sites. In 1986, CERCLA was amended by the Superfund Amendments and Reauthorization Act (SARA). The most significant short-term effect of SARA was to increase the size of the clean-up trust fund to $8.5 billion.

EPA developed a list of chemicals, which, when released, could cause serious harm to human health and the environment. Facilities having any of these acutely toxic substances on site at any one time, above certain threshold levels, are subject to the emergency planning provisions of SARA Title III. SARA Title III is composed of four parts:

- Sections 301–303: These sections provide for the establishment of state emergency response commissions (SERCs) and local emergency planning committees (LEPCs).
- Section 304: This section states that facilities must notify the proper agencies if there is a release of a hazardous substance that exceeds the reportable quantity for that substance. The lists of chemicals are found at 40 CFR 355 and 40 CFR 302.4.
- Sections 311–312 (Community Right-to-Know) Reporting Requirements: This section requires that material safety data sheets (MSDSs) be submitted to the local emergency planning committee, state emergency response commission, and the local fire department. These reports are called Tier I and Tier II reports. Facilities do not have to submit reports if they have less than 500 pounds or the threshold planning quantity (whichever is less) of extremely hazardous substances—or have less than 10,000 pounds of hazardous chemicals, as defined by OSHA's *Hazard Communication Standard*.
- Section 313: This section provides for annual reporting requirements for companies that manufacture, process, or use a listed material in quantities greater than specific threshold quantities. Approximately 175 of the Section 313 toxic chemicals have been designated "Section 313 Water Priority Chemicals." Regulated facilities must meet the minimum pollution prevention plan requirements and must also comply with special provisions for areas where water priority chemicals are stored, processed, or otherwise handled. These provisions include standards for appropriate containment, drainage control, and diversionary structures.

The Resource Conservation and Recovery Act (RCRA)

RCRA was passed by Congress in 1976. Its primary goals are to ensure that all wastes are managed in a way that protects human health and the environment, to promote waste reduction and minimization, and to encourage recycling and recovery of energy and natural resources. RCRA regulations provide for cradle-to-grave management of hazardous wastes, imposing regulations on those who generate, transport, treat, store, dispose of, and recycle hazardous waste.

Clean Air Act (CAA)

The Clean Air Act of 1990, along with other EPA regulations, set minimum pollution guidelines. All states have developed and implemented EPA-approved state implementation plans (SIPs), which detail how each state administers CAA regulations. It is the CAA that requires "air" permits for those who discharge certain pollutants into the air.

Clean Water Act (CWA)

The CWA was originally called the Federal Water Pollution Control Act Amendments of 1972. After it was amended in 1977, it was more commonly called the Clean Water Act. The CWA sets standards for surface water quality and industrial wastewater discharges. The Spill Prevention, Control, and Countermeasures (SPCC) regulation (40 CFR 112) was created in 1973 under authority of the Clean Water Act. This regulation established spill prevention procedures, methods, and equipment requirements for nontransportation-related facilities with aboveground oil storage capacity greater than 1320 gallons (or greater than 660 gallons aboveground in a single tank) or underground oil storage capacity greater than 42,000 gallons. Facilities regulated by SPCC include those at which an accidental discharge could reasonably be expected to reach navigable waters. These accidents might include facilities where, in the event of a spill, rainwater could wash the spill into a stream or enter the groundwater.

The CWA also established the National Pollutant Discharge Elimination System (NPDES) permit (40 CFR 122), a nationwide program that regulates the sources of discharged pollutants into waters. Under the authority of the Clean Water Act, EPA requires facilities to develop and implement stormwater pollution prevention plans and conduct site inspections. Facilities subject to SARA Title III are also subject to additional NPDES requirements. Many individual states oversee implementation and administration of this program in their state.

Oil Pollution Act (OPA)

OPA contains provisions for facilities and vessels that have the potential to discharge oil. The significance of OPA is that it establishes civil, criminal, and financial liability to the responsible party of facilities and vessels from which oil is discharged (or which pose a substantial threat of oil discharge). Responsible parties must demonstrate evidence of financial responsibility and are liable for most costs resulting from a spill or discharge of oil. OPA also establishes requirements for contingency and emergency response plans.

OCCUPATIONAL SAFETY AND HEALTH ADMINISTRATION

OSHA's Web site states that its primary goal is to protect worker safety and health (www.osha.gov/oshinfo/mission.htm). To this end, OSHA has promulgated regulations concerning numerous specific occupational safety and health hazards. In the event that a particular hazard is not directly covered by a standard, the Occupational Safety and Health Act contains a General Duty Clause that requires all American employers to provide a workplace free of recognized hazards that cause, or are likely to cause, serious harm or death to employees. The two most relevant OSHA standards pertaining to spills and releases of hazardous materials are the *Hazard Communication Standard* (HCS) and *Hazardous Waste Operations and Emergency Response* (HAZWOPER).

The Hazard Communication Standard (HCS)

The primary goal of the HCS (29 CFR 1910.1200) is to reduce the number of chemically related occupational illnesses and injuries. Employers who use hazardous chemicals must have on hand a written program that provides information to employees who may be exposed to hazardous chemicals under normal conditions or in a foreseeable emergency. The program must include a determination of the hazards present in the workplace and discuss measures that employees must take to protect themselves against those hazards, thus reducing exposure to hazardous chemicals. The HCS also requires employers to maintain copies of material safety data sheets (MSDSs) on each chemical they use.

When a good hazard communication program has been developed and implemented in the workplace, workers will be able to protect themselves in the event of a small spill. They will know how to find, read, and interpret pertinent information on MSDSs. They will have been trained on labeling/hazard recognition and will know what kind of personal protective equipment they need to protect themselves from the chemical hazards presented by the spill.

As of early 2010, OSHA is proposing to change the requirements of the HCS to comply with the recommendations of the *Global Harmonization System* (GHS) proposed by the United Nations. The proposed changes include changing the name and format of MSDS, additional hazard categories and rankings, and new labels (pictograms). Additional information may be found on OSHA's Web site at www.osha.gov/dsg/hazcom/ghs.html.

Hazardous Waste Operations and Emergency Response

As the name implies, the HAZWOPER standard (29 CFR 1910.120) covers two major categories of workers: those whose primary function is to perform hazardous waste operations and those who perform emergency response. Emergency response includes work relating to actual or threatened releases of hazardous substances regardless of the location of the hazard. Hazardous waste operations include the following:

- hazardous substance clean-up operations required by a governmental body at uncontrolled hazardous waste sites, including initial hazard investigations at government-identified sites
- clean ups at RCRA sites
- voluntary clean up of uncontrolled hazardous waste sites
- hazardous waste operations that are conducted at RCRA treatment, storage, and disposal (TSD) facilities
- emergency responses without regard to location

An *uncontrolled hazardous waste site* is an area on either public or private land where the presence of hazardous substances creates a threat to people or the environment. To be considered an uncontrolled hazardous waste site, the site must be designated as such by a federal, state, or local government agency.

As used by OSHA, the term *emergency response* alludes to response efforts by employees or others (such as the local fire department) from outside the immediate release area to an emergency that results, or could result, in an uncontrolled release of a hazardous substance. Generally speaking, if the spill or other release is incidental and can be managed by employees in the immediate area or by maintenance personnel, the response effort is not covered under this standard, but it would still be covered under the HCS and perhaps under other standards, depending on the circumstances.

There are exceptions to the standards and regulations, so one must always read the full standard or regulation carefully to determine which parts apply to one's particular situation. For example, under certain conditions, conditionally exempt small-quantity generators do not have to comply with parts of the HAZWOPER standard.

The HAZWOPER standard specifies that an employer should have an emergency response plan in effect that would include pre-emergency planning; required training, personnel roles, all lines of authority, and communication; emergency recognition and prevention; designated safe distances and places of refuge; site security and control; evacuation routes and procedures; any decontamination procedures that are not covered by the employer's comprehensive site safety and health plan; provisions for emergency medical treatment and first aid; emergency alerting and response procedures; lists of personal protective and emergency equipment; and a critique of response and follow up.

In practical terms, the HCS mandates that employers have an MSDS for all hazardous materials used in the workplace, and that all employees must be trained on the nature of the hazards and how to protect themselves from those hazards. The HAZWOPER standard addresses pre-emergency planning, emergency equipment and procedures, and training for personnel. If all employers develop and implement the plans, programs, and training required by these two standards, spills and other releases—whether small or large—will likely be managed in a safe and efficient manner.

FEDERAL ASSETS AND SOURCES OF INFORMATION

Two essential requirements for any hazardous material spill response planner are: (1) technical details and properties of the materials for which the plan is being developed and (2) a sense of how the operation should be conducted—an operational definition of *good*. There are several federal government Web sites that provide information to meet both of these requirements.

These Web sites are useful for new planners who are looking for basic information as well as for personnel revising or updating existing plans. The list below is not intended to be exhaustive, but rather to provide entry onto the information superhighway.

Organization: Agency for Toxic Substances and Disease Registry

Web site: www.atsdr.cdc.gov
Typical information:
- Hazardous substances
  - ToxFAQs: These are chemical-specific fact sheets that provide answers to frequently asked questions about exposures to hazardous substances found around hazardous waste sites and the effects of exposure on human health.
- Information Sources
  - The HazDat database includes the hazardous substances release and health effects database.
- Emergency Response
  - This provides information on training recommendations and technical databases for hazardous substances.
- Publications
  - These are lists of publications available for downloading or in printed format.

Organization: Centers for Disease Control and Prevention

Web site: www.cdc.gov
Typical information:
- Health and Safety Topics
  - These topics cover emergency preparedness and response, including preparation and planning information and chemical emergency information.
  - The focus is often on chemical emergencies, including an MSDS database from the Department of Energy.

Organization: Department of Justice

Web site: www.justnet.org
Typical information:

The basic concepts in numerous publications are based on the needs of law enforcement and corrections, but the documents provide concise and useful information for planners and emergency responders.

- Publications
  - *Draft NIJ CBRN Protective Ensembles for Law Enforcement*
  - *Comparative Evaluation of Protective Gloves for Law Enforcement and Correction Applications*
  - *Guidance on Emergency Responder Personal Protective Equipment (PPE) for Response to CBRN Terrorism Incidents*
  - *Guidance for the Selection of Chemical and Biological Decontamination Equipment for Emergency First Responders*

Organization: Department of Transportation

Web site: www.phmsa.dot.gov
Typical Information:

Emergency Response Guidebook (ERG). This emergency responders' guide is intended to assist in quickly identifying the specific or generic characterization of a hazardous material in an incident and to assist in protecting emergency responders during the initial response phases of an incident.

Organization: Federal Emergency Management Agency

Web site: www.fema.gov and www.usfa.fema.gov (U.S. Fire Administration)

Typical information:

–Typical information covered is incident management, including information on creating response management systems and coordinating plans with local and federal agencies.

Organization: National Institute of Occupational Safety and Health (NIOSH)

Web site: www.cdc.gov/niosh

Typical information:

NIOSH Pocket Guide to Chemical Hazards (NPG). This is a concise source of general industrial hygiene information for workers, employers, and occupational health professionals on 677 chemicals or substances commonly found in the work environment.

Organization: Occupational Safety and Health Administration (U.S. Department of Labor)

Web site: www.osha.gov/dep/etools

Typical information:

–Information covered is the Health and Safety Program, electronic format (e-HASP). An important message is that a safe response must be a planned response. This site shows than an excellent tool either for drafting new health and safety plans or for reviewing existing plans is the electronic health and safety plan. The following is a brief outline of the online plan. See the *E-Hasp$_2$ Software User's Manual* for complete information and details on each element.

- Organizational Structure: Documents how the authority, responsibility, and duties are divided among the various agencies and members of a response team.
- Job Hazard Analysis (JHA): This is a technique used to help identify, then reduce or eliminate, hazards. JHAs focus on the relationship between the worker, the task, the tools, and the work environment.
- Site Control: This plan shows how to define boundaries of contaminated zones and work areas. It also explains how to identify safe work practices, methods of routine and emergency communication, methods of controlling entry into contaminated areas, and methods of controlling the migration of site contaminants.
- Training Program: The training program identifies the jobs and tasks that require training, and how much and what type of training is needed for each. It describes how changing site-specific conditions or information will be communicated to employees and other site workers. It also tells where and how training documentation will be maintained.
- Medical Surveillance Requirements: This aspect describes various requirements and techniques, such as physical examinations, biological testing, the collection of workplace exposure data, and other needs that are mandated by various OSHA standards. A good resource for medical surveillance information is the Web site www.osha.gov/SLTC/medicalsurveillance/index.html.
- Personal Protective Equipment (PPE): What is described here is how PPE is selected, fit, used, stored, and maintained. This site tells how personnel will be trained for proper use and how one can ensure that workers are physically capable of using PPE under routine and extreme conditions, such as during emergencies or periods of extreme heat or cold.
- Exposure Monitoring: This part discusses how and when monitoring for hazardous

contaminants will be conducted. Included is a discussion of the monitoring instruments that will be used and how they will be calibrated and maintained. If an accredited analytical laboratory will be used, one can find how to describe sampling procedures and sample handling procedures.
- Thermal Stress: This describes measures to be taken to protect site workers from the effects of heat and cold stressors.
- Spill Containment Program: What is provided here is detailed information about the actions that will be taken in the event of a spill or a leak. Included is information about the equipment that is to be used to control and contain the released material; where tools and equipment are located; the personnel who are to respond; how and when to obtain off-site assistance; and other site-specific information.
- Decontamination Program: Described here are procedures to decontaminate personnel and equipment. Also explained is how disposable and reusable equipment will be managed and how to ensure decontamination is effective.
- Emergency Response Plan: This is a written plan that identifies the actions employees will take in the event of a chemical release, fire, accident, injury, or other type of emergency that may occur at the site.
- Standard Operating Procedures: Here, one can learn how to develop procedures to ensure safe, consistent, work practices that will minimize employee contact with hazardous substances and provide compliance with applicable standards and regulations.
- Confined Space Programs: If confined spaces are a potential site hazard, refer to 29 CFR 1910.146, Permit-Required Confined Spaces, to determine whether the circumstances necessitate the development and implementation of a written, confined-space-entry program.
- Hot Work: If welding, cutting, or other hot work is to be performed at the site, develop safety and operating procedures; list worker roles and responsibilities, and describe the location(s) where the hot work is to be conducted.
- Lockout/Tagout: If applicable, and based on site conditions, one can develop specific procedures that can be used to protect workers from the unexpected start up or energization of machinery and equipment and from the release of hazardous energy during equipment maintenance or other activities where energy could be suddenly released.

Organization: U.S. Coast Guard

Web site: www.uscg.mil/vrp

Typical information:

–Shipboard Oil Pollution Emergency Plans (SOPEP) and Shipboard Marine Pollution Emergency Plans (SMPEP).
- The Oil Pollution Act of 1990 (OPA-90) and the international treaty, MARPOL 73/78, require owners/operators of certain vessels to prepare a Vessel Response Plan (VRP) and/or Shipboard Oil Pollution Emergency Plans (SOPEP) approved by the U.S. Coast Guard. In addition, for certain vessels carrying noxious liquid substances, MARPOL 73/78 requires owner/operators to prepare and submit Shipboard Marine Pollution Emergency Plans (SMPEP), effective January 1, 2003. Access to information and key elements contained in those plans is available from the above Web site.
- These plans provide lists of the types of information and formats that good plans, even those not involving marine spills, should include.

PUBLIC AND COMMUNITY ASSETS

Many public and private community assets exist, both for providing assistance in emergency spill response situations and for providing help or guidance to facilities that want to ensure that they are doing everything possible to prevent spills and respond adequately in the event of a spill or release. The following assets are examples of the types of services that could be available in your area.

Public Service Agencies

In many cases, emergency responders to large spills or transportation spills will include some type of public service agency, such as the local police, fire, and/or emergency medical service (EMS) department. Local police departments generally do not participate directly in incident management, but may assist by securing the scene, managing traffic, routing emergency equipment, or notifying other local or state emergency response agencies. Approximately 65 percent of all fire departments provide EMS services and often have hazardous material teams whose members are trained and equipped to manage many types of emergency spills and releases (BLS, 2007).

Communication and preplanning with the local fire department are often required by state or local law, usually for facilities that have larger quantities of hazardous materials. Facilities of any size that use or store materials that pose unusual hazards during a fire should coordinate with the local fire department to discuss those hazards. For example, firefighters need to know if a material is water-reactive *before* they use water to try to extinguish it. Telling them after the ensuing explosion is useless. Likewise, local doctors, hospitals, and other medical facilities should be contacted prior to an emergency and made aware of the types of injuries and illnesses they can expect to see in the event of a spill or release so they are able to prepare adequately.

Industry-Related Assets

Responsible Care® (www.responsiblecare.org) is a voluntary initiative developed by the chemical industry. The Responsible Care initiative is a comprehensive environmental, health, and safety management system composed of ten key elements through which participating companies work together to improve their environmental, safety, health, and security performance.

Many chemical companies also participate in the Community Awareness and Emergency Response (CAER) program (described at www.caer-mp.org). Each CAER member-company has developed and implemented an emergency response program that enables it to respond quickly and effectively to emergencies at its facility. CAER members also have community outreach programs to address questions and concerns about any safety, health, and environmental issues concerning their product or process.

The International Organization for Standardization (ISO) (www.iso.org) developed a set of standards—a complete management system—that helps facilities adopt a proactive approach to managing environmental issues. By developing and implementing programs and best practices found in ISO 14000 and the Occupational Health and Safety Assessment Series (OSHAS) 18000, any type of facility or organization—large or small, public or private—can improve its safety and environmental programs. Sound environmental management results in cost savings such as reduced raw materials and energy consumption and less hazardous and nonhazardous waste generation and disposal. Sound safety and environmental management will reduce the likelihood of spills and releases and result in more efficient management of incidents if and when they occur.

Community Assets

Local emergency planning committees (LEPCs) are typically composed of emergency responders (both public and private), local industry, emergency management agencies, and the community. LEPCs take an active role in community emergency planning and are responsible for developing a community emergency plan for response to chemical emergencies. They often provide services such as the review of a facility's contingency plans, public education, industry outreach, and development and implementation of emergency drills and exercises. For more information about LEPCs, or to find out what services, if any, your LEPC offers, visit www.fema.gov/hazard/hazmat/hz_cres.shtm or search for your state's Web-site listing.

Federal Notification and Reporting Requirements

The National Response Center (NRC)

The NRC is the sole federal point of contact for reporting regulated oil and chemical spills. The NRC maintains a 24-hour-per-day, 7-days-per-week, 365-days-per-year Operations Center, where all information is received via a toll-free number entered directly into an online database system, and electronically disseminated as part of the National Response System. Information such as the material involved, mode of transportation, injuries, damage, and fatalities will be disseminated to select federal agencies within 15 minutes of receipt. When any of the following incidents occur, the NRC should immediately be contacted by the responsible party via the toll-free number. Anyone who sees or discovers an oil spill or release of chemicals, even if he or she is not the responsible party, should immediately contact the NRC with whatever information is available.

- Oil spills in or along U.S. navigable waters: The definition of "navigable waters" found in 40 CFR 112.2 is rather broad and lengthy. Generally speaking, however, the term includes *all* waters that are currently used, were used in the past, or may be susceptible to use in interstate or foreign commerce, including territorial seas, rivers, ponds, streams, wetlands, wetlands adjacent to waters, lakes, impoundments, prairie potholes, wet meadows, and other areas in which the use, degradation, or destruction of which could affect interstate or foreign commerce.
- CERCLA requires that all releases of hazardous substances exceeding reportable quantities be reported by the responsible party to the NRC. Title 40 CFR Part 302 promulgates reportable quantities and reporting criteria. All the Extremely Hazardous Substances (EHS) that overlap with the CERCLA-listed chemicals table (40 CFR Part 302.4) should also be reported.
- Certain transportation accidents (see below under Department of Transportation).
- Others, including gas and liquid pipeline releases and discharges from a hazardous waste treatment or storage facility. Abandoned dump or waste sites should be reported by anyone having knowledge of such a site.

Department of Transportation

To comply with 49 CFR 171.15, incidents of the following types that occur during the loading, unloading, or storage of hazardous materials in commerce must be reported to the NRC by telephone by the person who has physical possession of the hazardous material(s) as soon as possible, but no later than 12 hours after the incident:

1. Incidents where, as a direct result of a hazardous material,
   - a person is killed
   - a person receives an injury requiring admittance to a hospital
   - the general public is evacuated for an hour or longer
   - a major transportation artery or facility is closed or shut down for at least an hour or the operational flight pattern or routine of an aircraft is altered
2. Incidents where breakage, spillage, or suspected radioactive contamination occurs involving a radioactive material
3. Incidents where breakage, spillage, or suspected contamination occurs involving an infectious substance other than a diagnostic specimen or regulated medical waste
4. Incidents where a release of a marine pollutant occurs in a quantity exceeding 119 gallons (450 L) for a liquid or 882 pounds (400 kg) for a solid
5. Incidents where a situation exists of such a nature that, in the judgment of the person in possession of the hazardous material, it should be reported to the National Response Center, even if it does not meet the above criteria

For incidents involving infectious substances, the report may instead be forwarded to the Centers for Disease Control and Prevention in Atlanta, Georgia, at (800)232-0124. Each report must include the following information:

- name of the reporter
- name and address of the person represented by the reporter
- telephone number where the reporter can be contacted
- date, time, and location of the incident
- extent of injury, if any
- if available, the proper shipping name, hazard class or division, and quantity of hazardous material involved
- type of incident and nature of hazardous material involvement and whether a continuing danger to life exists at the scene

Within 30 days of the incident, the person who makes the report must also file a written report on DOT Form F 5800.1.

DOT also requires that a written report be made when there has been an unintentional release of hazardous materials from a package (including a tank), or when any quantity of hazardous waste has been unintentionally discharged during transportation. Reports of hazardous waste discharges must include a copy of the hazardous waste manifest and other information, such as an estimate of the quantity of the waste removed from the scene, the name and address of the facility to which it was taken, and the manner of disposition of any removed waste. There are some exceptions to the reporting requirements, so refer to the full text of 49 CFR 171.16 for details.

Environmental Protection Agency

Under 40 CFR 302.6, EPA requires persons in charge of facilities (including transport vehicles, vessels, and aircraft) to report any release of a hazardous substance in a quantity equal to or greater than its reportable quantity, as soon as that person has knowledge of the release, to the National Response Center at (800)424-8802 or (202) 267-2675. The term *reportable quantity* (RQ) means the quantity, as set forth in 40 CFR 302, the release of which requires notification pursuant to the regulations contained in 40 CFR 302.

STATE REQUIREMENTS
Federal "States' Rights" Legislation

Some environmental laws are national in applicability. Deviations from these federal laws are not allowed. For example, transportation laws regulating hazardous materials may not be altered. All states must follow DOT regulations and standards because only Congress, as authorized by the U.S. Constitution, may regulate commerce between states. Bulk and nonbulk packages of hazardous materials must meet the manufacturing and quality assurance standards set by DOT at 49 CFR 178. Labels and placards must meet federal specifications set by DOT at 49 CFR 172. Some laws, however, allow states to add to, but not delete from, federal standards. For example, the document that must accompany shipments of hazardous waste—the Uniform Hazardous Waste Manifest (40 CFR 262)—was created by the Resource Conservation and Recovery Act (RCRA). All states must use the Uniform Hazardous Waste Manifest, but space is allotted on the form for state-specific waste codes. Lists of state-specific variations and additions are available at EPA regional offices or state environmental compliance agencies.

At the federal level, generators of hazardous waste may not store hazardous waste more than 90 days with a storage permit. Generators, at the federal level, may, however, use satellite accumulation areas, at or near the point of waste generation and under the control of the operator of the process generating the waste, to accumulate up to 55 gallons of waste without a time limit. Some states, however, do not allow satellite sites. In those jurisdictions, generators must ship all waste off site within 90 days or obtain a storage permit. This interplay of federal regulations and state-specific requirements tends to confound spill response plans and procedures because states and regional authorities within states may set specific standards that differ from federal requirements. Many state and federal regulations contain provisions for resolving conflicts between regulatory bodies. In the case of contradictory requirements, the more restrictive regulation generally applies. If in doubt, ask one or both of the agencies involved for a written, legal interpretation of the regulation(s) in question.

Personnel Licensing and Registration

Some states have established licensing and registration requirements for companies and individuals assessing the severity of a specific situation, conducting spill response operations, or determining the need for additional remediation efforts after the majority of the spilled material has been recovered or removed. For example, California's Environmental Protection Agency Department of Toxic Substances Control has published a *Preliminary Endangerment Assessment Guidance Manual*. Only individuals qualified as and recognized as a registered environmental assessor (REA) may complete a preliminary endangerment assessment (PEA) to determine if a spill or release site is *clean* or needs additional remediation. The Connecticut Department of Environmental Protection has established Remediation Standard Regulations. Connecticut also qualifies, tests, and recognizes environmental professionals. When organizations with only a single facility plan a spill response to include determining whether the spill or release has been remediated, contacting a single state environmental regulatory organization will be sufficient. For national organizations with facilities in numerous locations, spill response plans must include state and regional contacts, registration, and licensing requirements for specific operations and individuals. Check with your state's environmental agency to determine whether licensing or registration is required.

Notifications and Response Actions

Virtually all jurisdictions within the United States require notification of a spill or release based on the specific material(s) involved and the amount and location of the spill. The agency to which the notification is sent may be the local fire department, a state agency, or a statewide notification center. Generally, the emphasis is on responding quickly and safely to the spill or release. A spill response planner must be aware of the type(s) of notification(s) required, the organization(s) to which the notification should be sent, and the format of the notification(s), and should include this information in the spill response plan. Nationwide commercial organizations must include this information for specific facilities. Planners who write specific response plans must contact the local fire department or state environmental agency to verify reporting and notification requirements.

POST-CLEAN-UP RESPONSE REQUIREMENTS

After the initial spill response actions have been completed, there is generally a requirement to assess, examine, or test the spill site to determine whether any harmful residual levels of the spilled materials or contaminants remain. As noted earlier, various states and regional authorities may have product-specific standards in certain areas of the United States. These authorities must be consulted, and their approval, if required, obtained before any long-term remediation work is initiated. In most jurisdictions, the sampling and analytical procedures in *Test Methods for Evaluating Solid Waste* (Physical/Chemical Methods) EPA Publication SW-846 (www.epa.gov/epaoswer/hazwaste/test/main.htm) must be followed. Because sampling involves specific procedures, methods, and sometimes health or safety hazards, only personnel with the appropriate knowledge should be permitted to obtain samples. Many environmental service companies and laboratories offer sampling services. Additionally, several good references are available. One is EPA publication EPA530-D-02-002, *RCRA Waste Sampling Draft Technical Guidance—Planning, Implementation, and Assessment* (August 2002). Another good resource is *ASTM Standards on Environmental Sampling*, now in its third edition (2006), which is published by ASTM International (www.astm.org).

For any post-clean-up issues concerning building safety or reoccupancy, consult local building codes or contact the local fire department for guidance.

Soil Decontamination

Soil decontamination is important for its own sake as well as to prevent cross-media contamination. Spill residues entrained in soil may volatilize and become airborne clouds of gases and vapors. On the other hand, contaminated soil may dry and be displaced by the wind, creating clouds of hazardous particulate matter. Soils highly contaminated by releases or spills may be removed during the emergency phase of the response, making decontamination a moot point. More likely, low levels of contamination will exist on the horizontal and vertical peripheries of the spill. Those are the soils that must be decontaminated. As in all phases of spill response, knowing the nature of the contaminant may indicate the type of decontamination that will be most efficient. Some heavy metals, such as arsenic, tend to be relatively soluble and migrate through the soil. Thus a 100-square-foot area of arsenic-contaminated soil after a spill may become a 1000-square-foot decontamination problem if not addressed quickly. Dense nonaqueous-phase liquids (DNAPLs) will migrate through soil, sink through the groundwater in the saturated soil zones, and cause both soil and groundwater decontamination problems.

A spill of elemental or white phosphorus results in extensive soil contamination. Because white phosphorus is a spontaneously combustible material, repeatedly tilling the contaminated area over a period of weeks forces the phosphorus to the surface, where it simply burns itself out. In a case like this, cross-media contamination (air contaminated by burning phosphorus) is determined to be less of a human and environmental health and safety concern than allowing the phosphorus to remain in place.

Groundwater

Groundwater decontamination is nearly always difficult. Especially in the case of sole-source aquifers, contamination must be reduced to extremely low levels. This reduction may be accomplished by pumping the contaminated groundwater to surface treatment units or, in some situations, by biological or chemical processes, using bacteria to degrade the contamination in place, or using chemicals to either oxidize or reduce the contamination. Depending on soil conditions, it may be necessary to inject the decontaminating chemicals directly into the groundwater. Or, it may be more efficient to build porous barriers in the soil, allowing contaminated groundwater to flow through the decontaminating barrier or reactive zone. The contaminants will be oxidized or reduced as they are carried by the water through these subsurface structures.

Building and Equipment

There are some specific clean-up standards in EPA regulations. The clean-up standard for polychlorinated biphenyls (PCBs), for example, is published at 40 CFR 761 and includes acceptable residual levels of PCBs. Experience often has shown, however, that there is no specific standard. Cleaning to background levels or method detection limits in SW-846 may be extremely expensive without providing any benefit to human health or the environment. OSHA standards may be used to provide some guidance for decontamination in industrial or commercial facilities. Recognizing human health and safety are the primary concerns; there will probably be requirements to clean processing equipment so that manufactured goods meet specifications and are not contaminated with spill residues.

APPLIED SCIENTIFIC AND ENGINEERING PRINCIPLES IN ENVIRONMENTAL MANAGEMENT

Chemical and Physical Properties of Hazardous Materials

The physical state of the material being dealt with will often determine the seriousness of a spill or release. Solids tend not to disperse as rapidly in the environment as liquids or vapors. Powdered solids, however, may become airborne quickly and create contaminated environments, both locally affecting spill response workers and, downwind from the release site, creating hazardous areas for people, the environment, and continuing operations.

When *water-insoluble liquids* that are lighter than water are spilled on water, they tend to spread over wide areas because these materials are dispersed by wind, current, or tidal flow. Water-insoluble liquids that are heavier than water tend to sink directly to the bottom and may form localized, concentrated, highly contaminated areas. The extent of the contamination depends to a large extent on bottom conditions and current characteristics.

Water-soluble liquids, when spilled on water, may be impossible to remove from the environment completely because the entire water column, from top to bottom, is contaminated. Water-soluble liquids, when spilled on soil, tend either to permeate the soil or to dissolve in precipitation and sink into the soil until groundwater is encountered. They tend to contaminate large areas.

Water-insoluble liquids spilled on soil tend to spread more slowly than water-soluble materials. These contaminated areas will be relatively small.

Water-soluble solids, when spilled on water, may be impossible to remove. As with water-soluble liquids, they contaminate the entire water column. Water-insoluble solids, when spilled on water, will either float or sink. Water-insoluble solids that are lighter than water tend to spread over wide areas because these materials are dispersed by wind, current, or tidal flow. Water-insoluble solids that are heavier than water tend to sink directly to the bottom and may form localized, concentrated, highly contaminated areas.

Spilled solid materials tend not to penetrate soils very deeply. However, water-soluble solid materials that are spilled on soil may dissolve in precipitation and act as a liquid, contaminating large areas.

The *boiling point* (BP) of a liquid is the temperature at which a liquid turns to vapor. Materials with a boiling point below ambient temperatures will evaporate rapidly, forming vapor clouds that may endanger both responders and people, operations, and the environment downwind from the spill or release (Bowling Green State University 2008).

The *lower explosive limit* (LEL) and the *upper explosive limit* (UEL) establish the range of flammability. The LEL is the minimum concentration of a material in air that will support combustion, given an ignition source. A synonym for LEL is LFL (*lower flammable limit*). Below the LEL, the material-to-air mixture is too lean to burn. The UEL is the highest concentration of a material in air that will support combustion, given an ignition source. Above the UEL, the material-to-air mixture is too rich to burn.

The instrument that measures the concentration of flammable vapors in air is called a combustible gas indicator (CGI). It is generally calibrated to either methane or pentane and displays contamination as a percentage of the LEL (%LEL). The highest level that OSHA has determined as safe for entry into confined or poorly ventilated spaces is 10% LEL. CGI readings are generally displayed as large numbers—percentages in air or tens of thousands of parts per million. Permissible exposure limits (PELs) and threshold limit values (TLVs) are generally small numbers—often only tens or hundreds of parts per million. It is critical that, after an atmosphere is tested for flammability with a CGI, it is tested for low levels of hazardous vapors with direct-reading organic vapor instruments to determine proper personal protective equipment. Because a CGI measures flammability, not toxicity, a toxic atmosphere may exist, but it might not be detected.

The *flash point* (Fl. P.) of a material is the temperature at which sufficient vapors are generated to support combustion, given an ignition source. Materials with flash points well below ambient temperatures pose extreme risk of fire and explosions to response workers. An extremely low flash point often determines both what and how emergency responders conduct operations, at least until the source of the flammable vapors is controlled.

The *ionization potential* (IP) of a material is the amount of energy, measured in electron volts (eV), that is required to form an ion. An instrument commonly used during spill responses to measure vapors in air is a photo ionization detector, or PID. A PID can detect many solvents, but only if the ionization lamp in the instrument produces more electron volts than are required by the molecule(s) of concern to form ions. Thus a PID with a low energy bulb may give very low readings when in high concentrations of vapor(s) with high ionization potential(s). PIDs are commonly calibrated to isobutylene in the low parts-per-million range. One should always refer to the manufacturer's instructions when interpreting instrument readings because a specific material may cause an instrument response that is significantly different from the actual levels of contamination. PIDs can be used to determine the need for, and type of, respiratory protection.

Specific gravity (Sp. Gr.) is the weight of a material relative to water (water being defined as having a specific gravity of 1). Materials with a Sp. Gr. of less than 1 will float on water and may spread significantly from the original release site. Such materials released onto soil tend to permeate or diffuse into the soil to the top of the water table, then float on underground water. This forms large pools of contaminated water that often require extensive and lengthy remediation efforts. Materials with a Sp. Gr. greater than 1 will sink in water. If such a material is released onto surface water, clean up or removal may be impossible without herculean efforts. Materials with a Sp. Gr. greater than 1 released onto soil may permeate into the ground, sinking through groundwater until a confining layer (a layer of geologic material such as clay, rock, or compressed silt that has little or no permeability) is encountered.

Vapor density (VD), sometimes expressed as the *relative vapor density* (Rel. VD), is a ratio of the density of the released gas(es) or vapor(s) compared to air, with the density of air equaling 1. Materials with a vapor density less than 1 will tend to rise and disperse. Materials with a density greater than 1 will tend to form pockets in low or poorly ventilated areas. Thus storm drains near a spill or release may contain hazardous concentrations of spilled, high-density gases and vapors. These drains may form dispersion pathways, allowing the spilled materials to contaminate large areas. Vapor density should always be used as a very general measure of the ability of a vapor to disperse. For example, mercury has a VD of 13.5, but air currents caused by personnel walking near a spill site will cause mercury vapors to rise and disperse in air (Bowling Green State University 2008).

Vapor pressure (VP) is the pressure, generally measured in millimeters of mercury (mm Hg) in equilibrium with the liquid or solid phase of the same material. VP will affect both on-site and off-site operations. Low vapor-pressure materials may produce relatively small contaminated areas with relatively low inhalation risks and small, if any, downwind hazard areas. On the other hand, high vapor-pressure materials may create large areas of high contamination, requiring the on-site use of respiratory protection equipment for long periods. In addition, high vapor-pressure materials may create large, long-lasting hazard areas downwind of the spill site.

Viscosity is the resistance of a liquid to flow or move. Highly viscous materials cling to surfaces—including personal protective equipment worn by response workers—the soil surface, and any equipment or structure in the spill or release site. High-viscosity fluids are typically difficult to decontaminate. Low-viscosity fluids may tend to disperse rapidly on soil or surface waters.

Miscibility is the ability of two liquids to form a uniform blend. For example, the DOT *Emergency Response Guidebook* (ERG) uses miscibility in lieu of solubility. The term may be used as a synonym for *solubility*. The water solubility, or miscibility, of a spilled material affects how the material will spread from the release site. A water-miscible material that is allowed to contact water will probably never be recovered. Surface waters will spread the material, creating huge areas with huge volumes of contaminated water. Controlling access to the contaminated water until natural forces dilute the spill to acceptable levels will probably be the remediation technique used. Groundwater aquifers contaminated with a water-soluble material may be abandoned, thus requiring new water supplies. It may not be possible, in some cases, to remediate the groundwater.

Water-immiscible materials may be either lighter than water (having a specific gravity less than 1) or heavier than water (having a specific gravity greater than 1). Water-immiscible, low-specific-gravity liquids will float on surface water until they degrade or meet a physical barrier. A gasoline spill on a river is an example of a water-immiscible material. If this type of material is allowed to soak into the ground and contaminate the aquifer, extensive decontamination will be required.

Water-immiscible, high-specific-gravity materials will sink to the bottom of any body of surface water. Removing these materials may be physically and financially impossible. Contaminated sediments and sludges in industrial harbors are examples of these materials. Water-immiscible, high-specific-gravity liquids are so difficult to remove from groundwater that they have been given a specific name: *DNAPLs, or dense nonaqueous-phase liquids*. Again, time is critical. Keeping these materials contained at or near the spill site can prevent major pollution events. Responding slowly, allowing these materials to seep into the soil, can create conditions that require decades to restore or remediate.

Nature of the Spilled Material—Measures of Toxicity

Common measures of toxicity that affect an exposed population are called the lethal dose (LD) for a liquid or solid and the lethal concentration (LC) for a gas or vapor. The dose that kills 50 percent of the organisms in a test for skin contact or ingestion is called the LD_{50}. The concentration (in air) of a gas or vapor that kills 50 percent of the organisms in a test of respiratory exposure is shown as the LC_{50}. The proposed Global Harmonization System (GHS) expands the measure of toxicity to include target organ systemic toxicity (TOST) for either a single exposure or repeated exposures (UNECE 2005).

The *permissible exposure limit* (PEL) is the exposure ceiling set by OSHA that most workers can be exposed to based on 8-hour workdays and 40-hour work weeks. A PEL is measured as a *time-weighted average* (TWA). A TWA is the mathematical average value of a chemical exposure over the course of an 8-hour work shift. Longer exposure times—more than 8 hours per day or 40 hours per week—will cause an overexposure, even if the actual exposure is within permissible exposure limits.

The *threshold limit value* (TLV) is the exposure, measured as a TWA, set by the American Congress of Governmental Industrial Hygienists (ACGIH) and based on 8-hour workdays and 40-hour work weeks. Owing to differences in standard development, the TLV for a specific substance may vary significantly from the PEL. Both PELs and TLVs tend to be small numbers, measured in parts per million (ppm) or in milligrams per cubic meter (mg/m^3).

The *short-term exposure limit* (STEL) is the exposure workers may safely be exposed to under the following conditions: (a) the exposure is limited to 15 minutes, (b) the exposure at this level may not occur more than four times within an 8-hour workday, and (c) exposures at the STEL level must be separated by at least one hour. STELs must be included in any calculations for the TLV® or PEL.

Chemical levels are considered to be *immediately dangerous to life or health* (IDLH) when they are present in the atmosphere in concentrations that pose an immediate threat to life, would cause irreversible adverse health effects, or would impair an individual's ability to escape from a dangerous atmosphere. Response workers should never be allowed to enter an IDLH atmosphere without adequate personal protective equipment or without proper rescue equipment and personnel on site, who are ready to provide support to injured or trapped workers immediately.

Nature of the Affected Area or Environment—Geology and Hydrology

Near-surface soils affect the impact a spill has on the environment. Tight, nonporous, low-permeability soils tend to limit the diffusion or permeation of spills that migrate downward into the soil. Loose, porous, high-permeability soils offer little resistance to permeation or diffusion. A spill of a highly viscous material (a thick, tarlike substance) will tend to form puddles at or near the spill site on nonporous soils. Given a moderate surface slope, these materials will move slowly, if at all, down the slope or downward into the ground. On the other hand, a low-viscosity material (thin and watery, like fingernail polish remover) spilled on highly porous soil tends to move quickly down the slope and downward into the ground.

Saturated soils tend to retard the movement of water-insoluble materials into the ground. The water filling the spaces between soil particles acts like a dam, blocking the movement of spilled materials as they are pulled downward by gravity. On the other hand, saturated soils tend to accelerate the movement of water-soluble materials by acting as a dispersion pathway. The near-surface water may be connected to, and recharge, groundwater, forming a direct link between spilled materials on the surface and subsurface aquifers.

Basic soils, or soils derived from limestone, also influence how spilled materials affect the environment. Basic soils may assist in neutralizing spilled acids, minimizing the impact of the spill. Karst topography forms over limestone, dolomite, and gypsum and is characterized by sinkholes, caves, and underground drainage. This underground drainage actually allows spilled material to escape from the accident site in miles per hour in underground streams in caves.

Soils are rarely a uniform layer of a single material. Often there are lenses, beds, and other complex structures that may, in some instances, retard the movement of material away from a spill site and, in other instances, accelerate the movement of materials. Time is of the essence in spill response. A few hours' difference in response times can mean the difference between controlling a spill on or near the surface in one or two days or spending months attempting to remediate underground soils and water.

Nature of the Affected Area or Environment—Meteorology

As a general rule, the higher the ambient temperature, the faster spilled liquids tend to evaporate. Low temperatures may allow a spill response team adequate time to effectively contain spilled liquids, creating small downwind hazard areas. Higher temperatures tend to increase vapor pressure and evaporation, providing spill response teams very little time to contain and control liquid spills before a significant downwind hazard area is formed.

Some basic knowledge of atmospheric stability also can help predict the dispersion of contaminants in the atmosphere. A common classification of atmospheric stability is known as the Pasquill-Gifford (P-G) stability class system, which assigns a classification based on factors such as wind speed, solar radiation, and cloud cover. Seven classes are designated by letters: A (for unstable or turbulent conditions) through G (for very stable conditions). Sometimes the numbers 1 through 7 replace the letters. Neutral conditions are class D (or 4).

Very low winds (up to approximately 3 miles per hour) tend to limit the generation of a large downwind hazard area. High winds (above approximately 17 miles per hour) also limit the generation and spread of a large downwind hazard area. Wind speed and direction typically change after sunrise, during the warmest time of the day (approximately 10 AM to 4 PM), and after sunset.

The *Emergency Response Guidebook* (2008), available from the PHMSA Web site, uses a simplified, two-stage stability system to create protective action distances downwind from a spill site. This system consists of day (sunrise to sunset) and night. During the night, the air is generally calmer, corresponding to P-G class D to G (4 to 7) conditions. These conditions cause vapors to disperse less and therefore create a more toxic, but smaller, danger zone. During the day, P-G class A to D (1 to 4) conditions, vapors are generally dispersed by a more active atmosphere. The downwind danger zone will be larger, but generally have a lower toxicity level.

An atmospheric inversion, when warmer air aloft tends to trap cooler air near the surface, will cause large downwind hazard areas to be created quickly. Heavy cloud cover or other inversions will cause vapors or dust released from a spill to be carried miles downwind. This downwind hazard area may force the evacuation of large populations from large areas as well as posing environmental threats.

Nature of Response Operations

Ideally, a properly trained, equipped, and managed spill response team will respond instantaneously to any spill or release of a hazardous material. Unfortunately, time of day, weather conditions, spill location, and the characteristics of the material may prevent or delay response. Specific techniques and equipment used at a spill or release site must be based on actual conditions and the materials involved. In general, the following actions should be taken in any spill situation:

- Identify necessary emergency response equipment and supplies such as PPE, sorbents, hand and power tools, solvents, shovels, pumps, fire extinguishers, and any site-specific equipment or supplies and ensure that it is in good working order and readily accessible.
- Do not underestimate the seriousness of the situation. The first responders may need additional equipment, personnel, and expertise to safely and successfully respond to a situation.
- Control the leak or release as soon as possible. Small spills are always easier to clean up. Stopping the release of a material establishes safer working conditions and limits off-site effects.

- Contain spilled material. Material may escape from a spill site by numerous pathways. Contain vapor clouds, spilled liquids and solids as much as possible as soon as it is safely possible.
- Pump downhill, if possible, to increase efficiency. Working in personal protective equipment is difficult, especially in hot or cold conditions. Increased efficiency will benefit both personnel and the overall response effort.
- Keep hose lines as straight as possible. Again, the increased efficiency will significantly affect spill response operations. Curved or sharply bent hoses limit the efficiency of any pumping system.
- Do not make the situation worse. A spill is a complex situation. Stopping response operations to rescue improperly trained or equipped personnel increases risks to people, the environment, and operations. Using incompatible materials may cause additional spills or hazards such as fire, explosions, or the release of more toxic materials and spread contamination from the original spill site.

BENCHMARKS AND PERFORMANCE APPRAISAL CRITERIA

Several benchmarks exist against which various aspects of spill and release responses may be measured. The most commonly available benchmarks are for responder training, for development of response plans, and for measurements of effectiveness of the response effort.

Training Benchmarks—Sources of Information

For training, the most basic benchmark is set by OSHA in the form of regulatory minimums for response personnel (see the "Personnel Training" section later in this chapter). OSHA very clearly lists the minimum knowledge and skills required to participate in emergency response and hazardous waste operations. Levels of training vary according to the employee's role in an emergency. To supplement these benchmarks, refer to National Fire Protection Association (NFPA) Publication 472, *Standard for Professional Competence of Responders to Hazardous Materials Incidents* (2008). NFPA 472 provides benchmarks for each level of responder, from the first responder at the awareness level up to incident commander, in several performance categories, including analyzing the incident, planning the response, implementing the planned response, evaluating progress, and terminating the incident. NFPA 472 also describes competencies for private-sector specialist employees, technicians for several types of tanks (e.g., tank cars, cargo tanks, and intermodal tanks), and others.

Plan Development Benchmarks—Sources of Information

There are several excellent resources that assist in developing new plans or evaluating existing plans. Many of these resources are available online.

First, the National Response Team has information at www.nrt.org. Of particular interest to planners are these guides:

- *Hazardous Materials Emergency Planning Guide* (NRT-1)
- *Criteria for Review of Hazardous Materials Emergency Plans* (NRT-1a)
- Update of the *Hazardous Materials Emergency Planning Guide*

Using these documents in the order listed provides a historical basis for benchmarking existing plans and illustrates how the planning process and the information sources have evolved. The documents provide a checklist to ensure that plans are comprehensive and complete.

Second, the Environmental Protection Agency's site (www.epa.gov/ceppo) provides significant, useful information, including the NRT-Integrated Contingency Plan Guidance ("One Plan"), which is intended to be used by facilities to prepare emergency response plans. Again, the information can be used as a checklist or benchmark to measure a facility's plan.

Also included on the EPA's Web site is information on local emergency planning committees (LEPC) created by the Superfund Amendment and Reauthorization Act (SARA). Larger facilities should have been coordinating plans with an LEPC since the 1990s. If plans have not been kept up to date, a new facility is being created, or an existing facility is being modified, using local emergency response organizations, as represented on an LEPC, is an excellent way to ensure that a facilities plan meets current standards and work.

Third, many insurance companies, as part of a risk assessment/risk management plan, work with specific facilities to design safe facilities and to develop (and keep current) emergency response plans. Also, many local cooperatives, commodity-specific organizations, and trade associations have prepared standards of good practice that are useful benchmarking tools.

Fourth, and finally, FEMA has developed an independent study course called "Exercise Design" (course number IS-139) that provides excellent information on exercise design, performance, and evaluation and that may be used as a benchmark for both the public and private sectors. This publication also may be used to assess performance and implementation of response drills and exercises.

Measures of Effectiveness

The effectiveness of spill and release response measures varies with the circumstances. For example, if a worker closes the leaking valve on a vat of acetone and the valve ceases to leak, the response is most likely a success. Other factors that could be considered in this example are the following:

- Was the worker or anyone else injured in the response?
- Was the material contained or prevented from spreading in accordance with the facility's emergency response plan?
- Was clean-up equipment readily accessible and in proper working condition?
- If the material leaked onto soil, was it completely removed, as demonstrated by sampling and analysis, or did it simply become an airborne or waterborne spill (caused cross-media contamination)?

The most basic goal of most spill response plans is to safely stop, control, or contain the spill or release and clean up any spilled material (whenever possible). The details of how to accomplish the goal varies from facility to facility and often depends on the characteristics of the material and the quantity of spilled or released material. Benchmarks and performance appraisal criteria should be developed from those details and from any applicable regulatory requirements. In the example above, one very important benchmark of spill clean-up effectiveness is the sampling and analysis of contaminated soil. If analysis of a soil sample revealed contamination in excess of regulatory limits, the clean up was not completely successful—an indication that the spill response plan should be reevaluated.

Operational Readiness

Once plans are determined to be current, comprehensive, and complete, they should be tested. Table-top exercises and other small-group drills are a logical starting place. In preparation for exercises and drills, it may be useful to develop a site-specific checklist to help ensure operational readiness. Some of the following questions may prove helpful in checklist development:

- Do individual workers know how to safely detect and report a spill? Putting a pound of dry ice in a small puddle of vinegar creates a smoking, low pH spill simulation.
- Do workers walk by, or do they investigate? If shift supervisors are responsible for notifying the plant security force that a spill has occurred, are the supervisors capable of transmitting on the same frequency as the security radios? If shift supervisors use an in-plant telephone system, can they get from their normal workstation to the telephone quickly enough?
- Equipment should be inspected. Are self-contained breathing apparatuses (SCBAs) usable and equipped with filled cylinders?

Are pumps and hoses stored so they can be immediately used, or do they need to be reconfigured?

- Are high-dollar items such as direct-reading instruments (photo ionization detectors, chemical-specific detectors) and response suits immediately available? If they are kept in locked cabinets for physical security (a smart procedure), where are the keys to the locks?
- Are people ready to respond to emergencies? Can the in-plant response team be mobilized five minutes before the end of a shift on Friday or the day before a holiday? If off-shift personnel are equipped with pagers for rapid recall, will they answer their pagers and respond at night and on weekends? Can in-plant personnel operate safely until off-site emergency personnel respond?
- Is the facility's management prepared to implement an emergency response plan at 2:00 A.M.? Do they have the authority to incur the expense of mobilizing a commercial response team if that is part of the plan? Will they actually call the fire department and emergency medical service, or will they have to wait for authorization from senior personnel?

Once small teams have had the opportunity to practice, the entire plan should be implemented. Are the planned command-site locations realistic, given the nature and quantity of material likely to be involved in a spill? Does the plan assume that more personnel and equipment are available than actually exist? If forklifts are included as response equipment, who will operate them? Are a sufficient number of vehicles available, or will one function take priority? For example, if one in-plant vehicle is scheduled to move injured personnel to the first-aid clinic, one in-plant vehicle is scheduled to move the response team from their normal workstations to the spill site, and one in-plant vehicle is scheduled to move emergency response personnel and equipment, are three in-plant vehicles available, or will one function (e.g., moving the injured) take priority?

During table-top exercises, small group drills, and the first or second full-team exercise, no fault should be assessed for failure to implement the plan. Many failures at this level are due to simple lack of training or awareness of the implications of the training. Honest critiques, pointing out deficiencies in implementing the plan, should be conducted to ensure that all personnel know what their individual, specific roles are. A lab technician or part-time security guard may be the initial incident commander and should understand exactly what that means. Benchmarking, or measuring the success of implementing the emergency response safely and efficiently, means that everyone involved should be able to effectively perform their emergency response role, from reporting the spill on a radio to obtaining and donning the correct PPE and plugging leaking equipment.

Performance Appraisal Criteria

Performance appraisals are essential for the effective management of an incident and for the evaluation of worker effectiveness, techniques, and equipment and supplies used for emergency response. Appraisals both during and after the incident (whenever possible) and during and after exercises and drills help improve the effectiveness of the response and provide valuable information for future responses. Once specific goals or actions have been identified in the response plan, devise a simple way to measure their effectiveness, such as a checklist or any other convenient format (e.g., a narrative).

Performance appraisals conducted during exercises demonstrate the strengths and shortcomings of the emergency response plan—such as the use of inadequate equipment, the need for further employee training, or the need for improved communications during an incident. For example, the emergency response plan of a fictitious company directs a particular employee to close a particular valve to stop a release. On the day of the planned exercise, the employee was absent, so the valve was not closed. This fact would have been noted during a post-exercise performance evaluation and the corrective measures implemented.

COST ANALYSIS AND BUDGETING

Preparing for 24-hour spill response—personnel selection and training, medical surveillance, personal protective equipment, increased staffing for immediate, around-the-clock response—is a major expense. Before any resources are committed to spill response, a risk determination and a cost-benefit analysis should be performed. What is the likelihood that a spill or release will occur? Consuming thousands of dollars and hundreds of man-hours to prepare for an event that is unlikely to occur may not be justified. On the other hand, what are the consequences of a spill or release? Even in the unlikely event of a spill, severe consequences may require some type of immediate response.

The accidents at Three Mile Island, Pennsylvania, and Bhopal, India, demonstrate the disastrous consequences of improperly evaluating a seemingly small, unlikely event. Do the materials known to be present or likely to be involved in a spill or release require immediate response? If oil from a failing tank is contained within a dike, responders have some time before the oil is recovered. On the other hand, an oil spill from a ship or shore-based facility can result in tens of thousands of dollars in damages if an effective spill containment and control plan is not implemented within minutes. A small chemical reactor in a laboratory may release only a few liters of a spontaneously combustible catalyst. The ensuing fire may destroy thousands of dollars of equipment if it is not controlled immediately. Perhaps designing the plant to operate on a lower inventory of hazardous materials or using diluted, less hazardous materials may be a more efficient use of resources.

Assessment of Risk

There are numerous computer programs and planning processes that can assist in predicting the spread of a hazardous material and its effects on people, property, and the environment. The following discussion is not intended to replace these planning tools, but rather to present additional concepts that can valuable in determining the need for developing a spill or release response plan.

Damage to People

Human health and safety are the prime concerns before and during the response to any type of spill or release. Spectacular, world-scale events such as the incidents at Chernobyl, Ukraine, or Bhopal, India, cause direct, measurable loss of life and damage to human health. Even less-publicized events, such as transportation accidents in the United States that released chlorine or ammonia, have killed or injured people at the site and downwind from the spill or release site. Response workers have also been at risk. During the sarin (an extremely toxic chemical) attack in the subway in Tokyo in 1995, significant numbers of response workers were adversely affected while attempting to aid injured commuters. One spectacular event, a boiling liquid–expanding vapor explosion, or BLEVE, has killed responders minutes or hours after accidents involving railroad tank cars of propane.

Risk assessment during a chemical spill response must begin before the incident. Basic questions need to be asked and answered. What types of materials are present or likely to be present? What quantities of materials are involved or likely to be involved? Are responders trained to recognize the presence of these materials and amounts and the hazards involved in the response? Do the response workers have the equipment and training to work with these materials under poorly controlled situations that typically exist during the initial phases of a response? Do the response workers actually know how to use their equipment during adverse conditions?

Planning saves lives and protects health. Before materials are brought to a site, plans should be prepared and practiced for normal operations as well as spills or releases. Even if a facility is not required to comply with the provisions of section 112(r) of the Clean Air Act, using it and the implementing regulations at 40 CFR 68 (Risk Management Program) may indicate shortfalls in planning for the safe storage and use of a specific material. The off-site consequence analysis (OCA) in 40 CFR 68 is one way to plan for possible off-site or downwind consequences of a spill or release of material. Environmental laws and safety regulations such as the Superfund Amendment and Reauthorization Act (SARA) Title III, also known as the Emergency Planning and Community Right-to-Know Act (EPCRA), and the OSHA process safety management standard, 29 CFR 1910.119, should be studied not just for legal compliance but also from the respond-on-Sunday-afternoon-in-90°F-weather or the Friday-night-in-freezing-rain perspective.

Consider the materials expected to be present; are spills or releases likely to generate flammable atmospheres? How will response workers control the release and contain released materials if flammable vapor clouds are present? Are the materials, in the quantities likely to be involved in a spill, expected to generate vapor clouds above the permissible exposure level or threshold limit value? Will workers be expected to wear air-purifying respirators or air-supplying respirators (SCBA or air lines with escape bottles)? In addition to off-site consequence analysis, the on-site procedures and techniques to prevent a release and respond safely, efficiently, and quickly if a release occurs, should be closely examined to ensure that response workers have the tools, knowledge, and skills to complete their assigned tasks.

Damage to Property

Just as spills and releases pose risks to people, they also pose risks of damage to property. A spill of a reagent or raw material represents not only the loss of that product but also of adjacent materials in storage, awaiting processing or use. Concentrated acetic acid leaking from a feed line into a processing building was allowed to leak into the soil. The spill created not only a dangerous situation to people but also corroded through the fire main to the building, causing it to fail. The failure of the fire protection system forced the closing and evacuation of the processing building. The loss of the product was only a minor expense compared to the unplanned, forced shutdown; replacement of the fire main; and restart of the system. A spill of methyl ethyl ketone peroxide resulted in a fire. The fire destroyed thousands of dollars of spill response equipment that was stored in the hazardous materials warehouse, near where it was expected to be used. Planning and practicing the plan would have indicated the raw material and the response equipment were too close to each other. Again, the loss of the product was only part of the total loss.

Spills and releases damage more than just raw materials. Loss of operating capability can greatly exceed the cost of the materials that were spilled—and this involves any type of material, not just hazardous materials. For example, heated sugar syrup was kept in insulated tanks in a manufacturing plant. Since sugar syrup is not a "hazardous material," there was no planning for any spills or responses. When a transfer line was ruptured by a forklift, the syrup immediately overflowed the poorly designed containment system and oozed from the warehouse into the manufacturing part of the plant. Because there were no provisions for containing this hot, viscous mass, it was allowed to cool before clean up began. Unfortunately for the plant, the only door between the warehouse and the manufacturing section was in the path of the spill. Even worse, that one door had been effectively sealed shut for three days. In the rush to restart manufacturing, forklifts moving raw materials from the warehouse were driven over the partially cleaned floor. The second clean up, removing crystallized sugar syrup from all parts of the plant, took longer and cost more than the initial, poor response and greatly exceeded the cost of the syrup. Even more severe consequences may result from the release of truly "hazardous" materials.

Finished materials may also be at risk. Solvents and building maintenance materials were spilled and spread over hundreds of thousands of dollars of finished aircraft parts during a fire. Unpacking the parts, cleaning and repackaging them, and disposing of the contaminated packaging not only closed the facility but cost more than the products and initial fire and hazardous materials response. Planning the storage of hazardous materials, in the amounts typically present in the plant or facility, makes spill response quicker, safer, more efficient, and saves money.

Critical infrastructures can also be damaged during spills or releases. Sewage treatment plants may be forced to close to prevent petroleum products, activated sludge-killing materials, and heavy metals from contaminating the plant, killing all the bacteria, and being released into the environment. Highways and railways may have to be closed during spill response work to protect workers and allow equipment to operate on site. A transportation spill or a release from a facility near a bridge may affect the community for extended periods. Again, there must be plans to safely, quickly, and efficiently respond to spills.

Damage to the Environment

Critical habitats can be severely damaged during hazardous material spills. Petroleum products spilled into or onto wetlands can destroy precious, nearly irreplaceable environmental assets, as well as consume thousands of dollars in clean up and remediation. Love Canal is one example of how releases of hazardous materials damaged the environment to such an extent that people could no longer safely live in their homes. Leaking underground storage tanks are another example of hazardous material releases damaging the environment—in this case groundwater—and requiring extensive and expensive remediation efforts.

Conclusion

There are a variety of commercial planning tools, laws, and regulations that can assist in estimating the damage to people, property, and the environment from hazardous material spills and releases. Spill response plans should address not just compliance with legal requirements and costs of response, but should also address safety concerns in a realistic, ethical manner.

BEST PRACTICES IN ENVIRONMENTAL MANAGEMENT–SPILL PREVENTION AND RESPONSE

Spill Prevention and Response Plans

Spill prevention, planning, and response programs or plans are required by several federal standards. In many cases, the development and implementation of one comprehensive plan will satisfy all of the applicable federal regulatory requirements. For example, if a facility has a contingency plan, as required by EPA regulations, and that plan addresses all elements required under the HAZWOPER standard, the contingency plan may be used to satisfy the HAZWOPER emergency response plan requirement.

Employers who evacuate employees from the facility during an emergency and do not allow employees to help in managing the emergency do not have to have an emergency response plan, as required by the HAZWOPER standard, as long as they provide an emergency action plan that complies with the applicable regulation (e.g., 1910.120, 1926.35).

The following is a partial list of federal standards and regulations that require some type of emergency prevention, planning, or response plan or program. This list is not inclusive; however, it is intended to demonstrate the wide range of regulations that may require a plan.

- DOT (49 CFR): Part 130—Oil Spill Prevention and Response Plans
- EPA (40 CFR): Part 68—Chemical Accident Prevention Provisions
- OSHA (29 CFR): *General Industry:* 1910.38—Emergency Action Plans, 1910.119—Process Safety Management of Highly Hazardous Chemicals, 1910.120—Hazardous Waste Operations and Emergency Response, 1915.502—Fire Safety Plan, 1917.30—Emergency Action Plans, 1918.100—Emergency Action Plans *Construction:* 1926.35—Employee Emergency Action Plans, 1926.64—Process Safety Management of Highly Hazardous Chemicals, 1926.65—Hazardous Waste Operations and Emergency Response, 1926.150—Fire Protection

Nearly all industry-accepted best practices stress incident planning, written plans, and practice exercises as essential elements of a successful emergency response. Best practices include general concepts such as planning, PPE, mitigation, and decontamination, but these must always be adapted to provide for any site-specific conditions and contingencies.

Several references are available to assist organizations in the development of site-specific best practices. Some of these are listed here:

- NFPA 471 *Recommended Practice for Responding to Hazardous Materials Incidents*, 2002 edition

- NFPA 1600 *Standard on Disaster/Emergency Management and Business Continuity Programs*, 2010 edition
- National Response Team NRT-1 *Hazardous Materials Emergency Planning Guide*, 2001 edition
- OSHA *Best Practices for Hospital-Based First Receivers of Victims from Mass Casualty Incidents Involving the Release of Hazardous Substances*, 2005 edition

The basic steps in developing an effective spill prevention and response plan that incorporates industry-accepted best practices include performing a hazard assessment, identifying ways to eliminate or reduce the hazards, developing plans and procedures to be taken in the event of an emergency, and training personnel in their particular role in an emergency and in execution of the plan. To be effective, spill prevention and response plans should be site-specific. Because all facilities are not necessarily subject to all regulations, and because the regulations have varying requirements, it is not possible to provide one plan that fits all facilities and circumstances, but the plan elements discussed below will provide a good foundation for most facilities.

Hazard Prediction Model

General Behavior Model (GEBMO) is a hazard prediction model developed by Ludwig Brenner. Given a particular set of circumstances and conditions, predictable outcomes will result. GEBMO can be used to plan responses to virtually any situation: a broken syringe or vial in a biohazard lab, small-volume spills of low-hazard material, or large-volume spills of high-hazard material. As shown in Figure 1, GEBMO considers seven factors. GEBMO is a valuable tool for predicting outcomes when completing a hazard assessment.

Hazard Assessment

Hazards may be separated into three basic types: physical, chemical, and natural. Physical hazards are those that pose a threat to human physical well-being. Examples of physical hazards are fire, explosion, noise, slips, falls, release of hazardous energy (e.g., electrical, steam, pressurized hydraulic or other fluids), entrapment, heat and cold, and others. Some physical hazards, such as fire or explosion, may cause a spill or release of hazardous materials or hinder response efforts.

Chemical hazards, radiation, and biological agents pose an external or internal physiological threat to one or more parts of the human body. Chemical hazards can cause short- and long-term health and physical effects, the severity of which depends on several factors, such as route of entry, toxicity, amount, and duration of exposure. Poisons, corrosive materials, anthrax, and asbestos are examples of chemical hazards. During emergency response and mitigation of a spill or release, personnel must take the appropriate precautions to protect themselves from the chemical hazards associated with all of the spilled or released material(s).

Natural hazards are those found in nature and that either affect such living things as animals and insects or are caused by or exacerbated by electrical storms, earthquakes, and wildfires. Natural hazards may cause or contribute to a spill or a release or may impede emergency response and clean-up efforts.

The hazard assessment should begin with a walk-through of the site or facility. Next, determine and

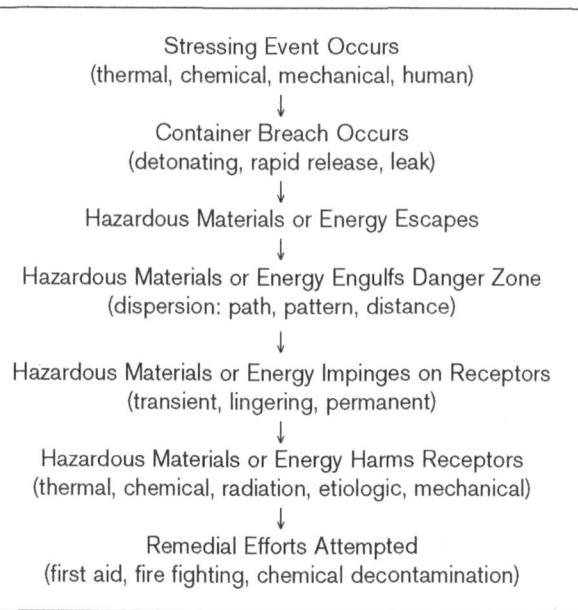

FIGURE 1. General Behavior Model (GEBMO)

document the actual or potential chemical hazards, including chemical names, locations, quantities, and packaging (e.g., bulk and nonbulk containers, underground and aboveground storage tanks, process vats, and compressed gas cylinders). In the event of an emergency, some scenarios to consider are:

- Will a spill or release harm people or the environment or both?
- If spilled, can the material reach a body of water?
- If the released materials commingle, what will the results be?
- Is it likely that a natural disaster, such as an earthquake or hurricane, will result in a release of material?
- Will response efforts be hindered by physical hazards such as confined spaces, fire, release of electrical or other hazardous energy, flooding, etc.?
- Will off-site significant structures, such as buildings, bridges, tunnels, water treatment plants, schools, houses, and the like, be affected by a release?
- Is there a downwind hazard, and if so, how far does it stretch?
- In the event of a major catastrophe, what is the likelihood that personnel evacuation would be hindered?
- What off-site resources (e.g., fire departments, hazmat teams, rescue squads, commercial response companies) are available that could respond in a timely manner?
- Which federal, state, and local agencies require notification during or after a spill or release?
- Does the facility have some response capability? If so, what types or sizes of spills or releases can personnel manage? Have personnel been properly trained? Is the correct equipment available?

After the hazard assessment has been performed, decide what procedures or actions can be used to reduce or eliminate the actual or potential hazards. The three most common hazard-reduction tools are engineering controls, administrative controls (including safe work practices), and the use of personal protective equipment (PPE). These tools are primarily aimed at increasing worker health and safety, but are very valuable in reducing the likelihood of an accidental spill or release because a safer workplace results in fewer accidents. The responsible party should try one or more of the following:

- Engineering Controls: Engineering controls are usually the most effective measures because they are used to control the hazard at its source. If possible, design the equipment or process so that it is less hazardous. This is sometimes accomplished by substituting a hazardous material with one that is less hazardous. Some engineering controls are quite simple. For example, enclosing a hazard may remove it completely. Barriers, spill containment, blast shields, automatic monitoring and shut-off equipment, and local ventilation are other ways to reduce or eliminate hazards.
- Administrative Controls: Administrative controls are measures that are designed to reduce employee exposure to hazards. Common measures include rotation of workers, exercise breaks, shorter shifts, heat/cold stress management, the use of additional relief workers, and others. Administrative controls are often used with other controls, such as PPE, that more directly prevent or control exposure to the hazard.

Safe work practices are often considered forms of administrative controls. These controls are generally presented as employer-specific and operation-specific rules, such as written operating procedures, the use of buddy systems, training, use of permits (e.g., hot work and confined space permits), warning signs, alarms, and the like.

- Personal Protective Equipment: PPE should be used as the last resort (after engineering controls and administrative controls) to protect personnel from hazards at the site or facility. The use of PPE requires its own hazard assessment to determine what kind of equipment is needed to protect against the hazards of the job. It is very important that employees are trained on the selection, use, and maintenance of PPE. They must understand that PPE does not eliminate the hazard. If the equipment is not the correct equipment for the job, or if it fails, exposure to the hazardous material(s) will occur. Again, keeping workers safe will help reduce accidents, including spills and other surprise releases.

It is very helpful to elicit worker input during this stage of emergency planning. Employees who actually work with the materials often have valuable suggestions that may greatly assist in developing hazard analysis and ways to mitigate those hazards.

Develop Written Plans and Procedures

Once the hazard analysis is complete and hazard reduction tools have been considered and implemented, as indicated, the written plan may be developed. The plan should be reviewed and evaluated every year and updated, as necessary. At minimum, the following plan elements should be addressed:

Facility or Site Description. This section should include the facility address and a general description of facility function. It should include topography (if applicable), the surrounding population, facility layout, off-site concerns (e.g., waterways, downwind hazard zones, significant structures), and a general description of the types and quantities of hazardous materials on site.

Personnel Roles and Communication. This section should describe the roles all personnel will play in the event of an emergency. Roles may be described by department (e.g., Maintenance Department or Radiation Department), job function (e.g., mechanic or administrative), title (e.g., vice president or safety manager), and/or by name. Lines of personnel authority and a description of how communication will take place should also be included.

Describe medical and security duties for those employees who are to perform them. The role of some personnel or departments may be simply to evacuate. If that is the case, clearly state that in the plan. List who will be responsible for ensuring all employees have been safely evacuated and who will be responsible for federal, state, and local notifications. Also include in the plan the names or job titles of persons who can be contacted for an explanation of personnel roles and responsibilities or for questions about the plan.

Evacuation Routes and Procedures. Obtain a site map or diagram of the facility. On the map, mark evacuation routes, exits, locations of emergency supplies and equipment, locations of emergency shutoffs, floor drains, bodies of water, safe meeting places, hazardous locations, and any other information that would be pertinent in an emergency. Depending on the size and type of the facility, a lockbox located outside the facility, which contains MSDSs, a site map, emergency contact information, and facility keys, may be required by the local fire department. If such a lockbox is used, be sure to note its location on the map so that, if necessary, local responders may be directed to the box by the person reporting the emergency. Post the map in several locations throughout the facility, as appropriate.

Describe the conditions and procedures for reporting incidents to local, state, and federal governmental agencies. At some facilities, workers may be trained to respond to small spills and leaks, but also may depend on outside sources for help with management of larger spills. Because the meanings of *small* and *large* are relative, be sure to define those terms in the plan. Reporting procedures should include initial emergency reporting as well as any required written or follow-up post-incident reports.

Develop written procedures to be followed by employees who are to remain behind to operate or shut down critical plant operations or equipment before they evacuate. Develop procedures to account for all employees after an emergency evacuation has been completed and what to do if not all personnel can be accounted for.

Emergency Procedures. In this section, clearly describe, step by step, all procedures that should be used during a spill or other emergency involving hazardous materials. Each topic should be addressed in logical steps or bulleted lists so that during an emergency, when stress is likely to be high, the procedures are very clear and easy to follow. Some of the procedures may be redundant, but this section is meant to be clear, simple, and easy to follow during emergencies. For some facilities, the emergency procedures may consist only of two steps—evacuate all personnel and call 911—but for most facilities, the procedures will be more in depth. For very large facilities with multiple types of concurrent operations, a flow chart may be useful for showing how emergencies in one area do or do not affect other areas of the facility. These facilities may also benefit from having several smaller emergency response plans in various areas of the plant, with a master plan maintained by the administration or safety office.

Clearly describe the following, as applicable to the facility or site, as well as any other site-specific procedures that are needed:

- Emergency alerting and notification procedures: Outline how the emergency will be communicated to other facility personnel and to outside agencies, if necessary.
- Security: Spell out how to secure and control the spill or release site and how to secure and control the facility or any off-site locations.
- Evacuation/safe distances: Delineate where and by what route personnel are to go so they are a safe distance from the release.
- Outline facility, process, and equipment shutdown procedures.
- Lay out specific steps and methods to stop, contain, or confine the spill or release, including the necessary PPE and emergency equipment and supplies.
- List the monitoring frequency and methods.
- Emergency medical treatment and first-aid procedures: If medical treatment and first aid are to be administered only by trained outside professionals, state that; if injuries may be treated by facility personnel, this section may contain procedures for categories of injuries, such as burns, cuts, punctures, and others.
- Decontamination procedures: Detail routine and emergency decontamination procedures.

Post-Response Actions. Once the spill or release emergency response and clean up is complete, it is very useful (and required by some regulations) to perform an incident investigation and to critique the response actions. This investigation is a tool that is useful for discovering hazards that were either inadequately addressed or completely missed in earlier stages of planning. The ultimate purpose of accident and incident investigation is to make the system better—to uncover and correct the root cause of the problem and to prevent future occurrences—not to place blame.

Another post-response action that may be required by federal or state regulations (e.g., the HAZWOPER standard and others) is a follow-up report. Consult the applicable agency or regulation(s) to ensure that the required information is submitted in a timely fashion.

Personnel Training

Before any spill response or other emergency plan is implemented, all affected personnel must receive training, the level of which depends on the employees' responsibilities during an emergency. For employees who are not likely to have contact with hazardous materials and who will have no responsibility other than to evacuate, minimal training is needed. These people need to be trained to understand the general contents of the plan and when and how to evacuate. Also, an appropriate number of people should be trained to help with the safe evacuation of employees during an emergency.

As the level of responsibility goes up, so does the amount and type of training. At a minimum, OSHA's *Hazard Communication Standard* training will apply, and depending on the type of site or facility, it is likely that training requirements of the HAZWOPER standard will also apply. Most hazardous waste site workers (including those who respond to emergencies at those sites) will need 40 hours of training plus an annual refresher, as detailed in 29 CFR 1910.120(e).

Employees who respond to hazardous material spills and releases at sites other than hazardous waste sites are required to have the appropriate level of training found in 29 CFR 1910.120(q). The five levels of training (which also require an annual refresher) and a brief description of duties found in this section include the following:

- First responder awareness level: These are workers who are likely to witness or discover a spill or release and whose only responsibility is to notify the proper authorities of the release.
- First responder operations level: These are workers who respond initially to help protect nearby people, property, and/or the environment from the effects of the release. They do not specifically try to stop the release, but instead try remotely to contain or stop the spread of the release.
- Hazardous material technician: This is a worker who more aggressively tries to stop the release by patching, plugging, or using some other method.
- Hazardous material specialist: This is a worker whose duties are similar to the hazardous material technician. The specialist has more of a specific knowledge of the material or process and provides support to hazardous material technicians. They also have the authority to act as the site liaison with federal, state, local, and other government authorities regarding site activities.
- On-scene incident commander: He or she assumes control of the incident scene and is able to implement the employer's emergency response plan and incident command system and local emergency response plan. The commander also has a thorough knowledge and understanding of the risks and hazards involved when employees are working in PPE (including decontamination procedures). In addition, the on-scene incident commander must have knowledge of the state emergency response plan and of the federal Regional Response Team.

At a minimum, personnel should be trained when the plan is first developed, whenever worker responsibilities or procedures change, and whenever the plan is changed or revised. For information on training benchmarks, see the "Training Benchmarks—Sources of Information" section earlier in this chapter.

Practice drills are recommended to familiarize workers with the procedures and to reinforce behaviors that are necessary during emergencies. Critiques of the drills can be used to discover and improve plan weaknesses.

Medical Surveillance

Medical screening and medical surveillance are two basic, distinct methods used to monitor and help protect worker health. The purpose of medical screening is the early detection, diagnosis, and treatment of an individual worker who has been exposed and adversely affected by an incident. As in pre-employment screening, the purpose of medical screening is to provide a baseline of the worker's current medical condition so that later changes resulting from workplace exposures can be detected. The main purposes of medical surveillance are to detect, then eliminate, the underlying causes of specific, work-related health problems and to detect exposure trends, often across groups of workers.

Numerous OSHA standards require some type of medical screening/surveillance. See OSHA's Web site (www.osha.gov) for more information and additional medical screening/surveillance resources. Personnel engaged in hazardous waste or emergency response operations must be covered under a medical surveillance program. Generally speaking, the employer must institute a medical surveillance program for any of the following employees:

- employees who are or may be exposed to hazardous substances or health hazards at or above the established permissible exposure limit, published exposure level (without regard to the use of respirators) for 30 or more days a year
- all employees who wear a respirator for 30 days or more a year
- all employees who are injured, become ill, or develop signs or symptoms as a result of an overexposure involving hazardous substances or health hazards from an emergency response or hazardous waste operation
- employees who work with specific substances (e.g., lead, arsenic, benzene, and many others)
- employees who are members of hazardous material teams

Personal Protective Equipment

The classic hierarchy of safety techniques is engineering controls, administrative controls, and personal protective equipment (PPE). Engineering controls are physical modifications of the work site to protect workers. During spill or release responses, engineering controls will be extremely difficult to establish. By the very nature of a spill or release, engineering controls have either failed or cannot be established until the response action is nearly complete. Similarly, administrative controls, although helpful in setting safe work conditions, will not provide adequate protection to response workers. Therefore, personal protective equipment, generally the last choice in protecting workers, becomes the prime, and sometimes the only, reliable way to protect workers during the initial phases of spill responses.

Table 1 lists the four levels of protection specified in the *Hazardous Waste Operations and Emergency Response* (HAZWOPER) standard, published at 29 CFR 1910.120, Appendix B. The table also lists selection criteria and some disadvantages for each level of protection. There are several factors that greatly enhance the safety provided by PPE. These include, but are not limited to, the following:

- Chemical compatibility: Any item of PPE—body protection, gloves, boots, accessories—must be resistant to the materials present or likely to be present in a spill. There are two measures of compatibility: breakthrough time and permeation rate. Breakthrough time, simply put, is the time it takes an item of PPE to leak. This time interval between first contact on the outside and detection of the material on the inside of the PPE is critical to proper selection. Some materials will cause virtually instantaneous failure of PPE. Obviously, this provides no protection to workers. The longer the breakthrough time, the better the PPE is suited for a particular response. The second measure of compatibility is the permeation rate. Again, simply put, this is the rate PPE leaks, once breakthrough has been achieved. The lower the permeation rate, the better the protection provided to workers. Virtually all manufacturers provide breakthrough times and permeation rates for their particular brands and models of PPE. Do not use equipment without this information. Additional sources of information include NIOSH, the National Fire Protection Association (NFPA), and numerous commercial spill response manuals.

- All levels of PPE should be considered a complete ensemble. If the fabric of a Level A suit provides hours of breakthrough time when exposed to a specific chemical, but the facepiece fogs instantly when exposed to the same material, the ensemble fails. Outer gloves and boots or boot covers must provide the same breakthrough time and permeation resistance as the suit.

- Size: A 100-pound, 5-foot-tall worker cannot safely wear the same PPE that fits a 250-pound, 6-foot-tall responder. PPE selection is often based solely on chemical compatibility. Workers who cannot safely move on a spill site are not protected—they are just wearing a chemical resistant wrapping that creates slip, trip, and fall hazards.

- Suitability for the task: Full-facepiece respirators worn under a chemical protective suit with a hood and built-in facepiece provide excellent chemical protection but effectively destroy all peripheral vision. Most Level A suits, properly sized, will not allow the wearers to see their feet or what they are walking on. PPE must address all hazards on the spill site. Workers who need corrective lenses may not be able to achieve a proper fit with some half-mask respirators. Full-facepiece respirators with spectacle kits inside the mask may be required.

- Training: Life is different and difficult inside PPE—even something as simple as Level C splash suits and half-mask respirators. Breathing is more difficult and voice communications are limited. Workers must be comfortable enough and confident enough in PPE to work safely and efficiently. This comfort and

TABLE 1

Personal Protective Equipment

Level	Selection Criteria	Respiratory Protection	Body Protection	Limitations
A	• The greatest level of eye, skin, and respiratory protection is required • Substances with a high degree of hazard to the skin are known or suspected to present, and skin contact is possible • Operations are being conducted in confined, poorly ventilated areas and the absence of conditions requiring Level A have not yet been determined	Pressure-demand, full-facepiece SCBA or pressure-demand supplied-air respirator with escape SCBA, NIOSH-approved	• Totally-encapsulating chemical protective-suit • Inner and outer chemical-resistant gloves • Chemical-resistant, steel-toe and shank boots Optional items: • Coveralls • Long underwear • Outer boots or boot covers • Hard hat (under suit)	• Fully-encapsulating suit material must be compatible with the substances involved • Movement is restricted • Induces heat stress
B	• The highest level of respiratory protection is necessary, but a lesser level of skin protection is needed. • The atmosphere contains less than 19.5% oxygen • The presence of incompletely identified gases are indicated by a direct-reading instrument, but they are not suspected of being harmful to the skin	Pressure-demand, full-facepiece SCBA or pressure-demand supplied-air respirator with escape SCBA, NIOSH-approved	• Hooded, chemical-resistant clothing (hooded one- or two-piece suit; disposable chemical-resistant overalls) • Inner and outer chemical-resistant gloves • Chemical-resistant steel toe and shank boots Optional items: • Coveralls • Long underwear • Outer boots or boot covers • Hard hat (under suit)	• Use only when exposure to materials will not adversely affect the skin • Suit, outer gloves, and boots must be chemically compatible with materials present • Induces heat stress
C	• The concentration(s) and type(s) of airborne substance(s) are known, and the criteria for using air-purifying respirators are met • Atmospheric contaminants, liquid splashes, or other direct contact will not adversely affect or be absorbed through the skin • The types of air contaminants have been identified, concentrations measured, and an air-purifying respirator is available that can remove the contaminants	Full-face or half-mask NIOSH-approved respirators	• Hooded, chemical-resistant clothing (hooded one- or two-piece suit; disposable chemical-resistant overalls) • Inner and outer chemical-resistant gloves • Chemical-resistant steel toe and shank boots Optional items: • Coveralls • Long underwear • Hard hat (under suit)	• Atmospheric concentrations of chemical must not exceed IDLH levels • The atmosphere must contain at least 19.5% oxygen • May not protect workers from sudden, drastic changes at the work site
D	• A work uniform providing minimal protection; used for nuisance contamination only • The atmosphere contains no known hazards • Work functions preclude splashes, immersion, or the potential for unexpected inhalation of, or contact with, hazardous levels of any chemicals	None required	• Coveralls • Chemical-resistant steel toe and shank boots Optional items: • Gloves • Hard hat • Safety glasses or chemical splash goggles • Face shield • Escape mask	• This level should not be worn in areas where chemical exposures are likely • The atmosphere must contain at least 19.5% oxygen • May not protect workers from sudden, drastic changes at the work site

(*Source*: National Institute for Occupational Safety and Health 1985)

The standard for personal protective equipment (PPE) is at 29 CFR 1910.120, Appendix B. It is important to note that this appendix includes the statement: "... Combinations or personal protective equipment other than those described for Levels A, B, C, and D protection may be more appropriate and may be used to provide the proper level of protection."

confidence comes only through repeated training exercises, under conditions likely to be encountered during spill responses. Training in the actual suits to be worn during a spill response may damage the suits. It may be necessary to dedicate specific suits to training use while saving other suits, of the same model, for actual responses.
- Disposable versus reusable: Reusable PPE may offer some long-term cost savings. But after exposure to specific materials, it may not be possible to completely decontaminate reusable PPE. Given that PPE is often stored for weeks or months between responses, small amounts of contaminants missed during decontamination may permeate through suits, gloves, etc., exposing responders as soon as they don the "protective" equipment.

Spill Kits

Spill kits can solve many problems in an emergency. While planning the response, two important questions to be answered are (a) Who will use the kits? and (b) How big is the potential spill? A 5-gallon bucket of sorbents will not control most spills from a rail car. An 85-gallon overpack drum full of rubber suits, goggles, shovels, and sorbents is useless in the hands of unskilled or untrained personnel.

Components of spill kits can be divided into two sections—PPE and containment and recovery tools. PPE should include head, body, hands, and feet protection. Relatively inexpensive coated and hooded Tyvek or PVC coveralls may be sufficient. Inner surgeon's gloves and long gauntlet outer gloves and boot covers, if resistant to the spilled chemicals, may complete the skin protection equipment. Respiratory equipment will range from half-mask disposable respirators to positive-pressure, full-facepiece SCBAs, depending on the vapor pressure of the spilled material, the toxicity of the spilled material, and the location of the spill. Other items include splash aprons, goggles, hard hats, and thermal protection, depending on the nature of the spill.

Containment and recovery tools are sorbents (absorbents and adsorbents), diking and patching materials, tools to deploy and recover them, and containers. Again, the type and amount of materials depends on the vapor pressure of the spilled material, the toxicity of the spilled material, the size of the anticipated spill, and the location of the spill. Materials generally useful on spills include the following:

- oil dry or some type of expanded clay (in 40- to 50-pound bags): used for general purpose diking and solidifying liquids
- granular activated carbon (in 40- to 50-pound bags): used to absorb and adsorb vapors and liquids from spill materials with high vapor pressure
- garden lime (in 50-pound bags): used to neutralize and solidify spilled liquid acids
- food-grade granular citric acid (in 50-pound bags): used to neutralize spilled liquid bases
- shovels, scoops, dust pans, and brooms to apply the material and to recover it once it has been used
- absorbent/adsorbent pads and pillows
- drums to hold everything ready for use and to contain used sorbents
- containment and sorbent boom if a spill is expected near water or if drains need to be blocked off
- plastic bags to contain used sorbent materials
- DOT-specification drums to contain and transport spill clean-up materials
- overpack drums if leaking drums are included in the plan
- warning barricades (tape, cones, portable barriers)
- documentation on transporting hazardous wastes—labels, manifests, and placards

The previous list is not exhaustive. Many products such as corn oil, vinegar, household hydrogen peroxide, liquid chlorine bleach, baking soda, soda ash, and sodium carbonate may be useful in certain cases. As mentioned previously, the components of the spill kit should be based on a realistic assessment of likely spill situations and the size and competence of the crew using the kit.

Site Layout

A spill or release site is typically divided into work zones to provide better control of the incident and to increase worker safety. In very general terms, a spill response contains three zones, as shown in Figure 2.

Hot Zone: Also called the work zone or the exclusion zone, it is the area of highest known or anticipated contamination. There may be areas of higher contamination or different types of contamination within the hot zone. For example, if a process building was damaged during a fire and explosion, each reactor vessel or broken pipe may be designated a separate high-risk area within the hot zone. Each drum or pallet of drums released from a truck or train may be designated a high-risk area, or there may be different risk areas (flammable, toxic, corrosive, oxidized) within the overall hot zone for a transportation accident. All personnel not wearing the proper personal protective equipment should be barred from entering the hot zone.

Warm Zone: Also called the contamination reduction zone or buffer zone, it is an area of reduced contamination or potential for worker exposure. Air monitoring to determine evacuation distances and soil and water sampling to determine the extent of contamination are significant activities conducted within the warm zone. As with the hot zone, only personnel wearing the proper personal protective equipment should be allowed to enter the warm zone.

Cold Zone: Also called the support zone or administrative zone, it is an area of no known contamination or no anticipated exposure to hazardous materials. The command post, first-aid station, equipment storage area, maintenance areas, media briefing area, and break areas are typically located within the cold zone. Keeping unwanted or unnecessary personnel from the cold zone can become a major activity if security is not maintained. Maintaining security on the site can be very difficult in urban areas, production facilities, and research laboratories.

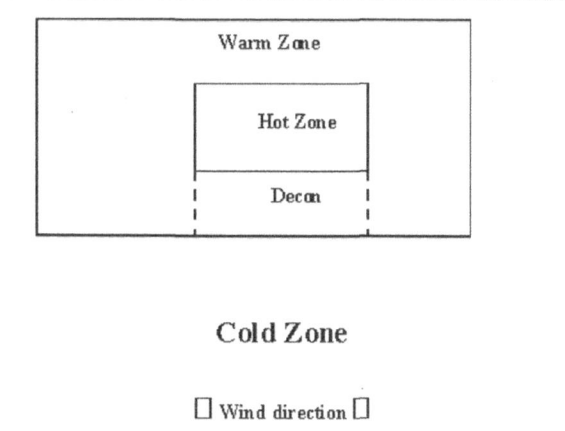

FIGURE 2. Spill response work zones (*Source*: NIOSH 1985)

Decon: Also known as the contamination reduction corridor or the personnel/equipment decontamination station, the decon area is where chemical contamination is removed from personnel, tools, instruments, and equipment before any person or any item is allowed to enter the cold zone. Decon, discussed elsewhere in detail, is a sizable subject. In general, the same level of personal protective equipment is used on decon and in the hot zone: Level A decons Level A, Level C decons Level C. Occasionally, it may be possible to step down one level: Level B decons Level A, Level C decons Level B. Decon personnel should always wear at least Level C. Improper or incomplete decon endangers personnel, property, and the environment by allowing contamination to escape into the general, uncontrolled environment. On multiple-day responses, every reasonable attempt should be made to keep decon uphill and upwind from the hot zone.

Wind Direction: If at all possible, the site should be established so that the wind blows from the command post in the cold zone, through decon, onto the hot zone. On the downwind side of the hot zone, the warm and cold zones should be large enough so that personnel outside the spill response site are not in risk of contact with either atmospheric (airborne) or physical (liquid, solid) contact with chemical contaminants.

It is important to realize that work zones are *never* uniformly shaped circles and rectangles. Rooms, hallways, buildings, roads, fences, streams, and other physical structures always make establishing work zones difficult. When establishing work zones, maximum use should be made of physical items. "Thirty feet" from the doorway is a meaningless expression in an emergency. Traffic cones, colored barricade tape, chairs laying on their sides, curbs—virtually any physical object—should be used to establish the work-zone boundaries.

Air Monitoring

When hazardous or toxic vapors are a concern at a spill or release site, the use of air-monitoring instruments is necessary to ensure the safety of both on-site and off-site personnel. To adequately sample the air at the site of a spill or release, air-monitoring instruments should be placed at various locations throughout the work site. In addition to semipermanent air samplers, area monitoring stations may also include direct-reading instruments (DRIs), such as photo ionization and flame ionization detectors, which are equipped with recorders and operated as continuous air monitors. Area monitoring stations should be placed in the following locations:

- *Upwind.* Many hazardous incidents occur near manufacturing facilities or highways that generate air pollutants. Air must be monitored upwind of the site, and wherever there are other potential sources of contaminants, to establish background levels of air contaminants.
- *Support or Cold Zone.* Air must be monitored near the command post or other support facilities to ensure that they are maintained in a clean area.
- *Contamination Reduction or Warm Zone.* Air should be monitored along the contamination control line to ensure that personnel are properly protected and the on-site workers are not removing their protective gear in a contaminated area.
- *Exclusion or Hot Zone.* The exclusion zone presents the greatest risk of exposure to chemicals and requires the most air sampling. The location of an air-monitoring station should be based upon the hot spots or source areas detected by DRIs, types of substances present, and potential for airborne contaminants.
- *Fence Line/Downwind.* Air-monitoring stations should be placed downwind from the site to determine whether any air contaminants are migrating from the site. If there are indications of airborne hazards in populated areas, additional monitors should be placed downwind.
- *Periodic Monitoring.* Site conditions and atmospheric chemical conditions may change following the initial characterization. Periodic monitoring should be conducted when the possibility of a dangerous condition has developed or when there is reason to believe that exposures may have risen above PELs since prior monitoring was conducted. The possibility that exposures have risen should be seriously considered when any of the following occurs:
    1. work begins on a different portion of the site
    2. different contaminants are being handled
    3. a markedly different type of operation is initiated (e.g., drum opening, as opposed to exploratory well drilling)
    4. workers are handling leaking drums or working in areas with obvious liquid contamination (e.g., a spill or lagoon)

Personnel Monitoring

The selective monitoring of any high-risk workers (i.e., those who are closest to the source of contaminant generation) is required by 29CFR 1910.120(h). Because occupational exposures are linked closely with active material handling, personal air monitoring is not necessary until site operations have begun. If any employee is exposed to concentrations over PELs, monitoring must continue to ensure the safety of all employees likely to be exposed to concentrations above those limits.

Meteorological Considerations

As an integral part of any air-monitoring plan, data concerning wind speed and direction, temperature, barometric pressure, and humidity, or a combination of these, are needed for selecting air-sampling locations, calculating air dispersion, calibrating instruments, and determining population at risk of exposure from airborne contaminants.

Control and Clean Up

Spill Containment

Containment is the process of stopping a release or preventing its spread through mechanical means without adding chemical or biological agents. Containment methods may include patching and plugging the leaking container; building dikes, berms, or dams; reorientation of the leaking container; overpack drums; portable collection vessels; or others, as appropriate.

Containment devices or substitute containers may be useful in stopping a leak. Be sure the containment device is chemically compatible with the leaking substance. Build dikes, berms, or dams, using earth or sand. A container such as a plastic swimming pool or inflatable raft may be useful. Dig a pit or trench to stop the slow flow of liquids. Use sorbents to slow or stop the flow of material. Placing the leaking container in a larger container (overpack) and filling any space with absorbent materials is an effective means of containment.

Portable collection vessels are usually containers of a size that can be easily transported to the spill site. These may be used to catch the substance as it spills out. This method is often an interim measure used while the leak is being patched. Containment should be the first response considered when a spill occurs because it provides the following advantages:

- minimizes damage to the environment
- allows for on-site clean up
- prevents spilled material from flowing into the waterways or entering into sewers, streams, and subsurface water supplies

Sorbents

Sorbents are materials that physically remove liquid chemicals from surfaces (including the surface of other liquids, such as water). Generally, synthetic sorbents *adsorb* liquids, and natural sorbents *absorb* them. Absorption is the process of taking up a hazardous liquid material. Adsorption is the process in which materials adhere to the surface. Sorbents may be used to slow or stop the flow of material and are often also used as clean-up tools.

Patching and Plugging

If possible, attempt to patch or plug the leak to prevent further releases from occurring during the clean up. The degree of difficulty involved in patching or plugging a leaking container depends on the hazards of the substances involved and the size and location of the leak. For smaller containers, turn it so the leak is on top, then patch or plug with any suitable, chemically compatible material, such as wood plugs or golf tees, pieces of rubber (e.g., patches made from inner tubes), pieces of thin scrap metal, or commercially available kits and devices. Sometimes materials may be solidified or frozen to stop a leak. It may be possible to create an internal patch or barrier with matting or other material. Through proper planning, a plug and patch kit should be available and easily accessible.

Forklift Punctures

Because drums are heavy, they are frequently handled by forklifts. Consequently, many incidents are caused by the forks puncturing the drum about five inches from the bottom. If this occurs, the forklift should be withdrawn from the hole and the drum rotated so the hole is above the product level. The following sequence may be used to patch forklift or other holes:

- Use a wire brush to roughen the area over the hole, removing all paint down to bare metal. Be careful to consider flammability before creating friction and possibly sparks.
- Drive a wooden wedge into the hole with a hammer. Do not drive the wedge completely inside the drum. If lead wool is available, it

should be packed around the wedge to afford a tight seal. Cut the wedge flush with the drum.
- Put aluminum tape over the wedge.
- Put epoxy over the tape and smooth the surface even with the drum.
- Place the drum in a DOT specification overpack "salvage drum" before transporting.

Compressed Gases

Preparing for an emergency involving compressed gases is not possible without familiarity of the properties of the gases on site. After the hazards are identified, develop an emergency response plan that includes, at the minimum, procedures for managing leaks, first aid, and fire prevention. Positive-pressure SCBAs, PPE, fire extinguishers, and other emergency equipment should be readily available for use by trained personnel.

Fires

First, evacuate all personnel who are not actively involved in fire fighting. If a fire has started that is being fed by a flammable oxidizing gas, turn off the supply of gas *only* if it is safe to do so. If a flammable gas fire is extinguished when the valve is still open, explosive mixtures of flammable gas and air may be formed. Never enter an enclosed area unless it has been adequately ventilated and checked with an air monitor.

Once the fire is out, cool the cylinders and surrounding area with water spray (or other material, as indicated on the MSDS). Indiscriminate use of water on fires involving cryogenic liquids can produce icy surfaces. If the fire is coming from the cylinder, it is often best to let it burn itself out. Again, know the chemical and physical properties of the gases on site. Never put a cylinder that has been involved in a fire back in service.

Leaks

Do not attempt to control or repair a leak without the proper equipment and training. Never attempt to manage a leak without knowing the chemical and physical properties of the gas.

First, check the valve; it may not be fully closed. For flammable, inert, and oxidizing gases, notify the appropriate response personnel. Move the cylinder to an isolated area with adequate ventilation. Post warning signs that describe the hazard(s). For corrosive and toxic gases, notify the appropriate response personnel. Don the proper PPE and move the cylinder to an isolated area with adequate ventilation. If possible, direct the gas into an appropriate chemical neutralizer, such as a plastic drum filled with lime or a caustic soda solution. Post warning signs that describe the hazard(s).

Treatment

Depending on the type and amount of material released, one or more treatment or clean-up methods may be available. Spilled or released materials may be treated by chemical, biological, or physical means. Many times, acids and bases can be neutralized (chemical treatment) to make clean up safer and easier and to lessen disposal costs. Oxidation or reduction reactions are another example of chemical treatment. Biological treatment methods may include aerobic or anaerobic degradation, the use of specific fungi or bacteria, the use of abiotic technologies, and others. Coagulation, air stripping, clarification, and burning are examples of physical treatment methods.

DECONTAMINATION

Decontamination is the process of removing or neutralizing contaminants that have accumulated on personnel, PPE, tools, instruments, samples, vehicles, and all other equipment and supplies used on site. Proper decontamination protects all site personnel by minimizing the transfer of hazardous substances into clean areas, and it protects the community as a whole by preventing the transportation of contaminants from the site.

Everything—all personnel, clothing, equipment, samples, and so on—leaving the contaminated area of a site must be decontaminated to remove any contaminants that may have adhered to them. Decontamination methods either physically remove any contaminants, inactivate them, or remove contaminants by a combination of both physical and chemical means. Many factors, including availability, ease of use, site resources, and cost, influence the selection of decontamination equipment and methods. To be safe and effective, ensure that the selected decontamination methods are effective for the type of contamination present and that the decontamination methods do not pose additional health or safety hazards.

The best way to minimize the amount of necessary decontamination is to work as cleanly as possible. Here are seven ways to *work clean*:

- Minimize contact with contamination—do not walk through puddles, do not touch obviously contaminated surfaces.
- Use remote tools and equipment as much as possible. Be careful that you are not just contaminating equipment instead of people.
- Protect tools and equipment as much as possible by bagging or wrapping in disposable plastic.
- Wear disposable outer gloves, boot covers, head gear, and suits that are relatively quick and easy to change.
- Cover tools and equipment with strippable coatings that can easily be removed, taking any contamination with them.
- Contain the contamination—use overpacks, plastic sheeting, barrier foams, or thin layers of clean soil to cover contaminated ground.
- Whenever possible, use the least hazardous material/method when working (e.g., use water-based solvents; use a household neutralizer, such as vinegar, instead of a stronger acid).

Contaminants may be found on the surface of personal protective or other equipment or may have permeated the material. Surface contaminants are often easy to see and remove, but contaminants that have permeated a material are very often extremely difficult or impossible to detect and remove. Contaminants that have permeated a material such as gloves or coveralls, and remain undetected, can cause an unexpected, potentially serious exposure when the contaminant reaches the skin. The extent of permeation is determined by the following:

- *Contact time.* The longer the contact time, the greater the probability and extent of permeation. Minimizing contaminant contact time is one of the most important objectives of a decontamination program.
- *Concentration.* As concentrations of contaminants increase, the potential for permeation increases. One way to minimize this problem is to reduce worker contact time in areas of high contaminant concentration.
- *Temperature.* Generally, the permeation rate increases as temperatures increase.
- *Physical state of contaminants.* In general, gases, mists, vapors, and low-viscosity liquids tend to permeate more quickly and easily than high-viscosity liquids or solids, just as coffee (low viscosity) permeates your shirt faster than fudge sauce (high viscosity).
- *Molecule and pore space size.* As the size of the contaminant molecules decreases, the rate of permeation increases. Also, as the pore space of the material increases, the rate of permeation increases. Because flour has a relatively small particle size, it will pass easily through a flour sifter, but rice would not go through the same sifter as readily, if at all. But if you increase the size of the holes by using a spaghetti strainer, the rice will pass through much more easily.

Decontamination Plan

A decontamination plan should be developed and decontamination equipment should be staged before personnel enter areas where the potential for exposure exists. The decontamination plan should include at least the following information regarding:

- the types, amounts, and concentrations of expected contaminants
- ways to protect clean areas and prevent the spread of contamination both on and off site
- routine and emergency decontamination procedures, including personnel and equipment needed, the number and layout of decontamination stations, and methods that minimize personnel (both workers and decon personnel)

contact with hazardous substances during removal of PPE
- methods of disposal of contaminated clothing, equipment, and wash/rinse solutions

Decontamination Methods

Physical Removal. Removal of particles, vapors, and volatile liquids often may be accomplished by brushing, scrubbing, rinsing, wiping, or evaporating. Other physical removal methods, such as the use of pressurized air or steam jets, can spread contamination and cause injury and are generally not recommended, except under special circumstances.

Contaminants such as resins, adhesives, and other sticky materials are often more difficult to remove. Try scraping, brushing, or wiping. Some adhesive materials are easier to remove when frozen or melted. If the material is highly viscous, it may help to absorb or adsorb it into or onto a chemically compatible material before attempting removal.

Chemical Removal. After removing any gross contamination, follow with a wash and/or rinse, using an appropriate cleaning solution. Always use the least hazardous cleaner or solvent that will accomplish the task. In some cases, this may be merely ordinary household soap or detergent and water. Be sure the cleaning solvent is chemically compatible with the item being cleaned. Be especially careful when cleaning PPE because it can be damaged or destroyed by the use of an incompatible cleaning solvent.

Emergency Decontamination. It is essential to establish and train personnel on emergency decontamination procedures, including methods which will be used to protect emergency aid providers. Whenever possible, delay medical treatment until decontamination has been performed; otherwise, emergency aid providers may become contaminated, which could result in their being unable to perform their duties and result in more victims. In extreme situations where immediate medical treatment is necessary to save a life, delay decontamination until the victim has stabilized as long as it is safe for emergency aid providers to do so (NIOSH, 1985.) Never jeopardize the lives of several people unless absolutely necessary.

Disposable PPE. In order to save time, consider the use of disposable PPE. In this system, all outer wear (boot covers, gloves, suits) is cut or rolled away from personnel while going through the decontamination process. The used, disposable PPE is packed in DOT-authorized containers for transportation and disposal, generally as an RCRA-regulated hazardous waste. While this process consumes more PPE, total cost in terms of manpower for the decontamination system, containment structures for decontamination fluids, laboratory testing, and transportation and treatment of contaminated wash and rinse waters is often considerably more.

Disposal

During the early stages of a spill response, three planning functions should occur simultaneously. Once the spilled materials are established, each of these functions should ensue:

1. Planning tactics to be used during the spill response should be developed. What are the best procedures and tools to be used to stop the release and control the released product?
2. Planning should begin on the type of personal protective equipment to be used and the material(s) that the equipment is made from. What level of protection is required by the response workers?
3. Planning should begin on how to manage—package, transport, and recycle or dispose of—the released material(s) and the sorbents or decontamination products.

The Resource Conservation and Recovery Act (RCRA) regulates the management of all hazardous wastes. There are three broad options under RCRA—storage, treatment, or disposal. Storage of a hazardous waste implies that the waste will be shipped at some future date. This is generally not a viable option for materials left after a spill response.

Treatment, at its simplest level, means the waste is going to be changed into a less hazardous or a nonhazardous material. One common form of treatment is wastewater treatment. If this is the planned waste disposal technique, keeping all spilled liquids in a liquid form, and not solidifying them, is the best tactic to be used. Planning on using pumps to transfer spilled material(s) to transportation containers (drums, vacuum trucks, tank trailers) will produce the desired results with the least handling and minimize risks to workers. If the treatment technique used will be incineration, keeping spilled liquids in a liquid form or adsorbing them on combustible sorbents will result in lower disposal costs. Because of air emission standards on hazardous waste incinerators some materials, such as mercury-containing wastes, must be packaged in relatively small containers. Planning, before the response begins, to place these free or solidified liquids in a container size accepted by incinerators will minimize repackaging after initial containment. Other forms of treatment, such as chemical oxidation, may be possible with either liquid or solid wastes. Again, planning for this option before the spill response begins will result in less waste-handling, minimizing risk to workers and lowering disposal costs.

The third option for hazardous waste management is land-based disposal, either land farming or land filling. Land farming is generally not a viable option for spill residues. Land filling hazardous wastes that have been solidified with nonbiodegradable sorbents is generally more acceptable than land filling wastes solidified with biodegradable materials. Because of land disposal restrictions (LDRs) (also called land bans), hazardous waste may require some type of treatment prior to land filling. As mentioned earlier, knowing the most effective and efficient way to manage the wastes generated by a spill response is vital for preparing response workers to conduct specific procedures and use specific types and sizes of containers. Failing to plan for disposal of spill residues often results in repackaging the waste, which can increase worker exposure and risk. Failing to plan for disposal may result in higher waste packaging, transportation, and management costs.

TRANSPORTATION SPILLS AND RELEASES

According to the U.S. Department of Transportation, there are more than 800,000 hazardous material shipments daily in the United States, of which about 315,000 are petroleum products. On the average, more than 3 billion tons of hazardous materials are shipped each year. In terms of the number of shipments, the vast majority are by truck. In any given year, with the exception of catastrophic air and rail disasters, truck incidents involving hazardous materials usually result in more deaths, injuries, and financial losses than all other modes of transportation combined.

The DOT's definition of *transport* and *transportation* is the movement of property and the loading, unloading, or storage incidental to that movement. It is clear, then, that transportation incidents happen at times other than when hazardous materials are actually being conveyed over the roadways. Improper loading, unloading, or transloading account for many transportation-related spills and releases of hazardous material. Examples of improper loading or unloading are dropped packages, loading incompatible materials together, incorrect packaging, punctured packages, improper bracing or blocking of the load, and so on. An example of *transloading* is transferring a hazardous material from a bulk packaging to a nonbulk packaging for the purpose of continuing the movement of the hazardous material in commerce. Since loading and unloading are literally in the hands of people, human error is most often the cause of these incidents. Luckily, people also have the ability to help prevent these types of incidents by ensuring that hazardous materials are properly loaded, segregated, and braced; vehicles are in sound working condition; and that drivers and equipment operators have the appropriate level of knowledge, skills, and experience to safely manage the load.

Operator Emergency Response Capabilities

The outcome of any hazardous material transportation incident is based, to a greater or lesser extent, depending on the circumstances, on the capabilities of the driver or equipment operator. In order to safely and successfully respond to a transportation incident, drivers and equipment operators must have adequate training, equipment, and other resources necessary to manage the spill or release.

DOT Training Requirements. Anyone who loads, unloads, handles, or otherwise prepares hazardous materials for transportation; operates a motor vehicle that transports hazardous materials in commerce; is responsible for the transportation safety of hazardous materials in commerce; or whose duties directly affect the safety of hazardous material transportation, is required to meet the DOT minimum training requirements found in 49 CFR 172.704. Motor vehicle operators must also comply with the training requirements of 177.816. Additionally, individual states may impose more stringent driver training requirements on those who live in that state as long as the requirements do not conflict with DOT training requirements.

DOT training includes four general areas: general awareness, specific functions, safety, and security awareness training. General awareness training familiarizes employees with DOT's training requirements and ensures that they are able to recognize and identify hazardous materials and know what measures to take to protect themselves from those hazards.

Function-specific training is just that: employees must be trained in their specific job functions. As an alternative, employees may be provided with mode-specific training, such as that required by the International Maritime Dangerous Goods (IMDG) Code (IMO, 2006) or the International Civil Aviation Organization (ICAO) (www.icao.int) Technical Instructions, as long as the training addresses the requirements of 49 CFR 171.12 (Import and Export Shipments) and 171.11 (Use of ICAO Technical Instructions).

Training may be provided by qualified in-house personnel or by outside companies or contractors. Many trade organizations, such as the American Petroleum Institute (www.api.org), the Association of Oil Pipelines (www.aopl.org), the American Chemical Society (www.acs.org), International Air Transport Association (www.iata.org), and International Institute of Ammonia Refrigeration (www.iiar.org) offer training programs or publications.

Equipment. The amount and type of available spill response equipment should be selected on the basis of the quantity, size, and type of container(s) being transported, the hazards posed by the materials, the training and experience level of the operator, and the mode of transportation. It is of little value in an emergency to include equipment the operator does not know how to properly and safely use or that is inappropriate for the potential spill or release.

The following list contains equipment and supplies that are useful for response to various types and sizes of transportation spills and releases. The first several items can be useful in nearly all transportation spill/release scenarios; the remaining items may be more useful for management of specific types and sizes of spills.

- personal protective equipment, including chemical-resistant and/or fire-resistant outer garments, gloves, boots, respiratory protection, safety glasses/goggles, and other chemical-specific equipment, as necessary
- first-aid kit
- reflective traffic vests
- fire extinguishers
- leak sealing/patching/plugging kit
- sorbent pads, rolls, or boom
- trash bags, rags and paper towels
- traffic cones, reflective warning devices
- caution tape
- communication devices such as cellular telephones, radios, and so on
- shovels, picks, rakes, brooms, squeegees, and so on
- flashlights or portable lights
- tape: duct and electrical tape have many potential uses at a spill scene
- camera, binoculars
- reference materials, such as material safety data sheets, DOT's *Emergency Response Guidebook*, and others, as applicable to the material(s)
- clean water, brushes, soap, and buckets for decontaminating small tools and equipment
- hand tools such as hammers, crescent and pipe wrenches, bolt cutters, pliers, saws, socket sets, drills, bung wrenches, utility knives, chisels, screwdrivers, vice grips, crow bars
- combustible gas indicator (or other air-monitoring instrument depending on the load) with spare batteries
- fall protection harness

- disinfectant, spray bottles, and biohazard bags
- hand and/or transfer pumps with any hoses, clamps, or necessary fittings
- spark-proof tools
- grounding cables
- dome clamps, hatch cones, valves, camlock adapters, and other specialized equipment and fittings
- plastic or metal pails
- rope
- overpack and salvage drums
- ladder

Other Resources. In some cases, other resources may be needed that are beyond the scope of what the driver or local fire or hazmat team can provide. Some spills or releases require specialized equipment such as cranes, vacuum trucks, compressed gas cylinder overpacks, specialized fire-extinguishing media, specialized valves, or leak-sealing equipment. For large spills and releases, it is likely that outside, contracted help will be needed. Some spills and releases require assistance from highly trained and specialized management teams. Are these resources available to the driver or operator? Does the driver or operator have a list with telephone numbers and points of contact that are available at various points along the route? Does the driver or operator have the authority to contract for emergency assistance? If not, can he or she reach the person with the appropriate authority at all times? Does the driver/operator have the authority to make statements or answer questions from the media? If not, to whom shall he or she refer them?

Driver/Operator Response Actions

If a spill or release of hazardous materials occurs during transport, a driver or operator must perform several tasks within the limitations of his or her training, experience, available equipment, and other resources. It is extremely important that drivers know and understand their personal limits in terms of response capabilities and the limitations of their equipment. Drivers and operators should only attempt control, containment, and other emergency spill response activities that they are fully trained and equipped to manage.

Begin the response action by analyzing the incident and planning the initial response, if it is safe to do so; otherwise, evacuate, call for help, then secure the scene to ensure that others are not injured. When evaluating the situation and gathering pertinent information, note product identification (chemical name), physical and health hazards associated with the product(s), type of container damage (e.g., puncture, crush, leak), extent of the spill or release (e.g., container size and type and the quantity of release), whether the spill or release is complete or ongoing, and whether there are factors that could change the nature or severity of the incident (e.g., the potential for fire, explosion, or the commingling of products).

If outside assistance is needed, notify local authorities, the owner, or other responsible party, and if applicable, the spill contractor or other response organizations. Provide information about the nature of the emergency, including location, product(s) involved, type of vehicle (if pertinent), approximate quantity of spilled or released material, any injuries, any special hazards (e.g., water reactive or radioactive), and any other relevant information.

If possible, provide responders with a method of contact, such as the driver's cellular telephone number or the availability of a citizen's band (CB) or other radio, to be used in the event responders need to contact the driver, which might be the case if the responders are delayed or have a difficult time finding the location of the spill or release.

For bulk containers, determine the safest method to off-load the product and where to position a vacuum or tank truck that will receive the off-loaded product. Possible bulk product removal methods include removal through vapor recovery lines, external or internal valves, unloading lines, or through the dome or hatch covers. Each method has both advantages and disadvantages, so this issue should be preplanned.

Next, secure the scene to ensure that other persons or vehicles are protected from inadvertently entering the area. Equipment and measures to secure the scene may include reflective warning devices, flares (if fire is not a potential hazard), barrier tape, traffic cones, signs, verbal warnings to bystanders or those in nearby dwellings, and so on. If fire is a hazard, turn off the vehicle and shut down other vehicle electrical systems (if so equipped), and remove all other possible sources of ignition.

Begin spill or release mitigation by donning the proper personal protective equipment. If relevant to the spill or release, set up air-monitoring instruments and a fire watch. For rail and tank cars carrying flammable materials, perform bonding and grounding to prevent buildup of static electricity. Perform spill or release control and/or containment procedures, which may include the following procedures, or others, in accordance with the company's spill response plan and procedures:

- Rotate the damaged container so the leak is at the top.
- Turn the container upright.
- Close valves and shut off all pumps.
- Seal storm sewers; dig containment ditches or construct earthen dikes; deploy sorbent pads, socks, or boom.
- Patch or seal leaks or holes.

It cannot be stressed enough that drivers and operators must recognize the limitations of themselves and their equipment. They must be able to recognize the need for more or advanced levels of personal protective and other equipment and the need for more response personnel or for those who are capable of managing more complex incidents. If drivers and operators do not recognize their limitations, it is very possible someone will be injured or, in the case of large or extremely hazardous substance releases, that the spill or release could escalate to the point of being catastrophic.

Incident Termination

When the emergency has passed and all hazardous materials are contained, contaminated equipment and supplies must be decontaminated. This may be accomplished at the scene if the driver/operator has the necessary supplies. If the necessary supplies are not available, contaminated items may be placed in drums or sealed in bags for later decontamination. If these items are contaminated with a hazardous waste, as defined by RCRA regulations, the wash and rinse water from decontamination must be managed as hazardous waste along with the other hazardous waste produced at the scene.

The last step of an incident close-out is to file all required reports. These may include reports to the responsible party (DOT, state agencies, and others), depending on the type, quantity, and location of the spill or release. Refer to the "Federal Assets and Information Sources" section for more information on notifications and reporting.

ABBREVIATIONS

ATSDR	Agency for Toxic Substances and Disease Registry
BLEVE	Boiling Liquid–Expanding Vapor Explosion
CAER	Community Awareness and Emergency Response
CERCLA	Comprehensive Environmental Response, Compensation, and Liability Act
CFR	Code of Federal Regulations
DOT	Department of Transportation
EPA	Environmental Protection Agency
Fl. P.	flash point
HASP	health and safety plan
HCS	hazard communication standard
HAZWOPER	hazardous waste operations and emergency response
HMT–USA	Hazardous Materials Transportation–Uniform Safety Act
IP	ionization potential
ISO	International Standards Organization
LC_{50}	lethal concentration 50%
LD_{50}	lethal dose 50%
LEL	lower explosive limit
LEPC	local emergency planning committee
LFL	lower flammable limit
MSDS	Material Safety Data Sheet
NFPA	National Fire Protection Association
NRT	National Response Team
OPA 90	Oil Pollution Act of 1990
OSHA	Occupational Safety and Health Administration (U.S. Department of Labor)
PPE	personal protective equipment
PEL	permissible exposure limit
PHMSA	Pipeline and Hazardous Materials Safety Administration (U.S. Department of Transportation)
PID	photo ionization detector
RCRA	Resource Conservation and Recovery Act
RSPA	Research and Special Projects Administration (U.S. Department of Transportation) (now part of PHMSA)

SARA	Superfund Amendments and Reauthorization Act
STEL	short-term exposure limit
Sp. Gr.	specific gravity
TLV	threshold limit value
TWA	time-weighted average
UEL	upper explosive limit
UFL	upper flammable limit
VD	vapor density
VP	vapor pressure

REFERENCES

American Society for Testing and Materials (ASTM) International. 2005. *ASTM Standards on Environmental Sampling*. 3d ed. West Conshohocken, PA: ASTM International. www.astm.org

Bowling Green State University. 2008. *Mercury Vapor Experiment*. wbgustream.bgsu.edu/bgsu/epa/index-fl.html

Bureau of Labor Statistics (BLS). 2007. *Occupational Outlook Handbook*. 2006–2007 ed. Washington, DC: U.S. Department of Labor, Bureau of Labor Statistics. www.bls.gov/oco/

Environmental Protection Agency (EPA). 2002. EPA530-D-02-002, *RCRA Waste Sampling Draft Technical Guidance—Planning, Implementation, and Assessment*. Washington, D.C.: EPA. www.epa.gov

Fatah, Alim A., et. al. 2001. *Guide for the Selection of Chemical and Biological Decontamination Equipment for Emergency First Responders*. vol. 1. Washington, D.C.: U.S. Department of Justice, Office of Justice Program, National Institute of Justice. www.ncjrs.gov/pdffiles1/nij/189724.pdf

Federal Emergency Management Agency (FEMA). 2007. *FEMA Independent Study Program: IS-139 Exercise Design*. www.training.fema.gov/emiweb/IS/is139.asp

International Civil Aviation Organization. 2007. *Technical Instructions for the Safe Transport of Dangerous Goods by Air*. 2007–2008 ed. Montreal, Quebec. www.icao.int

International Maritime Organization. 2006. *International Maritime Dangerous Goods Code*. London: International Maritime Organization. www.imo.org

International Organization for Standardization (ISO). 2007. ISO 14000, *Environmental Management Systems: Requirements for Guidelines with Use* (retrieved 2007). www.iso.org

Investigation Process Research Resource Site. 2010. *The Story of GEBMO* (retrieved June 30, 2010). www.iprr.org/HazMatdocs/GEBMO/GEBMO.html

National Fire Protection Association (NFPA). 2002. *Hazardous Materials Response Handbook*. 4th ed. Quincy, MA: NFPA. www.nfpa.org

_____. 2008. Standard 472, *Professional Competence of Responders to Hazardous Materials Incidents*. Quincy, MA: NFPA.

National Institute for Occupational Safety and Health (NIOSH). 1985. Publication No. 85-115, *Occupational Safety and Health Guidance Manual for Hazardous Waste Site Activities*. Washington, D.C.: Government Printing Office. www.cdc.gov/niosh/pdfs/85-115.pdf

Occupational Safety and Health Administration (OSHA). 1997. *Hazardous Waste Operations and Emergency Response* (Publication 3144). Washington, D.C.: U.S. Government Printing Office. www.osha.gov/Publications/OSHA3114/osha3114.html

_____. 2007. *e-HASP$_2$ Software User's Manual*. www.osha.gov/dep/etools/ehasp/ehasp2_usermanual.pdf

Pipeline and Hazardous Materials Safety Administration (PHMSA). PHMSA 06-25885 (HM232F), *Hazardous Materials: Risk-Based Adjustment of Transportation Security Plans*. Washington, D.C.: PHMSA.

U.S. Congress. 1970. Occupational Safety and Health Act, Section 5(a), Public Law 91-596, codified at 29 U.S. Code 654. www.osha.gov/pls/oshaweb/owasrch.search_form?p_doc_type=oshact

_____. 1976a. Resource Conservation and Recovery Act, Public Law 94-580, codified at 42 U.S. Code 6901. www.epa.gov/regulations/laws/rcra.html

_____. 1976b. Toxic Substance Control Act, Public Law, 94-469, codified at 15 U.S. Code 2601. frwebgate.access.gpo.gov/cgi-bin/usc.cgi?ACTION=BROWSE&TITLE=15USCC53

_____. 1977. Clean Air Act. Public Law 95-95, codified at 42 U.S. Code 7622. www.epa.gov/regulations/laws/caa.html

_____. 1980. Comprehensive Environmental Response, Compensation, and Liability Act. Public Law 96-510, codified at 42 U.S. Code Section 9601. www.epa.gov/regulations/laws/cercla.html

_____. 1986. Superfund Amendments and Reauthorization Act, Public Law 99-499, codified at 42 U.S. Code 9662. www.epa.gov/regulations/laws/cercla.html

_____. 1987. Clean Water Act. Public Law 100-4, codified at 33 U.S. Code 1344. www.epa.gov/regulations/laws/cwa.html

_____. 1990a. Hazardous Materials Transportation–Uniform Safety Act of 1990, Public Law 101-615, codified at 49 U.S. Code Chapter 51.

_____. 1990b. Oil Pollution Act of 1990, Public Law 100-380, codified at 33 U.S. Code 2701. www.epa.gov/regulations/laws/opa.html

_____. 1996. Federal Insecticide, Fungicide and Rodenticide Act, Public Act 108–199, codified at 7 U.S. Code 121. www.epa.gov/regulations/laws/fifra.html

United Nations Economic Commission for Europe (UNECE). 2005. *The Globally Harmonized System of Classification and Labelling of Chemicals (GHS)*. Blue Ridge Summit, PA: U.N. Publications.

U.S. Department of Transportation. 2002. *Hazardous Materials Transportation Enhanced Security Requirements* (Publication DHM50-0030-0903). hazmatonline.phmsa.dot.gov/services/Pub_Free.aspx

_____. 2004. *Emergency Response Guidebook*. www.phmsa.dot.gov/hazmat/library/erg

_____. 2006. Immediate Notice of Certain Hazardous Materials Incidents. 49 Code of Federal Regulations, 171.15. www.access.gpo.gov/cgi-bin/cfrassemble.cgi?title=201049

Hazard Communication and Right-to-Know Regulations

James M. Miller

6

LEARNING OBJECTIVES

- Learn how to implement and comply with the OSHA *Hazard Communication Standard* 29 CFR 1900.1200 (OSHA 1983).

- Become familiar with hazard communications for products, environments, and locations *not* within an OSHA-controlled workplace, including established methods for providing general chemical product information (ANSI Z129.1 2010); standards for environmental, facility, and product signage and labeling (ANSI Z535 series 2011); and standards more closely related to vehicular applications (*Manual on Uniform Traffic Control Devices* 2009).

- Learn how labeling and material safety data sheet (MSDS) standards and guidelines are gradually changing to the Globally Harmonized System (GHS).

THIS CHAPTER IS concerned with hazard communications, with an emphasis on the standards and regulations that address such communications. Most of the chapter addresses the Occupational Safety and Health Administration's promulgated *Hazard Communication Standard* (HazCom or HCS), dealing primarily with chemical hazards. But it also includes a broader overview of warnings applicable to several other types of hazard communications that are often confronted in one's work and nonwork environments.

Hazard communication should be viewed as a broad term that identifies information about hazards of many types. The goal of such information is to create an awareness that will help protect not only human safety and health but also physical property, vehicles, machinery, processes, and the environment. Ultimately, any hazard communication is directed toward humans with the hope that they might respond in a way that will increase the likelihood of avoiding a particular hazard. The common channels through which such information is conveyed include environmental and facility signing, product labeling, operator and instruction manuals, specialized safety documents, formalized training, and personal communications. All of these typically have imbedded within them both warning and instructional information. Think of hazard communications as both "warnings" about the possible presence of hazards and "instructions" for remedial action to avoid or minimize the risk associated with such hazards.

The modern movement toward providing hazard communications started to gain momentum in the 1960s and early 1970s with the passage of congressional acts such as the Consumer Product Safety Act (CPSA), the Motor Vehicle Safety Act (MVSA), and the Occupational Safety and Health Act (OSH Act). The health regulations promulgated under OSHA in the mid-1980s, section

29 CFR 1910.1200, focused on the premise of the *worker's right to know*, and that section was titled "Hazard Communication." In retrospect, using this term was unfortunate; it probably should have been more specifically identified as "Health Hazard Communication." As a consequence, in any type of chemical health setting, the term "hazard communication" has been broadly used to refer to the OSHA promulgated 29 CFR 1910.1200 (OSHA 1983). However, outside of the OSHA setting, the term is used more generally to refer to all of the types of communications about many hazards. Therefore, within this or any writings about hazard communications, one must correctly identify the type of hazard being addressed. For example, there are environmental hazard communications, safety hazard communications, health hazard communications, processing hazard communications, and equipment hazard communications, to name a few. This chapter turns first to a discussion of early health hazard considerations that led to the OSHA (Health) *Hazard Communication Standard* (HazCom) (OSHA 1983).

Early History of Chemical Hazards
Chemical Hazards in the Pre-OSHA Era

Providing information about chemicals to users is a tradition that goes back centuries. Manufacturers and distributors have always had an interest in defining the characteristics of the chemical products they make and distribute. Chemical manufacturers are in business to sell chemicals, and such chemicals will not be bought if manufacturers do not have specification data that deal with the functional and physical characteristics of each chemical. Thus, there were early versions of abbreviated chemical data sheets that had information about health and safety hazards along with physical properties. Such safety data, until recently, was voluntarily developed and distributed as a part of doing business as a chemical manufacturer or distributor. That there are now regulatory requirements for such information has only slightly changed the format of these earlier safety data sheets and the types of information they provide. However, there are those who allege that the purposes of these sheets should be much broader in scope than tradition or current regulations require. Thus, an understanding of the development of the chemical data sheet is essential, particularly in the legal environment, to appreciate what it was intended to do, both historically and currently.

The formative period in the history of chemical data sheets was from the early 1900s through about 1968. As this period evolved, professional, trade, industrial, university, insurance, and government organizations gradually began to take an interest in providing information about both the physical characteristics and the potential health hazards associated with chemical usage. In 1938, the National Conference of Governmental Industrial Hygienists first issued maximum allowable concentrations of chemicals for human exposure. In 1944, the Manufacturing Chemists Association established their Labels and Precautionary Information Committee. A few years later in 1946, they began to publish what was to become a tradition for the next 30 years, their Chemical Safety Data Sheets, the first of which was for formaldehyde (Kaplan 1986).

One academic individual stood out in these early years, the industrial hygienist Warren Cook of the University of Michigan, who in 1947 compiled the early listings of maximum allowable concentrations (MACs). These were compiled among the industrial hygienists and toxicologists of that day. It was also in the 1940s that insurance companies had an interest in providing hazard information about chemicals through their American Association of Casualty and Safety Companies (AACSC). Initially called "Special Hazard Bulletins," they were renamed "Chemical Hazard Bulletins" in 1951 and were distributed to the AACSC's insured companies, who in turn distributed them to end users of hazardous chemicals (Kaplan 1986).

The U.S. government also took a role in providing health hazard information with initial efforts housed in the U.S. Department of Labor (DOL). In 1945, DOL began to publish a series of documents under the title "Controlling Chemical Hazards." The first of these was on ammonia. How exposure levels were measured and reported changed in the years 1958–59, and the term maximum allowable concentration was changed to threshold limit value. About ten years later, it was changed to time-weighted averages as OSHA and the industry began using the personal dosimeter, which could measure workplace exposure concentrations over a full 8-hour shift (Kaplan 1986).

One industry that received early attention from the government in the 1950s was the maritime industry. Because of the number of incidents, the DOL established a maritime safety office, headed by Joseph LaRocca and Edward C. March, to investigate maritime and dock accidents. They found the cause of many accidents to be related to hazardous chemicals and began researching the types of chemical data sheets used by the manufacturing industry. Some 18 years later, in August 1968, LaRocca and Van Atta produced the first governmental format for chemical information sheets with categories of recommended information. It was published in 33 FR 12008 as an amendment to 29 CFR, Parts 1501, 1502, and 1503 (Shipbuilding, Shipbreaking, and Ship Repairing) (Kaplan 1986). It was identified as Form No. LSB-00S-4, and employers in the covered industries were to collect information about the chemicals within their respective maritime workplaces. To do this, they were to use Form LSB-00S-4 or to collect these same categories of information and place them into optional formats. It was likely that these required types of information were solicited from chemical manufacturers, distributors, trade sources, and insurance companies. It is important to note that even these early regulatory responsibilities required employers to gather information but did not require manufacturers to provide it. There is no information on whether this requirement was enforced or whether the main intent of these efforts became absorbed into the regulations of the act that followed. This act was the OSH Act of 1970 and, with its enactment, the world of worker safety and health was forever changed.

Post-OSHA and Before the HCS Standard (1970–1985)

With the passage of Public Law 91-596 in December 1970, the Occupational Health and Safety Act, the OSH Act, as it is known today, was established. Relative to hazard communication, the act states that all occupational health and safety standards "shall prescribe the use of labels or other appropriate forms of warning as are necessary to insure that employees are apprised of all hazards to which they are exposed, relevant symptoms and appropriate emergency treatment, and proper conditions and precautions of safe use or exposure" (OSH Act, Section 6, Paragraph 7). This provision of the OSH Act was to be implemented by employers. It did not put requirements on manufacturers to provide chemical information. However, one can presume information from manufacturers was being requested by those employers at the same time manufacturers were voluntarily providing such information in conjunction with regular customer technical services.

To provide and further promote the idea of readily available chemical information, the form developed for maritime employers (LSB-00S-4) was considered as something that might be useful across many industries, so it was adopted by OSHA and renamed Form OSHA-20 in May 1972. Another step toward providing chemical information came in 1974 when the National Institute for Occupational Safety and Health (NIOSH) published a document intended for OSHA, "A Recommended Standard: An Identification System for Occupationally Hazardous Materials" (NIOSH 1974). It included recommendations for warning labels and chemical data sheets (48 FR 53280). It was OSHA's decision not to act on this proposal at that time, and the NIOSH recommendations did not become part of a proposed standard until several years later.

Then in 1976 Congressman Andrew Maguire of New Jersey and a health research group petitioned OSHA to issue a standard requiring the labeling of all workplace chemicals. During the same time period, the House of Representatives' Committee on Government Operations recommended that OSHA enforce the health provisions of the Occupational Safety and Health Act by requiring manufacturers to disclose any toxic ingredients in their products and to disclose this information to employees (47 FR 12092). By January 1977, OSHA responded and published in the Federal Register an advanced notice of proposed rulemaking (ANPR) regarding chemical labeling. The ANPR notice requested comments and recommendations from the public regarding the need for such a standard along with information that should be included in such a standard (42 FR 5372-5374, 34). Four years later, in January 1981, OSHA published a notice of proposed rulemaking (NPR) that would require employers to assess workplace hazards under a predetermined set of criteria. The proposed standard did not make material safety data sheets (MSDSs) mandatory, and it was withdrawn a month later for further consideration (48 FR 53280, 34). It was the following March 1982 that OSHA published a "final proposal" for the *Hazard Communication Standard*. It required chemical manufacturers to assess the hazards of all chemicals that they produced. Furthermore, all employers were to establish hazard communication programs for their employees. Under this proposed standard, an important change was that the MSDS would now be mandatory (47 FR 12092), but it was several years before this became a reality, due to various legal challenges.

THE HAZARD COMMUNICATION STANDARD IS ENACTED

On November 25, 1983, OSHA published in the Federal Register, Vol. 48, the actual *Hazard Communication Standard*, 29 CFR Part 1910.1200. This initial standard applied only to standard industrial classification (SIC) codes 20 through 39. As of November 25, 1986, it required MSDSs to be provided by only manufacturers and distributors for their customers and employees. Even prior to this effective date, during 1985, there was a judicial review of this same HazCom standard. Because this original standard covered only manufacturing and distributors, OSHA was asked by the U.S. Court of Appeals to reconsider this limited breadth. Then, in August 1987, OSHA published a final rule incorporating the changes suggested by the Court of Appeals. The revised standard expanded the scope to all industries where employees were exposed to hazardous chemicals (52 FR 31852). After various court challenges, it eventually became effective January 30, 1989. On another front, in September 1985, the OSHA staff published OSHA Form 174, a blank MSDS sheet that incorporated all of the MSDS requirements of the *Hazard Communication Standard*, although it was not necessary to use this form to provide the required information. When completed correctly, an MSDS prepared using Form 174 contains all the information required by OSHA. However, Form 174 does not use the more organized and comprehensive 16-section format and substantial changes that the Global Harmonization System (GHS) will require in the 16-section format. As noted earlier, Form 174 was structured after the earlier Form LSB-00S-4. An example of Form 174 appears as Appendix A.

HAZCOM STANDARD OVERVIEW AND RESPONSIBILITY

The *Hazard Communication Standard* was based on the philosophy that employees have both a need and a right to know the identities of chemicals and the associated hazards of those chemicals to which they are exposed when working. They also have a right to know what protective measures are available to prevent adverse effects from occurring. Dr. Eula Bingham, Assistant Secretary of Labor for OSHA in the late 1970s, was a strong promoter of this philosophy. The major administrative interpretations of the HCS were formulated during this period of time to provide employees with the information they needed to know about their workplace health hazards. The rules specifically address the evaluation and communication of chemical hazard information to workers. The standard has been represented by analysts as incorporating a "downstream flow of information," which means that producers of chemicals have the primary responsibility for generating and disseminating information, whereas users of chemicals must obtain the information and transmit it to their own employees.

It should be obvious to anyone who looks at a chemical's hazard information that the evaluation of chemical hazards involves a multitude of technical concepts, and this evaluation process is one that requires the professional judgment of experienced experts familiar with a particular chemical or a particular chemical family. That is why the HCS is designed so that employers who simply use chemicals but do not produce or import them are not required to evaluate the hazards of those chemicals.

Once a hazard determination is made, it continues to be the responsibility of the manufacturers and importers of the chemicals to provide updated hazard information to employers purchasing and using their chemical products. On the other hand, employers who do not produce or import chemicals need only to focus on those parts of the rule that deal with establishing a workplace program and communicating pass-through hazard information to their workers.

Because of the extensive compliance requirements within OSHA's health hazard communications standard, employers and chemical manufacturers carry a heavy burden of responsibility that is hardly matched by the requirements of any other type of health, safety, or environmental hazard regulation. The dominance of health hazard communication requirements within OSHA becomes further emphasized by OSHA's records, which reflect that violations of 29 CFR 1910.1200 have typically been second only to scaffolding in the number of citations issued annually by OSHA compliance officers.

Before moving into the next section, which provides some specifics of compliance, there are certain historical clarifications that should be noted. In the current forensic environment, workers' exposures to hazards are being reviewed retrospectively to include their past as well as their present and future work careers. The role that product hazard information in various forms has played in this review has come under scrutiny because hindsight seems so much clearer than foresight. During the period before 1987, some factions point to certain inadequacies of labeling or to MSDS material as not complying with OSHA. But before this time there was no compliance required by OSHA, as noted in several places in this chapter. On the other hand, even when compliance was not mandatory, there were extensive voluntary efforts by chemical producers, distributors, professional organizations, trade associations, and insurance interests to create the common practice of providing chemical hazard information to purchasers and users. But again, it was only after the enactment of the OSHA HCS from 1987–89 that it became mandatory to provide such information to employees. To summarize, before the November 1987–89 effective dates for the HCS, manufacturers, importers, and distributors were not required under OSHA to provide (a) any material safety data sheets for chemicals under their manufacture or distribution; (b) specific categories of health hazard information; or (c) health hazard information in a certain format.

Federal Versus State Program Requirements

As this chapter proceeds to discuss the implementation of the HCS requirements, there is one caveat that could affect certain practitioners. That is the existence of OSHA-approved state plans. When operating with employees in state plan states, one must obviously comply with that state's requirements, which may be slightly different from the federal requirements. However, to qualify for a state plan, a state must provide rules (regulations) that are "at least as effective as" the federal OSHA regulatory requirements. Some states, such as California, have selected requirements that go beyond those of the federal program. A few of the state-plan states actually had hazard communication or right-to-know laws prior to the effective date of the federal OSHA rule. Currently, about half the states have some type of OSHA-approved state plan. However, some states such as Connecticut, New Jersey, and New York, as well as the Virgin Islands, have plans that cover only public-sector (state and local government) employment. The specifics of state plans are not provided or further addressed in this chapter. Thus, employers in state-plan states should contact their respective state OSHA Offices or Web sites for applicable requirements.

The chapter next turns to a description of the OSHA *Hazard Communication Standard* as it now exists and how one can, in general, implement a plan that will likely satisfy the OSHA compliance requirement. Recognize that, over the next ten years, this standard is expected to evolve and resemble the GHS.

HazCom Standard Requirements under Federal OSHA

As of 2010, the HazCom standard applies to all businesses where hazardous chemicals are used in the workplace. A *hazardous chemical* is defined by OSHA as "any liquid, solid, or gas that could present a physical or health hazard to an employee" (OSHA 2002, 4–5). Examples of hazardous chemicals include cleaning agents, degreasers, flammables, greases, paints, pesticides, aerosols, and compressed gases.

The provisions outlining the hazard communication program compliance requirements are found in the standard located at 29 CFR 1910.1200 (OSHA 1983). A key focus of these requirements is the employer's HazCom program. The specifics of such a program are in paragraphs (e) through (h) in particular, but the following list of headings includes all paragraphs within 29 CFR 1910.1200, including (e) through (h):

(a) purpose
(b) scope and application
(c) definitions
(d) hazard determination
(e) written hazard communication programs
(f) labels and other forms of warning
(g) material safety data sheets
(h) employee information and training

Paragraphs (e), (f), (g), and (h) are frequently cited as the heart of the *Hazard Communication Standard*. However, 29 CFR 1910.1200(b), "scope and application," and 29 CFR 1910.1200(c), "definitions," should be used as references to help explain the breadth of coverage of all of the provisions. Volumes have been written for employers about how to comply with HazCom. The following version is a list suggested by OSHA (OSHA, 2000, 16):

- Obtain a copy of the HCS rule.
- Read and understand the requirements.
- Assign responsibility for tasks.
- Prepare an inventory of chemicals.
- Ensure that containers have labeling.
- Obtain the MSDS for each chemical.
- Prepare a written program.
- Make MSDSs available to workers.
- Conduct training of workers.
- Establish procedures to maintain the current program.
- Establish procedures to evaluate effectiveness.

This chapter identifies fives tasks that embody the essence of this list:

Task 1. Develop a written HazCom plan/program.
Task 2. Create an up-to-date hazardous chemical inventory.
Task 3. Have all hazardous chemicals properly labeled.
Task 4. Make accessible to employees an MSDS for every chemical that is covered by the standard.
Task 5. Properly instruct, train, and provide required information to all affected employees.

The chapter will now focus on assisting management in implementing these five primary tasks of a HazCom program. Each task involves a major commitment of time and resources from management.

Implementation of a HazCom Program

Task 1. The Written HazCom Program

For the fiscal year 2009, hazard communication was the third most frequently cited standard by OSHA. Failure to develop and maintain a written program was and is the most pervasive type of violation, with failure to provide training a close second. Establishing programs that include training will not only help eliminate these violations, but may also reduce other violations that are causally related to injuries and illnesses suffered by employees who are not receiving adequate training. Additionally, establishing written programs with training is likely to provide protection against many willful violation claims (Keene State College 2006, 2). One should be aware of OSHA's proposal in September of 2009 to align the standard with the United Nations' Global Harmonization System (GHS) of Classification and Labeling of Chemicals (OSHA 2009). This has yet to be acted upon in final rulemaking.

Consultants and OSHA administrators agree that the first task for employers using hazardous chemicals is to develop the written program, and the most important aspect of the written program is to designate a responsible administrator. That individual will be responsible for oversight and implementation of each of the five tasks listed above.

The overall written plan does not have to be lengthy or complicated. It is intended to be a blueprint for implementation of a program and to provide assurance to inside management and outside observers that all aspects of the HazCom requirements have been addressed. The written program must describe how the requirements for labels (and other forms of warnings), material safety data sheets, and employee information and training are going to be met in a facility.

Preparation of the written plan can be done most easily using good resources. Because there were so many citations issued for noncompliance with the HCS and many misunderstandings about the requirements, OSHA responded with extensive information to assist employers in their compliance efforts. To this end, there are many publicly available and reproducible bulletins offered by OSHA in electronic formats. Several of these have been used in the preparation of this chapter, and they are cited within. Among the key documents that would be useful to the program administrator are the following (OSHA 2000):

- All about OSHA, OSHA 2056
- Chemical Hazard Communication, OSHA 3084
- Consultation Services for the Employer, OSHA 3074
- Employee Workplace Rights, OSHA 3021
- Employer Rights and Responsibilities Following an OSHA Inspection, OSHA 3000
- How to Prepare for Workplace Emergencies, OSHA 3088
- OSHA Inspections, OSHA 2098
- Personal Protective Equipment, OSHA 3077
- Respiratory Protection, OSHA 3079

These and other OSHA documents can be located at www.osha.gov/ and www.osha-slc.gov/. Single hardcopies can be obtained free of charge from the OSHA Publications Office, P.O. Box 37535, Washington, D.C. 20013-7535; a self-addressed mailing label is requested along with your solicitation.

Integration into a Sample Program

Complying with the many OSHA guidelines involves compiling information and integrating it into a comprehensive written program. This integration might best be illustrated through an example program (see Sidebar). Several federal, state, and private example programs can be found via the Web. The example template program presented in the Sidebar has been adapted from a publicly available California Occupational Safety and Health Administration (CalOSHA) document intended to assist program administrators to satisfy both CalOSHA and federal requirements. Of course, employers must tailor this and any program to accommodate their individual operations and regulatory needs. Just reading through the template itself is an excellent tutorial for understanding the scope of the HazCom program and responsibilities placed on the administrators of the program.

Task 2. Hazard Evaluation and Chemical Inventory: A "Tiered" Approach

The second major task in setting up a HazCom program is the chemical hazard evaluation and inventory process. This process is intended to result in a complete inventory of chemicals used in a particular workplace and other chemicals to which employees might be exposed. In light of the hundreds of chemicals that could possibly be present in an employer's establishment, a systematic means is necessary to survey the candidate chemicals to determine those that have been identified as occupationally hazardous. To this end, OSHA has attempted to assist by creating a document titled "Draft Guidance for Hazard Determination" (OSHA 2002). This document attempts to provide a methodology for creating a hazardous chemical inventory list for an entire facility.

The hazard evaluation process recommended by OSHA has been labeled as a tiered step approach. This means that the thoroughness to which a chemical must be evaluated depends on factors such as

SIDEBAR

Example Program Template for the XYZ COMPANY

To enhance our employees' health and safety, our company has developed and implemented and now maintains a hazard communication program as required by federal OSHA 29 CFR 1900.1200 (and this state's regulations). The hazard communication manager, [insert name here], has full authority and responsibility for implementing and maintaining this program. We provide information about the hazardous substances in our workplace, the associated hazards, and the control of these hazards through a comprehensive hazard communication program that includes the elements in the following list.

1. List of hazardous substances

    (Person/position) will prepare and keep current an inventory list of all known hazardous substances present in our workplace. Specific information on each noted hazardous substance can be obtained by reviewing the MSDSs (see Attachment C, "Hazardous Substance Inventory List Sample" [not included in present chapter]).

2. Proposition 65 list of chemicals [California Only]

    (Person/position) is responsible for obtaining updates of Proposition 65 listed chemicals and providing new information to affected employees. In the case of newly added chemicals to the Proposition 65 list, warning requirements take effect twelve months from the date of listing.

3. Material Safety Data Sheets (MSDSs)

    [Person/position] is responsible for obtaining the MSDSs, reviewing them for completeness, and maintaining the data sheet system for our company. In the review of incoming data sheets, if new and significant health or safety information becomes available, this new information is passed on immediately to the affected employees by additional training sessions, posting of memos, and other means of communication. Legible MSDS copies for all hazardous substances to which employees of this company may be exposed are kept in [list all locations here]. MSDSs are readily available for review to all employees in their work area and during each work shift. If MSDSs are missing or new hazardous substances in use do not have MSDSs, or if an MSDS is obviously incomplete, please contact [person/position] immediately, and a new MSDS will be requested from the manufacturer. If we are unable to obtain the MSDS from the vendor within 25 calendar days of the request, we will either call or write to our local federal or state compliance office.

    If we use alternatives other than paper MSDSs—computer or microfiche machines with printers or telefax machines—we will make sure that employees have ready access to and know how to operate these devices for retrieval and printing of legible hard copies. Our back-up system in the event of failure of the primary MSDS retrieval system will require employees to request paper MSDSs by telephone. An MSDS hardcopy will be provided to the requester as soon as possible after the telephone request is made.

4. Labels and other forms of warning

    Before hazardous substance containers are released to the work area, it is the policy of our company that [person/position] will verify that all primary and secondary containers are labeled as follows:

    - Identity of the hazardous substance(s)
    - Applicable hazard warnings
    - Name and address of the manufacturer

    To address exposures to (California Proposition 65-type) chemicals, [person/position] will provide clear and reasonable warnings to individuals prior to exposure by means of posting signs conspicuously, labeling consumer products, and training employees. If applicable, [person/position] will arrange for labels, signs, and other warnings to be printed in other languages.

5. Employee information and training

    Employees are to attend a health and safety training session set up by [person/position] prior to starting work. This training session will provide information on the following:

    - The requirements of the hazard communication regulation, including the employees' rights under the regulation
    - The location and availability of the written hazard communication program
    - Any operation in their work area, including nonroutine tasks, where hazardous sub-

stances or Proposition 65 carcinogens or reproductive toxins are present and exposures are likely to occur
- Methods and observation techniques used to determine the presence or release of hazardous substances in the work area
- Protective practices the company has taken to minimize or prevent exposure to these substances
- How to read labels and review MSDSs to obtain hazard information
- Physical and health effects of the hazardous substances
- Symptoms of overexposure
- Measures employees need to put into practice to reduce or prevent exposure to these hazardous substances by engineering controls, work practices, and use of personal protective equipment
- Emergency and first-aid procedures to follow if employees are exposed to hazardous substances
- The location and interpretation, if needed, of warning signs or placards to communicate that a chemical known to cause cancer or reproductive toxicity is used in the workplace
- Additional training whenever a new hazard is introduced into the workplace or whenever employees might be exposed to hazards at another employer's work site

6. Hazardous nonroutine tasks

Periodically, our employees are required to perform hazardous nonroutine tasks. Prior to starting work on such projects, affected employees will be given information by their supervisor on hazards to which they may be exposed during such an activity. This information will cover the following:

- Specific hazards
- Measures the company has taken to reduce the risk of these hazards, such as providing ventilation, ensuring the presence of another employee, providing a respiratory protection program, and establishing emergency procedures
- Required protective/safety measures

7. Labeled/unlabeled pipes (if applicable)

Above-ground pipes transporting hazardous substances (gases, vapors, liquids, semi-liquids, or plastics) shall be identified in accordance with established standards for "Identification of Piping." The standard to be followed is ANSI A13.1, American National Standard Scheme for Identification of Piping Systems.

Other above-ground pipes that do not contain hazardous substances but that may have associated hazards if disturbed or cut (e.g., steam lines, oxygen lines) shall be addressed as follows:

Before employees enter the area and initiate work, [persons/position] will inform them of the following:

- The location of the pipe or piping system or other known safety hazard
- The substance in the pipe
- Potential hazards
- Safety precautions

8. Informing contractors

To ensure that outside contractors work safely in our plant and to protect our employees from chemicals used by outside contractors, [person/position/department] is responsible for giving and receiving the following information from contractors:

- For hazardous substances, including (California Proposition 65-type) chemicals, to which contractor employees may be exposed while on the job site as well as substances they will be bringing into the workplace, we will provide contractors with information about our labeling system and give them access to MSDSs.
- Precautions and protective measures the employees may take to minimize the possibility of exposure include the following: _____

If anyone has questions about this plan, please contact [person/position]. Our plan will be maintained by [person/position] to ensure that the policies are carried out and the plan is effective.

_____
(Signature of Owner or Management Representative)

(Adapted from California Department of Industrial Relations 2000, 17) the common knowledge regarding the chemical, whether its health effects are under scientific review, and how prevalent the chemical is in a particular workplace. This process can be systematized into the following tiered set of steps (OSHA 2002, 12):

Step 1. Create the Exhaustive Inventory List

Often one can start with the purchasing department to determine all the chemicals and chemical products that have been purchased. Nearly any powdered, gaseous, or liquid product and some solid products will qualify for this initial list. The list should not be limited to raw materials used in production but should also include items to which employees may be exposed through maintenance, construction, or even office-work contact. For items produced in a particular facility, there will be potential for chemical exposure during handling, shipping, storage, waste disposal, and recycling. And, of course, those chemical items being shipped to customers will have to include MSDS sheets, just as the chemicals received within the facility will have to have MSDS sheets. It quickly becomes apparent how large and complex these lists can become. In similar industries or places of business, it is common for lists to be shared, as long as proprietary information is not involved. Trade associations are often in a position to assist in providing such lists among their members that have similar chemical inventories.

Step 2. Identify the "Floor" Chemicals

At this second step, one begins to identify the hazardous nature of certain chemicals. It begins with determining from governmental sources whether the chemical is part of the "floor" of chemicals to be considered hazardous in all situations. This floor of chemicals has been identified as originating from three sources, which include the following:

1. Any substance for which OSHA has either a permissible exposure limit (PEL) in 1910.1000 or a comprehensive substance-specific standard in Subpart Z. (This includes any compound including these substances and where OSHA would sample to determine compliance with the PEL.)

2. Any substance for which the American Conference of Governmental Industrial Hygienists (ACGIH) has a threshold limit value (TLV) in the latest edition of their annual list and any mixture or combination of these chemicals.

3. Any substance that the National Toxicology Program (NTP) or the International Agency for Research on Cancer (IARC) has found to be a suspected or confirmed carcinogen or any substance that OSHA regulates as a carcinogen.

At this level of review one would also check the NIOSH Registry of Toxic Effects of Chemical Substances (RTECS) to see if any hazards are indicated that do not appear in the previously listed sources. If there are, further investigations should be done to evaluate the hazards. It has been noted by OSHA that the NIOSH-generated RTECS, though useful as a screening device, should not be considered a definitive source for establishing a hazard because it consists of data that has not been evaluated (OSHA 2002, 16).

Step 3. Analyze the Data Collected about the Chemicals

The third step involves analyzing the collected data. This step is the most demanding in technical expertise. The HCS requires that chemical manufacturers and importers conduct a hazard determination to determine the level to which physical or health hazards exist. It is likely to require the services of outside expert consultants.

Step 4. Document the Process and Results Obtained

This fourth step focuses on documenting the findings for each chemical. This is an important step because all other steps will be wasted if findings are not documented carefully. Good documentation will assist in preparing labels and MSDSs, maintain a record for future reference and updating, and defend the decision regarding how the chemical hazards are handled.

Keeping Inventory Current

A continuing challenge with any inventory is that it can change on a daily basis. This is true also with the chemicals passing through an organization. The HazCom manager must set up a system to track the new chemicals entering an organization and the ones no longer being used. An efficient way to do this is through monitoring the products and vendors passing through the purchasing department. In theory, most companies have formal procedures for what items are purchased and through which channels or vendors those items may be acquired. A close relationship with the purchasing department will greatly assist the manager of the chemical inventory list. Many companies are now using bar-coding systems to create the chemical inventory libraries. On the other hand, in small companies where there is no purchasing department, then the chemical list manager must communicate with the numerous persons who have the authority to order products for offices, production buildings, or anywhere on the premises.

Task 3. Proper Chemical Container Labeling

The third primary task in the HazCom program is making sure all chemical containers are properly labeled. Although most containers are typically thought of as being some type of open or closed can of a certain size, material within piping systems may also be thought of as a container. The following discussion first addresses the usual can-type containers. It will be followed by specific standards dealing with pipe labeling.

Based on OSHA standards, each individual container must be marked. The formal requirement comes under OSHA 29 CFR 1910.1200, *Hazard Communication Standard*, in paragraph (f), "Labels and Other Forms of Warnings": "Each container of hazardous chemicals is to be labeled, tagged or marked with the following: (i) Identity; (ii) Appropriate hazard warnings; (iii) Name and address of manufacturer" (OSHA 1994, 947).

Interpretations made by OSHA have been broader than these three requirements might imply. OSHA has administratively stated that the labels must also include hazard warnings appropriate for employee protection. The hazard information and warnings can contain any type of message, words, pictures, or symbols that provide at least general information regarding the hazards of the chemical(s) in the container and any targeted organs affected. Employers are required to use legible labels and other forms of warning that hopefully can clearly and quickly communicate the identity and hazards of chemicals in the workplace. Labels and other forms of warnings are to be conspicuously placed on containers so that the message is readily visible. If a business employs a large number of non-English-speaking employees, employers have the option to use a combination of symbols, warning signs in English and other languages, and any other means necessary to ensure that their employees understand the dangers present in the workplace. On stationary process containers employers can use signs, placards, and other options in lieu of labels as long as the required information is included. Finally, employers must also relabel containers whenever labels are damaged or defaced.

In California, additional labeling requirements are applicable for those specific chemicals listed under the substance-specific health standards as referenced in the California Code of Regulations at T8 CCR, Article 110, "Regulated Carcinogens" (California Department of Occupational Safety and Health, n.d.).

Labeling Exemptions (OSHA)

As has been suggested, there are exemptions to the requirement that each individual in-plant container be labeled (OSHA 1998, 6). This can be an unnecessary burden and may not lead to increased safety under certain circumstances. These exemptions are as follows:

- Employers can post signs or placards that convey the hazard information if there are a number of stationary containers in a work area that have similar contents and hazards.
- Employers can substitute various types of standard operating procedures, process sheets, batch tickets, blend tickets, and similar written materials for container labels on stationary process equipment if they contain the same information and if the written materials are readily accessible to employees in the work area.
- Employers are not required to label portable containers into which hazardous chemicals are transferred from labeled containers if the portable containers are intended only for the

immediate use of the employee who makes the transfer. This is sometimes interpreted as a chemical within a portable container that is for immediate use during a single shift by a single employee who performs the transfer himself or herself.

Chemicals regulated by the following acts do not require their own OSHA-style HAZCOM warning labels because the respective acts controlling them likely have their own labeling specifications. From 29 CFR 1910.1200(f)(4), the acts listed are as follows:

- Toxic Substances Control Act
- Federal Food, Drug, and Cosmetic Act
- Virus-Serum-Toxin Act
- Federal Alcohol Administration Act
- Consumer Product Safety Act
- Federal Hazardous Substances Act
- Federal Seed Act

Although OSHA is very strict about there being labels on chemicals in and around the workplace, the requirements for the actual formatting and content of the label are fairly broad. The general language requiring "appropriate hazard warnings" is very nonspecific. On the other hand the chemical manufacturers and affiliated organizations have been concerned for decades about the specifics of what information should be provided for a chemical. They have stated these recommendations through the American National Standards Institute (ANSI) committees responsible for the standard titled ANSI Z129.1, *American National Standard for Hazardous Industrial Chemicals—Precautionary Labeling* (2000, 6).

Labels for Chemicals Based on ANSI Z129.1

For any commercial- or industrial-type chemical, the most respected standard for communicating information about that chemical is ANSI Z129.1. This standard has evolved after extensive research and committee deliberations. That research had as its objective the construction of labels that would not only have the essential information about the chemical, but also provide hazard communication with language that the average chemical worker would likely understand. The requirements of the standard, though voluntary, have received wide support from the industry. The requirements themselves existed before the OSHA requirements and have continued concurrent to the OSHA HazCom standards. In fact, one of the reasons the OSHA chemical labeling requirements are minimal is that most chemical manufacturers followed the ANSI Z129.1 standard even before OSHA and have included extensive amounts of information about their product. Most managers can expect to find this more extensive information on the labels they encounter. Purchasers of chemicals would expect the types of information in the list following the next paragraph to be on the respective labels if the ANSI Z129.1 standard has been followed by the originator. If such information is not on the label, equivalent language can often be found on the MSDS sheet for that chemical. It would also be reasonable to request missing information from the chemical manufacturer or distributor.

The standard categories of information recommended in ANSI Z129.1 for labels are provided in the following list. Explanations of those categories are also provided as abstracted from the standard itself (ANSI 2006). There is no recommended format or order for these categories. Of course, how many of the different categories of information are included may depend on the space available on the container:

> ***Product Name or Identification (Identity of Hazardous Components).*** Identification of the chemical product or its hazardous components shall be adequate to allow selection of proper action in case of exposure. The chemical name should be used for a single chemical substance. For mixtures, use the chemical names of the components contributing substantially to the hazards of the mixture.
>
> ***Signal Word.*** The signal word shall indicate the relative degree of an immediate hazard in diminishing order and may use an exclamation mark for emphasis after the signal word.
>
> ***Statement of Immediate Hazard(s).*** The statement of hazard shall give notice of the hazard(s) that are present as determined by the hazard evaluation.

Precautionary Measures. These supplement the statement of hazard by briefly providing measures to be taken to avoid injury from physical or health hazards.

Delayed Hazard(s) Label Statement. Longer-term potential health effects.

Instruction in Case of Contact or Exposure (Including First Aid and Antidotes). Instructions in case of contact or exposure shall be included where the known or potential adverse effects of contact or exposure warrant immediate treatment and where simple measures may be taken before professional medical assistance is available.

Notes to Physicians. If a specific, effective antidote is known and can be administered by medical personnel, include it on the label.

Fire Instructions. Include simple and brief instructions in case of fire. These are intended to provide persons who handle containers during shipment and storage with appropriate instruction for confining and extinguishing fires.

Spill or Leak Instructions. Include methods for handling spills or leaks to allow immediate action to contain spills.

Container Handling and Storage Instructions. Include these to provide additional information for chemicals requiring special or unusual handling and storage procedures.

References. May include a reference to an additional label, MSDS, technical bulletin, and so on.

Additional Useful Statements. Reserved for any other statements the manufacturer chooses to include.

Name, Address, and Telephone of Chemical Company. Include the name and address of the manufacturer, importer, or distributor on product labels leaving the workplace and intended for outside sale or distribution.

(Adapted from ANSI 2006)

Special situations arise when chemicals are bought in large bulk volumes and then divided into smaller quantities by distributors, such as in 1-, 5-, and 50-gallon barrels for liquids or dry chemicals in smaller packages. Also, chemicals that are by-products of production processes and that are either in storage or in transition awaiting disposal or recycling have very special labeling and handling requirements. Such labeling is aimed at the protection of environment, water, personnel, and physical facilities. Regulations dealing with the management of such by-products exist at both the federal and state levels.

An extremely useful feature of ANSI 129.1 deserves special notice. This feature has been useful to label and sign designers, as well as those involved in warning-label and sign litigation. The standard has over 225 examples of hazard communication phrases that have been divided by the type of hazard one might want to address. Many of these phrases have been tested with worker populations for understandability. Consequently, the phrases have found their way into all types of safety communications, and the authors of such communications can rest somewhat easy in knowing that they are choosing phrases that have had some peer review and have possibly been tested.

Other Systems of Labeling

The safety manager will also see other systems of labeling on products entering the plant. These include the national fire rating (NFR), the hazardous materials identification guide (HMIG), and right-to-know (RTK) systems.

To satisfy the OSHA HazCom standard, personal preference determines which system or combination of systems are adopted since OSHA does not require a specific format as of this printing. RTK labels list the chemical name, common name or synonym, signal word, hazard information, precautionary measures, first-aid procedures, and the CAS number. No chart for interpretation of hazards is necessary. Personal protection pictorials can be added to the RTK system for additional worker awareness (Lab Supply Safety 2007).

The NFR system uses a hazard-rating colored diamond code for ranking the health, flammability, and reactivity of hazardous chemicals in the presence of fire. Substances are assigned a rating of 0–4, with 4 being the most hazardous. Several pictorials alert workers to hazards such as water reactive and radioactive (Lab Supply Safety 2007).

The HMIG system is similar to the NFR system, except the label is in a color bar format and is rectangular, rather than diamond, in shape. The definition of the health ratings is not based on fire exposure, but on acute and chronic hazards present in normal day-to-day operations. It includes twelve icons for personal protective equipment (Lab Supply Safety 2007).

After reviewing these several types of chemical labeling, one can understand why OSHA has not been specific as to a given format and content. Each manufacturer has thus far had the right to choose the system that best fits a particular chemical. The safety manager will see all these types of labels in his plant, all of which will likely comply with OSHA. Unfortunately, a mixture of label styles will likely lead to some uncertainty and confusion on the part of the workers—just what the OSHA act seeks to avoid.

Labeling for Piping

A type of hazardous chemical labeling that is not addressed in OSHA is that which identifies chemicals contained in pipes. However, there are some specific standards dealing with above-ground pipe labeling. For example, in California, as noted in the example program template presented earlier, it is specifically stated that above-ground pipes transporting hazardous substances (such as gases or vapors, liquids, semiliquids, or plastics) shall be identified in accordance with T8 CCR, Section 3321, "Identification of Piping." This requires identification through one or more of the following methods (California Occupational Safety and Health n.d.):

1. Complete color-painting of all visible parts of the pipe may be used.
2. Alternately, color bands, preferably eight to ten inches wide, at various intervals and at each outlet valve or connection may be used. Where identification is provided by complete color painting or by color bands, a color code shall be posted at those locations where confusion would introduce hazards to employees.
3. One may also put several of the names or abbreviations of the transported materials lettered or stenciled on the pipe near the valves or outlets.
4. Finally, one may use tags of metal or other suitable material naming the transported material and fastened securely to the system on or near the valve. The tag legibility must be maintained.

On a national level there are voluntary consensus standards that recommend color-coding of pipes based on the materials they are carrying. Even where such identification is not required, it is still a good practice to install such an identification system. The U.S. national standard is ANSI A13.1-2007, the *American National Standard Scheme for Identification of Piping Systems* (2007).

The ANSI standard for pipe identification is a widely used guideline in determining pipe-identification requirements. The purpose of the standard is to "assist in identification of hazardous materials conveyed in piping systems and their hazards when released in the environment." Pipes are defined as "conduits for the transport of gases, liquids, semiliquids or fine particulate dust." This ANSI standard recommends that pipes be marked with a legend indicating the name of the contents and arrows showing the direction of flow of the material. A color is used in combination with the legend to identify the characteristic hazards of the contents. The labeling needs to be applied close to valves, flanges, branches, where changes in direction occur, wherever pipes pass through walls, and at 50-foot intervals on straight runs. In 2007, the new edition of the standard changed the color scheme requirements for labels. Previous versions of the standard included only four colors for identifying pipes. The new label color requirements are based on the characteristic hazards of the contents. These are the classification of materials and designated colors (ANSI 2007):

- Flammable Fluids (Color field: yellow. Lettering: black)

- Toxic or corrosive fluids (Color field: orange. Lettering: black)
- Combustible fluids (Color field: brown. Lettering: black)
- Potable, cooling, boiler feed, and other water (Color field: green. Lettering: white)
- Compressed air (Color field: blue. Lettering: white)
- Fire quenching fluids (Color field: red. Lettering: white)

Task 4. Chemical Material Safety Data Sheets (MSDSs) and Their Accessibility

The fourth major task in the HazCom program deals with material safety data sheets, and this can involve their design, collection, maintenance, distribution, and accessibility. As indicated in the early portions of the chapter, chemical (or material) safety data sheets are a vital part of employee right-to-know programs, such as the OSHA HazCom. The MSDS has legal significance relative to the tort liability of manufacturers or processors who actually develop chemicals for eventual use or distribution. The adequacy of MSDS information often comes into question in such litigation. However, the focus of the present discussion is on compliance with the OSHA health hazard communication requirements. It should be noted, however, that any proposed criteria used to test MSDS adequacy under litigation and the common law can be quite different from adequacy under OSHA, unless, at some point, there is a government-mandated pre-exemption.

The first step in designing how chemical information should be presented to users within an MSDS is to decide on a format within which to present the chosen information. A standardized format was early seen as a way to make the technical information easier for users to read. Therefore, as discussed previously, OSHA established a voluntary format for MSDSs in the 1970s and called it OSHA Form 20, and a later version of a standardized format appeared in 1985 as Form 174 (see Appendix A). This two-page form includes spaces for each of the items included in the MSDS requirements of the standard. It was to be filled in with the appropriate information as determined by the manufacturer or importer. However, some in the regulated community did not find the OSHA Form 174 suitable to their needs. They were looking for a more comprehensive, structured approach for developing clear, complete, and consistent MSDSs.

To accomplish this objective, the Chemical Manufacturers Association (now known as the American Chemistry Council) formed a committee to establish guidelines for the preparation of MSDSs under the committee structure of the American National Standards Institute (ANSI). This effort resulted in the development of what is now known as ANSI Z400.1, *American National Standard for Hazardous Industrial Chemicals Material Safety Data Sheets—Preparation* (2004). Employers, workers, healthcare professionals, emergency responders, and other MSDS users participated in this development process. The standard established a 16-section format for presenting information. If one follows the recommended format, the information of greatest concern to workers is featured at the beginning of the data sheet, including information on ingredients and first-aid measures. More technical information that addresses topics such as the physical and chemical properties of the material, along with toxicological data appears later in the MSDS. The 2004 revision included several changes, most importantly improving hazard communication and aligning the standard with the recommendations for safety data sheets in the Globally Harmonized System for Hazard Classification, Communication and Labeling (GHS) and reordering the MSDS sections so Hazards Identification appears before Composition Information. The major sections of the ANSI Z400.1 standard follow. A detailed description of each appears in Appendix B.

- Section 1: Chemical Product and Company Identification
- Section 2: Hazards Identification
- Section 3: Composition, Information on Ingredients
- Section 4: First-Aid Measures
- Section 5: Fire-Fighting Measures
- Section 6: Accidental Release Measures
- Section 7: Handling and Storage

- Section 8: Exposure Controls, Personal Protection
- Section 9: Physical and Chemical Properties
- Section 10: Stability and Reactivity
- Section 11: Toxicological Information
- Section 12: Ecological Information
- Section 13: Disposal Considerations
- Section 14: Transport Information
- Section 15: Regulatory Information
- Section 16: Other Information

The ANSI Z400.1 standard also includes guidance on the appearance and reading level of the text in order to provide a document that would likely be understandable to readers. OSHA allows this format to be used to comply with the HCS because it generally includes the OSHA required information (ANSI 2004).

These sixteen sections differ only slightly from comparable sections appearing in the OSHA Form 174. Table 1 compares the ANSI and OSHA formats for MSDS creation. Note that a manufacturer is allowed a wide judgment in choosing what to include in an MSDS, although certain specific items are mandatory.

An employer who is not a chemical manufacturer or supplier is not expected to generate the information for MSDS sheets. Rather, the section descriptions listed above represent the information an employer would expect to be provided in whatever format is chosen by a manufacturer for its MSDS.

Comparison to European Safety Data Sheet

The European Commission in its initial Commission Directive 91/155/EEC stated that it is "defining and laying down the detailed arrangements for the system of specific information relating to dangerous preparations in implementation of Article 10 of Directive 88/379/EEC (31991L0155)" (EC 1991). To implement this directive, Europe essentially adopted the ANSI Z400.1 approach with an identical set of sixteen required sections (ANSI 2004). However, in 2007, the European Union (EU) regulation concerning the registration, evaluation, authorization, and restriction of chemicals (REACH) came into force. This law overtook the EU's provisions for SDS; therefore, Directive 91/155/EEC was repealed. The statutory basis for SDSs is laid down in Article 31, "Requirements for Safety Data Sheets," of REACH, and Annex II details the requirements for the compilation of an SDS in accordance with this article. REACH still maintains the division into 16 sections; however, Section 2, "Composition and Information on Ingredients," and Section 3, "Hazards Identification," have been reversed in order (EC 2001). Although the titles to the sections are the same, the particular requirements are described in a more specific and less liability-guarded terminology. Those manufacturers supplying to Europe will also be interested in when and how the SDSs (safety data sheets) must be provided. This is stated in the most recent referred-to directive as follows. Note, however, that this directive is being revised due to various parts of the GHS proposals:

Article 1:1 ... the manufacturer, importer or distributor, shall supply the recipient who is a professional user of the substance or preparation, with a safety data sheet containing the information set out in Article 3 and the Annex to this Directive, if the substance or preparation is classified as dangerous according to Directive 67/548/EEC or European Parliament and Council Directive 1999/45/EC. (European Commission 2001, 2)

Article 3: The safety data sheet referred to in Article 1 shall contain the following obligatory headings: [Numbers 1–16 are listed in the standards at this point within the directive and are identical in title to the ANSI 400.1 sections]. (European Commission 1991, 2)

An interesting observation has been included in the EEC directive that reflects the reality of member-nation differences in language. The EEC openly recognizes language-translation differences and states, "Chemical safety data sheets are published under several names, such as: international chemical safety card, ICSC; chemical safety card; chemical info-sheet; material safety data sheet, MSDS; product safety data sheet; health and safety data sheet" (EC 1991).

It is also interesting that the EEC recognizes two different types of chemical safety data sheets: (1) chemical safety data sheets prepared by working groups of experts containing information based on

TABLE 1

Comparison of ANSI Z400.1, OSHA, and European MSDS Specifications

ANSI Z400.1(2004–) MSDSs–Preparation and Communication Standard, Directive 91/155/EEC (1991)–SDS Safety Data Sheets Directive	U.S. Dept. of Labor OSHA Hazard (29 CFR 1910.1200) Subpart Z	U.S. Dept. of Labor OSHA Form OSHA 174 (1985)
Section 1: Product and Company Identification	Identification	Identity
	Name, Address, Manufacturer Telephone # Date of preparation	Section I. Manufacturer Information
Section 2: Hazards Identification	Carcinogenicity: Listing of Hazardous Chemical	
Section 3: Composition/Information on Ingredients		Section II. Hazardous Ingredients/Identity Information
		Section III. Physical/Chemical Characteristics
Section 4: First Aid Measures	Emergency and First Aid procedures	
	Primary Routes of Entry OSHA PEL, TLV	
Section 5: Fire Fighting Measures	Physical Hazards (Fire, Explosion, and Reactivity)	Section IV. Fire and Explosion Hazard Data
Section 6: Accidental Release Measures		Section VIII. Control Measures
Section 7: Handling and Storage	Safe Handling and Use	Section VII. Precautions for Safe Handling and Use
Section 8: Exposure Controls/Personal Protection	Control Measures, PPE	
Section 9: Physical and Chemical Properties	Physical and Chemical Characteristics	Section III. Physical/Chemical Characteristics
Section 10: Stability and Reactivity	Physical Hazards	Section V. Reactivity Data
Section 11: Toxicological Information	Health Hazards (signs/symptoms, exposure)	Section VI. Health Hazard Data
Section 12: Ecological Information		
Section 13: Disposal Considerations		
Section 14: Transport Information		
Section 15: Regulatory Information		
Section 16: Other Information		

laboratory tests and checked knowledge and (2) chemical safety data sheets prepared by the manufacturer or retailer. EEC further suggests that "validated" data sheets on pure substances are available—for example, from the International Programme on Chemical Safety (IPCS) or from national institutions such as the Canadian Centre for Occupational Safety and Health. The EEC suggests that these can be used by manufacturers as basic information sources when they create chemical safety data sheets for their own products.

By way of comparison, this EEC approach to chemical information is presented along with the ANSI and OSHA formats in Table 1. It is noted, however, that the European and U.S. regulations are under revision as various provisions of the GHS are adopted. The reader should follow these developments, as they are not complete as of the publication of this Handbook.

Comparison to Canadian MSDSs

Canada's right-to-know legislation is the Workplace Hazardous Materials Information System (WHMIS) (Health Canada 1988). In Canada, every material that is controlled by WHMIS must have an accompanying MSDS. Nine categories of information must be present on an MSDS in Canada. These categories are specified in the Controlled Products Regulations (CPR) and include the following (Department of Justice Canada 1985):

1. Product information: product identifier (name) and manufacturer and supplier names, addresses, and emergency phone numbers.
2. Hazardous ingredients
3. Physical data
4. Fire or explosion hazard data
5. Reactivity data: information on the chemical instability of a product and the substances it may react with

6. Toxicological properties: health effects
7. Preventive measures
8. First-aid measures
9. Preparation information: who is responsible for preparation and date of preparation of MSDS

Many products are imported from and exported to the United States using the 16-heading format used under ANSI Z400.1. Canadian authorities have indicated that this 16-heading format is acceptable in Canada if two conditions are met. First, all the required information specified under Column III of Schedule I of the Canadian Controlled Products Regulation (CPR) must be addressed; also, all headings and subheadings that are on the MSDS must be addressed by providing the required information or by stating that the information is not available or not applicable, whichever is appropriate (Canadian Centre for Occupational Health and Safety 2006). Second, the statement "This product has been classified in accordance with the hazard criteria of the CPR, and the MSDS contains all of the information required by the CPR" must appear under the section heading "Regulatory Information" (Canadian Centre for Occupational Health and Safety 2006). This is an interesting type of self-certification not yet found in other countries.

A conclusion one could draw from this is that, for chemicals being shipped to Canada or abroad to Europe, one could use essentially the same MSDS as would be prepared for the United States under ANSI Z400.1, with some small changes to accommodate the local regulations or customs. It is noted, of course, that translations into country-specific languages may be necessary. Thus, although there are no multilingual requirements for chemicals distributed in the United States, there will be non-English-language requirements for some other countries.

In Canada, the GHS will affect how chemicals are classified, and label requirements will change with the addition of a few new requirements. An interim Canadian policy has been established to permit the use of GHS-formatted safety sheets in Canada. Regulatory proposals to update WHMIS were anticipated in 2010.

Global Harmonization System (GHS) Evolution

Hazard communication systems are rapidly evolving, as various governments and organizations consider the proposals brought forward within the Global Harmonization System (GHS). The goal of this chapter is to give the reader an introduction to what is happening and what may be coming with the GHS. Unquestionably, the GHS is rapidly becoming a factor in providing hazard communications about chemicals and other products around the world.

The GHS began as a result of the recognition by the United Nations for the need to harmonize the separate systems between countries. It began in 1992 at the United Nations, and its goal was to have a system in place by 2000. The work groups involved produced a proposal, which was adopted in December 2002 under what is now called the "Purple Book." While sizable, this is a very understandable document intended for use by practitioners, regulators, and standards committees. The GHS is slowly being adopted; New Zealand, Japan, Korea, and Taiwan have already adopted it. Also, provisions within the GHS are regularly included in standards in both Canada and the United States, and this proposal is likely to change the way hazards are communicated across the globe over the next twenty years. The GHS is an international system under the United Nations Subcommittee for GHS. It has as its objective the establishment of new rules for hazardous chemicals in transportation, workplace use, and consumer use, and there are special rules for pesticides. The GHS includes new MSDS or SDS requirements and new hazard symbols. Its scope includes classifying chemicals, symbols for hazards, labeling requirements, and MSDS requirements. The hope is that it will replace the patchwork of regulations across the globe, all of which cover uses of similar chemicals.

Key to the GHS system is its new chemical classification methodology, based on both the physical and health hazards associated with any particular chemical. It also establishes a new labeling program that includes such elements as: product identifier/ ingredient disclosure, supplier identification, symbols/ hazard pictograms, signal words, hazard statements, and precautionary information. Keep in mind that these are applicable to transportation, workplace, and consumer environments and would supersede the individual standards for each application that countries like the United States currently have in place.

The model for SDS or MSDS requirements is similar to the International Labour Organization (ILO) and ANSI 16-heading format, but is different from OSHA Form 174. It should be anticipated that chemical suppliers using OSHA Form 174 or some other arbitrary format will be rewriting their MSDS materials to the 16-section format within the next several years.

Chemical labeling will also have to be changed under the GHS. Standardized signal words, hazard symbols, and risk phrases will be required. Suppliers of labels under the GHS system will have to reevaluate their product's hazards and redo all their labels whenever the GHS is made mandatory, regardless of what format they are currently using.

The U.S. government is now in the process of adopting certain provisions of the GHS and looking at integrating various "building blocks" of the GHS into their present requirements. An Advanced Notice of Proposed Rulemaking (ANPR) came out in 2006, which stated the OSHA position relative to the GHS and how it might affect the current OSHA HazCom regulations. The U. S. Department of Transportation (DOT) has been more aggressive in considering parts of the GHS and has adopted several of its elements within rulemaking number HM-2151. The U. S. Environmental Protection Agency (EPA) is in the process of holding public meetings relative to the potential use of the GHS in its requirements. The U.S. Consumer Product Safety Commission (CPSC), which has responsibility for the Hazardous Substances Act, is also currently evaluating to what extent they want to follow or adopt certain aspects of the GHS.

Within the Canadian government, both Health Canada and Transport Canada have indicated a commitment to incorporating changes to their regulations that reflect the GHS proposal.

In summary, there are few parts of either the U.S. or Canadian government regulations pertaining to chemical and product hazards that will not be impacted by adoption of all or parts of the GHS. A monumental education process for suppliers and users will soon be forthcoming, as parts of the GHS are adopted. Such adoption will also put heavy burdens on the consensus standards organizations to modify their standards to reflect such global changes in hazard communication.

Employee Access to MSDS Data—Electronic Access

From the very onset of the employee-right-to-know movement in the 1970s, unions and other employee groups wanted to know the specifics about the chemicals to which they were being exposed. However, once this information was collected by employers and input into possibly hundreds of sets of MSDS sheets, how was the employer to make this information practically available to workers in any location where an employee might be working? Adequate distribution and the continual updating became quite the challenge. How physically close this information had to be to any particular employee became open for compliance interpretation. Fortunately, the electronic era assisted in accommodating this concern in the late 1990s, and OSHA compliance administrators have cooperated. A 1998 news release from OSHA addressed the issue within the title "New OSHA Directive Makes It Easier for Employers to Comply with Hazard Communication Standard" (OSHA, April 7, 1998).

The directive addresses the issue of electronic access to MSDSs, indicating that in addition to hardcopies, employers may provide MSDSs to employees through computers, microfiche machines, the Internet, CD-ROM, and fax machines. It does insist that employers using electronic means must ensure that reliable devices are readily accessible in the workplace at all times; that workers are trained in the use of these devices, including specific software; that there is an adequate back-up system in the event of the failure of that system, such as power outages or online access delays; and that the system is to be part of the overall hazard communication program for the workplace. Additionally, the employees must be able to access hardcopies of the MSDSs and, in medical or fire emergencies, employers must immediately be able to provide copies of MSDSs to medical or fire personnel.

OSHA believes this type of electronic implementation more fully carries out the intent of the regulation by allowing a much broader and more user-friendly access, and it facilitates employers and chemical manufacturers in timely updating and enhancements. It also facilitates an information channel that can expand its coverage well beyond the mandatory requirements of the HazCom itself.

Trade-Secret Protection

Some chemical manufacturers understandably resist the idea of providing overly specific information about products that they consider trade secrets. This concern has been recognized by both the federal government and certain states. It is covered under 29 CFR 1910.1200(i):

> The chemical manufacturer, importer, or employer may withhold the specific chemical identity, including the chemical name and other specific identification of a hazardous chemical, from the MSDS.

Under the trade-secret provision, manufacturers, importers, or employers who wish to withhold the specific identity of a hazardous chemical from the MSDS must meet specific requirements as outlined in 29 CFR 1910.1200(i), including the following: (a) the MSDS must state that the specific identity of the chemical mixture is being withheld as a trade secret, but all other MSDS categories must be addressed; and (b) trade-secret information must be released in certain circumstances.

Information on the specific chemical identity of a trade-secret substance may be requested in medical emergencies as well as in nonemergency situations. In the case of a medical emergency, the chemical identity must be immediately disclosed to medical personnel. In nonemergency situations, disclosure shall be made to health or safety professionals and to employees and their designated representatives upon a written request that explains why the disclosure of the specific chemical identity is essential and describes the procedures by which the disclosed information will be kept confidential. It is also noted that a trade secret cannot typically include chemical identity information that is already discoverable through laboratory qualitative analysis (OSHA 2005).

Employee Understanding of MSDS

One of the more controversial issues is the difficulty some employees have understanding a label, MSDS, or other type of work chemical specification. A training program will have as one of its objectives the explaining of this information to the employees. The International Labour Organization (ILO) has proposed a useful set of questions that could either be asked of workers to determine their level of understanding or be used by workers as a self-test.

General
   Do you have the right safety data sheet for the chemical of interest?
   Do you have an up-to-date sheet?

Potential Hazards
   Can this chemical explode?
   Is this chemical unstable? If so, under which conditions?
   Can this material react with other chemicals? If so, which ones?
   Is there a possibility of mixing during storage?
   Can this chemical harm your health?
   Do you know the symptoms which may warn you of overexposure?

Preventive Measures
   Does your worksite need engineering controls?
   Does this material require special handling precautions?
   Do you need protective equipment?
   Do you need to be careful when mixing this chemical with any other chemicals?
   Does this material require special storage conditions?

Emergency Measures
   Do you know what to do in case of a fire or explosion?

Do you know the fire-extinguishing method for this chemical?

Do you know the first-aid measures needed in case of an overexposure?

Do you know what to do in case of a spill or leak?

Do you know where the emergency response equipment is and how to use it?

(ILO 2004, 10)

Online Access to MSDS and Other Information

The availability of MSDS and other information has mushroomed in the past few years. There are Web sites now advertising free availability to literally millions of MSDS sheets and other HCS materials. Not only have general lists been compiled, but individual companies and manufacturers also have freely made MSDS information available for the products they are responsible for. The reader wanting a quick overview of MSDS availability via the Internet is encouraged to visit the following URL: www.ilpi.com/msds/# Internet. In addition, Table 2 has been compiled by this author as an extensive Web-site listing of sites, active as of this writing, that provide access to vast amounts of MSDS and other HCS materials.

Task 5. Training Programs

The heart of right-to-know legislation is the training and education that provides knowledge in a form workers can appreciate, understand, and apply. Because of the importance of this education, there is an abundance of commercially purchasable materials and services to satisfy these requirements. Considerable free material is also available online from private organizations willing to provide training services. The material that follows in this chapter is intended to give insight into (a) OSHA requirements, (b) the OSHA criteria established to measure compliance, and (c) assistance OSHA provides to employers for the purposes of complying. From the employer's perspective, training has been a significant financial burden because of the paid time away from work that employees spend in such programs. However, this burden may be lightened with an improved safety and health record for the workforce, which may in turn reduce other costs such as worker compensation rates.

OSHA compliance activities for the HCS in general have focused strongly on the required training programs under the act. Consequently, failure to have adequate training has become a major source of noncompliance citations. Compliance officers are given the following guidelines to look for when examining an employer's training program. An OSHA publication, *Inspection Procedures for the Hazard Communication Standard*, outlines these guidelines by indicating what a training program is expected to contain (OSHA 1998):

- a summary of the standard and this company's written program
- the chemical and physical properties of hazardous materials (e.g., flash point, vapor pressure, reactivity) and methods that can be used to detect the presence or release of chemicals (including chemicals in unlabeled pipes)
- the physical hazards of the chemicals in the work area (e.g., potential for fire, explosion)
- the health hazards, including signs and symptoms of exposure, of the chemicals in the work area and any medical condition known to be aggravated by exposure to these chemicals
- procedures to protect against chemical hazards (e.g., required personal protective equipment and its proper use and maintenance; work practices or methods to ensure appropriate use and handling of chemicals; and procedures for emergency response)
- work procedures to follow to assure protection when cleaning hazardous chemical spills and leaks
- the location of the MSDSs, how to read and interpret the information on labels and MSDSs, and how employees may obtain additional hazard information

Designing a Training Program

At the time of the introduction of the HCS, the OSHA training requirements of the regulation were not well defined and not well understood. Currently, these requirements are carefully specified and examples of complete programs, including visuals, are available through numerous sources. Many training programs are accessible online free of charge. In 2003, OSHA took the lead by providing a "Draft Model Training Program for Hazard Communication" (2003). This model is complete with a day-by-day subject outline, PowerPoint slides, movies, and study/test questions to assure that the students have an adequate level of understanding. The program is available online at www.osha.gov. Of course this generic program cannot satisfy the detailed operations of specific employers. Thus, each program must be customized regardless of whether the OSHA model program is used or not. Such customization requires the HAZCOM program manager to be aware of the individual requirements of training. Such training must explain and reinforce the information presented to employees through the written mediums of labels and material safety data

TABLE 2

Sources of Online Information for MSDSs, Labeling, and Training Programs

	Locating or Providing MSDSs	
Web Site Address	**Organization**	**Description**
www.msds.com/	MSDS Solutions	Site houses over 2,000,000 MSDSs—English, German, Chinese, Dutch, Spanish, and French.
www.ilo.legacy/english/protection/safework/cis/products/icsc/dtasht/index.htm	International Occupational Safety and Health Information Centre	Describes what chemical safety cards are and their purpose.
http://www.rmis.com/db/dbchemicals.htm	Risk Management Internet Services	Conduct online searches of numerous chemical databases to obtain information related to material safety data sheets (MSDS). Has some international links.
www.ccohs.ca/products/msds	Canadian Center for Occupational Health and Safety	MSDS database gives instant access to the most up-to-date (more than 280,000) MSDSs from 2,000 North American manufacturers and suppliers. Provides link for MSDSs in French.
www.msdssearch.com/backgroundN.htm	MSDS Search	Find links/information on every aspect of MSDSs, including how to read, write, understand, and train employees to meet the HazCom standard.
http://hazard.com/msds/	Vermont Safety Information Resources	Searchable MSDS database of chemicals and chemical compounds.
www.ilpi.com/msds/index.html	Interactive Learning Paradigms Incorporated—Safety Emporium	Contains a listing of more than 100 free sites you can access to find MSDSs on the Internet.
	Creating an MSDS	
Web Site Address	**Organization**	**Description**
www.ess.co.at/RISK/MSDS/msds.html	Environmental Software and Services	Site provides a listing of the 16 articles required by EU's Directive 91/155/EEC.
2001/58/EC- http:eur-lex.eu/smart/cgi/sga_doc?smartapi!clexapi!prod!CELEXnumbdoc&numdoc=201L0058&model==guichett&lg=en http:eur-lex.europa.eu/LexUriServ/LexUriServ.do?uri=CELEX:31998L0024:En:HTML		Can download Directive 2001/58/EC, which amended 91/155/EEC from the European Union Web site. Sets out the requirements for the information that should be included in a safety data sheet. Employer responsibilities outlined in detail in Directive 98/24/EC.
http://ccinfoweb.ccohs.ca/help/msds/msdsINTGUIDE.html	Canadian Centre for Occupational Health and Safety	Site provides a summary of "The MSDS; A Basic Guide For Users—International Version."

Creating an MSDS (Continued)

Web Site Address	Organization	Description
www.ilpi.com/msds/ref/chip.html	Chemicals Hazard and Information and Packaging for Supply Regulations (CHIP). Interactive Learning Paradigms Incorporated- Safety Emporium	Great Britain's law governing MSDSs (among many other items) is the Chemical Hazard and Information and Packaging for Supply Regulations (CHIP)
www.ilpi.com/msds/ref/ghs/html	Safety Emporium	Provides links to several sites/pages detailing the Globally Harmonized System (GHS).
www.ccohs.ca/oshanswers/legisl/msds_prep.html	Canadian Centre for Occupational Health and Safety	Aids writers in identifying the specific types of information required in MSDSs used in Canada, the United States, and the European Union.
http://ccinfoweb.ccohs.ca/help/msds/msdsCDNREQE.html		Site provides a brief summary of Canadian requirements.
www.msdssearch.com/backgroundN.htm	MSDS Search	Find links/information on every aspect of MSDSs.

Chemical Labeling

Web Site Address	Organization	Description
www.rmis.com/sites/chemichemi.php	Risk Management Internet Services	Guidance on the required information for chemical hazard label systems for DOT, HMIS, NFPA diamond.
www.apps.kemi/se/nclass/default.asp	Nordic Council of Ministers (European Chemicals Bureau)	Provides up-to-date list of the legally required harmonized classifications and labelling for substances in the EU.
www.umanitoba.ca/admin/human_resources/ehso/WHMISHandbook.pdf	University of Manitoba	Site provides link to a Workplace Hazardous Materials Information System (WHMIS) handbook.
www.hc-sc.gc.ca/ewhisemt/occup-travail/whmis-simdut/index_eng.php	Health Canada	Canadian legislation overing the use of hazardous materials in the workplace. Closely parallels the U.S. Hazard Communication Standard.
http://ecb.jrc.ec.europa/eu/classification-labelling Click on the "Search ClassLab" tab and then the "Search Annex 1 button" to perform the search.	European Commission Joint Research Centre	Provides informationand links to classification and labelling requirements for dangerous substances and preparations.
www.msdssearch.com/backgroundN.htm	MSDS Search	Find links/information on every aspect of MSDSs, including how to read, write, understand, and train employees to meet the HazCom standard.
www.hc-sc.gc.ca/ahc-asc/intactiv/ghs-sgh/implement/tor/ghs1_e.html	Health Canada	Provides information on the Globally Harmonized System for Hazard Classification and Labeling, defining and classifying hazards, and communicating information on labels and safety data sheets.
www.osha.gov/dsg/hazcom/global.html	Occupational Safety and Health Administration (OSHA)	OSHA's information page; links to information on the GHS.

Hazard Communication Program Training

Web Site Address	Organization	Description
www.freetraining.com/osha/hazcom/hazmenu.htm		Free hazard communication training course covers labeling, MSDSs, physical hazards, health hazards, and protective measures.
www.osha-safety-training.net	National Safety Compliance	Offers OSHA compliance and training resources for all workplaces and employers.
www.free-training.com/		Offering free online training courses available in various formats.
www.lni.wa.gov/Safety/TrainTools/Trainer/kits/hazcom	Washington State Department of Labor and Industries	Free hazard control training kit containing Powerpoint presentation and script.
www.msdssearch.com/backgroundN.htm	MSDS Search	Find links/information on every aspect of MSDSs.

sheets. They must also learn how to apply this information in their workplace. Labels and material safety data sheets will be successful only when employees understand the information presented and are aware of what actions should be taken to avoid or minimize both exposure and the likely occurrence of adverse effects.

Training helps to integrate and classify the many pieces of information that relate to chemical hazard communication. In a typical workplace, a worker may be confronted with posted hazard warnings, signs, tags, incoming labels, workplace labels, MSDSs, manuals that explain the company hazard communication program, lists of chemicals, and information furnished by the union. This wide variety of communications will differ in format, content, and reading level. These differences can obscure the important hazard communication message; thus, integration of such information through training programs is essential.

Training sessions also provide a forum for employees to share their health and safety concerns and to obtain answers from managers and occupational health and safety professionals. Employees can also share their ideas and job experiences, which often include acquired expertise in dealing with potentially hazardous situations in their work environments.

Specific Requirements

Paragraph (h) of the HCS (29 CFR 1910.1200) addresses employee information and training. The requirements reflect the overall purpose of the standard. There are certain key words and phrases in this requirement on which OSHA has focused. (They are indicated in bold.) These key words and phrases have been identified in this integrated version of paragraph (h) (OSHA 1994):

a. First, employers shall provide employees with **effective** information and training on hazardous chemicals **in their work area** at the **time of their initial assignment**, and whenever a **new physical or health hazard** that employees have not been previously trained about is introduced into their work area. Information and training may be designed to cover **categories of hazards** (such as flammability or carcinogenicity) or **specific chemicals. Chemical-specific information must always be available through labels and material safety data sheets**.

b. Second, employees shall be **informed** of: the requirements of this section; any **operations in their work area** where hazardous chemicals are present; the **location and availability** of the written hazard communication program, including the required list of hazardous chemicals, and material safety data sheets that describe them.

c. Third, employee **training** shall include at least: **methods and observations** that may be used to detect the presence or release of a hazardous chemical in the work area (such as monitoring conducted by the employer, continuous monitoring devices, visual appearance or odor of hazardous chemicals when being released, etc.); the **physical and health** hazards of the chemicals in the work area; the **measures employees can take to protect themselves** from these hazards, including specific procedures the employer has implemented to protect employees from exposure to hazardous chemicals, such as appropriate work practices, emergency procedures, and personal protective equipment to be used; and the **details of the hazard communication program** developed by the employer, including an explanation of labels and material safety data sheets, and how employees can obtain and use the appropriate hazard information.

OSHA's Interpretation of Key Training Requirements

In order to give guidance to both employers attempting to comply and officers active in compliance activities, OSHA has provided some interpretation of the key words/phrases from the previous extract.

Effective means that the information and training program must work. Employees must carry the knowledge from the training into their daily jobs. For example, if asked, they should know where hazardous chemicals are present in their work area, and should also know how to protect themselves.

In their work area means just what it says. The information and training must be specific to each work area. You cannot inform only at training about general hazards found in work areas; you have to address the potential hazards that employees are actually going to encounter.

Time of initial assignment. This means that new employees must be informed and trained before going on the job, so that they are not faced with unknown hazards.

New physical or health hazard. Sometimes new hazardous chemicals are introduced into the workplace, and sometimes employees are assigned to new jobs that involve potential exposure to new hazards. Either way, no employee should be in the position of encountering unfamiliar or unknown hazards.

Categories of hazards. OSHA is aware that workplaces may contain so many different chemicals that it would be difficult and confusing to attempt to train employees about each one separately. Fortunately, many chemicals fall into categories, such as flammables or acids and bases. In these instances, it is not only acceptable but also more effective to discuss the hazards of the category as a whole. If individual chemicals within a category present a special safety or health hazard, these unique properties must be pointed out.

Specific chemicals are those that don't belong in a category or should be singled out for some other reason. For example, they may present a special hazard, or be represented in great quantity in the workplace.

Informed. Providing information is not quite the same as training, but we have included both under the general term "training" in this Model Training Program. It means that employees must know what the standard means and where things are kept. Information can be furnished with the help of signs, notices, handouts, or other means. Whatever information measures are chosen, however, they must be effective. For example, employees should be able to tell you where the written program is housed, and also to locate the material safety data sheet collection.

Operations in their work area. This phrase points again to the need to be specific in the information and training program. Generalities about operations that have no relevance to specific employees are not sufficient.

Location and availability must again be specific. For example, the written hazard communication program may be kept in Building A or in the supervisor's office, where it must be available at **all** times. Employees should know exactly where it is and how to gain access.

Training. This term covers anything that is done to impart new knowledge or skills or to refresh employees' memories on previously learned knowledge or skills. It can best be imagined as bridging the gap between what employees know now and what they have to know to identify hazards and protect themselves against chemicals. Many different training methods and media can be used to achieve this goal.

Methods and observations are any active or passive means that can be used to detect the presence or release of a hazardous chemical. For example, some chemicals can be detected by their odor, color, or other unique properties.

Physical and health hazards. These terms apply only to the physical and health hazards of chemicals. A physical hazard is associated with a chemical that is a combustible liquid, a compressed gas, explosive, flammable, an organic peroxide, an oxidizer, pyrophoric, unstable or water-reactive. All these can harm as a result of physical reaction. **Health hazard**

means that exposure to the chemical can cause acute or chronic health effects. Examples are carcinogens and eye irritants.

Measures employees can take to protect themselves. These can include any type of control, including everything from learning the meaning of emergency signals to observing "No Entry" areas or selecting the correct personal protective equipment.

Details of the hazard communication program. This allows employees to learn what label statements mean, what information can be found in the material safety data sheet, and how to find out if a chemical presents a potential hazard. (OSHA 2003, I-2.)

As indicated earlier, to assist employers with limited technical resources and to illustrate training that would satisfy the regulation, OSHA developed an example training program. This is complete with a schedule of topics, slides to accompany lectures, and quizzes to measure comprehension. This program can be obtained directly from OSHA.

Eight lessons have been developed within this program. These lessons and the approximate time for each are listed below.

Lesson A:	1 hour	Understanding the Hazard Communication Standard
Lesson B:	1 hour	Understanding the Material Safety Data Sheet
Lesson C	1 hour	Understanding Labels
Lesson D	1 hour	Understanding Health Information
Lesson E	90 minutes	Understanding Flammables and Combustibles
Lesson F	1 hour	Understanding Corrosives
Lesson G	90 minutes	Understanding Reactive Chemicals
Lesson H	1 hour	Understanding Toxic Chemicals
	9–10 hours	Approximate total lesson time (not including breaks)

The proposed contents for each of these lessons are listed in Appendix C. The topics within the contents provide what OSHA expects of employers in the way of a comprehensive training program. Such expectations are not to be taken lightly by the safety or health professional in charge of such training, and strong consideration should be given to using the OSHA model training program as a foundation from which to work.

Compliance Results and Assistance from OSHA

Over the years the General Accounting Office (GAO) and OSHA have done surveys and analyzed inspection data to determine levels of compliance with HCS. They found a substantial number of employers out of compliance, especially small employers with fewer than twenty employees. OSHA inspections of particular work sites are often selected because of accidents, complaints, or the hazardousness of the industry. In the early 1990s, OSHA found 26 percent of all inspected work sites out of compliance with at least one HCS requirement (United States GAO 1991, 3). In surveying a random sample of employers, GAO found 58 percent of small employers and 52 percent of all employers to be out of compliance with key requirements of HCS (United States GAO 1991, 3).

GAO issued reports identifying the difficulties small employers were said to be experiencing in complying with the HCS. The findings were based on the results of the employer survey mentioned previously. Forty-five percent of those in compliance with the HCS considered the standard to have a positive effect on employees, compared with only 9 percent who viewed the effect as negative. Almost 30 percent of employers reported that they had replaced a hazardous chemical with a less hazardous chemical substitute because of information presented on an MSDS (United States GAO 1991, 4).

Almost 70 percent of small employers complying with the HCS reported no difficulty in maintaining MSDSs and providing access for employees. Larger employers reported comparatively more difficulty, likely because of a need to manage a larger quantity of MSDSs and to provide access to a greater number of employees. Half of all large employers reported that they had 250 or more MSDSs. With regard to training, almost 80 percent of small employers complying with the HCS reported some difficulty. Insufficient training expertise and complex MSDSs were cited as particular problems (OSHA, March 2004).

The GAO findings generally indicated that noncompliance with the HCS resulted largely from lack of knowledge about the requirements of the standard, rather than difficulty in complying with the provisions of the standard. These results pointed toward greater outreach assistance efforts as a way to improve compliance. After these studies, OSHA continued to make extensive efforts to provide helpful materials to assist employers to comply with the various provisions of the HCS. This is reflected in the materials offered on their Web site and through hardcopy versions available for the referenced materials within this chapter.

This completes the chapter's five tasks addressing hazard communication compliance with OSHA. However, one can see from the listing of desired training topics proposed by OSHA (see Appendix C) that the expected scope of employee knowledge about safety and health goes well beyond that which is only within the OSHA regulations. Other standards and regulations that will be encountered by employees both on and off company premises are included within the topics of the suggested training materials. Consequently, the following sections have been developed to cover standards addressing several of the other types of hazard communication that are not covered under OSHA, for example, accident-prevention signs, general chemical labeling, safety posters, lockout tagging, barricade tapes, and highway hazard signs and vehicle communications.

OTHER HAZARD COMMUNICATIONS: SIGNAGE AND LABELING

Pre-OSHA Signage

The importance of accident-prevention signs to worker safety had been recognized by the early 1900s. By the 1930s to 1940s, the National Safety Council and insurance companies had assumed an important role in creating, promoting, and distributing safety-related information such as posters. During this time there was little research as to what type of signage design might be the most effective under a particular circumstance and context. Today, extensive research has suggested four attributes can be analyzed in any safety- or health-related labeling, signage, or other instructional materials. These include text (and cognitive aspects of messages), symbols (usage and meaning), format (layout and presentation), and location (geographical placement and environmental factors). For every type of safety communication developed, these attributes have to be addressed, and the number of such communication types is vast. One can think of scores of examples where persons are exposed to signage in their daily occupational and personal lives. To appreciate the breadth of this exposure, Appendix D has been developed to list numerous types of primarily hazard communications. There are warning and instructional communications that have been given special attention through government and voluntary standards organizations. Only a few of them are discussed in this chapter, but the scope of hazard warnings is clearly very broad.

Coverage of Standards—Any Standard

Understanding and properly applying standards covering the areas in Appendix D requires knowledge of the intent of the various provisions within a standard, in terms of coverage and specificity. Signage standards range all the way from being extremely specific and very detailed to being very nonspecific and with limited details. It is useful to think about classifying whole standards, or provisions within standards, in terms of (a) coverage (horizontal versus vertical) and (b) degree of specificity (performance versus specification). OSHA refers to such a classification system in its publication 92-14 (May 1996), but such a classification system applies regardless of whether it is a voluntary consensus standard (such as ANSI or ASTM) or a mandatory government regulation (such as OSHA, EPA, or CPSC).

The concept of the *horizontal* standard indicates application to a breadth of industry or across product categories (e.g., all machine guarding, all chemical hazard warnings, or all electrical safety). On the other hand, a *vertical* standard means it is more specific to a particular industry, type of operation, or a specific chemical (e.g., shipbuilding, welding, woodworking machines, benzene, or asbestos).

Relative to a standard's degree of specificity, consensus organization's standards are more likely to be of a *performance* nature to give applicators a breadth of flexibility in achieving a design adaptable to their company (e.g., automobiles must meet a crashworthy test at 5 mph, regardless of their design). On the other hand, government-mandated standards are often of a *specification* nature that, among other things, facilitates enforcers to judge compliance more easily (e.g., worker exposure to benzene shall not exceed 1 part per million (PPM) as a time-weighted, 8-hour average).

Government and consensus organizations must determine whether each standard, subsection, and provision will have a horizontal or vertical scope and then determine if the specificity of it will be based on performance or design. Nearly all standards have within them a mixture of these classifications across their various provisions, and the practitioner must try to ascertain what the intent of the developers was relative to these potential formats.

Most signing standards promulgated by consensual organizations are horizontal in structure, applying to a breadth of signing categories (e.g., all environmental or facility signing). Consensus standards are also more likely to be of a performance nature to give applicators a breadth of flexibility in achieving a design adapted to their company.

Early Industrial Accident-Prevention Signs

Many think of the United States of America as being innovative in its approach to industrial safety and health communications since 1970. However, the reader may be surprised by some of the contents of a publication dated 1914 and published by the Accident Prevention Department of the National Association of Manufacturers. It is titled "Preventive Appliances," and the publication abounds with quotations that could well have been published contemporarily 98 years later. Consider the following example:

> The use of danger signs has a very important place in a campaign for safety, serving as a warning to point out an existing danger, and . . . with the weight of opinion among safety engineers and others connected with the safety movement . . . the color green having come into general acceptance as signifying safety . . . the red color that indicates danger. (National Association of Manufacturers 1914, 1)

The National Safety Council, in its early safety and health role, provided a large selection of safety posters covering a wide variety of potential hazards. This effort was well underway by 1927, as indicated by a *National Safety News* article from that era (Mathieu 1927).

> The National Safety Council (NSC) posters are too well known to be described here. The hundred of thousands ordered each month show they serve a useful purpose.
>
> It remains then for our silent salesman to bridge the gap between safety meetings and other safety activities. This silent salesman is the safety poster.
>
> Posters must be changed frequently, the oftener, the better, within reasonable limits.
>
> We must remember the danger of leaving it up too long, for this is one case where our adaptiveness will work against us. (Mathieu 1927, 17–18)

If one looks at examples of posters from this era, an appreciation is gained of how sophisticated the designs were, even without having the benefit of our *modern* research input. More recent research has only validated the experiential knowledge applied to the designs of accident-prevention signs created in this earlier era.

The NSC posters often used cartoon-type drawings to depict various safety circumstances, and they gave accompanying descriptions suggesting preventive actions. These cartoon-type drawings could be viewed as the predecessors of nontextual symbols used internationally today. The early signs also revealed an important recognition that has since been called *human factors*. Namely, there was a sensitivity for understanding the capabilities and limitations of the various target recipients of safety information—humans. For example, a 1937 National Safety Congress presentation focused on longshoremen workers. "Longshoremen, as a class, are distinct from types of men found in other industry. . . . there are posters with safety slogans that 50 per cent of them can neither read nor understand" (Ames 1937, 358).

The response to such a situation was to create cartoon characters, such as the "Ozzie" used by the Travelers Insurance Company. Ozzie would be shown performing unsafe acts leading to an accident. As an indication of how effective this portrayal was, workers who had tendencies to commit unsafe acts were themselves called "Ozzies" by other workers, and not in a complimentary way (Ames 1937, 358).

The standards for signing can easily be traced back 50 years. For example, the United States of America Standard Institute's (USASI) "Specifications for Accident Prevention Signs" was already in its second revision in 1968 (1968a). According to the standard, it was mutually agreed that signage was one of the "oldest items of safety equipment" used. Also, within this standard, there was evidence that the sponsors had identified objectives and desired outcomes that are currently known as *effectiveness*. For example, one part of the standard expressed, "Uniformity of signs, intelligently located and properly worded, should provide an automatic warning, caution, or notice to all employees no matter where they work with a meaning that is clearly understood immediately" (USASI 1968a, 7).

A Movement toward Uniformity

The above showed early recognition of the importance of uniformity in hazard communication signs at all industrial levels. Guidelines for this uniformity came in a 1941–42 version of an American Standards Association (ASA) standard, Z35.1, *American Standard Specifications for Industrial Accident Prevention Signs*. After many years of use and subsequent deliberations, this ASA Z35.1 standard was revised in 1959 under the same title.

The early versions of ASA Z35.1 standards were specifically developed for hazard communications in workplaces. It is interesting that in the 1959 revision of the same American Standard Z35.1, the now well-known radiation symbol first appeared after its approval by ASA (ASA 1959, 9).

Contrary to how plaintiff lawyers try to convince juries, these initial signing standards were never intended to be applicable to labels on products. This is understandable since there were no other safety communication standards applicable to product labels in this era. As a consequence, many attempted to extrapolate the specifications within the Z35.1 signage standards and apply them to product warning labels. It was not until the 1991 ANSI Z535.4 standard that consumer-product warning labels were specifically addressed (ANSI 1991a–e).

Signage Standardization

Evolution of ANSI (ASA to USASI to ANSI)

It was about the time of World War II that a renewed interest in safety signage began. With a preexisting organization like the ASA already in place, it was a logical place for additional signing standardization to begin.

Current-day researchers attempting to trace the changes in consensual signing standards throughout the years are confronted with the name changes of the standards-generating organizations. Namely, early standards for safety colors were developed as an American War Standard at the request of the War Department, which was in power throughout World War II. This color standard was adopted in 1945 by the previously mentioned American Standards Association (ASA). The ASA was reconstituted as the USA Standards Institute (USASI) in August 1966 and later as the American National Standards Institute (ANSI) in October 1969 (ANSI 1979). Interestingly, although an organization's name may change throughout the life of a given standard, the standard's designated number typically does not change.

Consolidation under the ANSI Z535 Series

The ANSI Z535 series (2011) has become a set of systematic guidelines for designing any type of word-based hazard communication, whether signs, labels, tags, tapes, manuals, or instructions. The series could have been written as one standard, rather than six separate standards, and covered all the listed types of hazard communication channels. Regardless of the communication type, the designer is confronted with the same set of general questions, which the current ANSI Z535 series is now able to answer:

1. *What should the parts of the communication be?* Answer: For one-page communications there should be a two- or three-panel display consisting of an enlarged signal-word panel; a panel with verbiage describing the hazard, potential consequences, and preventive measures; and, optionally, a symbol that may also have a few words with it identifying what hazard or preventive measure the symbol represents.

2. *What color combinations should be used?* Answer: The standard Z535.1 (2006, R2011) specifies which colors are recommended for different parts of the design.
3. *If one uses a symbol, what are the rules of use, and how should it be displayed?* The answer is in Z535.3 (2011b), which gives the criteria for safety symbol usage.
4. *Are there recommendations specific to the type of communication one is designing for a particular application?* Answer: Yes, although the design procedure is the same and uses similar criteria, there are slight differences based on the application. These slight differences are spelled out in the separate standards dealing with the following: Environmental and Facility Safety Signs (Z535.2, 2011a); Product Safety Signs and Labels (Z535.4, 2011c); Safety Tags and Barricade Tapes (Z535.5, 2011d); and Other Collateral Materials (Z535.6, 2011e).

A somewhat controversial fifth question could be asked at this point, even though it digresses from the present discussion:

5. *How will the Globally Harmonized System's (GHS) recommendations affect the design and acceptability of "Environmental and Facility Safety Signs" and "Product Safety Signs and Labels"?* Answer: As described later in this chapter, the international directions for such designs are slightly different from that described within the ANSI Z535 series. There are cultural reasons for many of the differences, which U.S. governmental and standardization organizations have been slow to recognize. As a result, there will be alternative formats, which are likely to be acceptable across international borders.

The scope of the GHS proposal will be discussed later in this chapter.

As noted, the first four of these questions could have been dealt with more efficiently in one standard with several sections. However, it was more feasible under the ANSI committee political structure to divide the guidelines into six separate standard areas and to assign appropriate experts to respective committees. The misfortune is that a designer will probably have to have all these standards available for study so that no specification is overlooked.

Many different hazard communication applications are portrayed in the various signs in Appendix D in this chapter. For all these applications, the U.S. signing designers had moved in a common direction. That common direction was the ANSI Z535 series. For nearly twenty years this series of standards has become universally respected, and it has been used for guidance across broad classifications of safety information. The series is obtainable in electronic or hardcopy versions from the ANSI organization at www.ansi.org or through the Secretariat for the Z535 standards (National Electrical Manufacturers Association, 1300 North 17th Street, Rosslyn, VA 22209).

This entire series of ANSI Z535 standards began with the ANSI Z35.1 1941–42 standard on accident-prevention signs:

- Z535.1 (2006, R2011)—**Safety Color Code** (This first historical standard was published as Z35.1 in 1941–42. It was updated in 1979 and combined into this present standard in 1991.)
- Z535.2 (2011a)—**Environmental and Facility Safety Signs** (ANSI Z35.1-1972 and Z35.4-1972 were updated and combined into this standard in 1991 with the latest revision in 2007.)
- Z535.3 (2011b)—**Criteria for Safety Symbols** (new in 1991 with the latest revision in 2007.)
- Z535.4 (2011c)—**Product Safety Signs and Labels** (new in 1991 with latest revision in 2011.)
- Z535.5 (2011d)—**Safety Tags and Barricade Tapes (for temporary hazards)** (ANSI Z35.2-1974 was updated and combined into this standard in 1991 with the latest revision in 2007.)
- Z535.6 (2011e)—**Product Safety Information in Product Manuals, Instructions, and Other Collateral Materials** (new in 2006.)

For the scholar and researcher as well as the serious applications person, there are excellent references provided at the end of each of these standards. Such references have been either cited within the standards themselves or utilized as foundations for specific provisions. Just looking over the list of these references allows one to appreciate how intertwined standards for signage have become. Such intertwining is positive because it has led to consistency across many, though not all, arenas and applications. Because of the importance of these references, they have been compiled and provided in Appendix E to this chapter, titled "References in the ANSI Z535-2011 Series."

This chapter is no substitute for having the complete set of ANSI Z535 standards available for review. It addresses only certain aspects of the standards. The focus of this chapter has been on the hazard communications dealing with the occupational and commercial applications as opposed to the household and consumer applications. Hence, the ANSI Z535.4 standard on product safety signs and labels will not be emphasized. Instead, the ANSI Z535.2 standard on environmental and facility signs will be used to illustrate the design options available. Within the Z535.2 standard there are about fifteen parameters that the sign designer has limited options to manipulate. As these are discussed, remember that they are the same parameters that are applicable to product labeling or almost any type of visual hazard communication.

About the ANSI Z535 Series

The major types of hazard communications covered in the ANSI Z535 series are environmental signage and product signage. The difference in these is spelled out in the following section.

Environmental or Product Safety Signs

Even among the safety communications experts, there remains an assemblage of terms whose definitions are still gray, including *warnings* (verbal, written, contextual, auditory, etc.), *warning labels, signs, signage, instructions, safety data sheets, placards, tags, safety information, important information, safety tape, paperless warnings,* and *computer on-screen product information.*

To distinguish environmental signing from product signage and labeling, one can think of products as completed functional units or components that are purchased from, or supplied by, an entity outside an immediate organization. As such, the signing that was placed on the product before it was delivered to a customer is usually referred to as *product labeling*. The supplied product then already has a type of signage (or labeling) prior to the time it enters onto a premise, into a facility, or anywhere in its applications environment.

On the other hand, *environmental signage* involves the communication of information that an end user, facilities manager, premise owner, or environmental administrator determines as necessary for the safety and health of humans (or other living organisms) in a particular domain. This differentiation will become apparent as the Z535.2 standard is discussed further.

From Z535.2, an "environmental safety sign" is a "sign or placard in a work or public area that provides safety information about the immediate environment" (ANSI 2007, 4). And a "product safety sign," is defined in the same Z535.2 standard as a "sign, label, or decal affixed to a product that provides hazard and safety information about that product" (ANSI 2007, 4).

Safety signs, both environmental and product, are categorized in ANSI Z535.2 as being in one of the following seven categories: (1) DANGER, (2) WARNING, (3) CAUTION, (4) NOTICE, (5) safety instructions or safety equipment location, (6) fire safety, or (7) directional arrow signs. Among these, the signal words in uppercase letters designate the level of hazard seriousness. The specific definition associated with each of these types of sign is provided in the following list (ANSI 2007, 4).

1. **DANGER sign:** Indicates a hazardous situation that is to be limited to the most extreme situations. If not avoided, it *will* result in death or serious injury.
2. **WARNING sign:** Indicates a hazardous situation that, if not avoided, *could* result in death or serious injury.

3. **CAUTION sign:** Indicates a hazardous situation that, if not avoided, could result in minor or moderate injury. It may also be used without the safety alert symbol as an alternative to "NOTICE:" "NOTICE" is the preferred signal word to address practices not related to personal injury. The safety alert symbol should not be used with this signal word. As an alternative to "NOTICE," the word "CAUTION," without the safety alert symbol, may be used to indicate a message not related to personal injury.
4. **NOTICE sign:** Notice signs are used for precautions not related to personal injury, and the safety alert symbol is not used with this signal word.
5. **Signs for safety instructions or safety equipment location:** Signs used to indicate general instructions relative to safe work practices or indicate the location of safety equipment.
6. **Fire safety signs:** Signs used to indicate the location of emergency fire-fighting equipment. (*Note:* These signs indicate the location of, but not the directions to, the equipment).
7. **Directional arrow signs:** Signs used to indicate the direction to emergency equipment, safety equipment, and other locations important to safety.

Designing Hazard Communication Signs

Unless mandated by government regulations, the use of signage for the environment or products is voluntary. Nevertheless, the use of signs and posters to provide hazard communications is widespread and often effective both in providing valuable safety and health information and in constantly reminding employees of actions they need to take for their own well-being. However, if it is decided to use signage, the consensus has been that it is preferable for such signage to be standardized along certain guidelines that might improve their potential effectiveness. To this end, the ANSI standard Z535.2 provides guidelines for sign designers.

A better understanding of the standard can be achieved if one arbitrarily divides it into four categories of features: (1) sign classification, (2) configuration of panels, (3) content of panels, and (4) display method.

If one analyzes the ANSI Z535.2 standard further, it becomes apparent that there are at least fifteen parameters regarding these features over which the designer has control as indicated below:

1. *Sign classification.* At the onset, the designer confronts the issue of what type of sign is needed (parameter 1). The choices are danger, warning, caution, notice, general safety, fire safety, or directional.
2. *Configuration of panels.* Signage is typically formatted in a 3-panel display layout. Although the standard notes several acceptable configurations for this layout, each of these layouts will typically include a signal-word panel (parameter 2), symbol/pictorial panel size (parameter 3) as specified in Z535.3 (ANSI 2007), and the word-message size (parameter 4). Even at this initial stage the designer must consider the overall desired or allowable physical size of the sign given environmental (or product-size) limitations.
3. *Content of Panels.* The panel content parameters include color choice (parameter 5) in accordance with Z535.1 (ANSI 2006), choice of signal word (parameter 6), shapes of directional arrows, if used (parameter 7), choice of symbols or pictorials (parameter 8), letter style (parameter 9) and letter size (parameter 10), choice of text message (parameter 11), and possible use of multilingual formats (parameter 12).
4. *Display Method.* This designation includes: sign placement within an environment so that persons might see it (parameter 13); illumination on a sign under limited natural-lighting conditions (parameter 14); and contrast (parameter 15).

As a beginning to the design process, there are twelve acceptable format or layout examples provided in Z535.2, suggesting the variety of ways the panel components—signal-word panel (#2), symbol/pictorial panel (#3), and word message (#4)—might be laid out. Only in the case of fire safety or signs and labels is a panel format without a signal-word panel (#2) recommended (ANSI 2007, 10, 17).

The preceding discussion illustrates that there is a very systematic way to conceive and design signs for various purposes. Dividing the decision making into the suggested fifteen parameters also provides a methodology for documenting how the various components of a sign (or label) evolved. It is noted that, if the question of "adequate warnings" arises in the litigation arena, the systematic approach laid out here leads to a documentation trail that, though optional, will be highly valuable in the litigation discovery process.

Safety Symbols

According to ANSI Z535.3, "Safety symbols are an *optional* component of the multi-panel safety sign, label, and tag formats described in the ANSI Z535.2, ANSI Z535.4, ANSI Z535.5 standards. Although the international trend is to rely much more heavily on symbols to transcend the language barriers, symbols usually consist of a black image (or safety red image for some symbols) on a white background" (ANSI 2007, 3).

If a safety symbol is utilized, it may be used with or without additional verbiage to describe the nature of the hazard being addressed by a particular symbol. The ANSI standard has a clear requirement that, if a symbol is to stand alone without explanatory verbiage, then it must have been tested for its "demonstrated understandability." This involves passing an "85% recognition test" as described in the ANSI Z535.3 standard (ANSI 2007, 21). There are 24 such pretested successful symbols provided as examples in the ANSI Z535.3 standard. These may be used by any designer without further testing. Along with these tested symbols, references are given as to which researcher or author conducted the successful testing (ANSI 2007, 40–53).

"Other symbols," as defined in the standard, are those that have not passed this level of "understandability" with a sample population. For all these other symbols that have not been successfully tested, it is required that additional explanatory word messages be provided to assist in explaining the intent of the symbol. Note that such testing can be done by private concerns, consultants, or research organizations, or taken from published results, as long as the procedural guidelines explained in ANSI Z535.3 have been followed. In support of these sections on ANSI Z535 labeling, three examples are provided. Figure 1 shows three symbols (labeled A, B, and C) that have been tested in accordance with ANSI Z535.3 and can be used without any text explanation as to their related hazard. The reader is cautioned that the philosophy

A

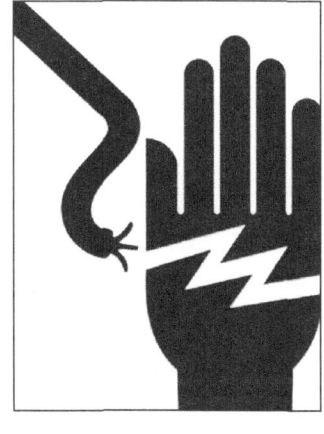
B

C

FIGURE 1. ANSI-tested safety symbols (*Source:* ANSI Z535.3, 2007)

and criteria associated with symbol usage is changing internationally even as this Handbook is published.

Figure 2 is the CPSC- and major manufacturers-approved ANSI Z535-style label that appears on all-terrain vehicles sold in the United States. It was developed and tested by this author not only for symbol recognition but also for user comprehension and understanding, where its score was in the 90 percent range. Figure 3 provides an example of an ANSI-formatted electrical hazard lockout label.

Choice of Signal Word

In any of the specifications for signs, labels, tags, or tape, emphasis has been placed on the choice of signal word for *alerting* persons regarding the level of hazard they may be about to face. Early research did *not* indicate a preferred signal-word prioritization scheme. The hypothesis has been that the continued, consistent use of certain signal words for particular purposes would eventually cause the exposed subject populace to learn the significance of these prioritizations (e.g., that DANGER always suggests a hazard with a greater potential consequence than WARNING). Although there are no recent studies to test this hypothesis, this differentiation continues to be the accepted convention. Consequently, the definitions and use of these signal words have become consensually accepted even outside the scope of ANSI. The following definitions are consistent with the types of signs presented earlier (ANSI 2007, 18–19).

> **DANGER** indicates a hazardous situation which, if not avoided, *will* result in death or serious injury.

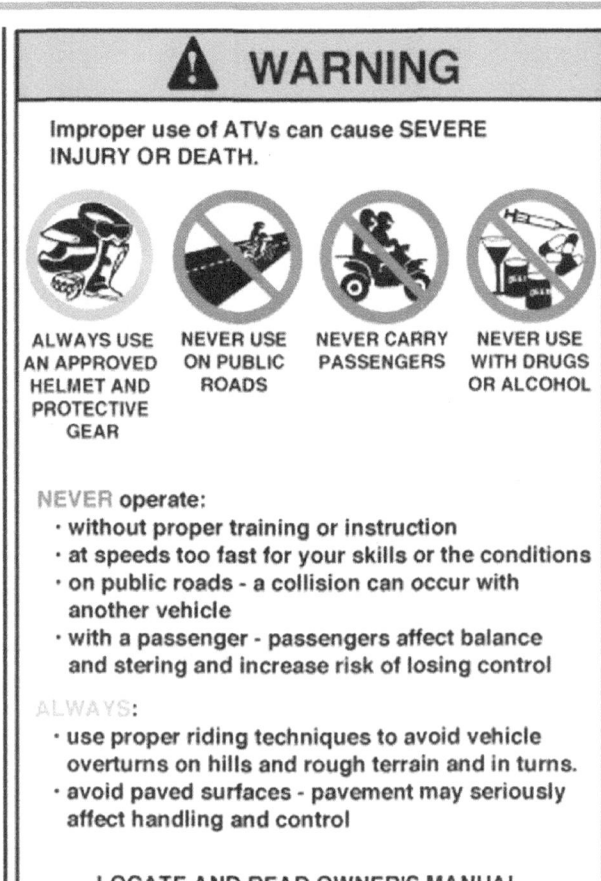

FIGURE 2. Example of ANSI-formatted ATV safety label (*Source:* ANSI Z535.4, 2007)

> **WARNING** indicates a hazardous situation which, if not avoided, *could* result in death or serious injury.
> **CAUTION (with the safety alert symbol)** indicates a hazardous situation which, if not

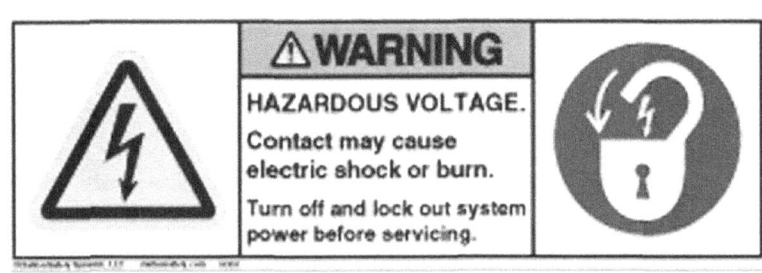

FIGURE 3. Example of ANSI electrical hazard lockout label (*Source:* ANSI Z535.4, 2007)

avoided, may result in minor or moderate injury.

CAUTION indicates a hazardous situation which, if not avoided, may result in minor or moderate injury. Without the safety alert symbol, it is used to address practices not related to personal injury.

NOTICE is used to address practices not related to personal injury.

Safety instruction or safety equipment location signs indicate general instructions relative to safe work practices or indicate the location of safety equipment.

The Safety Colors Standard

The use of colors in safety communication efforts has been extremely important. However, for those who have never reviewed the standard, there are many misunderstandings about the ANSI Z535.1 *Safety Colors* standard (2006), which neither indicates where a particular color should be used nor defines the significance of any given color. Rather, it is a specification standard that can be used to *manufacture* a certain color or verify that a given safety color has been achieved. There are ten such safety colors named. Where they are to be used is described in other standards. With this caveat in mind, the early history of the standard, described below, can be appreciated.

The Safety Color Code, was part of the *American War Standard*, which reportedly began in 1946 under committee procedures of the ASA and with the NSC as sponsor. This evolving effort was approved by ASA as the Z53 standard on September 11, 1953 (explaining the "53" designation). The 1979 version of ASA Z53.1 was the fourth revision and last in the series before the merging of several standards occurred under the Z535 series of 1991. The Z53.1 then took on the designation ANSI Z535.1, *Safety Color Code* (ANSI 2006, foreword, v). In 2006, the name of the standard was changed from *Safety Color Code* to *Safety Colors*.

In 1979, the ANSI Z53 Committee on Safety Colors was combined with the ANSI Z35 Committee on Safety Signs to form the ANSI Z535 Committee on Safety Signs and Colors. This committee still manages the entire ANSI Z535 series (ANSI 2006, foreword, v).

As indicated by this history, it was recognized early that individuals would learn to rely on the color coding, and such coding can even be applied to objects not featuring any word description, such as fire hydrants or facility piping.

The standard color specifications can be used across various types of safety information and safety-related objects, and they are frequently used within specifications originating from different governmental or organizational structures. They are also a mandatory reference for printers responsible for creating safety signage, labels, and other safety information.

As noted, other standards in the Z535 series recommend the circumstances in which a particular color from this set should be chosen. The standard color set itself is provided in Munsell Notation Specifications (ANSI 2006, 7) and also the Equivalent Commission Internationale de L'Eclairage (CIE), "Data Specifications" (ANSI 2006, 7). Besides specifying these colors, methods are given for testing, including visual evaluation. The set of ten primary color specifications for "safety colors" includes SAFETY RED, SAFETY ORANGE, SAFETY BROWN, SAFETY YELLOW, SAFETY GREEN, SAFETY BLUE, SAFETY PURPLE, SAFETY WHITE, SAFETY GRAY, and SAFETY BLACK. In addition to the color specs, the same Z535.1 standard provides recommendations for illumination and contrast (ANSI 2006).

The Z535.2 standard for environmental and facility signage utilizes a majority of the safety colors in its combinations of guidelines. Appendix F has been constructed to indicate the breadth of color combinations recommended in ANSI Z535.2. Each signal word is the beginning of the color combination for that respective type of sign. The required colors for background to the signal word, messages, background to messages, safety symbols, and background to symbols all have been specified for that type of sign. These combinations are shown on the table in Appendix F.

Signage Research References

The Z535 series standard has evolved from meetings where the communication scientists associated with signs and labeling and those persons actually involved in the design and application of such signage have tried to find common ground. Obviously, not all results found from research have made their way into these standard guidelines, and committees for such standards have not necessarily been in agreement as to what from the science should be included in any particular standard. Nevertheless, it is notable that the standards have listed in their appendices the primary references upon which some of the specifications were based. To assist the reader in being aware of these critical references, a table summarizing all the references cited by the ANSI Z535 committees has been prepared by this author and appears in Appendix E of this chapter under the title "References in the ANSI Z535 2006, 2007 Series." The various topics addressed in the standards, including the parameters used to design hazard communications, were further researched and presented in the book *Warnings and Safety Instructions—An Annotated Bibliography* (Miller and Lehto 2001), which reviewed 1200 such references.

Signage for Temporary Hazards—Tags and Tape

An early target in accident-prevention efforts was the class of accidents that occurred to persons involved in hazards created by temporary circumstances in the workplace. In 1968, USASI responded to these accidents with the initiation of standard USAS Z35.2, *Accident Prevention Tags* (1968b). This tracked the guidelines of its sister standard USAS Z35.1, *Accident Prevention Signs* (1968a). It found its way into the ANSI Z535 series of standards in 1991 as Z535.5, *Accident Prevention Tags (for Temporary Hazards)*, where it was made consistent with the other standards in this series. In the 2002 version of Z535.5, an additional type of signage was included, safety tags, and the standard was renamed: Z535.5 *Safety Tags and Barricade Tapes (for Temporary Hazards)* (ANSI 2007).

What distinguishes this type of hazard communication from others is discussed in the introduction to ANSI Z535.5 (2007): "Safety tags and barricade tapes are a means of alerting persons to temporary hazards often associated with construction, equipment installation, maintenance, repair, lockout or other transient conditions." It further explains that these are "not to be used in place of a permanent sign or label intended for hazards in normal use, operation or maintenance."

The same guidelines of design discussed under Z535.2, *Environmental and Facility Safety Signs*, can also be applied to both safety tags and barricade tape. Namely, the format includes a signal word, safety symbol, and message block. Thus, the fifteen parameters of design discussed earlier should also be considered in the design of accident-prevention tags and barricade tape. The barricade-tape format is unique in that it naturally has a more horizontal presentation and is expected to be repeated throughout the length of the tape. Thus the target audience of such tape may see the warnings repeated dozens of times.

Safety tags, besides providing warning information, are also used to signal the dysfunction of a piece of equipment. Some tags are attached to a lockout device for the equipment. This makes only the person named on the tag solely responsible for removing the tag before any energizing occurs because this person will have the only unlocking key. An interesting suggestion made in the appendix of the Z535.5 standard is that a photograph of the person responsible for the lockout be placed on the tag as an easier way to locate that individual on a large job site where workers may not be known by name (ANSI 2007, 18). Safety tags are also an important safety measure used in the ANSI and OSHA machine-guarding standards. Mechanical, chemical, and electrical systems having maintenance performed on them have been the subject of multitudes of accidents when they have not been safety tagged and locked out. Thus, the importance of this type of hazard communication cannot be overemphasized. Figures 4 and 5 represent examples of lockout and barricade tape warnings, respectively.

Other Types of Hazard Communication

Besides the requirements necessary for OSHA compliance in the workplace, there are many other circumstances within which hazard communication is important, and there were standards and practices in place to provide such warnings long before OSHA existed. One very prominent standard that was discussed earlier in the chapter was ANSI Z129.1, *American National Standard for Hazardous Industrial Chemicals—Precautionary Labeling* (2006). Another standard related to chemical hazard communication is the mandatory standard administered by the U.S. Department of Transportation, Bureau of Motor Carrier Safety (BMCS). It involves the labeling of vehicles that are carrying hazardous materials.

Placarding and Labeling of Hazardous Materials (49 CFR Chapter 1, Part 172)

The objective of this standard is to identify what chemicals are contained and being transported in over-the-road vehicles. It also addresses the level of hazard associated with the chemicals in those vehicles. The type of labeling and placarding required within these standards is very precisely defined in terms of colors, size, placement, and terminology. Because of the differences in jurisdiction and enactment dates, these standards have not been promulgated to be complementary to the ANSI Z535 series, ANSI Z129.1, or the *Manual of Uniform Traffic Control Devices* (MUTCD) standards, discussed in the next section. Colors are specified in accordance to Munsell notations and the Commission Internationale de L'Eclairage (CIE) specifications, but the colors are not the same as those referenced in the ANSI Z535.1 *Safety Color Code*. The description of all DOT hazardous chemical labeling and placarding requirements can be found in 49 CFR Chapter 1, Part 172 (1–704) and its appendices (OSHA 1976). Again, it is noted that these standards are in transition to make them consistent with international changes in signing.

Manual on Uniform Traffic Control Devices (MUTCD) Signage

The last of the U.S. standards addressed in this chapter is the MUTCD. It has importance in this discussion of hazard communication because of its extensive coverage and use. Although one sees a large volume of various signs and labels in relation to the work and home environments, there is also an incredible number of signs in the environment, which encompasses all highways and destination areas traveled to by the public.

The need for uniform standards in and around public highways and other public areas was recognized as early as 1927 for rural highways and 1930 for urban highways. At that time several early organizations joined efforts and eventually published the original edition of the *Manual on Uniform Traffic Control Devices* in 1935 (Federal Highway Administration (FHWA) 2009, I-1).

The MUTCD is underwritten by the Federal FHWA, which administers the MUTCD through the Code of Federal Regulations. All states are required to adopt a manual with specifications substantially similar to and consistent with guidelines provided in the current revision of the MUTCD (FHWA 2009, 2). Therefore, the MUTCD represents a mandated set of standards whose enforcement and implementation has been decentralized to state governments. Although its title might imply "traffic control," its scope goes

FIGURE 4. Example of ANSI-formatted lockout/tagout safety tag (*Source:* ANSI Z535.5, 2007)

FIGURE 5. Examples of barricade tape (*Source:* ANSI Z535.5, 2007)

far beyond that, and its guidance plays an important continuing role in hazard communication.

As was noted with placarding and labeling of hazardous materials (49 CFR Chapter 1, Part 172), the MUTCD actually originated before the ANSI Z535 series of standards.

Consequently, there has been no effort to make the MUTCD compatible with the ANSI Z535 series, and there probably is no necessity for the two to be complementary given that their respective functions are generally far removed from one another. On the other hand, the idea of standardizing signage formats, signal words, and colors so that people become uniformly knowledgeable about safety communications is somewhat undermined by the differences.

Unique to the MUTCD system is the importance of shape coding, which is not used in the Z535 series, but does appear in the current and proposed international signing guidelines. To accompany the MUTCD shape coding, there are colors that correspond to the shapes used. Anyone who has ever taken a state driver's license exam has been tested on MUTCD signage shapes and colors.

One area that does have some interesting overlap is the use of symbols. The ANSI Z535.3 requirement that symbols used alone must pass a recognition test is not specified as part of MUTCD. Instead, there are over 125 symbols that have been identified as acceptable for use across the various types of signage that MUTCD covers. One could conclude that the MUTCD is the most highly developed system for hazard communication in the United States. Its methods of communicating important safety and directional information are also likely the best understood of any safety system in the United States. The MUTCD special features involving designated colors and shapes have made this system unique. They have been summarized in Appendix G.

International Standards Organization (ISO) 3864—Safety Colors and Safety Signs

Many companies in this country are known as multinational corporations, or they do business with an international clientele. Consequently, such globalization requires the safety professional to recognize and sometimes accommodate for international standards for signage, labeling, and warnings. As noted in the discussions of the chemical MSDS materials, there has almost been a consensus regarding the content and format of hazard and physical properties information presented with chemicals. Europe and several other country groups have created standards quite similar to the ANSI 400.1 (2004). Hence, satisfying the chemical labeling and information requirements of these other countries is quite similar to satisfying the OSHA requirements in this country.

Existing in parallel to the ANSI Z535 series but quite different in content are some of the standards generated by the International Standards Organization (ISO). One such is the ISO 3864 standard *Safety Colours and Safety Signs* (2002). This standard was developed by the Technical Committee ISO/TC 80 in November of 1979. It was widely accepted by many countries, but countries such as the United States and Sweden initially disapproved of it (ISO 1984a, foreword). Today, it still maintains high acceptability among many countries, including most of Europe as well as Mexico and South Africa. This is the preferred format in the European community because of the concentration of diverse languages and because it focuses on universal symbols *without* words.

In 1998, the ISO subcommittee in charge of the ISO 3864 standard recognized the need to divide the standard into two parts: one for safety signs in the workplace and public areas and another for product safety labels (Peckham 2008, 1). ISO 3864, *Graphical Symbols—Safety Colours and Safety Signs: Part 1: Design Principles for Safety Signs in Workplaces and Public Areas*, was developed in 2002. Together with ISO 7010, it cancels and replaces ISO 3864:1984, which has been technically revised (ISO 2002, foreword). *Graphical Symbols Safety Colours and Safety Signs—Part 2: Design Principles for Product Safety Labels*, was first published in 2004 and reaffirmed without changes in 2010. The United States was instrumental in writing Part 2 of ISO 3864, the goal being to write a standard that would incorporate existing formats currently defined in both ISO product-specific standards and in the ANSI Z535.4 standard. In the ANSI Z535 standards, the safety alert symbol is used in the signal word panel to indicate the risk of personal injury. In ISO 3864, the triangle with an exclamation mark is defined as the general warning sign and indicates the risk of personal injury. When it came time to illustrate the use of signal words for product safety labels, the writers of ISO 3864-2 insisted that the triangle-with-exclamation-mark symbol appearing in the severity panel be identical to the ISO 3864-1 warning sign. As of the 2006 publication of ANSI Z535 standards, both ISO and ANSI have format options that are identical in every respect (Peckham 2008, 5).

The ISO is still responsible for publishing this standard, which defines the design criteria for *international* safety signs. It is a graphic-only approach intended to communicate the safety label's message quickly and without the use of words. Three geometric shapes are defined for use in graphic symbols. The circular form is used to surround symbols designating a prohibition or mandatory action, the triangle is used to designate warnings, and rectangular shapes are used to surround informational or instructional information (ISO 2002, 4). A color-coding scheme is also built into the standard: red for stop and prohibition, blue for mandatory action, yellow for caution and risk of danger, and green for a safe condition (ISO 2002, 4).

Figure 6 illustrates the three categories of ISO safety symbols, which are defined by both their shape and their color:

- Warning signs must be yellow triangles with a black border. The graphic must be black (Figure 6A).
- Prohibition signs are white circles with the familiar red circle and slash. Again, the graphic must be black. Each prohibition sign illustrates a prohibited activity (Figure 6B).
- The mandatory action signs are blue circles with white graphics and no border. Each sign indicates an action that must be performed for the safe use of the product (Figure 6C).

ISO 4196: Graphic Symbols—Use Of Arrows

An interesting companion document to ISO 3864, also with a first edition date of 1984, is the ISO 4196 *Graphical Symbols—Use of Arrows* (1984b). Based on its introduction, this standard was developed and agreed on to "promote the use of a reduced number of arrow forms as graphical symbols" (ISO 1984b, 1). Its scope was to "lay down the basic principles and the proportions to be adopted when designing graphical symbols which incorporate an arrow, or arrows, to indicate various movements, forces, or function to be indicated" (ISO 1984b, 1). Although it was international in its use and approved by European, Japanese, and South African countries, the United States neither approved nor disapproved of the standard (1984b, foreword). There is nothing comparable in the ANSI series of standards that deals only with arrows; however, ANSI Z535.2 includes a small section on arrow designation.

This introduction to international signs and labels suggests quite a different philosophy that other countries have relative to the design of signs and warnings. On the one hand, through U.S. standards committees

A

B

C

FIGURE 6. Example of ISO labels (*Source:* ISO 3864:1; ISO 3864:3)

and litigation, extensive amounts of information about a hazard have come to be expected on a label or sign. One expects an attention-getting signal word, description of the hazard, consequences in the form of potential injury, and what preventive action is in order. Other countries have products more likely to be distributed or exposed to nationals of several countries who may understand only a single native language. In such cases, repeating a warning in a multitude of languages may not be feasible with signage space restrictions. It is logical, then, that a system based on symbols and shapes would make more sense and likely be more effective among a multiple-language population of users.

One consequence of this philosophy is that hazard communications on equipment and nonchemical products that cross international borders into the United States will likely need to be reviewed and possibly modified by a safety professional. Label and signage changes may be necessary for products imported as well as for those exported. This necessity has been recognized by some of the ANSI signage committees, and changes have already been made to draft standards of the ANSI Z535 series that incorporate the international approach, placing more emphasis on symbols and shapes. While the above international standards were active as of the publication of this Handbook, the reader is strongly advised to stay abreast of the evolution caused by the Global Harmonization System (GHS) discussed earlier in this chapter. It may radically change the approach now used internationally for hazard warnings.

Advertising and Electronic Hazard Warnings

One contemporary type of hazard communication that often goes unmentioned in traditional safety research circles is that which accompanies advertising or which appears in some electronic form. Because of both governmental and common law, advertisers must provide warnings about certain potential hazards associated with the use of a product they are trying to sell.

The advertising that was used to sell products 50 years ago typically did not provide communications relating to the hazards intrinsic to a particular product. However, in the late 1960s the federal government started requiring safety information about smoking to appear in product advertising. Currently, safety information appears abundantly in the advertising of many product types. Such information is used to warn of the health or safety aspects of a product's use; to deter certain types of behavior (e.g., use of drugs, alcohol while driving, and cigarettes); and to prevent target groups of individuals from using certain products (e.g., "not intended for use by small children" or "use only with parental or adult supervision"). There are no known consensus standards that directly apply to solely advertising-type communications as of this printing.

Another type of contemporary hazard communication is that appearing in some electronic form, sometimes referred to as "paperless warnings." As an example, marketing people, in selling products for and through computers, are frequently not providing any paper warnings or operating instructions with their product other than what might appear on the packaging. Instead, the product may have only a CD containing warnings and instructions, or one may receive a video. On some products one is referred to a product Web site to find current information about new safety warnings, recalls, warranty, repair, maintenance, and operating instructions. Warnings are also now often being incorporated anywhere television-type monitors appear for public information, such as in retail stores, on electronic billboards, in airports and train stations, and at major sports arenas. Even facilities such as fast food restaurants and bowling alleys now heavily use monitors to provide various safety and instructional information. Finally, one cannot escape Internet searches with pop-up windows with various sorts of advertising and other unsolicited information, which also can contain hazard communications.

These expanding possibilities for providing hazard communication and training give safety and health professionals additional opportunities for bringing messages to employees and nonemployees in a facility as well as to the public outside the occupational environment. How this new era of electronic media will impact the hazard communication standards of such organizations as ANSI and ISO is only now being initially looked at by the respective committees, who in the past have been concerned only with static information appearing on signs, labels, or paper.

CONCLUSION

A first goal of this chapter was to provide guidance to those responsible for OSHA compliance with the *Hazard Communication Standard*, 29 CFR 1900.1200 (1983). The emphasis of this standard is, of course, the recognition and control of chemical hazards in the workplace and satisfying every employee's right to know about chemical exposure while working. As noted earlier, to accomplish this, the professional would have to accomplish five primary tasks: (1) developing a written health hazard communication (HazCom) plan/program; (2) creating an up-to-date hazardous chemical inventory; (3) having all hazardous chemicals properly labeled; (4) making accessible to employees an MSDS for every chemical that is covered by the standard; and (5) properly instructing, training, and providing required information to all effected employees. In this chapter, information useful to complying with each of these five steps was provided along with Internet and paper references for obtaining additional assistance.

Not every professional reading this chapter will be concerned with responsibility for HazCom compliance. Thus, a second goal of the chapter was to address hazard communication outside of the "OSHA box," that is, to review how hazard communication is accomplished for products, environments, and locations other than within a U.S. OSHA-controlled workplace. Consequently, the chapter introduced standards that establish methods for providing general chemical product information (ANSI Z129.1 2006); standards for environmental, facility, and product signage (ANSI 2006, 2007); and standards more closely related to vehicular applications and travel within this country (MUTCD 2009).

What is certain in this global economy is that one cannot avoid confronting the issue of imported or exported products (or workers). Thus, familiarization with hazard communication norms for other countries and other languages is becoming a necessity. Imported products will have to be reviewed as to the hazard information that accompanies them, and this information may have to be revised to meet new U.S. standards, which adopt some proposals within the Global Harmonization System (GHS). Products to be exported will also have to be modified to satisfy the new hazard communication standards of other countries, which may now reflect changes due to the GHS. Although the chapter discussed how similar MSDS standards were across countries, it also indicated how dissimilar on-product warnings were. The U.S. standards emphasize detailed verbiage to explain hazards, whereas the non-U.S. standards, such as those within the ISO, emphasize symbols and shapes. Achieving a higher level of international consistency is the goal of the GHS, which many countries are now in the process of reviewing for possible adoption.

Finally, it has been known for some time that presenting hazard information training through the use of videotape-type formats has been effective and useful. However, the expanded use of hazard communications through digital displays, monitors, computers, and other dynamic electronic means is an arena that has only recently started to get the attention of standards committees and researchers. Research may prove that these digital devices are the most effective means of communicating hazard information to a population that voluntarily gives priority attention to electronic visual media. Designers of hazard communications will undoubtedly have to incorporate these popular digital display devices into their warning, training, and instructional programs.

REFERENCES

Accident Prevention Department of the National Association of Manufacturers. 1914. "Signs and Their Value in the Prevention of Accidents." *Preventative Appliances, Supplement to American Industries,* May, pp. 1–4.

American National Standards Institute (ANSI). 1979. Z53.1-1979, *Safety Color Code for Marking Physical Hazards.* New York: ANSI

———. 2010. ANSI Z400.1/Z129.1-2010, *Hazardous Workplace Chemicals—Hazard Evaluation and Safety Data Sheet and Precautionary Labeling.* Washington, D.C.: Chemical Manufacturers Association.

———. 2006 (R 2011). Z535.1, *Safety Colors.* Washington, D.C.: NEMA.

_____. 2011a. ANSI/NEMA Z535.2-2011, *Environmental and Facility Safety Signs*. Washington, D.C.: NEMA.

_____. 2011b. ANSI/NEMA Z535.3-2011, *Criteria for Safety Symbols*. Washington, D.C.: NEMA.

_____. 2011c. ANSI/NEMA Z535.4, *Product Safety Signs and Labels*.Washington, D.C.: NEMA.

_____. 2011d. ANSI/NEMA Z545.5-2011, *Safety Tags and Barricade Tapes (For Temporary Hazards)*. Washington, D.C.: NEMA.

_____. 2011e. ANSI/NEMA Z535.6, *Product Safety Information in Product Manuals, Instructions, and Other Collateral Materials*. Rosslyn, VA: NEMA.

American National Standards Institute (ANSI)/American Society of Mechanical Engineers (ASME). 2007. A13.1-2007, *Scheme for Identification of Piping Systems*. New York: ANSI.

American Standards Association (ASA). 1941. Z35.1-1941, *American Standard Specifications for Industrial Accident Prevention Signs*. New York: ASA.

_____. 1959. Z35.1-1959, *American Standard Specifications for Industrial Accident Prevention Signs*. New York: ASA.

Ames, F. 1937. "The Value of Safety Posters in Accident Prevention." Transactions of 26th National Safety Congress, Kansas City, Missouri. National Safety Council, Inc., pp. 357–359.

California Department of Industrial Relations. 2000. *Guide to the California Hazard Communication Regulation*. Sacramento: California Department of Industrial Relations.

California Occupational Safety and Health Administration (CalOSHA). n.d. *Regulated Carcinogens*. Title 8 CCR, Article 10. Sacramento: CalOSHA.

_____. n.d. *Identification of Piping*. Title 8 CCR, Section 3321. Sacramento: CalOSHA.

Canadian Centre for Occupational Health and Safety (CCOHS). 2007. *OSH Answers, Material Safety Data Sheets (MSDSs)—Creating* (retrieved October 3, 2011). www.ccohs.ca/oshanswers/legisl/msds_prep.html

_____. 2009. *Globally Harmonized System (GHS)* (retrieved October 2011), www.ccohs.ca

Centers for Disease Control and Prevention (CDC). n.d. *International Chemical Safety Cards: Description*. NIOSH and International Programme on Chemical Safety (IPCS) (retrieved October 1, 2011). www.cdc.gov/niosh/ipcs/ipcscard.html

Chapanis, A. 1965. "Words, Words, Words." *Human Factors* 7: 1–17.

Compliance Center, Inc. 2011. *GHS Awareness for Canada and United States* (retrieved October 2011). www.compliancecenter.com

Department of Justice, Canada. 1985. *Hazardous Products Act, Part II. Controlled Products* (R.S. 1985, c. H-3) (retrieved November 2006). http://laws.justice.gc.ca/en/H-3

European Commission (EEC). 1991. *Commission Directive 91/155/EEC of 5 March 1991 defining and laying down the detailed arrangements for the system of specific information relating to dangerous preparations in the implementation of Article 10 of Directive 88/379/EEC* (retrieved October 2011) www.reach-compliance.eu/english/legislation/docs/launchers/launch-91-155-EEC.html

_____. 2001. *Commission Directive 2001/58/EC of 27 July 2001 amending for the second time Directive 21/155/EEC defining and laying down the detailed arrangements for the systems of specific information relating to dangerous preparations in implementation of Article 14 of the European Parliament and Council Directive 199/45/EC and relating to dangerous substances in implementaiton of Article 27 of Council Directive 67/548/EEC (safety data sheets)* (retrieved October 1, 2011) www.reach.sgs.com/documents_directive_2001_58_ex.pdf

Federal Highway Administration, U.S. Department of Transportation. 2009. *Manual of Uniform Traffic Control Devices (MUTCD 2009)*. Washington, D.C.: U.S. Government Printing Office.

Gullickson, R. 1996, May. *Reference Data Sheet on Material Safety Data Sheets*. Glenview, IL: Meridian Engineering and Technology.

Health Canada. 1988. *Hazardous Products Act*. Ottawa, Ontario: Health Canada.

International Labour Organization (ILO). 2004, November 11. "Chemical Safety Cards." In *Basics of Chemical Safety*. Geneva: International Occupational Safety and Health Information Centre (retrieved January 2007). www.ilo.org/public/english/protection/safework/cis/products/safetytm/msds.htm

International Standards Organization (ISO). 1984a. ISO 3864-1984, *Safety Colours and Safety Signs*. Switzerland: ISO.

_____. 1984b. *Graphical Symbols—Use of Arrows*. ISO 4196-1984(E). Switzerland: ISO.

_____. 2004. ISO 3864:2-2004, *Graphic Symbols—Safety Colours and Safety Signs--Part 2: Design Principles for Product Safety Labels*. Geneva, Switzerland: ISO.

_____. 2006. ISO 3864:3-2006, *Graphic Symbols—Safety Colours and Safety Signs: Part 3: Design Principles for Use in Safety Signs*. Geneva, Switzerland: ISO.

_____. 2011. ISO 3864:1-2011, *Graphic Symbols—Safety Colours and Safety Signs--Part 1: Design Principles for Safety Signs in Workplaces and Public Areas*. Geneva, Switzerland: ISO.

Kaplan, S.A. 1986. *Development of Material Safety Data Sheets*. 191st ACS meeting (retrieved 2006). www.phys.ksu.edu/area/jrm/Safety/kaplan.html

Keene State College. 2006. *Most Frequently Cited Serious Violations* (retrieved November 2006). www.keene.edu/conted/FY%202005%20MFC%20General%20Industry.ppt

Lab Safety Supply. 2007. *Labeling for Hazardous Communication: Document #200* (retrieved January 2006). www.labsafety.com

———. 2010. Document #203, *ANSI Pipe Marking Standards* (retrieved June 2010). www.labsafety.com

Mathieu, A. 1927, August. "Bridging the Gap in Safety Education." *National Safety News*, pp. 17–18.

Miller, J. M., and M. R. Lehto. 2001. *Warnings and Safety Instructions—Annotated and Indexed*. 4th ed. Ann Arbor, MI: Fuller Technical Publications.

National Institute for Occupational Safety and Health (NIOSH). 1974. *A Recommended Standard . . . An Identification System for Occupationally Hazardous Materials* (retrieved 2006). www.cdc.gov/niosh/75-126.html

Occupational Safety and Health Administration (OSHA). 1976. 49 CFR 172. *Hazardous Materials Table, Special Provisions, Hazardous Materials Communication*. Washington, D.C.: Office of the Federal Register.

———. 1983. 29 CFR 1910.1200. *Hazard Communication*. Washington, D.C.: Office of the Federal Register.

———. 1994. 29 CFR 1901.1200. *Hazard Communication, Final Rule*. Federal Register 59 (27). Washington, D.C.: OSHA.

———. 1996, May. *Setting Occupational Safety and Health Standards*. Washington, D.C.: OSHA.

———. 1997, May 23. *Hazard Communication: A Review of the Science Underpinning the Art of Communication for Health and Safety*. Washington, D.C.: OSHA.

———. 1998. OSHA 3084, *Chemical Hazard Communication* (retrieved 2006). www.osha.gov/Publications/osha3084.pdf

———. 1998, March 20. CPL 02-02-038-CPL 2-2.38D, *Inspection Procedures for the Hazard Communication Standard* (retrieved 2006). www.osha.gov

———. 1998, April 7. *New OSHA Directive Makes It Easier for Employers to Comply with Hazard Communication Standard*. OSHA news release. Washington, D.C.: OSHA.

———. 2000. *Hazard Communication: Guidelines for Compliance OSHA 3111* (retrieved 2006). www.osha.gov/Publications/osha3111.pdf

———. December 2002. *Draft Guidance for Hazard Determination* (retrieved 2006). www.osha.gov

———. 2003. *Draft Model Training Program for Hazard Communication* (retrieved 2006). www.osha.gov/dsg/hazcom/MTP101703.pdf

———. 2004, March. *Hazard Communication in the 21st Century, Executive Summary* (retrieved 2006). www.osha.gov

———. 2005. *A Guide to the Globally Harmonized System of Classification and Labeling of Chemicals (GHS)* (retrieved October 2011). www.osha.gov/hazcom/ghs.html

Nolan, T. J. 1960, October. "Revised Standards for Safety Signs." *National Safety News*, p. 206.

Peckham, Gregory. 2008. ISO 3864, *Part 2: The New International Standard for Product Safety Labeling* (retrieved November 2010). www.clarionsafety.com/assets/common/pdf/whitepapers/3864-2.pdf

United States of America Standards Institute (USASI). 1968a. USAS Z35.1-1968, *Standard Specifications for Accident Prevention Signs*. New York: USASI.

———. 1968b. USAS Z3521-1968, *Standard Specifications for Accident Prevention Tags*. New York: USASI.

United States General Accounting Office. 1991. GAO/HRD-92-8, *OSHA Action Needed to Improve Compliance with Hazard Communication Standard*. Washington D.C.: U.S. Government Printing Office. www.gao.gov/

Appendix A

OSHA Form 174

Material Safety Data Sheet
May be used to comply with
OSHA's Hazard Communication Standard,
29 CFR 1910.1200. This Standard must be
consulted for specific requirements.

U.S. Department of Labor
Occupational Safety and Health Administration
(Non-Mandatory Form)
Form Approved
OMB No. 1218-0072

IDENTITY *(As Used on Label and List)*	Note: Blank spaces are not permitted. If any item is not applicable, or no information is available, the space must be marked to indicate that.

Section I

Manufacturer's Name	Emergency Telephone Number
Address *(Number, Street, City, State, and ZIP Code)*	Telephone Number for Information
	Date Prepared
	Signature of Preparer *(optional)*

Section II - Hazard Ingredients/Identity Information

Hazardous Components (Specific Chemical Identity; Common Name(s))	OSHA PEL	ACGIH TLV	Other Limits Recommended	% *(optional)*

Section III - Physical/Chemical Characteristics

Boiling Point		Specific Gravity (H_2O = 1)	
Vapor Pressure (mm Hg.)		Melting Point	
Vapor Density (AIR = 1)		Evaporation Rate (Butyl Acetate = 1)	

Solubility in Water

Appearance and Odor

Section IV - Fire and Explosion Hazard Data

Flash Point (Method Used)	Flammable Limits	LEL	UEL

Extinguishing Media

Special Fire Fighting Procedures

Unusual Fire and Explosion Hazards

Section V - Reactivity Data

Stability	Unstable		Conditions to Avoid
	Stable		

Incompatibility *(Materials to Avoid)*

Hazardous Decomposition or Byproducts

Hazardous Polymerization	May Occur		Conditions to Avoid
	Will Not Occur		

Section VI - Health Hazard Data

Route(s) of Entry:	Inhalation?	Skin?	Ingestion?

Health Hazards *(Acute and Chronic)*

Carcinogenicity:	NTP?	IARC Monographs?	OSHA Regulated?

Signs and Symptoms of Exposure

Medical Conditions Generally Aggravated by Exposure

Emergency and First Aid Procedures

Section VII - Precautions for Safe Handling and Use

Steps to Be Taken in Case Material Is Released or Spilled

Waste Disposal Method

Precautions to Be Taken in Handling and Storing

Other Precautions

Section VIII - Control Measures

Respiratory Protection *(Specify Type)*

Ventilation	Local Exhaust		Special
	Mechanical *(General)*		Other
Protective Gloves		Eye Protection	

Other Protective Clothing or Equipment

Work/Hygienic Practices

Section IX - Special Precautions

Precautions to Be Taken in Handling and Storing

Other Precautions

Each MSDS must be reviewed for correctness and completeness every three years.

Reviewed by _____ Reviewed by _____

Revision date_____ Revision date _____

APPENDIX B

The ANSI Z400.1 Sections

Section 1: Chemical Product and Company Identification. Names the material and relates the MSDS with the label and shipping documents. Must also have a mailing address and telephone number for the manufacturer or distributor.

Section 2: Hazards Identification. Describes the material's appearance, odor, and health, physical, and environmental hazards that may be of concern for emergency response personnel.

Section 3: Composition, Information on Ingredients. Identifies the hazardous components of the material. If non-hazardous ingredients are listed, they should be listed separately. Chemical Abstract Service (CAS) numbers should be included, as well as OSHA permissible exposure limits and American Conference of Government Industrial Hygienists (ACGIH) TLVs. If the identity of any ingredient is claimed to be a trade secret, it should be so indicated in this section.

Section 4: First Aid Measures. This section should include emergency and first aid procedures. It should be in layman's language and easy to understand, and procedures for each potential route of exposure should be included. A "Notes to Physicians" subsection should be included if such information is available.

Section 5: Fire Fighting Measures. This section should describe fire and explosive properties of the material, extinguishing media to be used, and fire-fighting instructions. It applies to anyone who may be in the area of the fire.

Section 6: Accidental Release Measures. This section is intended for emergency response personnel.

Section 7: Handling and Storage. This section provides guidelines for minimizing any potential hazards from storing the material. It should include information to minimize handling when appropriate and conditions such as temperature, inert atmosphere, and conditions to avoid.

Section 8: Exposure Controls, Personal Protection. Discusses the degree of engineering control that may be needed when handling the material and the personal protective equipment that should be used if there is a potential for exposure above the regulatory or suggested limits. Exposure guidelines, such as OSHA PELs and ACGIH TLVs, should be included in this section.

Section 9: Physical and Chemical Properties. These properties should be included to assist users to determine proper handling and storage. Appearance, odor, physical state (liquid, solid, gas), pH, vapor pressure and density, melting and freezing point, solubility, and specific gravity should be included. Additional properties may be included if they are useful.

Section 10: Stability and Reactivity. This section should describe conditions that may result in a potentially hazardous reaction, such as evolution of hazardous gases, production of heat, or other hazardous conditions.

Section 11: Toxicological Information. This section should include any known information resulting from animal testing or human experience on the toxicity of the material. Also included would be information on its potential for causing cancer. Data should be included for acute, subchronic, and chronic exposures, if available.

Section 12: Ecological Information. This section should list impacts to the environment that may occur if the material is released to the environment or in evaluating waste treatment practices.

Section 13: Disposal Considerations. This section is intended to provide guidance to environmental and other technical people responsible for waste management for the product.

Section 14: Transport Information. This section should provide information concerning classification for shipping the material. It should include U.S. Department of Transportation (DOT) classifications or an indication that it is not regulated. It may include information for shipment into other countries.

Section 15: Regulatory Information. This section should contain information regarding the regulatory status of the material. It should include OSHA and EPA regulations. It may also include other regulatory agencies, and state agencies, if appropriate.

Section 16: Other Information. This section is intended for other material that the preparer feels is pertinent and that should not be included in the other fifteen sections. For example, it may include label information, hazard ratings, revision dates, and references to other related information.

APPENDIX C

Sample Training Program Contents

Lesson	Lesson module	Topics covered
Lesson A 1 hour	Understanding the Hazard Communication Standard	Identification of responsible staff Identification of hazardous chemicals in workplace Written program Labels and other forms of warning Material safety data sheets Information and training A training video and quiz are included in lesson
Lesson B 1 hour	Understanding the Material Safety Data Sheet	Purpose of the MSDS Contents of MSDS Requirements: identity used on the label Requirements: physical and chemical characteristics Requirements: health hazards Requirements: routes of entry Requirements: exposure limits Requirements: carcinogens/potential carcinogens Requirements: safe handling procedures Requirements: control measures Requirements: emergency and first-aid procedures Requirements: identity of responsible party and date of preparation A training video and quiz are included in lesson
Lesson C 1 hour	Understanding Labels	Requirements: three pieces of information Sample label Requirements: labels on incoming containers Requirements: stationary containers Requirements: transfer containers Exceptions Labeling and placarding systems: ANSI Labeling and placarding systems: NFPA Labeling and placarding systems: HMIS Labeling and placarding systems: DOT labels Labeling and placarding systems: DOT placards A training video and quiz are included in lesson
Lesson D 1 hour	Understanding Health Information	Dose–response relationship Exposure limits Routes of entry Acute effects Chronic effects Toxic and highly toxic chemicals Carcinogens Corrosives Irritants

Lesson	Lesson module	Topics covered
		Sensitizers
		Target organ effects
		Controls
		A training video and quiz are included in lesson
Lesson E 90 minutes	Understanding Flammables and Combustibles	
		Definitions of flammables and combustibles
		Types of flammables and combustibles
		Flammable aerosol
		Flammable gases
		Flammable gases: physical properties and hazards
		Flammable gases: health hazards
		Flammable gases: methods of detection
		Flammable gases: emergency and handling procedures
		Flammable gases: first-aid procedures
		Flammable liquids
		Flammable liquids: physical properties and hazards
		Flammable liquids: health hazards
		Flammable liquids: methods of detection
		Flammable liquids: personal protective equipment
		Flammable liquids: emergency and handling procedures
		Flammable liquids: first-aid procedures
		Combustible liquids
		Flammable solids
		Flammable solids: physical properties and hazards
		Flammable solids: health hazards
		Flammable solids: methods of detection
		Flammable solids: emergency and handling procedures
		Flammable solids: first aid procedures
		A training video and quiz are included in lesson
Lesson F 1 hour	Understanding Corrosives	
		Health effects
		Methods of detection
		PPE
		First-aid procedures
		Spill, leak, and disposal procedures
		A training video and quiz are included in lesson
Lesson G 90 mins	Understanding Reactive Chemicals	
		Reactive chemicals in the work area
		Physical properties and hazards
		Health hazards
		Methods of detections
		PPE
		Emergency and handling procedures
		First-aid procedures
		A training video and quiz are included in lesson
Lesson H 1 hour	Understanding Toxic Chemicals	
		Toxic chemicals/carcinogens in mixtures
		Toxic chemicals in work area

Lesson	Lesson module	Topics covered
		Routes of entry
		Physical hazards
		Health hazards
		Methods of detection
		PPE
		Emergency and handling procedures
		First-aid procedures
		A training video and quiz are included in lesson
9–10 hours	Approximate Total Lesson Time (without breaks included)	

Note: Adapted from *Draft Model Training Program for Hazard Communication*, by Occupational Safety and Health Administration, n.d.

APPENDIX D

A Taxonomy of Environmental, Facility, and Electronic Signing

Private-Residence Premise Signing
- swimming pools/spas
- trespassing prevention
- animal/property hazard

Commercial Premise Signing/Markings
- parking lots
- chemical storage (i.e., MSDS info)
- open areas/landscaping
- construction
- trespassing prevention
- informational/directional signs
- crosswalk/crossing vehicle

Signing Inside Commercial Buildings
- employee and visitor protection
    - danger/caution/safety signs
    - fire and emergency procedures (i.e., MSDS info)
    - personal protective equipment
    - informational/directional signs
    - accident prevention tags (safety tags/ barricade tapes)
    - temporary hazards
- process-related signing
    - process instructions
    - material handling procedures
    - environmental contamination prevention (i.e., MSDS info)
    - quality control procedures

Advertising and Electronic Media Warnings
- billboard footnote warnings
- magazine/paper footnote warnings
- software computer warnings
- e-commerce warnings
- product video tapes
- point-of-purchase video
- sports facility monitors

Public Notification Signing
- public buildings
    - informational/directional signs
    - fire and emergency signs
    - parking
    - egress/ingress
- recreational facilities signing
    - swimming pools/spas
    - parks/playgrounds
    - sports facilities
    - directional signs for hiking/bicycling trails
    - public boating, fishing, and beach areas
- public highway and road signs
    - traffic control and safety
    - pedestrian control and safety
    - informational/directional signs
    - temporary hazards/road construction
    - parking on city streets
    - school and pedestrian crossings
    - hazardous materials being transported

Environmental Dangers and Emergencies Signing
- weather warnings/natural disasters
- littering/landfill signs
- air pollution/smog warnings
- chemical spills and contamination (i.e., MSDS info)
- radiation/biohazard

APPENDIX E

References in the ANSI Z535 2006, 2007 Series

Author/Org	Title/Date	Primary Reference	Also Referenced In
Akerboom et al.	Products for Children: Development and Evaluation of Symbols for Warnings, 1995	Z535.3	
ANSI	D10.1-1966: Adjustable Face Vehicle Traffic Control Signal Heads, 1970	Z535.1	
ANSI	C95.2-1982: Radio Frequency Radiation Hazard Warning Symbol, revised 1999	Z535.1	Z535.2
ANSI	N2.1-1989: Radiation Symbol	Z535.1	Z535.2
ANSI	Z129.1-2000: Hazardous Industrial Chemicals—Precautionary Labeling	Z535.1	Z535.2, Z535.3, Z535.5
ANSI	A13.1-2002: Scheme for the Identification of Piping Systems	Z535.1	
ANSI/ASSE	Z244-2003: Control of Hazardous Energy Lockout/Tagout and Alternative Methods	Z535.1	
ANSI/ASTM	D1535-97: Standard Practice of Specifying Color by the Munsell System	Z535.1	
ANSI/NFPA	70 (1990) National Electrical Code	Z535.2	
ANSI/NFPA	70 (2002): National Electrical Code	Z535.2	
ANSI/SAE	S276.2: Slow Moving Vehicle Identification Symbol, 1968	Z535.2	
Assoc. of American Railroads	Standard Code—Operating Rules, Block Signal Rules, Interlocking Rules	Z535.1	
ASTM	D4956-95 99a: Standard Specification for Retroreflective Sheeting for Traffic Control	Z535.1	
ASTM	D1729-3 2003: Visual Appraisal of Colors and Color Differences of Diffusely-Illuminated Opaque Materials, 2003	Z535.1	
ASTM	D4086-92a(03): Visual Evaluation of Metamerism, 2003	Z535.1	
ASTM	E1164-02: Obtaining Spectrophotometric Data for Object Color Evaluation, 2004	Z535.1	
ASTM	E308-01: Computing the Colors of Objects Using the CIE System, 2001	Z535.1	
ASTM	D2244(2002): Test Method for Calculation of Color Differences from Instrumentally Measured Color Coordinates	Z535.1	
ASTM	E991-98: Color Measurement of Fluorescent Specimens, 1998	Z535.1	
Brugger	Public Information Symbols: A Comparison of ISO Testing Procedures, 1994	Z535.3	
CIE	39.2-1983: Recommendations for Surface Colours for Visual Signalling	Z535.1	
Code of Federal Regulations	Title 49, Parts 100–199: Hazardous Materials Warning Placards and Labels	Z535.1	
Collins	Use of Hazard Pictorials/Symbols in the Minerals Industry, 1983	Z535.3	
Collins et al.	Safety Color Appearance Under Selected Light Sources, 1986	Z535.2	Z535.5
Collins, Lerner, and Pierman	Symbols for Industrial Safety, 1982	Z535.3	

Author/Org	Title/Date	Primary Reference	Also Referenced In
Deppa and Kalsher	Safety Symbols in the ANSI and ISO Standards—Do People Understand Them? 2006	Z535.5	
Deppa and Martin	Human Factors Behind the Improved ANSI Z535.3 Label Standard for Safety Symbols, 1997	Z535.3	
Dreyfuss	Symbol Sourcebook—An Authoritative Guide to Z535.3 International Graphic Symbols, 1972		
FAA	AC 70 7460-1: Obstruction Marking and Lighting	Z535.1	
Federal Specification	KKK-A-1822: Ambulance Blue and Orange, 1994	Z535.1	
FMC Corp.	Product Safety Signs and Labels, 1978	Z535.3	
FMC Corp.	Product Safety Sign and Label System, 1985	Z535.4	Z535.5
Frascara and Yau	Evaluation and Development of Safety Symbols, Part 1: Evaluation of Existing Graphic Symbols for Safety, 1986	Z535.3	
Frascara and Yau	Evaluation and Development of Safety Symbols, Part 2: Evaluation of Safety Symbols, Appropriateness Ranking Tests, and Comprehension Recognition Tests, 1986	Z535.3	
General Services Admin.	Colors, Federal Standard 595B, 1994	Z535.1	
Grund	Lockout/Tagout, The Process of Controlling Hazardous Energy, 1995	Z535.5	
Hale Color Chart	Safety Color Tolerance Charts/Highway Color Tolerance Charts	Z535.1	
Howett	Size of Letters Required for Visibility as a Function of Viewing Distance and Observer Visual Acuity, 1983	Z535.2	Z535.4, Z535.5
ISO	3864: Safety Signs and Colors, 1984	Z535.2	Z535.3, Z535.5
ISO	3864:1: Graphic Symbols—Safety Colours and Safety Signs—Part 1: Design Principles for Safety Signs in Workplaces & Public Areas, 2002	Z535.3	Z535.5, Z535.6
ISO	3864:2: Graphic Symbols—Safety Colours and Safety Signs—Part 2: Design Principles for Product Safety Labels, 2006	Z535.3	Z535.6
ISO	3864:3 Graphic Symbols—Safety Colours and Safety Signs—Part 3: Design Criteria for Graphic Symbols Used in Safety Signs, 2004	Z535.5	
ISO	7010:2003 Graphical Symbols—Safety Colours and Safety Signs—Safety Signs Used in Workplaces and Public Areas, 2003	Z535.5	
ISO	11684: 1995 Annex D—Principles and Guidelines for Graphical Design if Hazard Pictorials	Z535.3	
ISO	Technical Report 7239: Development and Principles for Application of Public Information Symbols, 1984	Z535.3	
ISO	9186-2001: Graphical Symbols—Testing Methods for Judged Comprehensibility and for Comprehension	Z535.3	

Author/Org	Title/Date	Primary Reference	Also Referenced In
Lirtzman	Validation of Proposed Symbols for Precautionary Labeling of Hazardous Industrial Chemicals, 1987	Z535.3	
Magurno et al.	Iterative Test and Development of Pharmaceutical Pictorials, 1994	Z535.3	
Miller, Lehto, and Frantz	Instructions and Warnings, the Annotated Bibliography, 1990	Z535.5	
Munsell Laboratory	Munsell Book of Color	Z535.1	
Nat. Conf. On School Transportation	Minimum Standards for School Buses, revised 1970	Z535.1	
NFPA	291-1988: Uniform Marking of Fire Hydrants	Z535.1	
NFPA	1901-1985: Automotive Fire Apparatus	Z535.1	
NFPA	178-1986: Symbols for Fire Fighting	Z535.2	Z535.5
Olglay	Safety Symbols Art: Camera-Ready and Disk Art for Designers, 1995	Z535.3	
Olglay	Safety Symbols Art: The Testing Protocol, Materials & Results, 1996	Z535.3	
Smith	Letter Size and Legibility, Human Factors, 1979	Z535.2	Z535.4, Z535.5
Snap-On Tool Corp.	Safety Symbol Identification Survey, 1994	Z535.3	
Standard Solutions	The Standard Solutions Symbol Reference Manual, 1995	Z535.3	
Stds. Assoc. of Australia	AS 2342 Part 3: Test Procedures for Evaluating Graphic Symbols and Symbol Signs, 1980	Z535.3	
UL	UL969-1995: Standard for Marking and Labeling Systems	Z535.4	
U.S. Coast Guard	COMDTINST M16500.3A: Aids to Navigation—Technical	Z535.1	
U.S. Coast Guard	Colored Elastomeric Film, Specification G-ECV-473, 1992	Z535.1	
U. S. Dept. of Transportation, FHA	Manual on Uniform Traffic Control Devices for Streets and Highways, 2009	Z535.1	Z535.2
Virzi	Streamlining the Design Process: Running Fewer Subjects, 1990	Z535.3	
Westinghouse	Westinghouse Product Safety Label Handbook, 1981	Z535.4	
Wolff	A Study of the Effect of Context and Test Method in Evaluating Safety Symbols, 1995	Z535.3	
Wolff and Wogalter	Test and Development of Pharmaceutical Pictorials, 1993	Z535.3	
Zwaga	Comprehensibility Estimates of Public Information Symbols, 1989	Z535.3	
Zwaga et al.	Public Graphics, Visual Information for Everyday Use, 1994	Z535.5	

APPENDIX F

Color Combinations Used in ANSI Z535 Series
(Abstracted from ANSI Z535.2, 2007)]

SIGNAL WORD	SIGNAL WORD COLOR	SIGNAL WORD BACKGRND	SAFETY ALERT SYMBOL COLOR	SAFETY ALERT SYMBOL BACKGRND	MESSAGE COLOR	MESSAGE BACKGRND	OPTIONAL SAFETY SYMBOL/ PICTORIAL COLOR	OPTIONAL SAFETY SYMBOL/ PICTORIAL PANEL BACKGRND
DANGER	WHITE	SAFETY RED (rectangular background)	SAFETY RED	WHITE	BLACK or RED or WHITE	BLACK OR RED ON WHITE OR WHITE ON BLACK	BLACK, SAFETY RED, OR BLACK and SAFETY RED	WHITE
WARNING	BLACK	SAFETY ORANGE (rectangular background)	SAFETY ORANGE	BLACK	BLACK or WHITE	BLACK on WHITE OR WHITE on BLACK	BLACK	WHITE
CAUTION	BLACK	SAFETY YELLOW	SAFETY YELLOW	BLACK	BLACK or WHITE	BLACK on WHITE OR WHITE on BLACK	BLACK	WHITE
SIGNAL WORD	SIGNAL WORD COLOR	SIGNAL WORD BACKGRND	SAFETY ALERT SYMBOL COLOR	SAFETY ALERT SYMBOL BACKGRND	MESSAGE COLOR	MESSAGE BACKGRND	OPTIONAL SAFETY SYMBOL/ PICTORIAL COLOR	OPTIONAL SAFETY SYMBOL/ PICTORIAL PANEL BACKGRND
CAUTION (property damage)	BLACK	SAFETY YELLOW	none	none	BLACK or WHITE	BLACK on WHITE OR WHITE on BLACK	BLACK	WHITE
NOTICE signs	white italics	SAFETY BLUE	none	none	SAFETY BLUE or BLACK	WHITE	SAFETY BLUE or BLACK	WHITE

(ANSI 2007, 5–7)

APPENDIX G

Usage of Color and Shapes in MUTCD Signage Systems

(Abstracted from *Manual on Uniform Traffic Control Devices* 2009)

Color Code	Functional Uses	Color Uses	Shape Code	Sign Classifications
YELLOW	General warning	Used as background color for warning signs and for school signs	PENNANT SHAPE/ISOSCELES TRIANGLE (Longer axis horiz)—NO PASSING	WARNING SIGNS
RED	Stop or prohibition	Used only as background color for STOP, multiway supplemental plates, DO-NOT-ENTER messages, WRONG WAY signs and on Interstate route markers, as legend color for YIELD signs, parking prohibition signs, and the circular outline and diagonal bar prohibitory symbol	OCTAGON (STOP ONLY) EQUILATERAL TRIANGLE (1 point down)—YIELD	REGULATORY SIGNS
BLUE	Motorist services guidance	Used as background color for information signs related to motorist services and evacuation route marker	PENTAGON (Pointed up)—School, county route sign	MOTORIST SERVICE SIGNS, TOURIST-ORIENTED SERVICES
GREEN	Indicated movements permitted, direction guidance	Used as background color for guide signs, mileposts, legend color w/ white background for permissive parking regs and circular outline permissive symbol	RECTANGLE—Regulatory series, Guide series, Warning series	GUIDE SIGNS—CONVENTIONAL ROADS, EXPRESSWAY, FREEWAYS
BROWN	Recreational/cultural interest	Used as background color	TRAPEZOID—Recreational series	RECREATIONAL/CULTURAL-INTEREST AREA SIGNS
ORANGE	Construction and maintenance warning	Used as background color for construction and maintenance signs ONLY	DIAMOND—WARNING Series	CONSTRUCTION/MAINTENANCE
BLACK	Regulation	Used as background on ONE WAY signs, certain weigh station and night speed limit signs; also used as message. On white, yellow, and orange signs	CROSSBUCK (2 rectangles in an X configuration)—Grade Crossing	REGULATORY SIGNS

Color Code	Functional Uses	Color Uses	Shape Code	Sign Classifications
WHITE	Regulation	Used as background for route markers, guide signs, fallout shelter directional sign, and regulatory signs, except STOP signs, and for the legend on brown, green, blue, black, and red signs.	CIRCLE—GRADE CROSSING,	REGULATORY SIGNS
PURPLE				
YELLOW-GREEN	School signs	Used as background color		
LIGHT BLUE	Unassigned			
CORAL	Unassigned			

(FHWA 2009, 2A-1, 2N-09)

MANAGEMENT SYSTEMS

7

Robert R. Stewart

LEARNING OBJECTIVES

- Be able to explain the need for environmental compliance and the effects of noncompliance.

- Describe the basic components of an environmental management system (EMS).

- Discuss management theories that relate to EMSs.

- Outline the cultural and economic benefits of EMS implementation to an organization.

- List EMS cost factors and the reasons for higher or lower development costs within a particular type of organization.

- Describe several technologies available for processing, saving, and distributing EMS information across an organization.

ENVIRONMENTAL regulations, and their subsequent demands on the regulated community, have evolved steadily since their advent during the post–World War II years. One of the first environmental regulations in the United States addressed the need to prevent unauthorized excavation or filling operations that could interfere with water navigation (33 USC § 403). As the twentieth century progressed, increased public awareness of environmental issues led to the development of increasingly complex and stringent regulatory requirements. These regulations were designed by citizens, the regulated community, and government officials to assure a cleaner environment. For example, the Solid Waste Disposal Act (SWDA) of 1965 was amended by the passage of the Resource Conservation and Recovery Act (RCRA) in 1976. Additional waste management regulations were promulgated in 1984 (U.S. EPA 2007a).

Regulations are initiated as acts that are passed by Congress. Following the passage of an act, sets of regulations are designed specifically to implement the act for which they are written. Major environmental acts that are now law in the United States, in addition to the previously mentioned RCRA, include the Toxic Substances Control Act (TSCA 1976), Superfund Amendments and Reauthorization Act (SARA 1986), Resource Conservation and Recovery Act (RCRA 1980), Clean Water Act (CWA 1977), and Clean Air Act amendments (CAA 1990). All environmental requirements that a business or industrial entity must follow are derived to ensure compliance with an act.

The relatively rapid development of environmental acts and corresponding regulations has required industry and the regulated community to perform better environmentally (U.S. EPA 2005a). The need for a more organized approach rested with the regulated community to further ensure compliance with regulations and to better manage the economics of environmental affairs. A more efficient plan to preventing and mitigating environmentally damaging events, such as spills, accidents, and excess air-emission events, was clearly necessary.

Businesses are now expected by their surrounding communities to comply with environmental regulations. Communities have access to environmental performance information via the Internet (U.S. EPA 2002a). Internet resources, such as the U.S. Environmental Protection Agency's (U.S. EPA's) *My Environment* database, can provide up-to-date information on a facility's compliance status (U.S. EPA 2010). The Freedom of Information Act (FOIA) provides citizens with the right to access government environmental documents relating to a business, including inspection reports, monitoring and compliance assurance documents, and permits that are in control of the Agency (U.S. EPA 1992). However, FOIA access to many U.S. government technical documents was denied after the events of September 11, 2001 (Tien 2002). Permit applications and subsequent draft environmental permits for new pollution sources at industrial and commercial facilities are available for public review and comment before a final permit or authorization is issued. Draft permits are often available for review electronically, allowing a person to review a permit at any time from any location with Internet access.

Along with increased public scrutiny, many businesses are faced with the reality of high costs resulting from noncompliance with regulations. Such costs are in two forms, one financial, and the other through a potentially tarnished public image that can result in lost sales and increased liability through reduced public trust.

Noncompliance potentially carries high costs. For example, failure to notify the EPA before start-up of an air pollution source, a violation of the CAA, carries a potential fine of $27,500 per day (U.S. EPA 1999). In one case, the University of North Carolina was assessed a $19,633 penalty for several waste-handling violations, including failure to properly label waste containers (NCDENR 2006). Prosecutions of noncompliance with federal environmental laws involve businesses, organizations, and local government, but can also be directed toward federal facilities (U. S. EPA 2010).

The 1989 Ashland Oil tank collapse in Floreffe, Pennsylvania, released an estimated 750,000 gallons of heating oil into the Monongahela River. As a result, Ashland paid a penalty of $1.25 million (*Pittsburgh Post Gazette* 1998).

As evidenced thus far, good environmental management, including sound environmental engineering practice, is critical to the economic success of a business. Management of environmental affairs can no longer be thought of as a secondary function left to subordinates. Senior corporate management is now both responsible and accountable for the environmental actions of a company's employees. Case law has shown this to be true, with senior corporate officials being held criminally liable for their company's alleged failures in environmental management. For example, in 2006 four officials of a New Jersey pipe manufacturing company were found guilty of environmental crimes, among them being the regular discharge of oil into the Delaware River in violation of the CWA. Each official was subsequently sentenced to federal prison for a term ranging from 6 to 70 months (U.S. EPA 2009a).

As regulations evolved and enforcement became a reality for the regulated community, a systematic approach to environmental management was needed. The first environmental management systems, or EMSs, were derived from popular management concepts linked to quality control, such as ISO 14001 (Dimond 1996) and total quality management (TQM) (U.S. EPA 2006b). These concepts will be discussed later in the chapter.

The U.S. EPA has long supported use of the EMS as a positive overall management tool not only to achieve compliance, but to achieve beyond-compliance results in environmental performance. The Agency stated its formal position in 1998, which was reinforced in 2002 with its memo "United States Environmental Protection Agency Position Statement on Environmental Management Systems (EMSs)," dated May 15, 2002 (U.S. EPA 2002b), and again in its "Statement of Principles" dated December 13, 2005 (see Figure 1) (U.S. EPA 2005c).

Statement of Principles

EPA's overall policy on EMSs, as with the EMS approach itself, will continue to be guided by the principles of continual improvement and learning, flexibility, and collaboration.

- EPA will encourage widespread use of EMSs across a range of organizations and settings, with particular emphasis on adoption of EMSs to achieve improved environmental performance and compliance, pollution prevention through source reduction, and continual improvement. The Agency will support EMSs that are appropriate to the needs and characteristics of specific sectors and facilities and encourage the use of EMSs as a means of integrating other facility management programs.

- EPA will promote the voluntary adoption of EMSs. To encourage voluntary adoption of EMSs, EPA will rely on public education and voluntary programs.

- EPA will encourage organizations that use EMSs to obtain stakeholder input on matters relevant to the development and implementation of an EMS and to demonstrate accountability for the performance outcomes of their EMSs through measurable objectives and targets. Additionally, the Agency will encourage organizations to share information on the performance of their EMSs with public and government agencies and facilitate this process where practicable.

- EPA will encourage the use of recognized environmental management frameworks, such as the ISO 14001 Standard, as a basis for designing and implementing EMSs that aim to achieve outcomes aligned with the nation's environmental policy goals and the principles of this Position Statement.

- EPA will collaborate with other key partners – including states, other federal agencies, tribes, local governments, industry, and non-governmental organizations – as it implements this policy. EPA will support international EMS initiatives that facilitate the increased use of EMSs in the United States. The Agency will ensure that as it implements this policy, its decisions and work are transparent to all interested parties.

- EPA will lead by example, by developing, implementing, and maintaining EMSs at appropriate EPA facilities.

- EPA will foster continual learning by supporting research and public dialogue on EMSs that help improve the Agency's understanding of circumstances where EMSs can advance the nation's environmental policy goals. EPA will continue to collect improved data on the application of EMSs as it becomes available, including the efficacy of EMSs in improving environmental performance and the costs and benefits of an EMS to an organization and the environment.

DATE: DEC 13 2005

Stephen L. Johnson
Administrator
U.S. Environmental Protection Agency

FIGURE 1. Statement of Principles on EMSs (*Source:* EPA, December 13, 2005)

The U.S. EPA has accepted the development and implementation of EMSs as a form of injunctive relief to facilitate remedial actions and ensure ongoing compliance (U.S. EPA 2003). An EMS component has been used to bring many facilities into compliance, including multifacility companies, colleges/universities, and federal facilities (U.S. EPA 2003). Complaints involving one violation and those involving thousands of violations have been settled through EMS development and implementation.

To qualify for injunctive relief (i.e., to assure ongoing compliance), the EMS needs to follow guidelines listed in the U.S. EPA's Office of Enforcement and Compliance Assurance (OECA)—National Enforcement Investigation Center (NEIC) Compliance-Focused Environmental Management Systems (CFEMS)—Enforcement Agreement Guidance. The Guidance details twelve necessary components ("Elements") and provides draft settlement agreement language for regulators. Along with its use in enforcement, the CFEMS model is often used as a guide for development and improvement of EMSs in many types of organizations (NEIC 2005).

The use of SEPs for settlement negotiations is further detailed in the U.S. EPA guidance document entitled "Guidance on the Use of Environmental Management Systems in Enforcement Settlements as Injunctive Relief and Supplemental Environmental Projects," dated June 12, 2003 (U.S. EPA 2003). Typically a violator will negotiate an agreement with the agency to implement an EMS as a beyond-compliance initiative in exchange for a reduced cash penalty assessment. Such agreements, called Supplemental Environmental Projects, or SEPs, are used by violators to negotiate for reduced cash penalties and by agencies to produce tangible environmental improvements outside of the original citation or penalty assessment. An EMS is just one form of SEP. Many other ideas can be found by contacting U.S. EPA or by reviewing the U.S. EPA's brochure "Beyond Compliance: Supplemental Environmental Projects" (U.S. EPA 2001a).

The federal government is actively involved in developing and employing EMSs at federal facilities. In 2007, President Bush issued Executive Order 13423, requiring federal agencies to implement EMSs as part of an overall policy of sustainability and environmental management at the federal level (Federal Register 2007). The order details specific resource reduction targets, including those involving water, greenhouse gases, energy, and petroleum products. Those looking for assistance in EMS development can now find and review a federal agency's EMS to obtain ideas and guidance.

Organizations that self-audit are shielded from excessive financial and legal liability, as evidenced by companies' success in applying for and receiving relief under the U.S. EPA audit policy. For example, in 2006, National Railroad Passenger Corporation (AMTRAK) had total penalties of $319,875 waived entirely by self-disclosing known violations and by complying with U.S. EPA's audit policy requirements (U.S. EPA 2006a). By continually checking and auditing its compliance status, an organization is able to protect itself from being cited during an inspection. Violations of environmental requirements are systematically eliminated or corrected in a properly functioning EMS, and are prevented from recurrence through training and follow-up auditing. Implementation of an EMS can aid in reduction of negative public perception through the systematic removal of violations and associated negative impacts.

APPLIED SCIENTIFIC AND ENGINEERING PRINCIPLES
Management Theory

Several management theories have had an effect on the development of EMSs in the United States and elsewhere throughout the world. Additionally, key individuals have played important roles in the development of popular management theory. In *The Handbook of Project-Based Management*, the author discusses Dr. Edwards Deming, who believed in continuous improvement in products and services, along with Philip Crosby, who developed the concept of *zero defects*, and the idea that doing a task correctly the first time was always the least expensive option (Turner 1993). Other influential leaders in quality-management theory include Joseph Juran, Shigeo Shingo, and Armand Feigenbaum (Certo 1999). The concept of *Gemba Kaizen®*, or continuous improvement, has been applied successfully in both manufacturing and the service sector.

Total Quality Management

After World War II, Japan experienced a period of tremendous industrial and economic growth (CIA 2007). Part of the reason for the Japanese success was their development and use of quality control systems. American manufacturers took notice of the Japanese success in industry and began to develop quality systems to compete better globally.

Total Quality Management, or TQM, is the concept of involving all members of an organization in a continuous improvement process that reduces defects and increases quality (Certo 1987). Although originally conceived in the United States, TQM was expanded upon and applied actively and aggressively by the Japanese (Certo 1999). The Japanese effort resulted in U.S. manufacturers becoming eager to increase quality and decrease defects and mistakes. Japanese manufacturers using TQM produced products similar to those built in the United States, but at a much lower cost and with fewer after-sale problems owing to manufacturing defects.

TQM principles are needed to build an effective EMS (U.S. EPA 2006b). Implementing TQM and an effective EMS involves the concrete and unmitigated commitment by senior management (U.S. EPA 2006b) and the development of teams of individuals who are intensively trained in the appropriate management principles. An experienced outside consultant hired by the company often facilitates initial training and coordination. The consultant is usually an expert who works for a company that has successfully implemented TQM or an EMS. Teams of self-taught individuals in-house can also learn and implement TQM, but it should be understood by management and employees that a learning curve will be needed for personnel to develop the necessary expertise.

TQM training involves coaching and motivating employees to continually look for ways to solve problems; consequently, they become more productive employees (Padhi 2007). Brainstorming sessions by trained quality-improvement teams identify and solve quality problems (Padhi 2007). The teams of supervisors, initially selected and trained by the company, then take their training onto the floor and train all other floor employees not only to identify mistakes, but also how to prevent mistakes from happening. Progress charts are developed for each process in a plant that show, for example, the number of defects per 100 parts manufactured. The goal of TQM is to find the cause of each defect and resolve it, under the principle that *zero defects* is not only achievable, but that eliminating defects saves money and reduces the cost to produce a product. The same TQM concept of zero defects applies to EMS implementation for organizations that want to proactively manage their environmental affairs.

Gemba Kaizen®

A management philosophy that effectively implements TQM is Gemba Kaizen®, a technique employed initially with tremendous success by Japanese manufacturers and currently implemented internationally both by manufacturers and the service sector.

The focus of Gemba Kaizen® is the workplace, or *Gemba* in Japanese (Imai 1997). The underlying theory of Gemba Kaizen® is that the focus of management should be on the manufacturing plant or area where products are made or services are actually delivered (Imai 1997). Virtually all problems in manufacturing, and their resultant solutions, are found in Gemba.

Senior management often finds itself physically detached from Gemba, in offices far away from the workplace. Corporate offices and corporate managers are often located in different towns or cities, isolated from Gemba. Managers sometimes may not enter an actual manufacturing plant for months or years. The theory of Gemba Kaizen® is that this management detachment restricts a company from being more effective at resolving workplace problems, cutting costs, eliminating waste, or producing products more efficiently (Imai 1997). Gemba Kaizen® encourages managers to enter Gemba and spend time in the workplace.

There are many examples of how managing from the workplace floor, instead of the office, has tangible benefit. An environmental manager who is regularly on the shop floor can readily recognize an unpermitted stormwater discharge, a diesel-fuel-powered electric generating system that may need an air permit to operate, a waste container that is not labeled properly, or other regulatory noncompliance issues. Plant operations personnel who are not trained or aware of the regulatory requirements a manufacturing facility must meet on a daily basis can overlook serious noncompliance items such as these. That same environmental manager, while on the shop floor, can ask questions of floor operators, maintenance personnel, and supervisors to gauge their knowledge base regarding environmental requirements and to learn about conditions that may not be apparent to the casual visitor to the plant. For example, a maintenance person may be able to explain how he disposes of fluorescent bulbs, at which point an environmental manager can assess whether the U.S. EPA universal waste-handling requirements (40 CFR, Part 273) are being followed.

Another key practice of Gemba Kaizen® is for a manager, in focusing on a problem, to ask *Why* five times. The purpose of asking *Why* five times is to get at the root cause of a problem (Imai 1997). Here is an example of how it works:

General Manager (GM): *Why* did our company receive a Notice of Violation?
Environmental Coordinator (EC): Because we did not collect our annual stormwater sample by the required date.
GM: *Why?*
EC: Because we forgot we had to take the sample.
GM: *Why?*
EC: Because we did not have it listed on our compliance calendar.
GM: *Why?*
EC: Because we did not update our compliance calendar when we received our new stormwater permit.
GM: *Why?*
EC: Because we didn't read the permit when it arrived at the plant and subsequently transfer all conditions and action items to our compliance calendar.

From this dialogue a serious management deficiency is uncovered—failure of the environmental manager to read the permit and record key compliance dates and requirements on the environmental compliance calendar. Retraining in management skills would, in most cases, resolve this issue.

The Iowa Department of Management, Office of Lean Enterprise, a public-sector organization, has successfully employed the Gemba Kaizen® philosophy of eliminating waste and streamlining production processes throughout Iowa state government in the form of a *Lean*, or waste reduction, initiative. The organization's results show a significant improvement in government efficiency: collectively Iowa state agencies have completed over 100 Lean process improvements to reduce waste and to increase efficiency and customer satisfaction (lean.iowa.gov 2010). One example of the program's success is the Iowa Department of Natural Resources (DNR) Air Quality Program that reduced New Source Construction permit steps by 19 percent and handoffs by 33 percent (lean.iowa.gov 2010). Overall, the DNR has educated its permitting personnel to engage the regulated community in an immediate dialogue to ensure that applications can be administratively complete upon initial submittal, saving time in repeat submittals and technical reviews.

The use of Gemba Kaizen®, TQM, and related forms of management systems led to the creation of EMSs that could deliver the positive compliance results and company value that senior management, stockholders, and the public required. A look at EMSs follows; the first part will look at the ISO 14000 series of management systems, followed by overviews of similar systems.

Structure of an EMS

An EMS can be structured in many ways. Organizations often have EMS elements in place and desire additional structure to have a more complete system. The discussion below shows one suggested form of EMS. Because each organization has different needs, an EMS is bound to be completed and implemented in many ways. It is important to emphasize that any organization may deviate from the approach below to suit its individual needs.

An EMS is most often based on the Plan-Do-Check-Act principle (Figure 2), originated by Shewart and Deming (Stapleton, Glover, and Davis 2001).

The cyclical nature of this management system provides the user with steady improvement by continu-

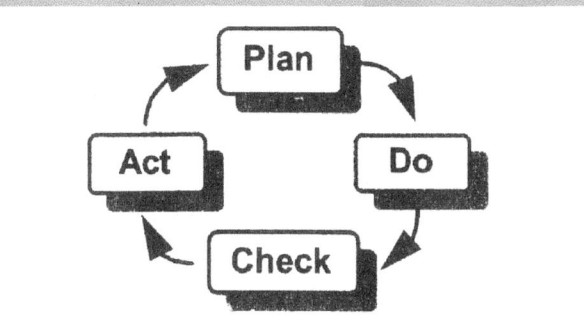

FIGURE 2. Plan-Do-Check-Act principle (*Source:* EPA 2006)

ally challenging the organization to review and revise its environmental objectives. Each step is described in detail below.

Step 1: Plan—Set goals and secure senior management commitment.

The ultimate success of any EMS is dependent on the organization's commitment to a realistic set of goals. This commitment must be demonstrated in a written form, so the company's environmental objectives will not be forgotten or misinterpreted. An implementation team is put together by the company's EMS "champion" (U.S. EPA 2006b) to define the organization's EMS goals and to review current compliance status.

After defining their organization's goals, most companies adopt the following protocol en route to publishing a written environmental policy statement, an example of which is shown in Figure 3.

Note the following characteristics, each of which is typical of a comprehensive environmental policy:

1. Endorsement by the company president or CEO, demonstrating senior management commitment
2. Compliance with all environmental standards, laws, and regulations as a primary objective
3. Promise of continuous improvement in environmental performance
4. Promise to engage in source reduction and recycling to the maximum extent possible

Depending on the level of commitment considered achievable by a company, it can expand the number of items in its policy statement. There is no standard format to an environmental policy statement; the only requirements are that it be in writing and be communicated throughout the organization (U.S. EPA 2006b). The EMS can have, along with the four statements listed here, some that are focused more on a specific industry or work practice in which the company engages. For example, a company that uses large volumes of water may have, as part of its policy statement, the promise to reduce water consumption to the maximum extent possible. Companies using large volumes of electricity, natural gas, coal, stone, or other natural resources could implement similar statements.

Producing an environmental policy statement is a necessary step toward building a successful EMS (U.S. EPA 2006b). The policy assures that a company's employees are certain of how management views environmental affairs; therefore, a standard policy has been set for both senior management and all employees to follow. With such a standard in place, little question remains as to where the company stands on environmental issues. This actuality is extremely important when dealing with those affected by the company's operations, including customers, the public, and the regulatory community.

Although the policy statement demonstrates the level of management endorsement, management must also endorse the necessary budget (which includes time, money, equipment, and tools) if the organization is to implement the EMS (U.S. EPA 2006b).

Once the company has produced a working environmental policy statement, it must take the next step, which is to *do*—in other words, follow through on how the company intends to carry out its strategy to achieve the goals planned and listed in the policy statement.

Step 2: Do—Decide on how to ensure that the EMS is focused on (a) forming a committee composed of representatives from all operating sectors of the organization and (b) developing a comprehensive set of aspects and impacts that the organization has to address in its management of environmental issues.

Forming a Committee

Based on the company *organization chart*, representatives from each operating segment of the company need to be selected to represent their segment in EMS

HESS CORPORATION
ENVIRONMENT, HEALTH AND SAFETY POLICY

HESS CORPORATION AND ITS SUBSIDIARIES RECOGNIZE THAT EXCELLENCE IN ENVIRONMENTAL, HEALTH, AND SAFETY PERFORMANCE IS AN ESSENTIAL PART OF OUR GOAL TO BECOME THE LEADING GLOBAL INDEPENDENT ENERGY COMPANY. TO ACCOMPLISH THIS, WE WILL:

- IDENTIFY, ASSESS AND MANAGE THE ENVIRONMENTAL, HEALTH AND SAFETY RISKS AND IMPACTS OF OUR EXISTING AND PLANNED OPERATIONS.

- SET OBJECTIVES AND TARGETS THAT RESULT IN CONTINUOUS IMPROVEMENT OF OUR ENVIRONMENTAL, HEALTH AND SAFETY PERFORMANCE.

- PROVIDE THE LEADERSHIP AND RESOURCES THAT WILL ENABLE OUR WORKFORCE TO MEET IMPROVEMENT OBJECTIVES AND TARGETS.

- REQUIRE EVERY EMPLOYEE TO TAKE PERSONAL RESPONSIBILITY TOWARDS MEETING ENVIRONMENTAL, HEALTH AND SAFETY OBJECTIVES.

- INCLUDE ENVIRONMENTAL, HEALTH AND SAFETY PERFORMANCE WHEN EVALUATING MANAGERS, EMPLOYEES AND CONTRACTORS FOR COMPENSATION, REWARDS, AND RECOGNITION.

- COMPLY WITH APPLICABLE ENVIRONMENTAL, HEALTH AND SAFETY LAWS AND REGULATIONS.

- RECOGNIZE THAT NO TASK IS SO IMPORTANT THAT IT BE PERFORMED AT THE RISK OF HEALTH AND SAFETY.

- PROVIDE INTERNAL STANDARDS FOR OUR MANAGERS AND EMPLOYEES WHERE CONTROLLING LAWS AND REGULATIONS DO NOT EXIST OR ARE CONSIDERED INSUFFICIENT.

- COMMUNICATE REGULARLY WITH THE COMMUNITIES WHERE WE OPERATE TO DEVELOP AND MAINTAIN A MUTUAL UNDERSTANDING OF GOALS AND EXPECTATIONS.

- PROMOTE THE CONSERVATION OF ENERGY AND NATURAL RESOURCES AND REDUCE WASTE.

- ROUTINELY MONITOR, ASSESS AND REPORT ON THE COMPANY'S ENVIRONMENTAL, HEALTH AND SAFETY PERFORMANCE AND ON OUR CONFORMITY WITH THIS POLICY.

John B. Hess
Chairman of the Board and Chief Executive Officer

May, 2006

FIGURE 3. Sample environmental policy statement (*Source:* Hess Corporation, May 2006)

Identifying Aspects	Evaluating Impacts
❏ Which <u>operations and activities</u> interface with the environment in a way that could result (or has resulted) in environmental impacts?	❏ Are the impacts <u>actual or potential</u>?
❏ What <u>materials, energy</u> sources and other <u>resources</u> do we use in our work?	❏ Are the impacts <u>beneficial or damaging</u> to the environment?
❏ Do we have <u>emissions</u> to the air, water or land?	❏ What is the <u>magnitude or degree</u> of these impacts?
❏ Do we generate <u>wastes</u>, scrap or off-spec materials? If so, does the treatment of disposal of these materials have potential environmental impacts?	❏ What is the <u>frequency or likelihood</u> of these impacts?
❏ Which characteristics or attributes of our <u>products or services</u> could result in impact the environment (through their intended use, end-of-life management, etc.)?	❏ What is the <u>duration and geographic area</u> of these impacts?
❏ Does our <u>land or infrastructure</u> (e.g., buildings) interact with the environment?	❏ Which <u>parts of the environment</u> might be affected (e.g., air, water, land, flora, fauna)?
❏ Which activities (for example, chemical storage) might lead to <u>accidental releases</u>?	❏ Is the impact <u>regulated</u> in some manner?
	❏ Have our <u>interested parties</u> expressed concerns about these impacts?

Identifying Aspects and Impacts: Some Questions to Consider:

FIGURE 4. Sample aspect and impact information (*Source:* Stapleton et al. 2001)

development to help develop a team concept within the organization (U.S. EPA 2006b). The person selected from each group must be willing to devote sufficient time and effort to identify the legal requirements as well as *aspects* and *impacts*. The time commitment by the members of this committee will be critical to the current and future success of the EMS.

Aspects and Impacts

Aspects are an organization's products or services and their interaction with the environment (Waters 1998). Some examples of aspects are a company's existing regulatory requirements, use of raw materials, and purchasing and disposal habits.

Impacts are the effects of aspects on the environment (Waters 1998). The effects can be either beneficial or deleterious. Examples of impacts are stormwater runoff, hazardous waste disposal to a permitted landfill, air emissions from a baghouse, and recycling of spent fluorescent light bulbs. Additional aspect and impact information is included in Figure 4.

Peer review is critical. All members of the committee should be given an opportunity to review the complete draft listing because each committee member will provide a unique perspective to any given aspect of the organization.

The committee members will be tasked with brainstorming ideas on how plant processes interact with air, water, or land; how their processes could potentially fail; and how emergency events could stop or impede operations. An example aspects identification checklist is included in Figure 5.

Checklists such as these can greatly simplify how an organization views its aspects and impacts.

Legal and regulatory requirements should be thoroughly reviewed, and the committee must assess the compliance or noncompliance of the organization with each regulatory requirement. Also, any promises or commitments made as part of a permit,

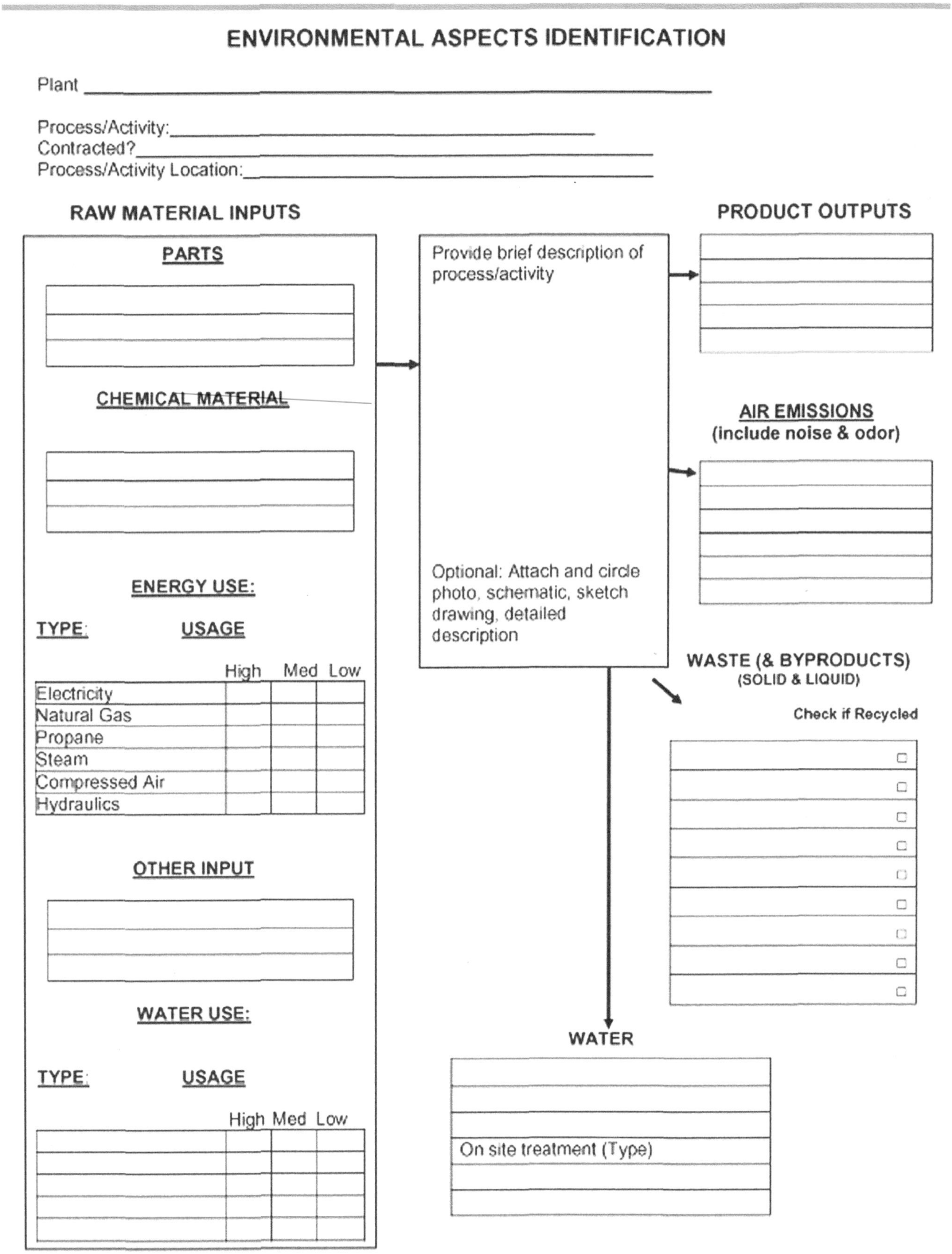

ENVIRONMENTAL ASPECTS IDENTIFICATION

Plant _____

Process/Activity: _____
Contracted? _____
Process/Activity Location: _____

RAW MATERIAL INPUTS

PARTS

CHEMICAL MATERIAL

ENERGY USE:

TYPE	USAGE		
	High	Med	Low
Electricity			
Natural Gas			
Propane			
Steam			
Compressed Air			
Hydraulics			

OTHER INPUT

WATER USE:

TYPE	USAGE		
	High	Med	Low

Provide brief description of process/activity

Optional: Attach and circle photo, schematic, sketch drawing, detailed description

PRODUCT OUTPUTS

AIR EMISSIONS
(include noise & odor)

WASTE (& BYPRODUCTS)
(SOLID & LIQUID)

Check if Recycled

WATER

On site treatment (Type)

FIGURE 5. Aspects identification checklist (*Source:* Stapleton et al. 2001)

authorization, or agreement should be included in committee review. Review and listing of legal and regulatory requirements should be documented as a formal procedure within the EMS (Stapleton, Glover, and Davis 2001).

Training

All personnel in the organization should be trained in environmental affairs as they relate to each employee's specific area of operations and job tasks (Stapleton, Glover, and Davis 2001). As such, operating procedures should be developed to ensure compliance with legal requirements (Stapleton, Glover, and Davis 2001). Employees involved in more than one area, or those in an emergency response role, must be trained further in multiple areas as well as in specific emergency response procedures.

A training matrix, such as the one in Figure 6, will become an integral part of an EMS because it helps the organization coordinate and ensure completion of all required and recommended training.

EMS Training Log (Sample)

Training Topic	Attendees*	Frequency	Course Length	Course Method	Comments	Date Completed
EMS Awareness						
Supervisor EHS Training						
Hazardous Waste Management						
Hazardous Waste Operations						
Spill Prevention & Response						
Chemical Management						
Emergency Response						
Accident Investigation						
Hazardous Materials Transport						
Hazard Communication						
Personal Protective Equipment						
Fire Safety						
Electrical Safety						
Hearing Conservation						
Confined Space Entry						
Lock-out/Tag-out						
Bloodborne Pathogens						
Job-Specific Training (list)						

Attendees Code
1: **All Employees**
2: **Supervisors / Managers**
3: **Operators**
4: **Maintenance**
5: **Material Handlers**
6: **Engineering**

FIGURE 6. Sample training matrix (*Source:* Stapleton et al. 2001)

Comparing Objectives and Targets - Some Examples

Objectives	Targets
Reduce energy usage	• Reduce electricity use by 10% in 2001 • Reduce natural gas use by 15% in 2001
Reduce usage of hazardous chemicals	• Eliminate use of CFCs by 2002 • Reduce use of high-VOC paints by 25%
Improve employee awareness of environmental issues	• Hold monthly awareness training courses • Train 100% of employees by end of year
Improve compliance with wastewater discharge permit limits	• Zero permit limit violations by the end of 2001

FIGURE 7. Sample objectives and targets (*Source:* Stapleton et al. 2001)

Objectives and Targets

Once the aspects and impacts of an organization have been drafted, reviewed, and finalized, the next step is to set objectives and targets, or clearly defined goals that demonstrate environmental commitment and reduction in environmental impact. For example, a company can commit to reducing dust emissions from its grinding operation by 10 percent in a 12-month period following implementation of the EMS, or installing fences around all of its aboveground storage tanks by the end of a specified year. Sample objectives and targets are shown in Figure 7.

A set of objectives and targets serves as the company "punch list" of specific goals for achieving and maintaining environmental compliance. The list must be reviewed periodically, at least annually, but preferably quarterly. Adhering to this review timetable will help ensure continuous improvement.

Documentation and Controls

How does an EMS get properly documented? The person in charge of managing the EMS must determine the most efficient and accurate way to complete and store all required documentation to validate the EMS. Documents include internal audit reports, inspection reports, analytical reports, and state or federal forms completed for a permit or authorization. Additional documents include standard operating procedures for environmental management, lists of objectives and targets, and emergency response procedures. An EMS manual can be a central location for compiling and storing documents that show the organization's EMS is working as planned (Stapleton, Glover, and Davis 2001).

A proven method of documenting responsibility is to create a responsibility matrix. A sample matrix is shown in Figure 8.

Each operating segment of the organization is listed, with associated duties in EMS development and implementation cross-referenced. Ideally, lead and supporting roles should be listed as well as the number of participants who are working in each area.

Current technology, such as spreadsheets and EMS software, can greatly reduce the time needed to organize an EMS and the ability of the organization to access EMS information. These concepts are discussed later in the chapter.

Environmental documents must be reviewed and updated periodically. Controls are written into EMS procedures to ensure that document updates and changes are standardized, apprehended by everyone, and easily located. Out-of-date or obsolete document management should be included in any document control procedure (Stapleton, Glover, and Davis 2001).

Emergency Preparedness

An organization must have a set of procedures to ensure life safety. Emergency response procedures are required by U.S. EPA Spill Prevention Control and

Responsibility Matrix

Legend:
L = Lead Role
S = Supporting Role

	Plant M'gr	EHS M'gr	HR M'gr	Maintenance	Purchasing / Materials	Engineering	Production Supervisor(s)	Finance	EMS Mg't Rep.	Employees
Communicate importance of environmental management	L	S					S			
Coordinate auditing efforts		L		S			S			
Track / analyze new regulations (and maintain library)		L								
Obtain permits and develop compliance plans		L				S				
Prepare reports required by regulations		L								
Coordinate communications with interested parties			L							
Train employees		S					L			
Integrate environmental into recruiting practices			L							
Integrate environmental into performance appraisal process			L							
Communicate with contractors on environmental expectations						L				
Comply with applicable regulatory requirements	L	L	S	S	S	S	S	S	S	S
Conform with organization's EMS requirements	L	L	S	S	S	S	S	S	S	S
Maintain equipment / tools to control environmental impact				L						
Monitor key processes		S					L			
Coordinate emergency response efforts	L	S								
Identify environmental aspects of products, activities, or services	S	L	S	S	S	S	S	S	S	
Establish environmental objectives and targets	L	S					S			
Develop budget for environmental management		S						L		
Maintain EMS records (training, etc.)		L								
Coordinate EMS document control efforts					S				L	

FIGURE 8. Sample Responsibility Matrix (*Source:* Stapleton et al. 2001)

Countermeasures (40 CFR, Part 112) regulations, Risk Management Plan (40 CFR, Part 68) regulations, and the Occupational Safety and Health Administration's (OSHA's) *Hazardous Waste Operations and Emergency Response* (29 CFR 1910.120) *and Process Safety Management Standard* (29 CFR 1910.119) regulations in applicable facilities (Federal Register1996). Because of similarities regarding emergency response aspects within these individual rules, the U.S. EPA has encouraged facilities covered by multiple emergency response requirements to use the Integrated Contingency Plan (ICP) format (Federal Register 1996). Emergency procedures should include: (a) assessments of the facility that has been designated for emergency potential, (b) roles and responsibilities of personnel, (c) existing levels of equipment and locations of emergency equipment, (d) levels of trained personnel within the plant, (e) evacuation measures, and (f) contact information for outside assistance. These procedures are an essential part of an EMS.

Spill prevention protects the environment, whereas fast and efficient emergency response minimizes damage to the environment; both save money and enhance third-party liability protection for the organization.

Step 3: Check—Continuous improvement of the EMS is necessary to meet the changing needs of an organization (Stapleton, Glover, and Davis 2001). Checking mechanisms should be included in an EMS to ensure this continuous improvement (see Figure 9).

Examples may include:

1. completion of plant environmental audits, with a corrective action checklist, follow-up responsibility, and target completion date
2. completion of routine (daily, weekly, monthly) environmental inspection reports

Plant audits should be completed at least annually (Stapleton, Glover, and Davis 2001). Auditors can be trained on the job or off site. Often an outside expert is used initially to help start the process. At least two trained plant auditors are recommended, if the company wishes to develop a team concept and provide continuity (Stapleton, Glover, and Davis 2001). Implementing a cycle of audit—review—corrective action within the EMS can ensure that the EMS is working as planned by providing evidence of issues that need to be addressed, or of environmental stewardship, cost savings, and success.

Step 4: Act—As stated earlier, periodic management review of completed audits and other EMS parameters may reveal deficiencies in either the EMS or in how quickly and efficiently action items are being completed. This step is perhaps the most valuable to the organization because it brings the process full circle and back to Step 1—the Plan stage (Stapleton, Glover, and Davis 2001). Acting on deficiencies forces the organization to evaluate root causes and to develop a plan of action to eliminate them. Note that if the organization's evaluation of the root cause is incorrect or inaccurate, then the problem may not be able to be resolved and will have to go through the cycle once again until it is ultimately changed or eliminated.

Management reviews can include the following action items:

1. Periodic management reviews of EMS team recommendations and employee suggestions (A sample management review procedure is shown in Figure 10.)
2. Periodic EMS team reviews of objectives and targets for completed items and new items needing attention
3. Review of audit reports
4. Review of comments from the public or other stakeholders
5. Investigation into why a violation occurred that was outside the established aspects and impacts for the organization

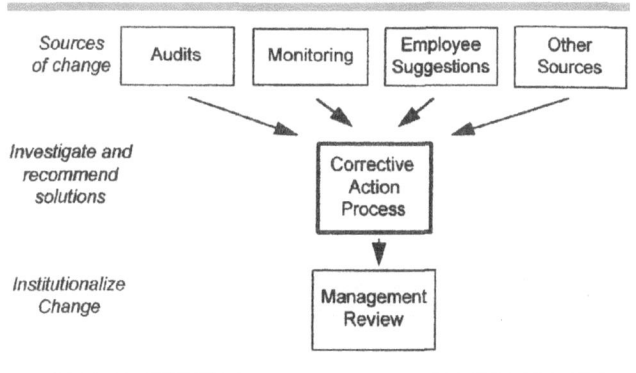

FIGURE 9. Checking mechanisms for continuous improvement (*Source:* Stapleton et al. 2001)

EMS PROCEDURE: MANAGEMENT REVIEW

I. Purpose

The purpose of this procedure is to document the process and primary agenda of issues to be included in the Management Review meetings for evaluating the status of the organization's environmental management system (EMS).

II. Scope

This procedure applies to all Management Review meetings conducted by the organization.

III. General

The Management Review process is intended to provide a forum for discussion and improvement of the EMS and to provide management with a vehicle for making any changes to the EMS necessary to achieve the organization's goals.

IV. Procedure

A. The ISO Management Representative is responsible for scheduling and conducting a minimum of two Management Review meetings during each 12-month period. The ISO Management Representative is also responsible for ensuring that the necessary data and other information are collected prior to the meeting.

B. At a minimum, each Management Review meeting will consider the following:

- suitability, adequacy and effectiveness of the environmental policy;
- suitability, adequacy and effectiveness of the environmental objectives (as well as the organization's current status in achieving these objectives);
- overall suitability, adequacy and effectiveness of the EMS;
- status of corrective and preventive actions;
- results of any EMS audits conducted since the last Management Review meeting;
- suitability, adequacy and effectiveness of training efforts; and,
- results of any action items from the previous Management Review meeting.

C. Minutes of the Management Reviews will be documented and will include, at a minimum the list of attendees, a summary of key issues discussed and any actions items arising from the meeting.

D. A copy of the meeting minutes will be distributed to attendees and any individuals assigned action items. A copy of the meeting minutes will also be retained on file.

FIGURE 10. Sample management review procedure (*Source:* Stapleton et al. 2001)

The frequency of management review meetings is best decided by the EMS team and the organization's senior management. To derive the best results, annual meetings are recommended (NSF 2001), although more frequent meetings may be needed early in the process. As the EMS becomes more familiar to the organization, fewer meetings should be needed.

Ultimately the process of Plan-Do-Check-Act will result in a highly efficient and sound EMS that will withstand repeated tests consisting of regulatory inspections, emergency events, and internal or external inquiries. In addition, as corrective action steps are taken, the organization should notice cost savings.

ISO 14001 EMS

The ISO 14001 *Environmental Management System* standard is a product of the International Organization for Standardization, a worldwide standards-setting body composed of standards-setting groups from each member organization (Waters 1998). The ISO 14001 standard is part of a family of ISO 14000 standards relating to environmental management. (The complete family of ISO 14000 standards is delineated in Figure 11.)

The ISO 14001 standard sets the framework for a company to develop and implement an environmental management system that is recognized internationally. Having an internationally recognized EMS is particularly advantageous to, and often required of, a company that operates both within the United States and globally. Overseas companies, as well as some U.S. companies, can require proof of ISO 14001 registration as a condition of doing business. Companies that fail to keep their registration can forfeit contracts and lose favored status with other companies. The U.S. automotive industry is a good example of an industry that has required ISO conformance of not only its own operating entities, but also of its suppliers. For example, Ford Motor Company required its preferred production suppliers' manufacturing facilities to acquire ISO 14001 certification by mid-2003 (Ford 2007). If a contract with an automaker is the primary income source for a parts supplier, achieving conformance with the ISO 14001 standard can be the difference between being profitable or going out of business.

Companies are not required to comply with ISO 14001 as part of any government regulatory requirement; however, agencies such as the U.S. EPA usually look at registration favorably as part of an overall regulatory compliance strategy. Additionally, although specific reductions in emissions of pollutants are not mandated, companies are required to set pollution reduction objectives and targets as part of an overall strategy of continuous improvement. In other words, a company's objectives, when met, should result in reductions in pollution.

Conformance to the ISO 14001 standard does not ensure environmental compliance. The standard is meant to set up the process of continuous improvement within an organization. Therefore, a company with a relatively poor environmental compliance record can, in fact, obtain ISO 14001 registration. By obtaining registration, the company can look forward to improved performance as the process of auditing and corrective actions required by the standard points out flaws and proposes solutions.

An ISO 14001 EMS contains the following five major elements: environmental policy, planning, implementation, checking and corrective action, and management review. Essentially, the organization is implementing its environmental policy through the actions carried out in the remaining four elements (Cascio et al. 1996).

Conformance with each element is demonstrated by publication of a company EMS manual. The manual describes each step that must be taken by the organization to establish and maintain compliance, along with personnel roles and responsibilities within the EMS, training requirements, objectives and targets, and audit requirements.

To acquire an ISO 14001 EMS, an organization must go through a rigorous registration process, usually assisted by the guidance of a registrar, who is an ISO-certified consultant with the credentials to award registration to successful applicants. The registration process involves showing the registrar the following:

- a corporate policy statement
- standard operating procedures
- a comprehensive set of objectives and targets
- a listing of personnel and their roles, along with responsibilities in environmental management

The registration process is completed once the registrar finishes interviewing key site personnel who will ultimately implement the EMS. The registrar will also review policies, procedures, and training records for any nonconforming issues (Cascio et al. 1996).

Registrars are often private consulting firms that specialize in providing ISO 14001 registration assistance to businesses and organizations. Such firms can help a company with all aspects, from initial consultation all the way through to final registration, and with each annual registration. Many private consulting firms offer ISO 14001 registration auditing and assistance. An Internet search under "ISO 14001" can

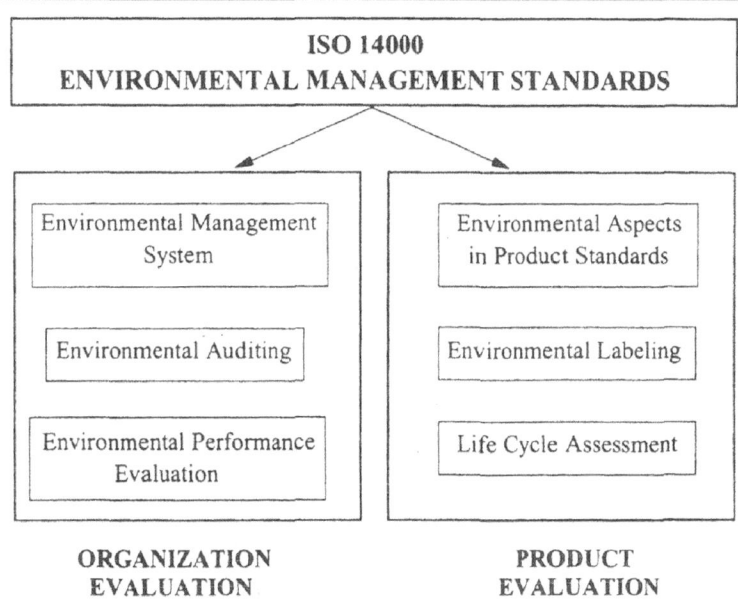

FIGURE 11. Complete family of ISO standards (*Source:* Cascio et al. 1996)

produce an extensive list of providers. A listing of public-based technical assistance providers that can help with EMS development and referrals to ISO 14001 registration providers can be found through the U.S. EPA's EMS Web site at www.peercenter.net (U.S. EPA 2007b).

Strategic Environmental Management

The idea of managing environmental affairs to produce minimum environmental impact is the basis for strategic environmental management (SEM) (Marcus 1998). Organizations that adopt SEM can reduce both regulatory liability and operating costs by converting environmental liabilities/costs into opportunities for competitive advantages in their businesses (Marcus 1998). SEM is summarized in Figure 12.

To properly implement SEM, an organization must actively work toward minimizing emissions and environmental impact. This often means an investment in new equipment or processes that produce less, or no, pollution; changing the company's public image to one of proactive environmental management; and compensating employees for environmental innovations (Marcus and Geffen 1998). An organization should be prepared to commit both capital and cultural investments to be successful at SEM. The results of successful SEM implementation can mean a more profitable business, an improved corporate public image, and a better corporate position for long-term success.

Benchmarks and Performance Appraisal Criteria

The effectiveness of an EMS can be measured by the results it provides to an organization. Such results can include fewer fines and penalties, reduced emissions, and lowered risk owing to increased auditing, checking, and corrective action implementation.

Current sustainability initiatives tie in well as measures of a functioning EMS. Sustainability measures such as tons of scrap recycled and energy use reduction targets show, when attained, that an EMS is serving its purpose by reducing impacts to the outside environment.

An ISO 14000 EMS registration is primarily reviewed annually, giving the organization an idea of how much improvement has been made. Sometimes, an EMS is reviewed more or less often, depending on the company and its auditor's recommendations.

Peer groups in the same industry can establish internal standards through their respective business associations to establish and promote best practices,

> **What Is SEM?**
>
> Strategic environmental management is the positioning of a business to take advantage of environmental challenges. It is the attempt to make these challenges into profit-making opportunities rather than threats that curtail business operations and prospects. Various companies have created value-adding programs in response to environmental issues. A list of some of the actions they have taken follows:
>
> **STRATEGY AND ORGANIZATION**
>
> - Cut back on environmentally unsafe operations.
> - Carry out R&D on environmentally safe activities.
> - Develop and expand environmental cleanup services.
> - Compensate for environmentally risky endeavors.
> - Purchase environmentally safe businesses.
> - Change structure, compensation, and other systems.
>
> **PUBLIC AFFAIRS**
>
> - Try to avoid losses caused by appearing insensitive to environmental issues.
> - Attempt to gain environmental legitimacy and credibility.
> - Collaborate with environmentalists.
>
> **LEGAL**
>
> - Try to prevent confrontation with pollution control agencies.
> - Comply early.
> - Take advantage of innovative compliance programs.
> - Rely on self-regulation rather than government requirements.
>
> **OPERATIONS**
>
> - Promote new manufacturing technologies.
> - Encourage technological advances that reduce pollution from products and manufacturing processes.
> - Modify production equipment and change manufacturing operations.
> - Eliminate manufacturing wastes.
> - Try to find alternative uses for wastes.
> - Recycle wastes.
>
> **MARKETING**
>
> - Tell the truth, the whole truth, and nothing but the truth about your products' environmentally friendly features; avoid being attacked for unsubstantiated or inappropriate claims.
> - Create consumer desire for environmentally friendly products as well as researching this market.
>
> **ACCOUNTING**
>
> - Demonstrate that anti-pollution programs pay.
> - Show all affects of pollution reduction programs.
>
> **FINANCE**
>
> - Gain the respect of the environmentally concerned investment community.
> - Recognize true liability.
> - Recognize business opportunities.
>
> Source: Buchholz, Rogene, Alfred Marcus, and James Post. *Managing Environmental Issues: A Casebook.* New York: Prentice-Hall, 1992.

FIGURE 12. Summary of strategic environmental management (*Source:* Marcus and Geffen 1998)

or benchmarks, throughout an industry. This method of benchmarking is beneficial because everyone in the group benefits. A primary example is the American Chemistry Council's Responsible Care® program, in which all American Chemistry Council member companies must participate (American Chemistry Council 2006).

Strategic environmental management (SEM) effectiveness will usually be measured by the amount of emissions reductions realized by the organization from year to year. Knowing that emissions reductions translate into reduced operating cost and regulatory liability makes SEM a reasonable add-on option for companies wishing to implement an EMS.

On June 26, 2000, the U.S. EPA established a public-private partnership called the National Environmental Performance Track that recognized companies that met predetermined performance goals with public recognition and low priority for routine inspection (U.S. EPA 2010). The program was terminated in 2009 with U.S. EPA working on new environmental leadership programs with both public and private stakeholders.

COST ANALYSIS AND BUDGETING
Budgeting for an EMS

Some organizations may have to develop an EMS out of necessity. A negative inspection report from a state or federal environmental agency can often provide enough impetus for corporate management to further refine their current environmental management strategy and enter into EMS development. Business associations voluntarily enter into EMS-like code programs, such as Responsible Care®, typically for two reasons:

1. To enhance public image
2. To show a clear difference between member and nonmember companies (NEETF 2000)

When entering into EMS development, a spending plan, or budget, should be developed to ensure that the organization is aware of and controlling costs. A budget for an EMS should include costs for the following items:

- staff time of site personnel, corporate personnel, and employees
- consulting expertise and assistance with program development and documentation
- training, including time spent on developing and delivering training

Costs can vary greatly, depending on the degree of personnel involvement, level of EMS detail, and desired level of registration. Internal labor accounts for the majority of costs for most organizations (U.S. EPA 2006a). However, an internally developed EMS can be accomplished at a relatively low cost. For example, an EMS developed by a Massachusetts Wastewater Utility produced significant cost savings and better customer service at a cost of $42,000. See Figure 13 for the EPA's comments regarding the City of Lowell Wastewater Utility EMS project.

The EMS focused on waste stream management, chemical use management, energy reduction, odor control, and industrial notification. Energy reduction alone resulted in a savings of $7000 over a 10-month period. Other benefits include improved communication at all levels of the organization, greater participation in decision making, more creative solutions, employee empowerment, as well as increased operation efficiencies and better service to customers (U.S. EPA 2006a).

Consultants will usually increase direct costs (Darnall and Edwards 2006), but will bring expertise to the process and free up internal staff time for their day-to-day work needs. Obtaining not-to-exceed cost and technical proposals from several consultants will give the company an idea of how much a consultant will cost versus how much is in the budget. A clearly defined scope of work will minimize additional charges as a company progresses with EMS development and implementation.

EMS adoption costs may be reduced by two means: having a good existing pollution-prevention program, and making use of government assistance. Additionally, those organizations with prior TQM experience usually have lower costs than those without (Darnall and Edwards 2006).

The type of company ownership may affect EMS cost. One study found that publicly traded organizations spent the least per employee ($268), whereas

---

The City of Lowell, Massachusetts, Lowell Wastewater Utility was selected as a project participant in the USEPA EMS Pilot Program for Local Government Entities. The Utility is an activated sludge wastewater treatment facility providing primary and secondary treatment to 170,000 users in five communities. The EMS focused on waste stream management, chemical use management, energy reduction, odor control, and industrial notification. Energy reduction alone resulted in a savings of $7,000 over a 10-month period. Other benefits include improved communication at all levels of the organization, greater participation in decision making, more creative solutions, employee empowerment, and increased operation efficiencies and better service to customers. These improvements resulted from a rather modest expenditure of about $42,000. For more information contact Mark Young, (978) 970-4248, e-mail: myoung@ci.lowell.ma.us.

FIGURE 13. A model cost-effective EMS

privately owned organizations ($531) and government spent more ($1,372). This cost variation may be attributed to the level of internal skill within the organization (Darnall and Edwards 2006).

Costs for ISO 14001 Registration

Development and implementation costs for ISO 14001 registration include the following:

- registrar (consultant)
- internal staff time
- external consultant costs to train employees as internal auditors
- EMS development costs
- EMS registration costs

Design costs for an ISO 14001 EMS are usually less than $100,000 (Duke 2000). These costs are readily paid back in increased organization, decreased risk of fines and penalties, and positive public image for the company. Beyond design costs, initial registration fees are usually under $50,000 (Duke 2000). In one EPA study, a company reported an average cost of $89,000 per plant to achieve initial registration (Dimond 1996).

Given the broad range of expenses between an internally developed EMS and a fully registered ISO 14001 EMS, an organization must carefully plan on the basis of what level of management it desires. As mentioned previously, the decision may already have been made for the organization by a parent company, the board of directors, a member association, a customer, or the shareholders. In other cases, the organization will have to make the decision on which type of EMS to develop. In either case, a properly functioning EMS should provide a financial and social benefit to an organization.

EMS Information Management

Advances in technology have enabled environmental managers to streamline the many record-keeping and management requirements demanded by an EMS. Examples include:

- spreadsheet applications
- secure shared drives
- online communication systems

Each example is discussed below.

Spreadsheet Applications

Current spreadsheet applications are ideal for organizing a facility's environmental information. Spreadsheets can be used for the following:

- aspects and impacts
- legislative requirements
- training information
- objectives and targets
- responsibility matrix
- permit requirements

Spreadsheets allow the user to efficiently manage and save environmental information. Additionally, spreadsheet cells can be modified with formulas to automatically perform calculations or functions. Cells can also be linked to cells on another spreadsheet, allowing the user to potentially complete multiple tasks with a single action. For example, with a spreadsheet application a user can fill in the amount of product manufactured in a day. That spreadsheet cell can be linked to other cells that will calculate the facility's greenhouse gas emissions, fuel usage, and related parameters for the day. Daily data can be organized and summarized in a variety of ways to provide useful information, for example, annual emissions data, or annual fuel-usage data needed for air quality permit compliance reports. For example, a typical emissions calculation spreadsheet for a brick manufacturing plant is shown in Figure 14.

In addition, there are a number of commercially available, web-based online EMS applications. A discussion of these applications is beyond the scope of this chapter.

Secure Shared Drive

Many organizations offer their employees secure access to the company's computer system to conduct company business. In a typical application, an employee logs in (provides user identification and password) to the system, the system then grants access to a secure area where documents can be stored and information can be shared. The area, often called a shared drive, is accessible to all employees, but not to the public.

For EMS applications, a shared drive can offer many benefits. For example, the corporate Environmental Policy and EMS manual can be stored on the shared drive, and thus be available for instant access to any employee. Recent agency inspection reports can be posted to alert other facilities of any issues found at a particular location. Training presentations, policies, and standard operating procedures, when posted, can be used to provide consistency throughout the organization. The costs for providing a shared drive are low, as the needed systems are normally already in place at an organization.

Online Communication Systems

Online training and meetings can be conducted with an online communication system. A high-speed internet connection and telephone-conferencing capability are usually necessary. Typically the meeting organizer sets up an account with a commercial provider. To hold a meeting, the organizer enters the provider's Web site, selects the date and time of the meeting, enters attendee e-mail addresses, and chooses a dial-in phone number to provide the meeting's audio component. The system then sends a Web link to all attendees with the meeting's date, time, and dial-in phone number.

The meeting begins with the organizer logging in to the meeting and signaling to the system to allow the organizer's computer screen to be seen by the attendees. When attendees log in to the Web site using the web link provided earlier, they will see the organizer's computer screen in live mode, meaning any actions taken by the organizer will be viewed by

Unit ID	Description	Control Device	Emission Limit		Control Device Required to Meet Limit?	Uncontrolled PTE > 100 ton/yr?	Subject to CAM?
101	Tunnel Kiln 1	N/A	PM:	0.04 gr/dscf	NO	NO	NO
		N/A	SO_2:	500 ppmdv	NO	NO	NO
		New Dry Limestone Absorber (DLA)	HCl:	0.26 lb/ton b	YES	NO	NO[1]
		New Dry Limestone Absorber (DLA)	HF:	1.2 lb/hr	YES	NO	NO[1]
102	Tunnel Kiln 2	N/A	PM:	0.04 gr/dscf	NO	NO	NO
		N/A	SO_2:	500 ppmdv	NO	NO	NO
		New Dry Limestone Absorber (DLA)	HCl:	0.26 lb/ton b	YES	NO	NO[1]
		New Dry Limestone Absorber (DLA)	HF:	1.2 lb/hr	YES	NO	NO[1]
104	Quarry Crusher	N/A	N/A		NO	NO	NO
105	Grinding/Screening/Manufacturing	C01: Sand Mixing Op. Fabric Collector	PM:	0.04 gr/dscf	YES	NO	NO
		C02: Shale Grdg Ln#2 Fabric Collector	PM:	0.04 gr/dscf	YES	NO	NO
		C03: Shale Grdg Ln#3 Fabric Collector	PM:	0.04 gr/dscf	YES	NO	NO
		C04: Fine Silo-Shale G Fabric Collector	PM:	0.04 gr/dscf	YES	NO	NO
		C05: Colonial Making Fabric Collector	PM:	0.04 gr/dscf	YES	NO	NO
		C08: Wirecut Sand B&S Fabric	PM:	0.04 gr/dscf	YES	NO	NO
		C10: Moldsander/Drysaw Fabric	PM:	0.04 gr/dscf	YES	NO	NO
106	Sand Dryer	C09: Sand Dryer Fabric Collector	PM:	0.04 gr/dscf	YES	NO	NO
		N/A	SO_2:	500 ppmdv	NO	NO	NO
107	Proctor Dryer	N/A	PM:	0.04 gr/dscf	NO	NO	NO
108	Space Heaters	N/A	N/A		NO	NO	NO
109	Shapes Dryer	N/A	PM:	0.04 gr/dscf	NO	NO	NO
		N/A	SO_2:	500 ppmdv	NO	NO	NO
110	Brick Shuttle Kiln	N/A	PM:	0.04 gr/dscf	NO	NO	NO
		N/A	SO_2:	500 ppmdv	NO	NO	NO
		N/A	HF:	0.91 tpy	NO	NO	NO
111	Emergency Generator No. 1	N/A	PM:	0.04 gr/dscf	NO	NO	NO
		N/A	SO_2:	500 ppmdv	NO	NO	NO
112	Emergency Generator No. 2	N/A	PM:	0.04 gr/dscf	NO	NO	NO
		N/A	SO_2:	500 ppmdv	NO	NO	NO

[1] Pursuant to §64.2(b)(1)(i), the emission limit is exempt from CAM requirements since it originates from the Brick MACT. MACT standards proposed after 11/15/90 already contain sufficient monitoring to assure compliance with the limitation.

FIGURE 14. Typical emissions calculation spreadsheet for a brick manufacturing plant (*Source:* All4, Inc. 2010)

Association	Code name and year established
Chemical Manufacturers Association (CMA)	Strategies for Today's Environmental Partnership (STEP), 1990
American Petroleum Institute (API)	Responsible Distribution Process^{SM} (RDP), 1991
National Association of Chemical Distributors (NACD)	• Encouraging Environmental Excellence (E3), 1992
American Textile Manufacturers Institute (ATMI)	• Quest for the Best, 1993
National Association of Chemical Recyclers (NACR)	Responsible Recycling, 1993
American Forest & Paper Association (AF&PA)	• Sustainable Forestry Initiative (SFI^{SM}), 1994
National Paint and Coatings Association (NPCA)	• Environmental, Health and Safety Principles, 1995
Responsible Care,® 1989	Coatings Care,® 1996

FIGURE 15. Associations with codes of conduct (*Source:* NEETF 2000)

	ATMI's E3	CMA's Responsible Care®	NPCA's Coatings Care®	Responsible Distribution^{SM}	SOCMA Responsible Care®	API's STEP	AFPA's SFI^{SM}
Regulatory Compliance Required	Yes	No	No	Yes	No	No	Yes
Demonstrate Continuous Improvement	Yes	Yes	Yes	No	Yes	Yes	Yes
Community Involvement	Yes	Yes	Yes	Yes	Yes	Yes	Yes
Product Stewardship	Yes	Yes	Yes	Yes	Yes	Yes	Yes
Participation mandatory	No	Yes	Yes	Yes	Yes	Yes	Yes
3rd Party Verification	No	Voluntary	No	Yes	Voluntary	No	Voluntary

FIGURE 16. Certain aspects of codes of conduct (*Source:* NEETF, 2000)

the attendees. The corresponding dial-in number allows a conference call to take place along with the visual presentation.

The medium is ideal for holding update meetings or group discussions and can be used to rapidly and efficiently complete EMS training needs or information updates across an organization.

Subscriptions to the online service provider and telephone-conferencing service are required. At the same time, the savings in travel costs often translate into reduced overall costs for EMS implementation and ongoing training.

BEST PRACTICES

Best practices are commonly developed through the sharing of information between businesses through peer associations and business/government partnership (U.S. EPA 2007b). Peer associations with environmental best-practice codes of conduct are shown in Figure 15.

Member companies are often required to comply with association codes of conduct or have their membership revoked (NEETF 2000). Certain aspects of codes of conduct may also be voluntary, as shown in Figure 16.

There have been numerous business/government collaborations on EMS development and best-practice sharing. U.S. EPA grants have been used to fund best-practice initiatives for public use; these include the following:

- The Development of the 1998 document "Environmental Management Systems" by Jean S. Waters, Pollution Prevention Institute. This step-by-step EMS guidance document for small businesses was developed with help from a grant from the U.S. EPA to the Kansas Department of Health and Environment, under contract to the University of Kansas Center for Continuing Education (Waters 1998). It provides the user with a thorough discussion of EMS benefits, along with a review of each step in EMS development and implementation. Additional external information sources are included.
- The NSF International report titled "Environmental Management System Demonstration Project—Final Report," dated December 1996 (NSF 1996). This document summarizes the experiences of eighteen organizations in their quest for ISO 14001 EMS registration. The project was funded by a two-year grant from the U.S. EPA, which recognized the public need for information on EMS development. The participants included sixteen private companies, one government agency, and the U.S. Postal Service. Of the fifteen individual companies completing both the initial and final self-assessment, twelve reported positive progress toward EMS implementation over the course of the project (p. 18). The report can be of significant value to a company of similar size to any in the study.

Best practices on EMS implementation are shared on the U.S. EPA Web site, www.epa.gov/ems. Along with useful discussions, the Web page contains reference documents, case studies, policy statements, and other tools to assist virtually any organization in its EMS development and implementation.

Also, EMS best practices are being shared at industry association work groups, technical committee meetings, and local/state pollution prevention roundtables. Sample EMS documents, outlines, case histories, and spreadsheets can often be located through membership in these types of associations, or through government Web sites beyond EPA, such as the Public Entity EMS Resource (PEER) Center Web site (found online at www.peercenter.net) (U.S. EPA 2007b).

Typical best practices may include a detailed training matrix, an audit schedule, and a comprehensive aspects and impacts listing developed for a particular organization or line of business. Having this type of documentation allows an organization to take advantage of a time-tested format to develop a successful EMS implementation strategy.

Ongoing development of best practices is necessary to ensure the highest level of EMS performance, the greatest reduction in emissions, and the maximum cost savings. Technical committees and business associations will play a large part in development and implementation of best practices within their respective business sectors. Government will play a role in recognizing need and establishing funding mechanisms for best-practice development and sharing to assist the public.

The overall benefits of an EMS to an organization are obvious—improved environmental performance, better public image, and reduced costs (U.S. EPA 2007b). All organizations should have some form of EMS in place, not only to better manage their organization, but also to better compete in a global economy.

REFERENCES

A114, Inc. 2010. "Emissions Calculation Spreadsheet." Kimberton, PA: A114, Inc.

American Chemistry Council (ACC). 2006. *About Responsible Care and the American Chemistry Council.* www.responsiblecare-us.com/about.asp

Cascio, J., G. Woodside, and P. Mitchell. 1996. *ISO 14000 Guide: The New International Environmental Management Standards.* New York: McGraw-Hill.

Certo, Samuel C. "The Push for Quality." *Business Week*, June 8, 1987, p. 131.

_____. 1999. *Modern Management*. 8th ed. New York: Simon & Shuster.

Darnall, Nicole, and Daniel Edwards, Jr. 2006. "Predicting the Cost of Environmental Management System Adoption: The Role of Capabilities, Resources, and Ownership Structure." *Strategic Management Journal*, January 2006, p. 305.

Delmas, Magali A. 2000. "Barriers and Incentives to the Adoption of ISO 14001 in the United States." *Duke Environmental Policy and Law Forum* 11(1):25.

Dimond, Craig D. 1996. "Environmental Management System Demonstration Project. NSF International. Environmental Management Systems." 2006. Michigan Department of Environmental Quality (MIDEQ) fact sheet no. 9838, Michigan Department of Environmental Quality.

Federal Register. Part II, The President, Executive Order 13423—Strengthening Federal Environmental, Energy, and Transportation Management. National Archives and Records Administration. Friday, January 26, 2007.

Ford Motor Company. 2007. *Sustainability Report 2005/6—Suppliers*. www.ford.com/en/company/about/sustainability/2005-06/relSuppliers.htm

Hess Corporation. 2006. *Environment, Health and Safety Policy*. www.hess.com/ehs/policies/ehspolicy.pdf

Imai, Masaaki. 1997. *Gemba Kaizen: A Commonsense, Low-Cost Approach to Management*. New York: McGraw-Hill. (Process Improvement—Standard Permits). www.iowadnr.com/air/prof/kaizen/kaizen03jun23.html

Iowa Department of Management, Office of Lean Enterprise. 2010. *Lean Business Process Improvement in the Executive Branch of Iowa State Government*. www.lean.iowa.gov/results/index.html

Marcus, Alfred, and Donald Geffen. 1998. *Introduction to the Compendium on Strategic Environmental Management*. Ann Arbor, MI: National Pollution Prevention Center for Higher Education, University of Michigan.

North Carolina Department of Environment and Natural Resources. 2006. *Division of Waste Management, Hazardous Waste Section (civil penalty assessments, December 2006)*. www.wastenot.enr.state.nc.us/HWHOME/penalties/Dec06.html

Office of the Federal Register. 1996. "The National Response Team's Integrated Contingency Plan Guidance." Federal Register, 61 no. 109 (June 5): 28642.

Padhi, Nayantara. 2007. *The Eight Elements of TQM*. www.isixsigma.com/library/content/c021230a.asp

Pitz, Marylynne. "Fish Return after '88 Oil Spill, Study Says." *Pittsburgh Post-Gazette*, October 9, 1998. www.post-gazette.com/regionstate/19981009rivers5.asp

Public Entity Environmental Management System Resource Center. 2010. *About the Center*. www.peercenter.net

Stapleton, Philip J., Margaret A. Glover, and S. Petie Davis. 2001. *Environmental Management Systems: An Implementation Guide for Small and Medium-Sized Organizations*. Ann Arbor, MI: NSF International.

The Institute for Corporate Environmental Mentoring. 2000. *The Emerging Role of Associations as Mentors, National Forum on Defining Environmental Excellence*. Washington, D.C.: The National Environmental Education and Training Foundation (NEETF).

Tien, Lee. "Access to Information after 9/11." Paper presented at the Electronic Frontier Foundation's 12th Conference on Computers, Freedom and Privacy, San Francisco, April 16–19 2002.

Turner, J. Rodney. 1993. *The Handbook of Project-Based Management*. New York: McGraw-Hill.

U.S. Army Corps of Engineers. 1899. "Section 10 of the Rivers and Harbors Act of 1899," 33 U.S.C. 403. www.usace.army.mil/cw/cecwo/reg/rhsec10.htm

U.S. Central Intelligence Agency. 2007. *The World Factbook*. www.cia.gov/cia/publications/factbook/print/ja.html

United States Environmental Protection Agency (U.S. EPA). 1992. *EPA 1550—Freedom of Information Act Manual*. www.nepis.epa.gov

_____. 1996. *Companies Come Clean about Environmental Violations*. www.yosemite.epa.gov/opa/admpress.nsf/56d5d55f70218074852572a000657b5d/3902ba81651887908525721200522563!OpenDocument

_____. 1998. "Memorandum: Issuance of Supplemental Environmental Projects Policy." Office of Enforcement and Compliance Assurance. www.epa.gov/safewater/wsg/wsg_119.pdf

_____. 1999. *Roto-Die Company cited for Clean Air Act violations at Micrometrics Systems plant in Virginia*. www.yosemite.epa.gov/opa/admpress.nsf/56d5d55f70218074852572a000657b5d/78afaf2bf2cf7ef4852570d60070fa56!OpenDocument

_____. 2001b. Office of Enforcement and Compliance Assurance. *Beyond Compliance: Supplemental Environmental Projects* (EPA 325-R-01-001).

_____. 2001a. *Environmental Management Systems and the Clean Water State Revolving Fund* (EPA 832-F-00-075). www.epa.gov/OW-OWM.html/cwfinance/cwsrf/emsfs.pdf

_____. 2002a. *Environmental Management Systems, Your Business Advantage* (EPA 240-F-02-002). www.epa.gov/EMS/docs/resources/ems_business.pdf

_____. 2002b. *Position Statement on Environmental Management Systems (EMSs)*. www.epa.gov/EPA-GENERAL/2006/February/Day-02/g1423.html

_____. 2003. *Guidance on the Use of Environmental Management Systems in Enforcement Settlements as Injunctive Relief and Supplemental Environmental Projects* (accessed June 11, 2010). www.epa.gov/compliance/resources/policies/civil/seps/emssettlementguidance.pdf

_____. 2005a. *Compliance-Focused Environmental Management System—Enforcement Agreement Guidance* (EPA 330/9-97-002) (accessed June 11, 2010). www.epa.gov/compliance/resources/publications/incentives/emd/emd12elemr.pdf

_____. 2005b. *EPA Celebrates the Nation's Cleaner Environment on its 35th Anniversary."* www.yosemite.epa.gov/opa/admpress.nsf

_____. 2005c. *United States Environmental Protection Agency Position Statement on Environmental Management Systems (EMSs).* www.epa.gov/ems/position/position.htm

_____. 2006a. *EMS Costs and Benefits.* www.epa.gov/ems/info/costben.htm

_____. 2006b. *Key Management Systems Concepts.* www.epa.gov/ems/info/keyconcepts.htm

_____. 2006c. *Laws and Regulations.* www.epa.gov/epaoswer/osw/laws-reg.htm

_____. 2006d. *Plan, Do, Check, Act Model—Do.* www.epa.gov/ems/info/do.htm

_____. 2006e. *Plan, Do, Check, Act Model—Plan.* www.epa.gov/ems/info/plan.htm

_____. 2007a. *Envirofacts Data Warehouse—Overview.* www.epa.gov/enviro/html/ef_overview.html

_____. 2007b. *Gateway to International Best Practices & Innovations* (accessed June 11,2010). www.epa.gov/innovation/international

_____. 2007c. *Summary of Criminal Prosecutions, Fiscal Year 1999.* www.cfpub.epa.gov/compliance/criminal_prosecution/index.cfm

_____. 2009a. *Company and Four Senior Managers Sentenced for Environmental, Worker Safety Crimes After Longest Trial in Environmental Crimes History* (accessed June 11, 2010). admpress.nsf/www.yosemite.epa.gov/opa/d0cf6618525a9efb85257359003fb69d/41d5e11b5cc11a77852575a5005ed68f!OpenDocument

_____. 2009b. *National Environmental Performance Track.* www.epa.gov/performancetrack

_____. 2009c. *Next Steps for the National Environmental Performance Track Program and the Future of Environmental Leadership Programs* (accessed June 11, 2010). www.epa.gov/performancetrack/downloads/PerformanceTrackNextStepsMemoExternal-text.pdf

_____. 2010. *My Environment* (accessed June 11, 2010). www.epa.gov/myenvironment

_____. 2011. *Civil Enforcement* (accessed November 8, 2011). www.epa.gov/compliance/civil

Waters, Jean S. 1998. *Environmental Management Systems, Prepared for the Small-Business Leadership Program under a Grant from USEPA.* Manhattan, KS: Pollution Prevention Institute.

INDEX

A

AACSC. *See:* American Association of Casualty and Safety Companies (AACSC)
Accident-prevention signs, 196–199, 204
Accidents. *See:* Hazards *and* Incident investigations
ACEEE. *See:* American Council for an Energy-Efficient Economy (ACEEE)
Acid deposition, 10–12
Acid rain, 5, 10–11, 17, 19–20
Acid Rain Program, 11, 19
Acoustic Barrier Particulate Separation, 29
Activated sludge, 51
Acutely hazardous wastes, 105
Adsorption, 49
Aerated lagoons, 51
Aerobic landfills and wastewater, 66
Agency for Toxic Substances and Disease Registry, 130
Air abatement issues, 2
Air pollution
    acid deposition, 10–12, 19–20
    best management practices, 29–32
    Clean Air Act legislation and amendments, 3–15
    control, 1–32
    control technologies, 7, 20, 25–29
    hazardous air pollutants, 9–10
    hazardous material spills, 157
    history, 2–6
    human and environmental effects, 16–20
    National Ambient Air Quality Standards, 4–8
    overview, 1–2, 31–32
    research, 14–15
    risk, 16–20
    solid waste, 82–83
Air Pollution Control (Cooper & Alley), 1
Air Pollution Control Act, 1955, 3
Air Quality Act, 1967, 3
Air-quality control regions (AQCR), 3
Air Quality Standards, National Ambient, 4–8
American Association of Casualty and Safety Companies (AACSC), 170
American Council for an Energy-Efficient Economy (ACEEE), 29–30
American National Standards Institute (ANSI)
    A13.1 Standard, 182
    evolution of, 197
    eyewash and shower stations, 83
    hazard communication, 197–200, 204–206, 208–209
    Z129.1 Standard, 180–181
    Z400.1 Standard, 183–184
    Z535 Series, 197–204, 219–222
American Society for Testing and Materials (ASTM), 113
    E1527 Standard, 113–114
    ASTM Standard on Environmental Sampling, 136
American Standards Association (ASA), Z35.1 Standard, 197
Ammonia (NH_3), 8, 42
AMTRAK. *See:* National Railroad Passenger Corporation (AMTRAK)
Anaerobic digestion, 51
Anaerobic landfills, 66
Animals, solid waste, 77
ANSI. *See:* American National Standards Institute (ANSI)
AQCR. *See:* Air-quality control regions (AQCR)
Arrows, directional, 200, 207–208
ASA. *See:* American Standards Association (ASA)
Asbestos, 208
Assessment. *See:* Benchmarking *and* Performance
ASTM. *See:* American Society for Testing and Materials (ASTM)
Atmosphere, 20–23
Atomic Energy Act, 1954, 94
Autoclaves, 72

B

Backyard burning, 68–69
BACT. *See:* Best available control technology (BACT)
Bag-house collector, 26
Barricade tape, 204–205
Basic Physical Chemistry for the Atmospheric Sciences (Hobbs), 20
BAT. *See:* Best available technology (BAT)
Batteries, 44, 69

Benchmarking. *See also:* Performance
    hazardous materials, 142–144
    wastewater regulation, 53–54
Benefits and Costs of the Clean Air Act—Second Prospective Study from 1990 to 2020 (EPA), 15
Best available control technology (BACT), 4, 13
Best available technology (BAT), 39–40, 42, 56
Best conventional pollution-control technology, 42
Best management practices. *See:* Management *and specific fields*
Best practicable control technology (BPT), 39, 42
Best Practices for Hospital-Based First Receivers of Victims from Mass Casualty Incidents Involving the Release of Hazardous Substances (OSHA), 148
Bingham, Eula, 172
Bio-scrubber, 29
Biological oxygen demand (BOD), 41–42, 44, 48, 54, 56
Biological treatment, wastewater, 50–51
BLS. *See:* Bureau of Labor Statistics (BLS)
BMCS. *See:* Bureau of Motor Carrier Safety (BMCS)
BOD. *See:* Biological oxygen demand (BOD)
Boiling point (BP), 138
Bowater, Inc. case study, 30
BP. *See:* Boiling point (BP)
BPT. *See:* Best practicable control technology (BPT)
Budgeting. *See also:* Cost analysis, Costs, *and* Economic analysis
    environmental management systems, 243–244
    hazardous material spills, 145–147
    hazardous waste, 117–118
    wastewater regulation, 54
Bureau of Labor Statistics, 61–62
Bureau of Motor Carrier Safety (BMCS), 205
By-products, labeling issues, 181

C

CAA. *See:* Clean Air Act (CAA)
CAER. *See:* Community Awareness and Emergency Response (CAER) program
Canada, hazard communication standards, 185–186
Canadian Controlled Products Regulations (CPR), 185–186
Canadian Workplace Hazardous Materials Information Systems (WHMIS), 185–186
Carabell v. United States, 47–48
Carbon dioxide (CO_2), 6, 14, 19
Carbon monoxide (CO), 6–9, 17–18
Carcinogens, 17–18, 178
Category hazards, 192–193
CAUTION signs, 200, 202–203
CC. *See:* Construction completion (CC) report
CCTV. *See:* Closed-circuit television (CCTV)
CDC. *See:* Centers for Disease Control and Prevention (CDC)
Cementation, 53
CEMS. *See:* Continuous emission measurement system (CEMS)
Census of Fatal Occupational Injuries (CFOI), 61
Centers for Disease Control and Prevention (CDC), 92, 130, 134
CEQ. *See:* Council on Environmental Quality (CEQ)
CERCLA. *See:* Comprehensive Environmental Response, Compensation, and Liability Act (CERCLA)
CESQGs. *See:* Conditionally Exempt Small-Quantity Generators (CESQGs)
CFCs. *See:* Chlorofluorocarbons (CFCs)
CFEMS. *See:* Compliance-Focused Environmental Management Systems (CFEMS)
CFR. *See:* Code of Federal Regulations (CFR)
CGI. *See:* Combustible gas indicator (CGI)
Chemical hazards. *See also:* Material Safety Data Sheets (MSDS) *and* Hazardous spills
    category, 192–193
    documentation, 172–173, 178–179, 183–185
    exposure levels, 170–171, 178
    historical background, 170–172
    inventory lists, 175, 178–179
    labeling standards, 179–189, 191, 204–205
    transportation, 205
Chemical oxygen demand (COD), 41–42, 44, 48, 54
Chemical treatment, wastewater, 50
Chlorofluorocarbons (CFCs), 5, 13–14, 20, 28, 94
CIE. *See:* Commission Internationale de l'Eclairage (CIE)
CIP. *See:* Continuous improvement process (CIP)
Classroom training. *See:* Training
Clean Air Act (CAA), 1963
    achievements, 15–16
    acid deposition, 10–12, 19–20
    amendments, 1963, 3
    amendments, 1970, 4, 6–7, 225
    amendments, 1990, 4–16
    hazardous air pollutants, 9–10
    hazardous waste, 128
    human and environmental effects, 16–20
    legislation, 1970, 4
    legislation, pre-1970, 3–4
    National Ambient Air Quality Standards, 4–8
    research, 14–15
    violations of, 226
Clean Water Act (CWA), 1977
    hazardous waste, 94, 128
    safety engineering management, 225
    wastewater regulation, 38–46
Clean Water Restoration Act (CWRA), 1965, 38
Clear Skies Act (CSA), 5–6
Climate, 12–14, 19–20
Closed-circuit television (CCTV), 79
Coal, 12. *See also:* Air pollution control
COD. *See:* Chemical oxygen demand (COD)
Code of Federal Regulations (CFR), 125–126
Codes of conduct, 246
Cold zone, 156–157
Coliform, 42, 56

Color coding
    hazard communications, 198, 203, 222–224
    highway signs, 223–224
    ISO standards, 206–207
Combustible gas indicator (CGI), 138
Cominco America, Inc., case study, 30
Commission Internationale de l'Eclairage (CIE), specifications, 203, 205
Community Awareness and Emergency Response (CAER) program, 133
Community Right to Know Law. *See:* Emergency Planning and Community Right to Know Act (EPCRA), 1986
Comparative Evaluation of Protective Gloves for Law Enforcement and Corrections Applications (DOJ), 130
Compliance
    air pollution, 3–15
    environmental management, 226–228, 240–241
    hazard communication, 173–175, 194–195
    hazardous waste, 112–113, 116, 118
    water and wastewater, 41–46
Compliance-Focused Environmental Management Systems (CFEMS), 228
Composites, 44–45
Composting, 69–70, 73
Comprehensive Environmental Response, Compensation, and Liability Act (CERCLA), 1980, 91–92, 108, 113, 127, 134
Conditionally exempt small-quantity generators (CESQGs), 95, 98–101, 103
Construction
    hazardous waste, 115–116, 147
    solid waste, 67–68
Construction and Demolition (C&D) debris landfills, 67–68
Construction completion (CC) report, 116
Consumer electronics, disposal, 69
Consumer Electronics Association (CEA), 69
Consumer Product Safety Act (CPSA), 169
Consumer Product Safety Commission (CPSC), 187, 202
Container labeling, 101–102, 179–182
Containers, types and designs, 80
Continuous emission measurement system (CEMS), 12
Continuous improvement process (CIP), 228–229, 237–238
Control technology guidelines (CTGs), 13
Controlled-air incinerator, 71
"Controlling Chemical Hazards" (DOL), 170
Cook, Warren, 170
Cost analysis. *See also:* Budgeting, Cost-benefit analysis, *and* Economic analysis
    air pollution control, 30–31
    hazardous material spills, 145–147
    hazardous waste, 115–118
    wastewater regulation, 54
Cost Analysis for Pollution Prevention (Washington State Dept. of Ecology), 118

Cost-benefit analysis, hazardous waste, 117–118
Costs
    air pollution control, 23–25
    environmental management systems, 243–244
    of noncompliance, 226
Council on Environmental Quality (CEQ) report, 4
CPR. *See:* Canadian Controlled Products Regulations (CPR)
CPSA. *See:* Consumer Product Safety Act (CPSA)
CPSC. *See:* Consumer Product Safety Commission (CPSC)
Criteria for Review of Hazardous Materials Emergency Plans (NRT), 142
Criteria pollutants, 7–8
Crosby, Philip, 228
CSA. *See:* Clear Skies Act (CSA)
CTGs. *See:* Control technology guidelines (CTGs)
CWA. *See:* Clean Water Act (CWA)
CWRA. *See:* Clean Water Restoration Act (CWRA)
Cyanide gas, 42, 44, 53
Cyclone, 26

D
DANGER signs, 199, 202, 205
Dechlorination, 50
The Decision-Maker's Guide to Solid Waste Management, Vol. II (EPA), 74
Decon, 156
Decontamination, 132, 159–161
Deming, W. Edwards, 228, 230
Demonstrated understandability, 201
Dense nonaqueous-phase liquid (DNAPL), 137, 139
Depreciation, 24
Designer bacteria, 50
Directional signs, 200, 207–208
Dischargers, direct, 39
Distillation, 49
DNAPL. *See:* Dense nonaqueous-phase liquid (DNAPL)
DOE. *See:* U.S. Department of Energy (DOE)
DOJ. *See:* U.S. Department of Justice (DOJ)
DOL. *See:* U.S. Department of Labor (DOL)
Donora, Pennsylvania, 2
DOT. *See:* U.S. Department of Transportation (DOT)
Draft Model Training Program for Hazard Communication, 190–192
Draft NIJ CBRN Protective Ensembles for Law Enforcement (DOJ), 130
Drag force, 23
Dry tomb landfill, 66–67

E
Economic analysis. *See also:* Cost analysis
    air pollution control, 23–25
Effectiveness. *See:* Benchmarking *and* Performance

e-HASP, 131
Electric power plants, 6, 12
Electrolytic recovery, 53
Electronic hazard warnings, 208–209, 218
Electroplating case study, 51–53
Electrostatic precipitator (ESP), 26
Emergency Planning and Community Right to Know Act (EPCRA), 1986, 92–93, 146
Emergency preparedness and response, 236, 238
    community planning, 234
    hazardous materials, 127, 129–130, 134, 141–142, 147–151, 160–161
Emergency Response Guidebook (DOT), 100, 127, 131, 139, 141, 163
Employees. *See also:* Training
    access to MSDSs, 187–188
    informed, 171–172, 187–188, 193
    total quality management, 229
    understanding MSDSs, 188–189
Employers. *See also:* Management
    hazard communication responsibilities, 171–173, 194–195
EMSs. *See:* Environmental management systems (EMSs)
Encyclopedia of Occupational Health and Safety (ILO), 1
Enthalpy, 22
Environmental management systems (EMSs), 225–247
    aspects and impacts, organizational, 233–235
    benchmarking and performance, 241–243
    best management practices, 246–247
    cost analysis, 243–244
    documentation, 236
    emergency procedures, 236, 238
    information management, 244–246
    ISO 14001, 116, 244
    management review, 238–239
    management theory, 238–239
    objectives and targets, 236
    policy statements, 231–232
    regulations, 225–226
    responsibilities, 236–237
    strategic environmental management, 241–242
    structure of, 230–235
    total quality management, 229
    training, 235
"Environmental Management Systems" (Waters), 247
Environmental Protection Agency (EPA)
    air pollution, 1, 6, 8–12, 14–18, 29, 31
    environmental management systems, 226–228, 236, 238, 247
    and GHS, 187
    hazardous materials, 125, 127–128, 135, 142, 147
    hazardous spill regulations, 127–128
    hazardous waste, 92–93, 95–96, 99, 102–116
    landfills, 63–68
    mission, 127
    solid waste, 63–68
    wastewater regulation, 39–43, 45
    water quality, 37
Environmental professional, defined, 113–114
Environmental regulations, 225–226
Environmental safety signs, 198, 204
"Environmental Site Assessments: Phase I Environmental Site Assessment Process" (ASTM), 113
EPA. *See:* Environmental Protection Agency (EPA)
EPCRA. *See:* Emergency Planning and Community Right to Know Act (EPCRA), 1986
Equalization, 49
Ergonomics, 83
ESP. *See:* Electrostatic precipitator (ESP)
Europe, hazard communication standards, 184–185, 207–208
Evacuation plans, 150–151
Evaporation, 49
Exemptions, for hazard warning labels, 179–180
Export/import, hazard communication standards, 186, 207–208
Exposure, chemical levels, 170–171, 178

F

Fabric filter, 26
Falling-object protection (FOP), 79
Falls, 62, 81–82. *See also:* Slips and trips
Fatalities, solid waste occupations, 61–62
Federal Emergency Management Agency (FEMA), 131, 143
Federal Insecticide, Fungicide and Rodenticide Act (FIFRA), 1972, 188
Federal Water Pollution Control Act, 1956, 38
Feigenbaum, Armand, 228
FEMA. *See:* Federal Emergency Management Agency (FEMA)
FIFRA. *See:* Federal Insecticide, Fungicide and Rodenticide Act (FIFRA)
Filtration, 49
Finances. *See:* Budgeting, Cost analysis, *and* Economic analysis
Fire codes, 183, 215
Fire protection maps, 114
Fire safety signs, 200
First responders, hazard communication and, 152
Flammable gas fires, 159
Flash point (Fl.P.), 138
Flocculant, 49
Floor Chemicals, 178
Flotation, 49
Flue gas, desulfurization, 27
FOP. *See:* Falling-object protection (FOP)
Foreign languages. *See:* Language issues
Forklift punctures, 158–159
Fossil fuels. *See:* Air pollution control
Freedom of Information Act (FOIA), 226

Fuel blending, 108–109
Fugitive emissions, 31–32

G

GAO. *See:* General Accounting Office (GAO)
Garfield, Douglas K., 48
Gas Law, 21–22
Gas leaks, 159
Gemba Kaizen, 228–230
General Accounting Office (GAO), 194–195
General Duty Clause (OSHA), 128
Generators, waste, 96–101, 105–106
GHG. *See:* Greenhouse gas (GHG) emissions
GHS. *See:* Globally Harmonized System of Classification and Labeling of Chemicals (GHS), 2003
Globalization, climate, 12–14, 19–20
Globally Harmonized System of Classification and Labeling of Chemicals (GHS), 2003, 129, 140, 184–187, 198
Goals, environmental management systems, 236
Grab samples, 44–45
Gravity settler, 26
Great Lakes, air toxics, 11–12
Great London Smog, 2
Green building techniques, 67–68, 118
Greenhouse effect, 19–20
Greenhouse gas (GHG) emissions, 5–6, 14
Groundwater, 65, 137
Guidance for the Selection of Chemical and Biological Decontamination Equipment for Emergency First Responders (DOJ), 130
Guidance on Emergency Responder Personal Protective Equipment (PPE) for Response to CBRN Terrorism Incidents (DOJ), 130

H

Handbook of Environmental Health and Safety (Koren & Bisesi), 1
Handbook of Environmental Health and Safety Principles and Practices (Koren), 1
The Handbook of Project-Based Management (Turner), 228
HAPs. *See:* Hazardous air pollutants (HAPs)
Hazard categories, 192–193
Hazard communication
    Europe, 184–185, 208
    signal words, 180, 199–200, 202–203, 222
Hazard communication regulations, 169–209. *See also:* Globally Harmonized System of Classification and Labeling of Chemicals (GHS), 2003
    federal vs state, 173–174
    and GHS, 173
    HCS overview, 172–173
    historical background, 170–172
    labeling issues, 178–182

    MSDS, 183–189, 212–215
    non-OSHA standards, 204–208, 222–224
    overview, 169–170, 204–206
    signage and labeling, 195–206, 218–221
    training, 189–194, 216–218
    written program requirements, 174–175
Hazard Communication Standard (HCS)
    chemical hazards, 77, 169–170, 172–173
    hazard communication, 128–130
    incidental spill, 129
    OSHA compliance issues, 174–175, 192–195
    overview, 172–173
    training, 151
Hazard prediction model, 148
Hazard warning labels, 179–183, 197–199, 201–203
Hazardous air pollutants (HAPs), 9–10, 16
Hazardous and Solid Waste Amendments (HSWA), 1984, 90–91
Hazardous Material Emergency Planning Guide (NRT), 142, 148
Hazardous materials and waste, 89–119. *See also:* Resource Conservation and Recovery Act (RCRA), 1976
    acutely hazardous, 105
    benchmarking and performance, 116–117
    best management practices, 106–107, 118
    characteristics of, 95
    classes and divisions, 126
    cost analysis, 117–118
    generators, 96–101, 105, 135
    geology and hydrology, 140
    identification, 93–94
    legislation, 90–93, 113–114, 116
    management issues, 91, 93–107, 118
    meteorology, 141, 158
    overview, 89–90, 119
    record keeping, 104–105
    recycling, 106
    registration, facility, 93
    regulatory enforcement, 110–113
    remediation, 115–116
    signs and labeling, 195–206
    training, 151–162
    transportation of, 62, 77, 83–84, 107–108, 162–165
    waste profile sheet, 97
Hazardous materials identification guide (HMIG), 181–182
Hazardous Materials Transportation–Uniform Safety Act (HMT–USA), 107, 126
Hazardous Materials: Risk-Based Adjustment of Transportation Security Plan Requirements (PHMSA), 26
Hazardous spills, 125–166
    assessment, 148–150
    benchmarking and performance, 142–144
    best management practices, 147–159
    clean-up requirements, 136–137

Hazardous spills (*cont.*)
    confined space programs, 132
    containment, 155, 158
    cost analysis, 145–147
    decontamination, 132, 159–161
    disposal, 161–162
    DOT regulations, 126–127
    environmental management, 137–142
    EPA regulations, 127–128
    federal assets and resources, 130–132
    federal reporting requirements, 134–135
    hot work, 132
    OSHA standards, 128–130
    overview, 125
    public assets, 133
    response work zones, 156–157
    state requirements, 135–136
    training, 131
    transportation, 162–165

Hazardous Waste Operations and Emergency Response (HAZWOPER)
    hazardous spills, 125, 129–130, 147, 151, 153
    solid waste, 76

Hazards. *See also:* Chemical hazards
    hazardous waste, 101–102
    regulation and legislation, 90–93
    solid waste, 61–63
    temporary, 204

HazCom. *See: Hazard Communication Standard* (HCS)

"Haze and Visibility Rule" 1999, 5

HAZWOPER. *See: Hazardous Waste Operations and Emergency Response* (HAZWOPER)

HCS. *See: Hazard Communication Standard* (HCS)

Health and safety program (e-HASP), 131

Health Effects Notebook (EPA), 17–18

Health hazard communication. *See:* Hazard communication *and* Hazard communication regulations

Hess Corporation, environmental policy, 232

Highway signs, 205–206, 223–224

HMIG. *See:* Hazardous materials identification guide (HMIG)

HMT–USA. *See:* Hazardous Materials Transportation– Uniform Safety Act (HMT–USA)

Hobbs, Peter V., 20

Hot zone, 156–157

Household hazardous waste (HHW), 66, 70, 83

Hybrid bioreactor, 66

I

IAFF. *See:* International Association of Fire Fighters (IAFF)
IARC. *See:* International Agency for Research on Cancer (IARC)
ICAC. *See:* Institute of Clean Air Companies (ICAC)
ICAO. *See:* International Civil Aviation Organization (ICAO)
ICP. *See:* Integrated Contingency Plan (ICP)
Ideal Gas Law, 21
IDLH. *See:* Immediately dangerous to life and health (IDLH)
ILO. *See:* International Labour Organization (ILO)
IMDG. *See:* International Maritime Dangerous Goods (IMDG) Code
Immediately dangerous to life and health (IDLH), 44, 140
Impact grills, 80
Import/export, hazard communication standards, 186, 207–208
Incident investigations, hazardous materials, 134–135
Incineration, 74, 108–109, 111
Incremental rate of return, 25
Indirect dischargers, 39–40
Industrial waste landfills, 68
Inspection Procedures for the Hazard Communication Standard (OSHA), 189
Institute of Clean Air Companies (ICAC), 12
Integrated Contingency Plan (ICP), 238
Integrated Risk Information System (IRIS), 18
Internal rate of return (IRR), 23
International Agency for Research on Cancer (IARC), 178
International Association of Fire Fighters (IAFF), 166–167
International Civil Aviation Organization (ICAO), 163
International issues. *See:* Globalization
International Labour Organization (ILO), 188
International Maritime Dangerous Goods (IMDG) Code, 163
International Organization for Standardization (ISO)
    3864 Standard, 206–207
    4196 Standard, 207
    14000 Standard, 116, 133, 240–241
    14001:2004 Standard, 240–241
    environmental issues, 133
    family of standards, 241
    hazard communication, 206–207
    registration costs, 244
    wastewater regulation, 55
International standards. *See also:* Globalization
    labeling issues, 206–208
    MSDS, 184–186, 206–208
Investigations. *See:* Incident investigations
Ion exchange, 50
Ionization potential (IP), 138
IRIS. *See:* Integrated Risk Information System (IRIS)
ISO. *See:* International Organization for Standardization) (ISO)

J

Job hazard analysis (JHA), 131
Juran, Joseph, 228

L

Labeling. *See also:* Signs
    chemical hazards, 179–184, 187, 215
    exemptions, 179–180
    hazardous waste, 101–102
    international standards, 184–187, 198
Land disposal restriction (LDR), 91, 96, 108–109
Land treatment, 51
Landfill gas (LFG), 64, 66–67
Landfill Methane Outreach Program (LMOP), 64
Landfills, 63–68, 74
    aerobic, and wastewater, 66
    safety and health issues, 77–84
Language issues, hazard communication, 179, 184, 200, 206–208
Lapple, C. E., 22
Large-quantity generators (LQGs), 97, 99–106
LDR. *See:* Land disposal restriction (LDR)
Leachate, 64–65, 68, 95
Lead (Pb), 4, 7–9, 16–18, 52
Leadership in Energy and Environmental Design (LEED), 118
LC. *See:* Lethal concentration (LC)
LD. *See:* Lethal dose (LD)
Lee, Michael C., 48
LEED. *See:* Leadership in Energy and Environmental Design (LEED)
LEL. *See:* Lower explosive limit (LEL)
LEPCs. *See:* Local emergency planning committees (LEPCs)
Lethal concentration (LC), 140
Lethal dose (LD), 140
LFL. *See:* Lower flammable limit (LFL)
Listed wastes, 95
LMOP. *See:* Landfill Methane Outreach Program (LMOP)
Local emergency planning committees (LEPCs), 127, 133, 143
Lockout/tagout, 78, 132, 204–205
Love Canal, 90, 124
Lower explosive limit (LEL), 28, 44, 138
Lower flammable limit (LFL), 138
LQGs. *See:* Large-quantity generators (LQGs)

M

MAC. *See:* Maximum allowable concentration (MAC)
Machine-guarding standards, 204
MACRS. *See:* Modified Accelerated Cost Recovery System (MACRS)
MACT. *See:* Maximum achievable control strategy (MACT)
Maguire, Andrew, 171
Management
    wastewater regulation, 45–46, 55
    water quality, 37

Managing Your Hazardous Waste: A Guide for Small Businesses (EPA), 93
Manifest, 99–100
The Manual on Uniform Traffic Control Devices (DOT), 205–206, 223–224
Manufacturers
    hazard communication responsibilities, 170–173
    labeling issues, 206–208
    MSDS, 183–184, 187–189
Maritime industry, 171
Material and energy balances, 22–23
Material Safety Data Sheets (MSDS). *See also:* Written hazard communication program
    access and storage, 187–188
    alternate names, 184
    chemical inventories, 175, 178–179
    hazardous waste, 93, 127, 129–130
    international standards, 184–187, 206–208
    OSHA compliance issues, 172–173, 194–195
    product shipment and, 178, 183–185
    resources, 189–191
    specifications, 183–184, 212–214
    trade secret protection, 188
    training, 189–194
Maximum achievable control strategy (MACT), 5, 10, 12–13
Maximum allowable concentration (MAC), 170–171
Maximum contaminant level (MCL), 37, 57
Medical surveillance, 131, 152
Medical waste, regulated, 70–72, 105
Medical waste incinerators (MWIs), 71–72
Medical Waste Tracking Act (MWTA), 1988, 105
Mercury emissions, 6, 12
Metal finishing industry case study, 51–53
Methane, 14, 19
Meuse Valley, Belgium, 2
Miscibility, 139
Model Training Program, 190–194
Modified Accelerated Cost Recovery System (MACRS), 24
Motor Vehicle Safety Act (MVSA), 169
Motor Vehicles Air Pollution Control Act, 1971 (EPA), 3
MSDS. *See:* Material Safety Data Sheets (MSDS)
Municipal solid waste (MSW), 72–75
Municipal Solid Waste in the United States: 2005 Facts and Figures (EPA), 74
Municipal solid waste landfills (MSWLFs), 64–66
Munsell notations, 203, 205
MSW. *See:* Municipal solid waste (MSW)
MSWLFs. *See:* Municipal solid waste landfills (MSWLFs)
MVSA. *See:* Motor Vehicle Safety Act (MVSA)
MWIs. *See:* Medical waste incinerators (MWIs)
MWTA. *See:* Medical Waste Tracking Act (MWTA)

N

NAAQS. *See:* National Ambient Air Quality Standards (NAAQS)
NAICS. *See:* North American Industrial Classification System (NAICS)
National Aeronautics and Space Administration (NASA), Astrobiology Institute, 19
National Ambient Air Quality Standards (NAAQS), 4–8, 14
National Conference of Governmental Industrial Hygienists, 170
National Emission Standards for Hazardous Air Pollutants (NESHAPs), 4–5
National Environmental Policy Act (NEPA), 1969, 4
National Fire Protection Association (NFPA), 142, 153
National fire rating (NFR), 181–182
National Institute for Occupational Safety and Health (NIOSH)
    chemical hazards, 131
    hazard communication, 171
    personal protective equipment, 153–154
    water and wastewater, 44
National Pollutant Discharge Elimination System (NPDES), 38–39, 41, 57, 128
National Primary Drinking Water Regulations (NPDWR), 36–37
National Railroad Passenger Corporation (AMTRAK), 228
National Research Council (NRC), 20
National Response Center (NRC), 134–135
National Response Team (NRT), 142
National Safety Council (NSC), 195–196
National Safety News, 196
National Secondary Drinking Water Regulations (NSDWR), 36–37
National Toxicoloy Program (NTP), 178
NEPA. *See:* National Environmental Policy Act (NEPA)
NESHAPs. *See:* National Emission Standards for Hazardous Air Pollutants (NESHAPs)
Net present value (NPV) *or* net present worth (NPW), 23
Neutralization, 50
New source performance standards (NSPS), 4
NFPA. *See:* National Fire Protection Association (NFPA)
NFR. *See:* National fire rating (NFR)
NIOSH. *See:* National Institute for Occupational Safety and Health (NIOSH)
NIOSH Pocket Guide to Chemical Hazards (NPG), 131
Nitrogen oxides (NO_x), 4–6, 9, 11–13, 17, 19, 27–28, 30
Nitrous oxide (N_2O), 14, 19
Noise, 77, 82–83
Non-English speakers. *See:* Language issues
Nonpoint sources of pollution, 55, 57
North American Industrial Classification System (NAICS) codes, 61–63
NOTICE signs, 200, 203
NPDES. *See:* National Pollutant Discharge Elimination System (NPDES)
NPDWR. *See:* National Primary Drinking Water Regulations (NPDWR)
NPG. *See: NIOSH Pocket Guide to Chemical Hazards* (NPG)
NPV. *See:* Net Present Value (NPV)
NRC. *See:* National Research Council (NRC) *and* National Response Center (NRC)
NRT. *See:* National Response Team (NRT)
NSC. *See:* National Safety Council (NSC)
NSDWR. *See:* National Secondary Drinking Water Regulations (NSDWR)
NSPS. *See:* New source performance standards (NSPS)
NTP. *See:* National Toxicoloy Program (NTP)

O

Occupational Safety and Health Administration (OSHA). *See also:* National Institute for Occupational Safety and Health (NIOSH)
    emergency response, defined, 129
    ergonomics, 83
    hazard communication, 170–174
    hazardous material spills, 125, 128–131, 137, 140, 142, 147–148, 151
    hazardous waste, 129–130, 238
    HAZWOPER standard, 76, 125, 129–130, 147, 151, 153
    MSDS compliance, 183–184, 187–188, 212–214
Occupational Safety and Health Act (OSH Act) 169, 171
Odor, 77
Office of Pollution Prevention and Toxics (OPPT), 241
OHSMS. *See: Standard for Occupational Health and Safety Management Systems* (OHSMS)
Oil
    defined, 57
    recycling, 75
    spill plan, 132
Oil Pollution Act (OPA), 1990, 46, 92, 132
Optimization, 24
OSH Act. *See:* Occupational Safety and Health Act (OSH Act)
OSHA. *See:* Occupational Safety and Health Administration (OSHA)
Oxidation/reduction processes, 50
Ozone (O_3), 5, 7–8, 13–14, 17–18, 21

P

Pais, David, 24
Paperless warnings, 208–209
Particles, characteristics, 22–23
Particulate matter (PM10 & PM2.5), 5–8, 11, 17–18, 22–23, 25–27
Pasquill-Gifford (P-G) Stability Class System, 141
Payback period, 23
Payout period, 25
PCBs. *See:* Polychlorinated biphenyls (PCBs)

PDCA. *See:* Plan-Do-Check-Act (PDCA) cycle
PEL. *See:* Permissible exposure limit (PEL)
Perfluorocarbons (PFCs), 14
Performance. *See also:* Benchmarking
    environmental management systems, 241–243
    hazardous material spills, 142–144
    wastewater regulation, 53–54
Permissible exposure limit (PEL), 138, 157, 178
Personal protective equipment (PPE), 44, 76, 78, 83, 101, 131, 149, 153–155, 160, 161
Pesticides, 11
PFCs. *See:* Perfluorocarbons (PFCs)
Phase I Environmental Site Assessment, 113–114
Phase II Environmental Site Investigations, 114–115
PHMSA. *See:* Pipeline and Hazardous Materials Safety Administration (PHMSA)
Physical treatment, wastewater, 49–50
Pipeline and Hazardous Materials Safety Administration (PHMSA), 126
Pipes, labeling standards, 182–183
Placards, hazardous material, 205
Plan-Do-Check-Act (PDCA) cycle, 230–231, 238–239
PM. *See:* Particulate matter
Point source emissions, 1
Point sources of pollution, 39, 54, 58
Pollution. *See also:* Air pollution *and* Spill Prevention Control and Countermeasures regulation (SPCC)
    best conventional control technology, 42
Pollution Prevention Act (PPA), 1990, 106
Polychlorinated biphenyls (PCBs), 11, 115, 137
Posters, accident prevention, 195–197
Potentially responsible party (PRP), 113
POTW. *See:* Publicly owned treatment works (POTW)
PPA. *See:* Pollution Prevention Act (PPA)
PPE. *See:* Personal protective equipment (PPE)
Precipitation, 50
Preliminary Endangerment Assessment Guidance Manual (EPA), 136
Process fugitive emissions, 31–32
Product safety signs and labels, 198–200, 206–209
Product shipments, 178, 183–186, 207–208
Product warning labels, 179–183
Protective equipment. *See:* Personal protective equipment (PPE)
PRP. *See:* Potentially responsible party (PRP)
Publicly owned treatment works (POTW), 39–43, 45–46, 52, 54–55, 57–58, 94

Q
Quality assurance project plan (QAPP), 115

R
Rapanos v. United States, 47
RBCA. *See:* Risk-Based Corrective Action (RBCA)

RCRA. *See:* Resource Conservation and Recovery Act (RCRA)
RCRA Waste Sampling Draft Technical Guidance—Planning, Implementation, and Assessment (EPA), 136
Reactor/filter system, 29
Recommended exposure limit (REL), 44
Recommended Practice for Responding to Hazardous Materials Incidents (NFPA), 147
Records
    chemicals, 172–176, 178–179, 183–189
    hazardous waste, 74–75
Recycling, 72–75, 106, 108
Refineries. *See:* Air pollution control *and* Oil
Refuse Act, 1899, 38
Registry of Toxic Effects of Chemical Substances (RTECS), 178
REL. *See:* Recommended exposure limit (REL)
Reportable quantity (RQ), 135
Requirements for Quality Assurance Project Plans (EPA), 116
Resource Conservation and Recovery Act (RCRA), 1976. *See also:* Treatment, storage, and disposal facilities (TSDFs)
    environmental management systems, 225
    hazardous waste, 90–91, 93–94, 96–98, 111–112, 135, 161, 165
    purpose of, 74, 128
    solid waste, 63
Responsible Care program (ACC), 133, 242–243
"Restoring the Quality of our Environment" (EPA), 3
Return on investment (ROI), 23–24, 31
Reverse osmosis, 49
Risk, air pollutants, 16–20
Risk-Based Corrective Action (RBCA), 115–116
Rivers and Harbors Act, 1894, 38
ROI. *See:* Return on investment (ROI)
Roll-over protective structure (ROPS), 79
RQ. *See:* Reportable quantity (RQ)
RTECS. *See:* Registry of Toxic Effects of Chemical Substances (RTECS)

S
Safe Drinking Water Act (SDWA), 1974, 35–37
Safety Color Code, 198, 203, 222–224
Safety colors, 203, 222–224
Safety data sheets (SDS), 184–185
Safety equipment, signs, tags, and posters, 196–197, 199–200, 204–208
Sampling, water and wastewater, 37–38, 43–45
SARA. *See:* Superfund Amendments and Reauthorization Act (SARA)
Savings. *See:* Cost analysis *and* Economic analysis
SCBA. *See:* Self-contained breathing apparatus (SCBA)
Scrap tires, 74–75
Screening, wastewater, 49
SDS. *See:* Safety data sheets (SDS)

SDWA. *See:* Safe Drinking Water Act (SDWA), 1974
Seatbelts, 80
Security, transportation, 126–127
Sedimentation system, 49
Self-contained breathing apparatus (SCBA), 143, 146, 154–155, 159
SEM. *See:* Strategic environmental management (SEM)
SEPs. *See:* Supplemental Environmental Projects (SEPs) Policy
September 11, 2001, 3
SERC. *See:* State emergency response commission (SERC)
Seveso, Italy, dioxin incident, 2
Sewage. *See:* Wastewater
Shape coding, 206, 223–224
Shingo, Shigeo, 228
Shipboard Marine Pollution Emergency Plan (SMPEP), 132
Shipboard Oil Pollution Emergency Plans (SOPEP), 132
Shipping. *See:* Maritime industry *and* Product shipments
Short-term exposure limit (STEL), 140
Signal words, hazard communication, 180, 199–200, 202–203, 222
Signs. *See also:* Labeling
    accident-prevention, 196–197
    ANSI Z535 Series, 197–204, 219–222
    hazardous material placards, 205
    traffic, 205–206, 222–223
SIPs. *See:* State implementation plans (SIPs)
Slips and trips, 84–85. *See also:* Falls
Sludge. *See:* Wastewater
Small Business Liability Relief and Brownfields Revitalization Act, 2001, 92
Small-quantity generators (SQGs), 99–105
SMPEP. *See:* Shipboard Marine Pollution Emergency Plan (SMPEP)
Soil decontamination, 136–137
Solid waste, 61–85
    dangers associated with, 61–63
    defined, 93–94
    environmental strategies for, 73–74
    identification, 93–94
    landfills, 63–68
    litter, 78
    management issues, 93–107
    medical, 70–72
    municipal, 72–75
    overview, 84–85
    regulations, 63
    safety plan for, 75–76
Solid Waste Agency of Northern Cook County v. Army Corps of Engineers, 47–48
Solid Waste Association of North America (SWANA), 66
Solid Waste Disposal Act (SWDA), 1965, 63, 90–91, 111, 225
Solid waste management hierarchy, 104
Solvent extraction, 49–50
SOPEP. *See:* Shipboard Oil Pollution Emergency Plans (SOPEP)

Sorbents, 158
Special wastes, 94–95
Specific gravity (Sp. Gr.), 138–139
Spill kits, 155–156. *See also:* Hazardous spills
Spill Prevention Control and Countermeasures regulation (SPCC), 46–47, 128, 236, 238
Spills, hazardous material, 151–152
Spotters, 81
SQGs. *See:* Small-Quantity Generators (SQGs)
Stabilization ponds, 51
Standard for Professional Competence of Responders to Hazardous Materials Incidents (NFPA), 142
Standard on Disaster/Emergency Management and Business Continuity Programs (NFPA), 148
Standards on Environmental Sampling (ASTM), 81
State emergency response commission (SERC), 127
State implementation plans (SIPs), 4–5
STEL. *See:* Short-term exposure limit (STEL)
Strategic environmental management (SEM), 241–242
Stripping, 49
Sulfur oxides (SO$_x$), 4–8, 10–12, 17–19, 27
Superfund Amendments and Reauthorization Act (SARA), 1986, 89, 92–93, 113, 127–128, 143, 145, 225. *See also:* Comprehensive Environmental Response, Compensation, and Liability Act (CERCLA), 1980
Supplemental Environmental Projects (SEPs) Policy (EPA), 228
SWANA. *See:* Solid Waste Association of North America (SWANA)
SWDA. *See:* Solid Waste Disposal Act (SWDA)
Symbols, hazard communication, 206–208, 222–224

T

Tags, safety, 198, 204–205
Target organ systemic toxicity (TOST), 140
TCLP. *See:* Toxic Characteristic Leaching Procedure (TCLP)
Temporary hazards, 204
Test Methods for Evaluating Solid Waste (EPA), 136
Thermal treatment, 51
Thermoturbulence, 21
Threshold limit value (TLV), 44, 138, 140, 178
Time-weighted averages, 45
Titanium dioxide (TiO$_2$) Photocatalytic Air Treatment, 28–29
Tires, scrap, 74–75
TLV. *See:* Threshold limit value (TLV)
TMDL. *See:* Total maximum daily load (TMDL)
TOC. *See:* Total organic carbon (TOC)
TOST. *See:* Target organ systemic toxicity (TOST)
Total maximum daily load (TMDL), 43
Total organic carbon (TOC), 42, 53
Total quality management (TQM), 229
Total suspended solids (TSSs), 42
Total toxic organics (TTOs), 52

Toxic Characteristic Leaching Procedure (TCLP), 95
Toxic material disposal, 76
Toxic Substances Control Act (TSCA), 1976, 225
TQM. *See:* Total quality management (TQM)
Trade secrets, 188
Traffic. *See:* Transportation
Traffic signs, 205–206
Training
    environmental management systems, 235
    hazard communication, 189–194, 216–218
    hazardous material spills, 151–152
    hazardous material transportation, 162–165
    hazardous waste, 102–103, 106
    OSHA standards, 189, 192–194
Transfer containers, 102
Transfer facility, defined, 108
Transloading, 162
Transportation. *See also:* U.S. Department of Transportation (DOT)
    hazardous materials, 162–165
    hazardous waste, 107–108
    solid waste, 62, 77, 83–84
Treatment, storage, and disposal facilities (TSDFs), 89–90, 99–100, 107–111, 129
Trickling filters, 51
Trips, 84–85
TSCA. *See:* Toxic Substances Control Act (TSCA)
TSDFs. *See:* Treatment, storage, and disposal facilities (TSDFs)
TSSs. *See:* Total suspended solids (TSSs)
TTOs. *See:* Total toxic organics (TTOs)

U
UEL. *See:* Upper explosive limit (UEL)
Ultraviolet (UV) radiation, 13
Uncontrolled hazardous waste site, 129
Underground storage tanks (UST), 94, 111–112, 116
Uniform Hazardous Waste Manifest, 135
U.S. Coast Guard, 132
U.S. Department of Energy (DOE), 130
U.S. Department of Justice (DOJ), 130
U.S. Department of Labor (DOL), Bureau of Labor Statistics (BLS), 61
U.S. Department of Transportation (DOT)
    and GHS, 187
    hazard communication, 204–205
    hazardous materials, 125–127, 130–131, 134–135, 147, 162–165
    hazardous waste, 99–100, 102, 107–108
    mission, 126
    transportation, defined, 162
U.S. Geological Survey, 11
Universal wastes, 105–106
Upper explosive limit (UEL), 138
Used Oil Recycling Act, 1980, 92

UST. *See:* Underground Storage Tanks (UST).
Utility Mercury Reduction Rule, 12

V
Vapor density (VD), 139
Vapor pressure (VP), 139
Vaporsep Membrane Process, 28
Vehicle emissions, 8–9
Vehicle safety, 79–81
Vessel Response Plan (VRP), 132
Viscosity, 139
Volatile organic compounds (VOCs), 4, 8, 13–15, 17, 27–28
VP. *See:* Vapor pressure (VP)
VRP. *See:* Vessel Response Plan (VRP)

W
Warm zone, 156–157
Warning labels, 179–183
WARNING signs, 199, 202
Warnings. *See also:* Labeling *and* Signs
    paperless, 208–209, 218
    product safety, 199–200, 206–207
Warnings and Safety Instructions—An Annotated Bibliography (Miller & Lehto), 204
Waste, hazardous. *See:* Hazardous materials and waste
Waste minimization, 73, 103–104
Waste profile sheet, 97
Wastewater, 30, 38–46, 48–53
    regulation, 53–54
Wastewater management engineering, 47–51
Water and wastewater, 35–59
    benchmarking and performance, 53–54
    best management practices, 54–55
    clean up, post-spill, 136–137
    cost analysis, 54
    effluents from industry, 42–43
    Oil Pollution Act, 46
    overview, 35, 55
    permits, 42–43
    pretreatment standards, 40
    protective measures, 76
    quality regulation, 35–38
    spill prevention, 46–47
    terminology, 55–59
    wastewater management and treatment, 48–53
    wastewater regulation, 38–46
    wetlands management, 47–48
Water Pollution Control Act (WPCA), 1948, 38
Waters, Jean S., 247
Wet scrubber, 26–27
Wetlands, 59
Wetlands management, 47–48

WHMIS. *See:* Canadian Workplace Hazardous Materials Information Systems (WHMIS)
Wilson, Richard G., 48
Wind direction, 156–157
Work areas, 192–193
Workers. *See:* Employees
Workers' right to know. *See:* Hazard Communication regulations
Workplace Hazardous Materials Information System (WHMIS), 185–186
WPCA. *See:* Water Pollution Control Act (WPCA)
Written hazard communication program. *See also:* Material Safety Data Sheets (MSDS)
  chemical inventories, 175, 178–179
  example program, 176–177
  resources, 175, 178–179, 212–215
  signage and labeling, 179–183
  specifications, 192–194

Z

Z35.1 Standard, 197
Z129.1 Standard, 180–181
Z400.1 Standard, 183–184
Z535 Series, 197–204, 219–222
Zero defects, 228